American Critics at Work:

Examinations of Contemporary Literary Theories

American Critics at Work:

Examinations of Contemporary Literary Theories

Edited by

Victor A. Kramer

The Whitston Publishing Company
P.O. Box 958
Troy, New York 12181
1984

TABLE OF CONTENTS

PART ONE: Theory and Practice

ACKNOWLEDGEMENTS

Several essays in this book appeared originally in different versions in journals. Grateful appreciation of permissions granted to republish the revised essays is hereby acknowledged.

Nathan A. Scott, Jr's "Santayana's Poetics of Belief" first appeared in *boundary 2.*

William V. Spanos's "Retrieving Heidegger's De-struction" is reprinted from *SCE Reports.*

J. Hillis Miller's "Theology and Logology" originally appeared in *The Journal of the American Academy of Religion,* © copyright J. Hillis Miller.

Michael Sprinker's "Reinventing Historicism: An Introduction to the Work of Frederic Jameson" appeared in a different version called "The Part and the Whole" in *Diacritics.*

Matei Calinescu's "Imagination and Meaning: Aesthetic Attitudes in Mircea Eliade's Thought" is based upon earlier versions of two essays which appeared in *The Journal of Religion* 57:1 (1977), pp. 10-15, and 59:2 (1979), pp. 218-223 and is reprinted in the revised form by permission of The University of Chicago Press.

Ihab Hassan's "Parabiography: The Varieties of Critical Experience" first appeared in *The Georgia Review,* © copyright Ihab Hassan.

The essays by Murray Krieger, Vincent B. Leitch, Joseph Riddel, Norman Holland, David Bleich, Steven Mailloux and Giles Gunn first appeared in *Studies in the Literary Imagination,* 12 (Spring, 1979). They have been revised for this volume with the permission of the Publications Board of *Studies in the Lit-*

erary Imagination.

Gerald Graff's "Literature as Assertions" is reprinted with revisions by permission of the publishers of *American Criticism in the Post-structuralist Age.* ed. Ira Konigsberg, (Ann Arbor, MI: Michigan Studies in the Humanities, 1981).

Several sections of Vincent Leitch's essay are published with slight alterations in various chapters of his book *Deconstructive Criticism* (New York: Columbia University Press, 1983).

The remaining essays and postscripts were written for publication in this book.

PREFACE

This collection gathers some of the more significant contemporary literary criticism and theory being written in America today. This occurs at a juncture when critical activity frequently appears threatened with both a forgetfulness about the past as well as a fascination with strategies and techniques of the moment. Such appearances are deceptive, however, for cumulatively these essays demonstrate the necessity for critics to remain aware of the past while also taking advantage of the plurality of critical enterprises available at the present time.

The contributions to this book have grown out of my study of, and exchange with, various critics during the past several years. Seven of the essays were originally written for the *Studies in the Literary Imagination* issue "Critics at Work: Contemporary Literary Theory," published in 1979. That collection was the foundation for this volume. The present book is a natural outgrowth and expansion of the earlier project. When the *Studies* issue was edited one of the forces determining its contents was the hope to demonstrate that contemporary American critics were pushing "beyond formalism," by a variety of significant new methods. The earlier collection demonstrated such diversity, and the cooperation of a large number of critics who made suggestions for that venture has contributed to the editing of this considerably revised and expanded collection.

Correspondence, drafts, revision, suggestions, postscripts, and still more revisions have led to the present combination of essays. This book is therefore a genuine collaborative effort. Its final form is the result of many suggestions made by numerous scholars and critics. I am especially appreciative of the assistance which I received from those who commented upon the *Studies* issue and who also urged expansion. While the present book reflects my interests, it is the result of the encouragement and influence of many different readers, teachers, students, critics, and scholars. I am especially grateful for the suggestions made to me by Angel Medina, Thomas Gilmore and Robert Detweiler.

Victor A. Kramer
Georgia State University

INTRODUCTION

American Critics at Work: Examinations of Contemporary Literary Theories— Questions, Mediations, Speculations

by
Victor A. Kramer

The seventeen essays included here were chosen as an introduction to various areas of contemporary criticism and theory which seem of most value for today's student. While the essays reflect the editor's interests and the fact that many different concerns were in mind as they were gathered, always at the core of the project remained a desire to choose, or commission, essays which had practical uses. The goal of the *Studies in the Literary Imagination* collection, which first included seven of these essays, was to present original work by critics who were making contributions to current theory and practice through a wide variety of methodologies. For this expanded collection the same goal had been sought, but with a wider scope in mind which reflects still more of the controversy and opening up of approaches so frequent in contemporary theory. These essays represent therefore part of a dialogue in a continuing process of conscientious criticism by a diversity of critics. These are critics who have proven their abilities. Many are distinguished writers with sizeable bibliographies while others are younger critics of promise.

Today when academic life sometimes suffers from an absence of new ideas, and the enthusiasm and daring which is part of a younger generation can be almost hidden, it seems especially useful to provide essays by a considerable range of critics, not just in light of the subject, but above all in terms of spirit. This combination reflects the fact that contemporary criticism, like most human endeavor, profits from as wide a variety of background and approach as possible. Some of the writers included here are concerned about our apparent cultural forgetfulness;

others are concerned with the examination of, deconstruction of, and reaction to, particular texts; still others remind us of the complexity of reading, and of moving toward the future, but also of the need to avoid oversimplification. All of these approaches, using inherited traditions or devising new ones, collectively enrich our critical procedure. This is true even when much energy seems to be devoted to what David Bleich has termed "negotiated knowledge" in the study of criticism and literature. In his perceptive essay in this collection Bleich shows how critics approach issues, define terms, and come to an understanding of critical positions only through the arduous process of explaining and reexplaining. Wouldn't it be easier, a prospective reader of this collection of essays might ask, if such negotiation could be avoided? Wouldn't it be better to adopt clear procedures, and move on? But what we come to suspect is that no such easy answers are possible, and what David Bleich implies, and what the various critical approaches included in this collection make clear, is that as readers we must learn to recognize that the contemporary critical horizon includes many spheres which are in motion, all of which must be recognized as of value, and not merely tolerated as idiosyncratic. Thus, we ask as we approach this collection, what is on that horizon? And, is it possible for so many different, and frequently antagonistic, critics to be working at a common enterprise? Indeed, is modern critical endeavor even any longer a common enterprise? In my opinion, it is, but it can only be so when each critic, or theorist, is able to admit that his own enterprise must ultimately be recognized as a symbol of his isolation and of a need for still other kinds of criticism.

The field of contemporary literary theory sometimes appears to be almost a battleground. Groups of critics often seem to be working against each other, and then with this approach, or that, they seem to be fiercely engaged in battle against some seemingly "outmoded" way of reading a text. But to think in such terms is to miss what many contemporary theorists have come to honor: most importantly, the very complexity of a text necessitates actions different than battle with an emphasis on winning. A text, a poem, should bring critical engagement, ultimately, joy, pleasure, wonder, even amazement. When this occurs, critics frequently realize that a text—when read even in the most attentive of manners—can never be completely read (nor, on the other hand) completely de-structed. Just as

Giles Gunn, by way of Clifford Geertz and Lionel Trilling, reminds us in the essay included in this book that all of culture is a web, and we are as we are because we are in that web, so many contemporary critics and theorists keep celebrating the complexity of texts which reveal more than we might suspect, or even sometimes wish. This fact of surprise is basic to the critical act. As readers we may not want (at first) to admit of the complexity of what lies buried in a text—either in a poem or in an essay which reveals "a critic's job of work" as any particular text is unfolded. Whether it is Murray Krieger demonstrating how a poetic work is special, as he does in the opening essay, or whether it is Ihab Hassan, who in closing this collection reminds us that the critic himself is unique, the way is prepared for more precise reading. Krieger celebrates the mystery of the word; Hassan celebrates the mystery of being a celebrator of the word.

There is no doubt that in this gathering of critics we readily see that many are preoccupied with the "errors" of other critics. Thus a considerable amount of energy can be expended in analysis of the advantages and disadvantages of particular methods. This finally gives life to many of these essays and, in fact, it is what provides the basic structure for this anthology. The book is arranged in three parts. Its arrangement reflects the controversies basic to today's critical circles. In the first part we include essays which demonstrate the tension and threatened split which exists between traditionalists who insist that art is special, and those sometimes mistrusted "French-influenced" disciples of Derrida who seem to weaken tradition with their assertions which suggest the possibility of literature subsumed in a great sea of words—all ultimately meaningless if pressed to the extreme. In the second part of the collection we include various critics who, through particular focus on texts, are moving toward more precise ways of reading and methods of reconciliation. The concluding essays in the third section were chosen because they demonstrate both the need for an awareness of interconnections, and the fact that serious critics with interdisciplinary interests are making just such connections.

These diverse essays provide evidence of a range of criticism and theory considerably greater than might be suspected if one were to study some of the more specialized examples of criticism published in the past decade. Traditions continue, yet new trends emerge; still other patterns grow more visible as new emphases are stressed, but none of this negates what has been accomplished earlier. One of the values of this collection should be to illustrate that criticism remains a slowly evolving project and a cumulative gathering built down into the present and toward a future. The engagement of literary criticism and theory is a project, then, where no critic works alone, but rather in the knowledge that the work of reading well is always being done with many others. Ignorance of this communal enterprise means insulation. A real value of William V. Spanos' essay included in Part One is that he reminds us of the proximity of the abyss to some contemporary critical activities which seem to exist in isolation, and the fact that critics dare not forget the work of others.

This book is an introduction to significant criticism as currently practiced in American universities, but especially it exists as an indication of valuable diversity. While the book cannot seek to present a complete picture of the current scene, these selections provide teachers and students with striking demonstrations of current critical practices. I have frequently sought to obtain essays which allow critics to deploy critical thought in specific analyses. All of these essays might be thought of as demonstrations of the fact that contemporary criticism (as is always the case with successful criticism) is in process of change. These pieces raise questions about how best to approach a text; how to make better sense of the poem; and, most importantly, how to look for connections between and among the conflicting approaches, responses, assertions, and deconstructions of other critics. Above all, these diverse essays demonstrate contemporary engagement with the complexity of criticism, a task sometimes in the past dismissed as an exercise to be finished. What these critics, often self-consciously, remind us of is that we will never be done with careful reading. At the same time their analyses and engagement with one another help us to see, and to see more clearly, the complexity of critical writing, which itself is no longer something for a reader to do confidently feeling he has satisfactorily wrested "the" meaning from a text.

I

The fact that much stimulating critical theory is now flowing from Europe to the United States is important and revealing; and the presence of such innovative critical procedures
provides part of the background against which the present gathering of essays is made. Most importantly, Jacques Derrida has
forced us all to raise new questions about literature and critical
theory. A collection of essays recently edited by Josué V. Harari, *Textual Strategies, Perspectives in Post-Structuralist Criticism,* provides an example of the significance of this French influence. Yet there remain many other modes of inquiry which
cannot be forgotten. As Harari himself points out, structuralism
has already been in fashion for almost two decades, and its
very popularity has caused a certain "trendiness" in critical
theory; we now seem to be in danger of still another cycle
of critical production that follows what is merely fashion-
able.

No doubt readers of modern critical theory have come to
understand that the critic is "a producer of texts," but it may
still be debatable if critics were ever quite so satisfied as Harari
implies in his characterization of Leo Spitzer's critical attitude
as representative of earlier certainties. Harari states that "Spitz-
erian interpretation" is one which is satisfied in taking the text
at face value. Criticism then becomes "transparent communication." At the other extreme, Harari reminds us, Derrida believes:
"A text is a text only if it conceals, from the first glance, from
the first comer, the laws of its composition and the rule of its
game."[1]   Surely, there is a middle ground between, and it is
my hope that the variety of essays chosen for this collection
demonstrates a broad range of American preoccupations, sometimes more straight-forward and often more trusting of language
than the French assumptions so basic to *Textual Strategies.*
Harari correctly insists that "to posit that a text operates in the
mode of concealment is to recognize that there is no autonomy
proper to the text, and thus that criticism is not a simple 'ad-
junct' to the so-called primary text but it is a continuous activity which is instrinsic to and extends the text."[2]   It is precisely on such a point that the essays in Harari's collection and
those in Part One here often agree. Thus both Vincent Leitch
and Joseph Riddel, with a full awareness of both American

critical history and deconstruction, indicate by their willingness
to add post-scripts to their essays that the critical enterprise
is, significantly, a continuing activity. There is a joy in what
Leitch and Riddel accomplish, but its very open-endedness
can appear to be a threat to other critics. A real need is to
find ways to take advantage of such new "games," while also
remembering the rules of still other methods of critical discourse. At the heart of the controversy which exists between
the defenders of the deconstructionist activity and more traditional ways of approaching the poem is what Nathan Scott,
Jr. in his essay calls "the problematique of symbolic forms."
The need is both to recognize the value of the poem and the
continuing activity of the critic who is more and more aware
that his work is never really ever completed.

Murray Krieger's task in "Literature vs. *Écriture:* Constructions and Deconstructions in Recent Critical Theory" is to remind readers of the threat of too quickly losing sight of the
unique quality of a poem. It should not become submerged
in the sea of *écriture* upon which the deconstructionists float.
Krieger asks the question, can poetry survive if it loses its unique
idenity? Must it be perceived as something other than just
one more text? A similar point is made in the essay by Nathan
Scott, Jr. whose "Santayana's Poetics of Belief" examines
the loss to humanistic studies if we, as critics and teachers, are
willing to ignore the legacy of Santayana whose theory of the
imagination insists on a relationship of symbolic forms and
"the world of which we are members."

Both Krieger and Scott are aware of the great influx of
continental criticism and its influence upon current critical
method, yet for them the paramount question remains what
does the critic do next? What critical approaches can be util-
ized which illuminate the task of the critic but also help him
retain a faith and delight in literature? For while all writing
may well be enigmatic, poets do communicate. Critics such
as Krieger and Scott, who to some might seem merely "traditionalists," insist on examining issues which continue to bring critics
into contact with the living presence of the word. For such
critics the very fascination of deconstructionist critics with
techniques of finding hidden meanings threatens to bring about
a loss of focus on the poem as something unique and as a form

which leads readers back to the world. They would remind us, as does Walter J. Ong, that the poem is ultimately a cry of the heart, and that to approach it is to be made aware of the person who informs it.

An awareness of the need to approximate what the poet has accomplished brings us to the considerations of Gerald Graff who has elsewhere argued that literature must be about those things which poets (and critics) take seriously. In his essay, included here, "Literature as Assertions," Graff argues that although literature may well be difficult to comprehend it always sets out to accomplish particular goals. He insists that "literature is propositions." In addition, he argues that readers clearly understand such a fact. Graff would therefore hold that when instructed by what Joseph Riddel designates the "fate of interpretation," and even when confronted by many deconstructive readings of literature, we must not ignore the value of what is accomplished by the poet in the poem, or by critics who insist on the mystery of the transforming word—for the poet and critic do assert truths. This is, we remember, also an important accomplishment of all the systematic work of Murray Krieger, and his essay, included here, attempts to stand back from and scrutinize the poem as a made thing which remains special. Poetic truth for Krieger is determinate and knowable.

The questions is, how does a position like Krieger's differ from that of a more skeptical critic such as Vincent Leitch, or others associated with Yale University such as J. Hillis Miller? The fact is that the members of the so-called "Yale school" are not nihilists. They manifest a consistent interest in poetic truth as knowable, and have provided valuable insights. (Yet what we come to know can be a surprise.) Most importantly the work of critics such as Paul de Man and J. Hillis Miller is a link between the critics of consciousness of Geneva and other more speculative attempts to understand and explicate the hidden characteristics of literary works. J. Hillis Miller's recent writing performs such a service, even though some readers seem to be disturbed at Miller's fascination with turning a text upside down to yield its implications. Perhaps Miller, among those critics who practice at Yale, is the most concerned with the complexity of ambiguities within the western literary tradition. His "Theology and Logology in Victorian Literature," included here, reveals the implications we as readers always seem to have sensed but had not formulated. Interestingly, Joseph Riddel's current investigation of an American poetics has a related value. Critics such as Miller, Leitch, and Riddel do not deny the complexity of the text. They insist upon it. These "deconstructionists" remind us that whenever any theory of criticism operates, there deconstruction questions.

Riddel's analysis of the interaction of H. D.'s life and writing is an exercise in the examination of the sedimentation that exists in any writing project. As he strips away meaning, in "H. D.'s Scene of Writing—Poetry as Analysis," we can better see implications, and we come to recognize, as did the poet, that Being (as we come to know it through language) is a myth to be examined, but never to be fully reassembled through systematic study; it is to be taken apart so that we can begin to build again. Critical activity, then, reading poetry, does not explain so much as it arrests our attention. In this way, Riddel forces us to re-examine how the language of a poet *and* critic is employed. He reminds us of the complexity of any critical act, and we realize through what is not said that the poet who seeks to express the inexpressible sometimes achieves that very goal. And strangely, what the poet sets out to assert she often does. But for any reader to do the same, she must follow steps which approximate those of the poet. It is in this way that one has to approach the essay provided here by Vincent Leitch, "The Book of Deconstructive Criticism," in which he provides a partial cartography of deconstruction.

Leitch writes with a wry gesture of enjoyment; he embraces the idea that one of the roles of the contemporary critic is *not* to rest assured in finding any definitive answer. He does not deny the possibility of critical truth; but he rather seeks to remind us of a need to be uneasy, as are Derrida, and de Man, and Miller with easy truths. Leitch instructs us therefore to look more carefully at the implications of any literary, critical, or textual activity. He does this within the context of an American critical tradition which beyond the "New Criticism" has striven to make use of insights provided by structuralists and advocates of the "nouvelle critique," yet also by not abandoning what earlier critics and theorists have accomplished.

Critics such as Leitch and Riddel would clearly argue that what they are doing is extremely revealing; indeed, maybe more is so accomplished than by placing a text within a single tradition or context. What they also remind us of, in the words of Joseph Riddel, is that what we learn about writing is applicable to both poetry and criticism.

In Part One of this collection, then, two quite different types of essays are represented. Some might dismiss Krieger, Scott, or Graff as reactionary, and others might want to label the methodology of Leitch, Riddel, or Miller as iconoclastic; but a more accurate way to view these writers is to see that both the "traditionalists" and "defenders of the *nouvelle-critique*" have cogent points to make about the complexities of literature and theory. Such critical diversity is essential if we are going to participate in the complexity of a world in which critics are no longer certain of procedures. Finally, these quite different approaches demonstrate that all arbitrary boundaries about meaning are problematic, while they also remind us that some meaning can be communicated or, at least, puzzled through. Krieger and Scott remain rightly troubled that, during the past decade especially, critics have become excessively preoccupied with system, while often these systems appear to have grown out of an isolated preoccupation with various European methods. While there clearly are advantages to the adoption of structuralist and post-structuralist principles, as Leitch, Riddel and Miller make clear, we must simultaneously be aware that some contemporary analysis, almost what seems to be a post-mortem examination of literature, has frequently been done in relative ignorance of what earlier literary critics accomplished. We must be reminded that the rather peculiar result of critical isolation is that many valuable insights provided by men such as John Crowe Ransom and Cleanth Brooks can be overlooked, even dismissed as simplistic.

II

With the two types of critics included in Part One we see an opposition which is inherent in approaches which range from an affirmation of the presence of the word to a denial that we will ever be able to isolate that very presence (which in a sense remains absent). Above all, if such positions are to be reconciled, perhaps what is needed is a greater sense of awe for what the poet and critic do accomplish. Such a need brings us closer to the chief concern of Part Two of the collection. In Part One William V. Spanos examines some of the apparent problems which Derridean critical procedure sometimes involves— the writer never really being able to say what he wishes to say— but Spanos asserts this is a result of oversimplification of Heidegger's text. Different from the Heideggerian destruction from which it seems to take its origin, the Derridean impulse (sometimes further simplified by avid disciples) tries to maintain that texts exist *only* to be dismantled. In such a simplified sense, deconstruction threatens to become elaborate exegesis, and Spanos rightly warns critics against a playing with analysis which can finally be merely a witty, playful, "negative and ineffectual play of dialectics," a kind of critical activity which would not really help to understand either the text or ourselves.

In the second part of this collection we include examples of critical procedures which seek to get at various levels of meaning, yet which also admit of the mystery of the text. It should be observed that in some ways this is a legacy from an earlier era when, as Cleanth Brooks noted in *Modern Poetry and the Tradition*, we needed to build scaffolds so that we could investigate the complexity of a poem, but we also have to remember to dismantle those scaffolds so that we can enjoy the poem. What some tend to forget about the legacy of the "New Criticism" is that those thinkers clearly insisted on the mystery of the word, while they also knew it was essential for readers of poetry to be aware that critical insight was furthered by systematic classification and description of the elements within a poem. Rigorous procedures help readers to experience the poem, but when Robert Penn Warren speaks of pure and impure poetry, Allen Tate describes tension in successful poetry, or John Crowe Ranson alludes to the need for an ontological critic, each has in mind the fact that poetry is finally a mysterious mode of communicating.

What sometimes happens in literary theorizing is that any sense of the mystery of poetry is quickly omitted from discussion, while a corrolary assumption often seems to be that poetry should be treated in precisely the same manner as all other types of discourse. In this way we invite closure, yet I do not believe that The New Critics ever felt quite this way, nor do poets think of poems in such a limited manner. The critics represented in Part Two of this collection are all aware of such a fundamental complexity. They often urge us to return to the poem with the same openness as the poet, yet to do so we have to become that involved reader which C. S. Lewis described in his *An Experiment in Criticism*. Lewis suggested that there are really only two modes of reading. The first is with the wonder of a child. The second, and, unfortunately more common method, is to read for information, as we might a newspaper. Lewis' point is basic: a story properly told, or read, invites re-reading; often a child upon hearing a story will ask that it be repeated. However, such pleasure seldom occurs when the emphasis of reading is on obtaining information or mis-information. What fascinates Lewis is the dearth of readers who retain a sense of wonder in an information oriented world where it has become difficult to maintain a sense of delight. Is it that we are caught up in too many other activities? To oversimplify: while critical theory has moved beyond the concerns which we once labeled "formalism" and has focused increasingly upon the controversies about what a text is, or hides, or what a reader's relationship to a text is, there still remain many questions about how readers experience the meaning buried in a text which both radiates presence (Krieger) and is sedimentation (Riddel). It is not an accident that the metaphor "buried" occurs since in a sense any text is dead; such is the nature of a typographical society. The critics in the second part of this collection seek to work out procedures for getting at the wonder of what is a text, yet at the same time they often seem to move in quite different directions as they search for what is signified—either in objective or subjective terms. As Norman Holland reminds us the contemporary critical imagination is moving away from a sense of closure.

E. D. Hirsch, Jr., sometimes referred to by other critics in this book such as Gerald Graff and Michael Steig, has long been concerned with problems of how one interprets a text. Hirsch has examined such issues in his essay "Objective Interpretation" where finally he rejects modes of interpretation which do not provide clearly limited principles of exclusion on the grounds that it is essential that methods be challenged which "hamper the establishment of normative principles in interpretation which thereby encourage the subjectivism and individualism which have for many students discredited the analytical movement." Graff's investigation of the nature of language and literature, as has been suggested, builds along similar lines. What he and Hirsch find alarming is that if critics allow a text's meaning to be dependent on any reader's outlook, "we have not simply a changing meaning but quite possibly as many meanings as readers." Hirsch argues that it is quite important for poets and critics to be aware of concepts of genre, for then a text's "horizon" is specified: "the importance of the horizon concept is that it defines in principle the norms and limits which bound the meaning represented by [a particular]."[3] But although Hirsch admits that in a sense all poets are liars (and to some extent, therefore, speakers and critics as well) he insists that ordinarily a poetic speaker's public stance is not totally foreign to private attitudes. Irony in a successful work, therefore, is perceived as irony. It is not itself a worker of deception. Yet, if I read Hirsch and Graff correctly, understanding what a poet means is finally much more important than understanding precisely what every given word indicates. The major difficulty in construing meaning from a text lies in grasping implications and in avoiding the inference of false meanings within any particular reading. What Hirsch and Graff importantly warn us against is reading which is merely idiosyncratic.

Criticism which grows out of a phenomenological approach has attempted to get back to the essence of what the poet expresses. Hirsch's concerns represent a movement toward procedures for getting at meaning, a method altogether different from those of critics who seem primarily concerned with the semantics of misreading. With Hirsch we are assured (as is the case with the early work of I. A. Richards) that, while it is never possible to explain exactly what any text means, we ought to be able to develop certain procedures while we must also be able to trust the poet. I have lingered with this consideration of Hirsch's theory because of its bearing on the essays in Part One by Murray Krieger, Nathan Scott, Jr., and Gerald Graff as well as the deconstructionist approaches which deal with related issues and essays in Part Two which deal with how to read. Writers in Part Two remind us of the value of individual readings. These critics admit the difficulty of analyzing what a poem presents, yet they also indicate that in analysis we do come nearer to what a poet suggests. This brings us closer to understanding the second group of critics included here—those who in various ways are concerned with the act of reading and the fact of idiosyncrasy.

The fact that some contemporary theory seems to distance us from reality—rather than bring us closer to our world—is an important fact about the "nouvelle critique." Yet we wonder can such distancing be a final answer? Sometimes, says Norman Holland, all we seem to have are "French games." Yet we also realize "our" reading does make a text. The question remains what does this complexity mean, and what can a critic do to understand himself and the complexity of any text better? Some of the critics in the second section would say the text manipulates us; others argue that we manipulate the text. Again, however, just as in the opposition between traditionalists and deconstructionists exhibited in Part One, the truth seems to be somewhere in between. Our understanding of a text results from a combination of the peculiarities of that text and the peculiarities of individual readers. Surely we, as critics, make the text. But just as surely, in a definite way, it makes us too.

Once again, to use a concept of C. S. Lewis's, we seek critics who approach the poem with a sense of wonder and awe. They may not always be satisfied or even confident readers, yet they are imaginative readers, and they realize the complexity of their critical activity. Such concern with the complexity of the reading process is common to all the essays in Part Two. Just what happens when a reader approaches a text wonders Norman Holland? More specifically, what happens when Holland himself reads a poem as in "Transacting my 'Good-Morrow' or, Bring Back the Vanished Critic"? Or what happens when a group of critics react to one another, asks David Bleich? His essay stresses how difficult it is to locate a common epistemology. Or just what are the motivations behind a particular reading of a work of art, asks Michael Steig? To observe carefully and to read these answers is to be instructed in the difficulty of performing any critical act and to be reminded that the critical act is one of wonder. Holland is aware of the complexity which arises from a text. He also seeks to remind us that such complexity is so, in large part, because of the variables of individual temperament, interests, background, biography and even the changing moods of a reader or critic. Similarly, Steig maintains the impulse to interpret follows from an affective response. Thus, just as the structuralists and post-structuralists have forced us to look carefully at the complexity of a text, other critics insist that we cannot forget the complexity of the very process of reading which is primarily centered in the self. Critics such as Holland, Bleich, and Steig assume a responsibility to raise fundamental questions about the way literature, but also the very act of criticism, functions. Of primary importance is the process of reading itself.

All critics, probably all included in this collection, ask questions about reading. It is not, however, just a matter of degree of implicitness or explicitness of grounding that distinguishes one critic from another. The ground to which they are pointing is not a mere function in which man is objectified; the ground is the totality of human existence as the medium in which all such critical functions blend. Speech, intentionality, technique, expressiveness, blend and differentiate themselves from all others. In respect to this shift, it is not only true that man understands texts, but it is also true that texts help us understand man himself. (Some of the problems investigated by critics seemingly as different as Krieger and Holland, therefore, overlap. Both would instruct us to be amazed at the complexity of the text, at how we make it flow together in its unique context and thereby learn about ourselves and a poetic context.)

Michael Steig seeks to bring other, more personal, factors to bear on his analysis of how we read in "Motives for Interpretation." What motivations, he asks, do we as individuals, bring to a text? What combinations of personal and public factors bring about the intricacies of a particular reading? In a related way, Steven Mailloux guides us through some of the intricacies of Reader-Response Criticism, a variety of analysis which allows us to see that response is something which the author, to a significant degree, controls. In "Learning to Read: Interpretation and Reader-Response Criticism," Mailloux demonstrates that interpretation within certain established readings constitutes facts, not the reverse as we might want to imagine. Further, the reader's response is carefully anticipated by the author.

What Holland, Steig and Mailloux insist upon is that any creative act of reading is itself a process. As Samuel Alexander has insisted in his "The Creative Process in the Artist's Mind," a poem is not a translation of some abstract state of mind, but rather a matter of discovery. A poet as he writes finds his thought in the completion of his work: "As the scientific inquirer aims not at the truth but at the solution of his problems, the artist aims to express the subject which occupies his mind in the means which he uses." For Alexander, then, to enter into what the artist does we need to be caught up in a similar process. Another example may clarify: "In Michelangelo's unfinished statues of slaves in the Academy of Florence we can feel the artist not so much making the figure as chipping off flakes of the marble from the figure . . . concealed in it, and which he is laying bare."[4]   Such was also the way, Henry James insisted, he conceived of and executed his fictions, often beginning with the merest glimpse or intimation of what a story would mean. (We remember his prefaces to *Portrait of a Lady, What Maisie Knew,* and *The Ambassadors.*) Yet to appreciate fiction which is cut from an original insight apparently requires that readers enter into a process similar to that which James himself underwent as he composed his work. His books are, most of all, cumulative renderings of what it means to be surrounded by particular circumstances. Yet we know that if we try to explain fully what James (or Michelangelo) means we become perplexed, and must remember that early American deconstructionist's, Gertrude Stein's, maxim: "In a masterpiece there is no thought."

Georges Poulet instructs us in his "Phenomenology of Reading" (and we are again reminded of J. Hillis Miller's essay) that there is a presence within any poem which will not finally be captured by means of an "objectivity" brought to the text. Any grasp is rather a matter of a quality which hovers about the text—something which finally invades the reader. Poulet is, therefore, fascinated by the strange displacement which takes place when a reader absorbs a work, and he finally insists that "criticism, in order to accompany the mind in this effort of detachment from itself, needs to annihilate, or at least momentarily forget, the objective elements of the work, and to elevate itself to the apprehension of a subjectivity without objectivity."[5]

Thus when we read a novel by James or a complex poem, we can never be fully aware of all the conventions of the genre we bring to bear in our judgment, while we also are drawn into a participation in the work (in the very manner Poulet insists).

It is apparently possible for readers both to make judgements about a text, and at other times to be drawn in by that text, and individual personality is thereby displaced. This is what sometimes happens when we watch a drama, admire a piece of sculpture, or listen to music; we apprehend artistic intuition. In reading, too, is not intuition just as important as formal critical judgment? As we have seen, there is a need for utilizing the insights provided by Krieger and Graff, as well as the need for using methods of reading such as those outlined by Leitch, which can finally threaten to become complete subjectivity. Both are valid. Books come alive only when a reader makes them come alive, but it seems to me that critics (looking for facts, yet being drawn in) can over-intellectualize the process of how a reader extracts meaning from the text. Perhaps it is more accurate to speak not of extraction, but of absorption. This is precisely what many of the critics in Part Two insist upon. I am reminded of Gaston Bachelard, with his conception of the ontology of the poetic image. He suggests much of what is sometimes overlooked; the poet, says Bachelard, speaks on the threshold of being, and forces are manifested in poems "that do not pass through the circuits of knowledge."

Bachelard provides a key to many of the problems which interest contemporary theorists in both Parts One and Two of this collection. Poetry is neither wholly fact nor fantasy, neither presence nor absence, neither truth nor untruth; but a combination: "A poetic image eludes casuality." The same is true of life itself, says Bachelard: "Art, [however] is an increase of life, a sort of competition of surprise that stimulates our consciousness and keeps it from becoming somnolent."[6] Thus it is with poetry and with the imagination of a poet or critic which exists on a margin at the point where the function of unreality comes both to charm and disturb yet "always to awaken." A poem, whether the *Song of Roland* or Whitman's "Song of Myself," is startling precisely because it is a blending of history and fact with unreality. Literary works have meaning which can be defined in terms of literary traditions (genre), but we also enter

into them because of immensely complicated cultural and personal reasons. Perhaps within a successful poem reality is not
of primary importance and to expect a poem to provide some
complete discursive mode for structuring reality is therefore
unrealistic.

Almost a century ago, Oscar Wilde chose to examine such
a dilemma in his *The Decay of Lying*, where he asserted that
we only see the world through the frameworks which culture
provides. Art is therefore responsible for much of the way we
think about our world, but "truth in art is a matter only of
style." Wilde, whose culture had confidence in scientific and
discursive modes of structuring reality, viewed this insistence on
"truth" as alarming, while he ventured to insist all art is "lying."
Art, Wilde insists, "never expresses anything but itself," and
art is untruth. Such exaggerations still might serve as good
advice for today's reader caught between a desire for satisfaction on the one hand, and the real threat of ambiguity on the
other. What we need to admit is precisely what Wilde jokes
about: art is not truth; yet we all can (apparently) agree that
intelligent readers throughout the history of civilization have
been attracted to poems, constructions which in a fundamental
sense are untruth. Much criticism, implicity or explicitly, reduces a work to content, to abstract forms (and conventions),
to categories—thereby insulating readers from the possibility
of being subjectively involved in the apprehension of the work.
It is as if some critics are afraid to admit that "lying" and their
own reactions do have value. The value of lying is not in that it
provides us with puzzles to interpret; it has value because it
constitutes an existential predicament we ourselves can hardly
avoid, yet which we must condemn if communication is to be
possible. Truth between men, then, appears as more fundamental,
at least for Wilde, than truth in language. The essays in Part Two
examine related problems and attempt to provide answers to
questions about how individual readers interpret literary works.

The most important fact that any "psychological" approach
to literary theory reminds us of is that there are literally as many
ways to read as there are readers. But equally important is the
fact that a text demands to be read carefully for the poem literally provides a new place in which the reader comes to dwell.
Steven Mailloux shows this in his consideration of reader-re-

sponse. The essay by Charles Altieri, "Criticism as the Situating of a Performance: or What Wallace Stevens Has to Tell Us About Othello," demonstrates how a text demands a particular stance for an informed reading. For Altieri the mind creates a space in which to dwell, and within that space dynamic movement takes place.

In the other essays of Part Two we see critics dealing with ways of accounting for how individual readers approach a text, while always they emphasize careful reading. These range from the self-conscious and personal approach of Norman Holland, schooled in psycho-analytic theory, to the examination of textual problems which are created by unconscious changes made by an author as he manipulates his own text as outlined by Hershel Parker's study, "Cheap Thrills: Lost 'Authority' and Adventitious Aesthetic *Frissons.*" In this study of the author's revisions in texts by Twain, Crane, Fitzgerald and Mailer, Parker demonstrates that even the author, who presumably should know his text best of all, is no reliable guide when it comes to seeing the work as a whole. Parker's essay is of special value for all seeking information about contemporary critical practice. For of what use is sophisticated literary speculation if we are not clear about the text itself? Parker demonstrates, by means of his systematic examination of changes in texts, that authors themselves have difficulty reading their own work, and that our difficulties as critics are compounded if we do not realize this simple yet complicating fact.

Other critics in the second part of the book introduce us to still other problems having to do with aspects of reading. Whether one agrees with Norman Holland who stresses how we manipulate the text, or with Steven Mailloux who stresses how we respond to the text, as they theorize about how individuals are involved in making judgments line by line, one comes to learn that no two readers read in just the same way and that any text has implications beyond its textuality. Reading literature and criticism demands, therefore, that a critic be able to enter into the world imagined by the poet. If the semblance of the poem created by a critic's reading is accurate, he will be able to validate the insights of the writer, and thereby guide other readers. Yet, ironically, if the poetry is really a reflection of felt life, no critic will ever fully understand everything that is implied by any net of interrelationships which a poet provides and through which he recreates a semblance of his original intuition. An element of awe, celebration, and mystery will always remain at the core. The same has to be true of any particular reading. As critics we need both approaches.

Critics can sometimes seem to be caught up in isolated readings—so much so they overlook the cumulative power of a poem; they might do well to remember that the whole poem is the critic's object—not an understanding of separate elements. The poem is not an occasion for the critic merely to de-center it, or to replace the primacy of the poem with the pecularities of individual critical erudition. What critics throughout this collection, and especially in Part Two, acknowledge is the primacy of the literary work. They combine respect for the word along with specific analytical tools which have grown out of other approaches, including the New Criticism, religion, philosophy, psychology, textual bibliography, structuralism, poststructuralism, historicism, and finally criticism of culture itself. In all these ways we become aware of the poet's power to communicate things which are beyond full explanation. This means that a text cannot remain an object for play. True concern with the process of reading is something more than a game. Reading with awe becomes instead a way of perceiving ourselves, and a way of reading the culture itself.

III

With the questions in mind about method which have been raised by the essays in Parts One and Two, we approach the final group of essays in this collection. We should be reminded that Nathan Scott, Jr.'s treatment of Santayana or William V. Spanos' consideration of Heidegger might well have been placed toward the end of this collection for these essays, in their breadth of concern, are just as importantly interdisciplinary as the final four essays by Michael Sprinker, Matei Calinescu, Giles Gunn, and Ihab Hassan which make up the concluding section. While the essays in the first two parts of the book demonstrate a variety of current theoretical approaches, ranging from an insistence upon the value of New Critical accomplishment and Derridean play to an insistence that the critic must, as well, accommodate the idiosyncrasies of the individual reader, as well as the fact of reader-response, many other ways of approaching a text are also basic to today's horizon of theory.

In the concluding four essays the concern is with broader strategies which contemporary critics use to keep readers aware of the complexity of the critical and cultural enterprise. One danger that critics face (In Part One they accuse one another of this.) is of being too insular, too caught up in their own methods and not enough aware of the need for connections and interconnections. Each of the essays in the final part of the book forces readers to see that the poet and the critic must not be isolated from other modes of intellectual activity. These essays remind us that all writing and reading is a social act. The earlier pieces in Parts One and Two, already discussed, which deal with questions of the continuity of traditions, of deconstruction, and of reading and interpretation, all imply this.

The final group of critics stresses that the poet and critic must work together to help readers make connections between poetry and other elements in the culture. We learn, then, in Giles Gunn's analysis of the semiotics of culture and Clifford Geertz's understanding of the moral imagination that any reading of a work is a combination of trust and skepticism. Geertz calls for a link between artistic and cultural analysis. We are also, again, shown that an individual's peculiar interests account for some of the ways in which he reacts to any particular work. Further, our understanding of culture, and our ideological hopes, help to frame our critical approach. Thus, Michael Sprinker in his essay, demonstrates the plight in which Fredric Jameson, as Marxist critic, finds himself in a time when he can do little but lament what he considers the absence of a proper historicism.

Each of these concluding essays moves into territory unlike that explored in any of the preceding investigations. Marxism, Myth, Moral Imagination, Parabiography—in these domains many more questions are raised. An accomplishment of these interdisciplinary approaches to critical theory is to remind readers that the contemporary critic's world should never be an enclosed one. Critical insight must ultimately make connections with life beyond the realm of literature. (So often the critic's temptation is to remain within an hermetically sealed world of literary categories, while this has never really been possible). Poet and critic force us back out to make connections. Each of these concluding writers is intent on reminding us that poetry (and criticism) should be social acts. Yet as they remind us of this, they also remind us of the complexity of a world where the literary and cultural constantly overlap. Sprinker and Gunn remind us of the complexity of any critical enterprise and they force us to make connections with the past. All of these writers stress that poetry (and criticism) should be social acts. Matei Calinescu guides us through the work of Mircea Eliade, who has constantly refused to allow a reductionist simplification of man's place in the universe. Eliade's response to religion is an aesthetic, a vital one which emphasizes growth, continuity, and eternal return. If Calinescu would force us to make connections with the past, Ihab Hassan would force us to look toward the future.

For the *Studies* issue of 1979, Hassan provided an essay which was called "Desire, Imagination, Change: Outline of a Critical Project."[8]   That piece would make an excellent conclusion for the present book, especially since one of its values lies in how it suggests parallels between what the critic and the scientist do. We have chosen instead to end the collection with a newer essay by Hassan, "Parabiography: The Varieties of Critical Experience," which is a meditation about the varieties of critical responsibility. Hassan stresses the freedom of a critic both to be imaginative and to exercise moral force. He also emphasizes the fact that in our very search for the "roots of knowledge and being," we constantly risk discontinuity and "illusions of newness." Hassan's speculations because they are parabiographical draw us closer to others, and that too is a social act.

In a critic like Hassan we see the value of synthesis. Finally the critic becomes like the poet, and the connections between the criticism and the world criticized (text as/and actuality) are more clearly drawn. We are reminded by Hassan, once again, that a successful critic can neither put the work (or his critical act) in separate containers. Each leads to each. Reading a poem, or an autobiographical or critical essay must have a social function because it is not possible to read a work of literature within a vacuum. Even as solitary readers we still read within (or for?)

some imagined group.

Perhaps it is this social aspect of criticism which had been most in danger of being overlooked during the past decades while critics placed so much emphasis on how a text means, or what a text signifies. In a recent study of literature as social experience Gordon Mills meditates on some of the problems which result because readers trust both abstractions and intuitions. By way of qualification, Mills writes "our trust in the concrete and our trust in the abstract, [both] seem to me to be true. I presume the principles involved in both are incessantly at work in the literature we read and in our response to it. The incompatibility between the principles in these insights is probably only a reflection of the mystery of our situation in the universe. It would be a very different universe if we could trust either all our perceptions or all our abstract relationships."[9] To begin to get at the full significance of a literary work, it is necessary to realize that readers make certain assumptions *both* about the abstract and the concrete. (As critics we might do well to observe how popular culture is absorbed and transmitted. Critics as diverse as James Agee and William Empson have pondered these matters, and the implications of their thinking suggest that ideas within popular literature are transmitted both because of the rationality of their ideas and because of an ever-present ambiguity of emotional factors.) Judgment about literary work finally involves emotional, spiritual, and intellectual factors, surely combinations of mystery and understanding.

IV

This book has been devised as an introduction to some of the most significant activities in recent American criticsm. The critics included demonstrate the interests and responsibilities which they have assumed as the boundaries of criticism open up toward still wider areas of concern. Clearly critical theory can no longer be content with an isolation which sets it apart from the other enterprises of man. Yet many practical problems remain for readers who seek to find their way in this new and largely uncharted terrain. Among these problems is a breakdown of old distinctions between poem and criticism and the tentativeness of much modern criticsm. I close with still more questions: Could it be that today's critic is slowly coming to a view which is related to that which poets as diverse as Wordsworth, Hopkins, Rilke and Valery long ago reached? Could it be that this critic, so recently hopeful that he would explain and explicate, is slowly coming around to the view that he is foremost a mediator of the impossibility of complete mediation? Here Krieger, Holland, Steig and Hassan would agree! Could this be why so much of contemporary criticism sounds like parody? Does today's critic provide doubt, defense, and truth all at once? Here Scott, Riddel, Sprinker, and Parker are called to mind. Three words also come to mind: *parody, parados, paradox.* 1) *Parody* (from the Greek, a counter-song). A composition imitating the characteristic style of some other work. *Critics Singing.* 2) *Parados* (from the French, *para* and *dos* [dorsum] in military usage an embankment of earth at the back edge of a trench for protection against gunfire from the rear). An exercise in protection. *Critics Digging in.* 3) *Paradox.* (from the Latin, *paradoxum,* and the Greek, *paradoxon,* a statement that seems contradictory, unbelievable, or absurd, but that may actually be true in fact, or a statement that is self-contradictory, and, hence, false). We approach the truth, yet we may never understand. *Critics contradicting.*

Ultimately as critics (and as critics of critics) we seem to be coming closer to the view that there is more than we can ever unravel (deconstruct). It was a nice thought to hope we could unlock the secrets of writing, but would a poet be compelled to use metaphor and song if he thought and felt that such a cry would be explained? Here we approach the heart (soul? spirit? ghost?) at the center, yet we do not, Heidegger would remind us, feel at home, with such mysteries. Is it because we have earlier put such single-minded confidence in the word? Much of today's criticism seems to exist for its parts, and increasingly critics become specialists in the parts; but have we been like mechanics who have never seen the machine? Like factory workers who do not know what they make? Are we too busy with parody and parados? Are we critics who may never experience a sense of awe? And is this finally like talking about meditation? A perfectly innocent activity—but altogether different from *to be* centered.

Now what lies on the horizon? Could it be the possibility

of an acknowledgement of a desire to approach the center, a
place of quiet?   Yet must this be the acknowledgement of a
beginning and ending never to be fully judged, never to be fully
expressed in terms of law and concept?   Might it be that criticism's self-reflectivity is within a story far more complex than we
as critics can begin to tell?

There is nothing wrong with *parody* (maybe it makes us
look at the real thing); nor with *parados* (we should be prepared for attack from the rear).   But with fun, which suggests
a seriousness, and with a concern for protection, which suggests
more than anything else vulnerability, we can also be ready to
welcome the *paradox* of our critical activities as readers, seekers,
teachers, story-tellers, as persons living the continuity formed
because of the ghosts of the past, other critics and other poets.
To say we are in a haunted house could even be an asset, not a
liability.   What if we were in an *empty* house?

Could it be that today's critic is slowly coming round to
the view that he cannot fully mediate?   Yet at the same time,
might it be that he can express a yearning just as does the poet,
and that his criticism reflects that yearning?   Varieties of post-
structuralism in this world of museums may finally lead critics
and readers to an awareness of a beauty not perhaps of the
whole but of the fragments.   And through these fragmentary exchanges (exchange means to receive, or give, *for* another thing)
we glimpse what may be the whole, many different approaches,
not just one.   We dismantle so that we can be reminded that
we can also do the opposite.   In our exchanges we are reminded
that neither deconstruction or construction will ever be finished.
Above all, perhaps we are coming to learn that we must learn
to tolerate, and in so doing we can profit from the varieties of
theory and criticism available to us.

NOTES

[1] Harari, Josué V. *Textual Strategies, Perspectives in Post-Structuralist Criticism* (Ithaca: Cornell University Press, 1979), p. 69.

[2] *Ibid.,* p. 70.

[3] Hirsch, E. D. Jr. "Objective Interpretation," first appeared in *PMLA* 75 (1960), in *Critical Theory Since Plato,* ed. by Hazard Adams (New York: Harcourt, Brace, Jovanovich, 1971), p. 1178, p. 1179, and p. 1183.

[4] Alexander, Samuel, from *Beauty and Other Forms of Value* (1933), in *Critical Theory,* op. cit., p. 868.

[5] Poulet, Georges, first appeared in *New Literary History,* 1 (1969), in *Critical Theory,* op. cit., p. 1222.

[6] Bachelard, Gaston, *The Poetics of Space,* translated from the French by Maria Jolas (New York: Orion Press, 1964), p. xiii, p. xviii, and p. xx.

[7] A recent book collects theoretical statements on readers and reader-response. See *Reader-Response Criticism* ed. by Jame P. Tomkins (Baltimore: John Hopkins Press, 1980).

[8] *Studies in the Literary Imagination,* 12 (Spring, 1979), pp. 129-143.

[9] Mills, Gordon, *Hamlet's Castle, The Study of Literature as a Social Experience,* (Austin: The University of Texas Press, 1976), p. 109.

PART ONE

Theory and Practice

LITERATURE VS. *ÉCRITURE*: CONSTRUCTIONS AND DECONSTRUCTIONS IN RECENT CRITICAL THEORY

by
Murray Krieger

I want to begin by surveying in a brief compass the theoretical conflicts currently animating our academic literary criticism and to make clear my own attitude toward them. Since I want to be brief in my summaries, I shall have to oversimplify various critical positions in order to place the variety of statements within each of them into patterns that I hope are accurate, even if only generally so.

Since those days, now at least two decades back, when we could speak confidently about the dominance of American criticism by the so-called New Criticism, a number of contenders has arisen to claim the place of primary influence. Whatever the differences among them, they seem to share the role of exacting retribution upon the New Criticism for its excesses. We associate the New Criticism with an exclusive focus upon the isolated literary work to the neglect of its relations to its author, its audience, and the language of which it is representative. Thus New Critics overemphasized the discontinuity of the poem and the experience appropriate to it, rejecting any continuity with the experiences of its creator and its reader or its continuity with discourse in general. Each of these areas of neglect seems to have sponsored a variety of criticism which has claimed some following in these post-New-Critical days.

If their idolatrous approach to the insulated poem as something like a sacred object led some New Critics to ignore authorial consciousness and with it the act of writing, some post-New Critics turned from work to author with a vengence, blending the work into his consciousness. Others turned instead to to the passing moments of the actual and even wayward experience of the reader and dissolved the work into them. And since New Critics, in their exclusive concentration on the poem, conferred upon it a privilege which cut it off as a discrete entity from the rest of language, still other post-New Critics have tried insistently to reestablish the unbroken continuity of all our discourse, poems and non-poems, as they merge the aesthetic into the continuity of all our experience.[1]

In the later 1950's it was Northrop Frye who, with his followers, led a resurgence of interest in Romanticism which sought to undercut the antagonisms of the classic dispassion that characterized the New Criticism. Then the influence of newer Continental critical movements began to assert itself, first by the so-called phenomenological critics, more accurately called "critics of consciousness" after the model of the Geneva School, most often seen in this country as represented by George Poulet. Though there have been other, philosophically more faithful versions of phenomenological criticism after Husserl, Ingarden, and Merleau-Ponty, it was the freer, more subjectivistic variety introduced to us by Poulet that attracted the neo-Romantic mood already aroused by Frye. It also fed the neo-Romantic return to an interest in the writer and his world as his consciousness constitutes it for him. Those other critics we more accurately call phenomenological have usually preferred to concern themselves with the mental states of readers in their perceptions of literary works. Such reader-oriented criticism is reflected not only in the so-called School of Konstanz but—perhaps even more influentially among younger American scholars—in the critics trying to apply speech-act theory to the work's confrontation of its reader, and especially in the "affectivist" work of Stanley Fish. But on this occasion I cannot pursue these several directions since there is one other major movement on which I want to dwell.

Only with structuralism, together with post-structuralism, also derived from Continental sources, do we find a movement with the spread and attempted dominance to match the New Criticism's. Indeed, in the semiotic ambition that would synthesize all the "sciences of man," structuralism would claim far greater a hegemony. And its following among younger scholars threatens to become far more extensive, spreading as it does well beyond the precincts of literary study. Its power rests on totally new and revolutionary grounds that would destroy the basis of all traditional criticism which it would replace as it deconstructs. For, in its most forceful posture, it would do away with any distinction among the modes of discourse, indeed in its extreme form even the distinction between criticism and the poem which is its object: it would deny that criticism serves, as a secondary and derivative art, the primary art of poetry. Instead it would see them both, with all their sister disciplines, sharing—as coordinates and equals—the common realm of *écriture*. There are, of course, many different voices in the domain of structuralism and post-structuralism, and they are often raised in violent debate with one another, as we move from a Lévi-Strauss to a Lacan or a Foucault or a Derrida, or as we move through each of Barthes' new and changing pronouncements, as these debate with one another. And we must ask, with some of these writers, whether he is structuralist or not, as he protests his freedom from the movement. More generally, we must ask when post-structuralism ceases to be structuralist.

What these positions share derives from a Saussurean view of language, which, by way of its universal analysis of discourse into *langue* and *parole,* must come to the leveling of any privilege which poems have been granted. Man is seen as an identical speaker-writer in all his varied discourses, each built upon equally arbitrary signifiers, based upon a monolithic principle of differentiation. We are instructed to find the unity of all discursive disciplines in a common structure of signifiers, whatever their arbitrary signifieds may turn out to be. Thus our analysis of any of these disciplines rests on the methodological assumption that homology is all. However favorable our attitude toward interdisciplinary study may be, however intense our search for a unifying principle for the human sciences, this procedure may well suggest too easy and undifferentiated a series of analogies (or rather homologies), especially—we should add—for a theory expressly based on the doctrine of difference. Still, these theorists surely represent (among other things) history's egalitarian revenge upon the New Criticism's aristocratic worship of the poem as a privileged and hence elite object, an object as separate from all others as it is from our normal experience. (This socio-political language is intended more than figuratively as it is used by many in the structuralist tradition.)

In the extreme form of Barthean semiology, the literary work (as we may obsoletely term it) flows with all others into the sea of *écriture*, part of an anonymous universal and inter-textual code that is a single system. The structural sameness behind the disposition of signifiers, though they parade their would-be signifieds before us, should remind us that it is but a mythification for us to take those signifieds literally, as if they and their claims represented a conceptual "reality." For, instead of signifiers embracing their signifieds, they stand at a hopeless distance from them, with a relationship between the two that is arbitrary at best. And, for the post-structuralist, the world of discourse becomes as empty as the world itself. With this claim, we are reminded that the post-structuralist, if not the structuralist, impulse, though its motives seem to be linguistic, may be seen as springing from the metaphysical (or rather anti-metaphysical) anguish that accompanies our sense of the "disappearance of God." Verbal meanings seem to follow God out of our experience, the one abandoning our language as the other abandons our world. Thus in Jacques Derrida or Paul de Man we often see linguistic terminology disguising an existential sense of absence. It is a lingering Heideggerian impulse. If their literary theories seem breathtakingly new, the motivating notion of the death of God does not. (It is not difficult to understand the role of Nietzsche as one of the major prophets of the movement.)

In such theorists both world and language come to be seen as decentered since, in the grand marriage of Nietzsche and Saussure, the world is reduced utterly to language, a now-empty world of language defined as the disposition of signifiers alone. Both world and language are seen as decentered; for any of us to claim to find a center ringed by signifieds, concepts whose would-be meanings we reify into reality, is for us to resort to the mythology of metaphysics, ripe for deconstruction. But if *all* language, as the common *écriture*, is equally doomed to emptiness, then our long-standing convictions about poetic presence in the book and the word can be demystified and revealed as the pious delusions they are. The study of poems becomes, for such theorists, the study of such decentering, such emptiness. The critic, thus licensed (or thus deprived), must content himself with the absence rather than the presence of meaning, with verbal deferral rather than self-assertiveness, with poems as centrifugal rather than centripetal movements.   As in de Man, criticism studies the poet at a distance from himself and the world, sending forth words that acknowledge the gap, the awesome void, between themselves and their would-be objects.   Linguistics, having yielded to thematics, now claims a poetics, what Joseph Riddel, in the spirit of Derrida, terms "the poetics of failure," the failure of the word.   The "uncreating word" of the *Dunciad's* apocalyptic end has come again, this time heralded and theoretically shepherded.

As I have suggested by mentioning Nietzsche, this movement may well represent an extreme extension into poetics of the mood of wan despair that has been with us for over a century.   We may recall that Matthew Arnold's own concern to come to terms with the new *un*metaphysical realities, while retaining a special role for poetry, led him to grant to poetry the psychological powers lost by religion along with our belief in its claims.   If we share Arnold's loss of faith, we can go either of two ways: we can view poetry as a human triumph made out of our darkness, as the creation of verbal meaning in a blank universe to serve as a visionary substitute for a defunct religion; or we can—in our negation—extend our faithlessness, the blankness of our universe, to our poetry.   If we choose the latter alternative, then we tend, like de Man, to reject the first, affirmative humanistic claim about poetry's unique power, seeing it as a mystification arising from our nostalgia and our metaphysical deprivation.

Stubbornly humanistic as I am, I must choose that first alternative: I want to remain responsive to the promise of the filled and centered word, a signifier replete with an inseparable signified which it has created within itself.   But I am aware also thay my demythologizing habit, as modern man, must make me wary of the grounds on which I dare claim verbal presence and fullness.   And I am grateful for my recollection that the aesthetic domain—the domain of *aesthesis*, of *Schein*—has been, from Plato onward, acknowledged to be the world of appearance, of illusion, so that verbal power, under the conditions of the aesthetic, need not rely upon a metaphysical sanction to assert its moving presence.

I have before now in several places argued for the power of a poem to persuade us of its own verbal presence, even while its "theme" may well have been that of separateness and absence.[2]   The point I have been trying to establish is that the existential theme of absence, of distance, indeed of one's very failure to touch the world while being overcome by it—however moving and universal this theme has been in our time and earlier—need not lead to an equal absence, distance, and failure in the created language of the poet who deals with it. Critics used to believe that a mark of the great poet was his power to overwhelm with his expression the gaps in the commonplace language of the rest of us as we try to stammer out our sense of the human predicament. It does not require us to surrender our sense of that predicament if we claim that combinations of words can be created which permit us to grasp it as we cannot for ourselves. Although Yvor Winters was not one of my favorite critics, I begin to sympathize with the impatience with which he used to invoke "the fallacy of imitative form" to characterize the activity of the poet who deprived himself of the capacity to transcend (and thus to transform) his materials.

It may be instructive, as an indication of how criticism has moved from valorizing the formal overcoming of thematic distance to valorizing the formal (or rather the anti-formal) echo of it, to compare Cleanth Brooks' invocation of romantic irony to Paul de Man's.[3]   For Brooks, as the representative New Critic, the poet employs irony as his device to master—through the conflation of them within a word—the several separated and even opposed layers of meaning and being. For de Man, irony is a reflection of the subject's isolated and powerless state as he relates himself to the nature (object) from which he is alienated. Poetry cannot for de Man succeed in escaping the fate of laguage as a differentiating instrument, trapping itself within its speaker. So in de Man irony returns the subject upon himself, thereby guaranteeing the inefficacy of his language to touch the endlessly differentiated world—differentiated, most of all, from himself.   On the other hand, the irony of Brooks enables the speaker—whatever the dehumanized state of the outside world as it oppresses him—to capture it all in his word and thereby, at least aesthetically, to humanize it after all.   If neither's irony alters the fallen reality, at least that of Brooks asserts man's formal power to comprehend it, whatever his existential status as forlorn subject.

Now it is true that the New Critics tended to bestow this substantive ontological role upon the word too literally, so that a later linguistic skepticism provided a needed demystification. Still, within the provisional nature of our aesthetic habit of response, is there not an illusion of verbal presence which we can find in the poems which constitute our canon? And from here can we not move to the further illusion that existential space and its gaps are collapsed into the sensible unity contained in words exploited for themselves? Would these moves not seem to preserve literature as a kind of discourse which seemed to be performing differently from its fellows?

Can we, then, propose a theory of literature that allows for literature even while taking into account the warnings about mystification which the structuralist movement has effectively used to displace its precursors?[4] I see this as the major question I must answer since, as we saw at the opening of this essay, post New-Critical movements seem to have defined themselves by their opposition to one or another element of neglect (poet, reader, or discourse as a whole) indulged in by the New Criticism as it reified its object. Need all the gains bequeathed by this movement be washed away along with the metaphysical orthodoxy and epistemological naiveté that apparently made those gains possible?

Clearly, any defense of a separatist concept of literature must today be provisional, if not paradoxical, in that it must free itself to attend to an object in whose independent existence it cannot afford to believe. It is for this reason that I see the critic dealing with intentionalities and illusions, even though his attention to our habits of aesthetic perception and the history of artistic conventions permits him to salvage what he can of an art object—not altogether unstable—functioning within its culture and serving that culture's visionary needs. Under the literary man's pressure to do justice to the art he tends, but equally under the pressure of recent deconstructionist theory, I feel both the presence of the object and the phantom nature of that presence. In this way I hope that—if one is candid enough—it is possible to evade a wishful reification on the one side and the dissolution of the literary experience on the other.

So, despite contrary tendencies, I mean to urge not only our recognition of the poet's verbal power for humanistic affirmation even in the face of the blankness of our common language, but also the availability of the poet's product as a special sort of stimulus for our response. Still, I must emphasize our present instinct for demystification in order to remind us of the crucial phenomenological qualification which reduces the art object from ontology to illusion. As we yield to the prodding of our aesthetic experience which would have us reify literature as an autonomous entity, we dare not forget that its illusionary role must somehow allow for its existence within the indivisible domaine of écriture. It is thus the case that any concept of literature which recognizes its ties, before and after, to a continuum of language and experience will have to treat its status as literature most delicately if that status is to be salvaged at all.

Even a modified phenomenological defense of literature as a special mode of discourse is likely to depend upon some claim in behalf of a peculiarly literary use of language. Such a claim rests, in turn, upon an assumption that there is a "normal" use of langauge and that language becomes poetic through deviations from the norms of "non-poetic" language usage.[5] But the long-accepted doctrine about language norms and deviations from them has been steadily undermined in recent years. Stanley Fish's attack on "deviation theory" and its dependence on the concept of an "ordinary language" is only one—if one of the more effective—of such attacks.[6] The insistence of Hayden White that all language is tropological, that it all has a "swerve" in the direction of the peculiar figurative vision of the discourse, leaves no neutral linguistic ground for language to swerve *from*.[7] One could observe this general tendency in recent theorists who, with a neo-Kantian awareness of the constitutive nature of language and cognition, insist on seeing all language as revealing a version of reality rather than reality itself, a context-controlled shaping of verbal figures rather than a transparent show of universal meanings outside and independent of all language. So all language comes in recent theory to be seen as constitutive of its visions, creative of its fictions, in poetry and non-poetry alike. Consequently, any line between poetry and non-poetry is seen to be mythical as all discourse is similarly gathered under the blanket of *écriture*.

How, then, can I at this late date urge the deviationist claim for poetry which I need if I am to urge its separatist mode of functioning? For how—to ask the same question another way—can I still speak of "normal" discourse as a mythical background against which deviations are to occur? Perhaps my answer is summed up precisely by such an acknowledgment that the concept of normal discourse *is* mythical, though it is necessary fiction if we are to account for the effects which the poetry in the western canon is capable of producing in those of us who come to it with the trained habit of aesthetic response. Can recent arguments for a seamless *écriture* altogether wipe out our common-sense awareness of the distinction between those discourses which are predicated on the assumption that they are telling us about a "reality" outside language—that they are more or less "true"—and those which are self-consciously cultivated fictions? We of course approach made-up stories about imagined people differently from discourse which claims to say things directly to us about the world; and we do so in part in deference to what we assume the writer means to do with us and to us. Yet the sophisticated claim about the similar metaphoric fictionality of all discourse would lead us to deny any such "common-sense" distinction as naive.

I would urge our "common-sense" awareness of yet a second distinction, this one between discourse which seems anxious to sacrifice itself in order to transmit extra-linguistic notions available in several possible verbal sequences or languages and discourse which seems to generate its meaning out of the very internalized play of its verbal medium, so that its meaning is untranslatably locked in "these words in this order." Recent theorists may well argue that there is no synonymity in *any* discourse,[8] thus reinforcing the antagonism against a claim for a poetic discourse which would create its nature through its unique untranslatability; but shall we not distinguish between the grappling with language to generate meanings as special as the very words and the lazier, stereotyped thing most of us do most of the time? It is refreshing to recall that the one earlier and most universally recognized contribution of the New Criticism was its power to distinguish the originally creative use of the language from the general storehouse of stock expressions which appear, in borrowed form, in discourse. To call the latter "creative," whatever the epistemological likelihoods in the mind of man as language-user, is to engage in a basic misuse of the language of creation. (I thus acknowledge my belief that, even in my desire to say something original here, I am essentially discovering—picking up as best I can to satisfy my minimal verbal requirements at each step—the language I am using and not, in any way that suggests what the poet does, creating it in the sense of making it new.)

I argue, then, that most trained readers of poetry feel an acute difference between discourse characterized by a self-generating play of words which maximally exploits all that is potentially in them, exploding them into its meaning, and the loosely instrumental "use" of words selected from the bag of almost equal candidates for service which our culture places at our disposal to carry—one or another of them in its minimal way—a predetermined extra-linguistic meaning. Of course, this is a matter of degree rather than of kind, so that boundary cases will have to exist and be debated about—and perhaps with almost every case a potential boundary case. Yet the theoretical distinction is a crucial and felt one for so many readers that there is likely to be considerable agreement about poetic and prosaic extremes. Between extremes of verbal manipulations tending toward and away from synonymity, and all that synonymity implies about the verbal satisfactions of maximal or minimal requirements, there may well be difficult and confusing examples of discourse which may appear to some to ask to be read one way and to others another way. And these often turn out to be the not-quite-philosophical-not-altogether-"literary" texts at the center of much recent theoretical discussion. But, far from proving the non-existence of literature as a relatively separate entity demanding unique interpretive methods, such texts (as they have recently been treated) may rather be seen as broadening the applicability of literary methods, thereby enlarging the peculiarly literary domain of literature to include self-consciously reflexive writers whose fictions include the illusion that they are non-fictional.

So all discourse may indeed be a metaphorically derived fiction at its source, and its language may indeed be creative of its reality. But, in the face of such epistemological concessions as I make here, I still suggest the phenomenological distinctions which the differentiated structures of our verbal experiences present to us. The self-consciously developed fictional illusion of discourse to which we respond as aesthetic creates in its turn the illusion that there is a "normal" discourse from which it deviates. (Of course, we must grant that by this time there is nothing either shocking or blameworthy in our creating—among all the fictions we create—the fiction that there *is* a "normal" discourse or that, except in poetic discourse, there is a synonymity among words.) As we contemplate and seek to define what *can* happen in that fused linguistic "corporeality" which poetic discourse sponsors the illusion of attaining, our habit of finding (or making) binary oppositions may be pressed to the invention of another class of discourse, a prosaic sort that helps us mark by opposition the magical behavior we feel we have witnessed and been partner to in poetry. And we come up on the other side with the ruthless instrumentality of a neutral, normal discourse which is self-deceived in its intention to be self-effacingly referential. The structuralist insistence that the signifier cannot have more than an arbitrary relation to its supposed signified is perhaps the strongest way of putting this claim of universal synonymity—a claim that is supposed to allow me here, for example, to grab onto any word that satisfies the minimal requirements, from moment to moment, of the field of linguistic forces developing before me. The invention of binary oppositions as a structuralist principle can thus win the literary man's assent through his own need to have such a principle as one from which the uniquely monistic principle of poetic discourse can deviate, and with apparently magical results.

In behalf of this sort of literary man and his cherished response to his favored works, we have been doing little more than circling and recircling his one tautology: that a poem is a speech-act and writing-act which deviates radically from our non-poetic uses of speech and writing. It is seen as becoming a version of *parole* which has been made to deviate from others so significantly as to make it autonomous and self-regulatory such as no *parole,* by definition, can be. Thus the experienced and properly initiated reader of poetry may be encouraged by the successful poem to sense the generic language system, or *langue*, behind it as violated and distorted until what is before us is seen as a self-generating and self-responsive—in short, as a reflexive—system.[9] As this reader comes to view it, every deviation from normal usage is converted into a constitutive element of an apparently new system which can occur only this one time.   The minimal functions of language, which usually satisfy us as speakers and writers, are thus converted—as he watches— into maximal functions of the totally realized poem.

In this way the need to operate in a special way upon all that goes on in a poem forces this reader to retain the opposition between "normal" and "deviationist" models of discourse as his binary fiction. The contrary claim—that all *paroles* stand in a similar relation to their *langue* so that a poem is just another *parole* on the same level as all others—collapses the opposition, of course. If the *parole* is to the *langue* as the particular to the universal in the Platonic model, then all *paroles*—poetry among them—are equally subordinate, common subjects all. Structuralist uniformity, extending *parole* into *écriture*, here makes alliance with the claim of E. D. Hirsch in precluding—or at least demystifying in advance—the very concept of poetry as a kind of discourse.

Yet must we not resist such a denial to the extent that our literary experience is otherwise?   In the greatest literary works, those documents which have—throughout their history with us—been treated as elite, those which, in other words, constitute the literary canon in the western tradition, the illusion of an autonomous, self-generating reflexivity in language persists for those trained to read them appropriately (that is, in ways appropriate to our conventions for reading our elite literary works). We are persuaded toward viewing such a work as a self-sufficient system because we grant to it a peculiar status as a fiction, a freestanding fiction which seems conscious of that status, building that consciousness (which we grant it) out of the self-referential devices we claim to find in it. Skeptically aware these days of the literary man's propensities for mystification, we may be uncertain of the extent to which we have been hypnotized by it or merely self-hypnotized.   Yet the sensitive and knowing reading of the work which seems to do its work upon us somehow each time breaks through our wariness and our wilfully irreverent inclination for demystifying our idols.

In this discussion I have been using the terms *langue* and *parole* and other references to linguistics in a metaphorical sense far broader than what is meant technically by them. To those who know my work it should be clear that the norms I speak of, or the deviations from them and the systems constituted by those deviations, are not to be thought of as exclusively verbal, though surely in many poems the words are the major element of the literary medium being manipulated into its own constitutive form and into its own self-consciousness. But as we move outward from lyric to narrative and dramatic modes, we find a number of presentational elements which serve as the manipulable medium, whether the staged presence (at once real and unreal) in drama, the point of view in narrative, or the great variety of received conventions—stylistic, formal, topological, or tropological—in all the genres. In effect, the medium is anything which the poet can convert into his performance space within his fiction, within his radical of presentation, within his language. That is, it is the space within which he performs his reflexive play, and persuades us to join him in it. We learn the internally generated rules fabricated for the occasion, and what they give rise to—within that performance space, whatever the genre—is the special sort of fiction we call literature.

Still, once we have decided—with whatever qualifications—to separate out literature from *écriture*, we must concern ourselves with the placement of a theoretical dividing line between literature and non-literature. This problem is especially troublesome if we have acknowledged the authority of those arguments which would deconstruct any separatist notion of literature. But whatever the mystifications of its more idolatrous critics, literature itself is no enemy to the deconstructive impulse. Far from it. Indeed, one might well argue that in its reflexivity and self-consciousness literature not only deconstructs itself but is the very model for our use in the deconstruction of other discourse. Modern theorists may be anxious to undercut the privilege granted literature by levelling it into common *écriture*, but what they have for the most part done is to raise *écriture* (or at least those non-literary examples of *écriture* they are dealing with) into literature. If these critics argue against the exclusiveness of poetry (that is, fictions, "imaginative literature") as the proper subject for criticism, and rather seek to include a wide range of works by essayists, philosophers, and even social scientists, they do so by treating these works as texts to which techniques appropriate to literary criticism

may be applied.   Even more, their techniques of deconstruction, of "unmetaphoring" their texts, are to a great extent
echoes of what poems have always been doing to themselves
and teaching their critics to do to them.

It is for this reason I suggest that, instead of the
concept of literature being deconstructed into *écriture,*
écriture has been constructed into literature.   As a consequence, everything has become a "text," and texts—as
well as the very notion of textuality—have become as
ubiquitous as writing itself, with each text now accorded
the privilege mode of interpretation which used to be
reserved for discourse with the apparent internal self-justification of poetry.   But if the no-longer-elite object of
criticism has fewer characteristics which seem to deserve
this concentrated treatment, it is a boon to criticism (and a
boost to critical arrogance): as deconstruction ceases to be
an element in a work no longer reflexive and device-filled,
it increasingly becomes a central feature of the critic's
interpretive reading of it.   And the text of the critic, in its
deconstructive shrewdness, can now expect to outdo its
object-text, whose native qualities are no longer a match for the
critic's own.

Yet even in the face of this development in recent theory,
we still can seek a separate phenomenological definition for the
peculiar forms we call literature, those whose justification
for deconstructionist treatment appears to lie within themselves.
We can very well grant, with Hayden White, that all the varieties
of discourse are similarly constitued by their guiding tropes.[10]
We have already observed that, in theorists like White, the egalitarian principle works to claim, not that no discourse is art, but
that all discourse is art.   Each discourse is at its source creative:
each creates its own tropological fiction; even discourse which
pretends to deal "objectively" or "empirically" with its data
from the outset "emplots" that data in accordance with the fiction permitted by the trope.   What place, then, can there be for
a "literature" which has a peculiar tropological functioning of
its own?[11]

According to the tropological universalism of White, discourse (poetic or otherwise) as it comes under analysis may be

seen generally as tracing similar figurative patterns.   And all such examples are then equally literary as they present themselves for analysis by the critic of tropes.   Each is seen as moving from metaphor to metonymy to synecdoche to irony, although there is some ambiguity about whether, as observed in discourse, these are analytic coordinates or (as in Vico) progressive stages. The sequence of figures surely leads from the primitive to the sophisticated, from the instinctual to the cerebral, from the naive to the self-conscious, in what seems to be a common romantic and post-romantic pattern of the fall of man, usually the fortunate fall.[12]   The sequence seems to move from an immediate, prediscursive, subjective identity (metaphor) to the particularizing differentiation as of items in a contiguous series (metonymy) to the totalizing of particulars into generalizations (synecdoche) to the self-consciously subversive reflection upon the entire process (irony).   We seem here to be dealing with modalities of consciousness as much as with linguistic tropes (or is the first utterly reducible to the second?), and we seem to have a series marked by cumulative progression even though there is a temptation to valorize each stage on its own.

(This pattern of discourse is seen as a reflection of the psychic history of the individual human consciousness as well as the collective history of western consciousness.   So, besides being an instrument for understanding discursive structure, it seems to propose a way of accounting for human development, both individual and collective, and in an identical sequence which suggests the principle that phylogeny reproduces ontogeny.   No wonder, if all private consciousness and public history reveal these structures, that they invade all our varied discourses equally, or at least similarly.   Of course, such structural analogies may reflect our own monomyth based on a privileged plot we have invented and projected onto discourse, consciousness, and history alike.   White's own radical skepticism allows us to doubt that the ubiquitous pattern [like the pattern of the fall on which it appears to be based] is seen because the tropology reflects a true state of universal structuration [of consciousness as well as language, or of consciousness because of language] ; it rather allows us to suspect that the pattern is seen because of a romantic and post-romantic convention of thought of which this tropological claim is no more than a recent version.   From this perspective the pattern

accounts for so many poets and thinkers of the past two centuries not because we have unlocked the secret of their common
discursive structures, but because their conventional mytholo-
gies of emplotment have invaded our own discursive habits,
turning our own work into just another historically controlled
example of an influential tropological habit of writing.)

In this series of the four tropes, the crucial movement—
at least for getting discourse started—is from the first to the
second, from metaphor to metonymy. The metaphorical world
of similitudes and analogies must dissolve its unity of a universally mirrorized sameness, dissolve it into a differentiated sequence of separated entities, so that language and rational science
may begin. From individual verbal boundaries, carefully demar-
cated and observed, words can then be marshalled into the
generality of propositions, a new unity of synecdoche, but now
safely arrived at through the observance of the rational law
of verbal differentiation upon which the very beginning of discourse in metonymy was predicated. Beyond this would-be
scientific security, nothing is left except the occasional reminder, by an ironic wisdom, that this has all been a movement
only in the world of tropes, and that the clean scientific objective has been a deceptive one in that the continual urge for
differentiation, in depriving language of its metaphorical moment
with *its* urge for sameness, has also deprived itself of its content, has in effect emptied itself. Yet our skeptical awareness
of the tropological bent which diverted the referential preten-
tions of the discourse reminds us of its figurative basis, so that
structuralist analysis reveals it to be more literary than scientific.

It is here, in this universal model for the tropes of all discourse—the model which for all practical purposes is to turn
all the varieties of discourse into literature—that we find a
unique characteristic of literature as distinguished from non-
literature. It rests—as we should have remembered from Jakobson—on literature's special relation to metaphor, on its need to
overcome the normally differential character of language. We
must note, in White's scheme (whose elements seem to be as
much borrowed from Piaget as they are applied to Piaget),
that prior to the differentiating action of metonymy, the metaphoric stage—with its commitment to identity—was essentially
pre-linguistic. What I mean to suggest is that, if discourse nor-

mally must find its nature by making its way from identity (metaphor) to difference (metonymy), literature has the role of earning its way back to identity from the differential nature of normal discourse from which it deviates. Thus literature has the peculiar task of becoming a kind of discourse which, as discourse, can yet appear to occupy the normally non-discursive metaphorical stage.

As I conceive it, literature performs this feat, not by struggling toward an impossible return to naiveté in a romantic search for the origins of language, but by borrowing the appearance of a discourse of identity through an ironic self-consciousness which knows the metaphorical indulgence to be an illusion. Once we think beyond the nostalgic notion of literature as primal metaphor, like that of a Vico or a Shelley, we recognize that literature is not an innocent: it cannot be defined in terms of naive metaphorical identity because it has already known metonymy, springing as it does from the ordinary uses of language such as metonymy creates. An advantage of White's tropological model is that it permits us to see literature as an ironic discourse, transcending and transforming both metonymy and synecdoche, though it does so in the guise of metaphor. Seen thus, literature is a sophisticated, a beyond-metonymy, rather than a before-metonymy, discourse.

I prefer White's enumeration of the four traditional tropes to Jakobson's reduction to two because a binary distinction between metaphor and metonymy restricts poetry within the former, thereby failing to account for the post-metonymic character of poetry which masks itself as metaphor. The romantic opposition between metaphor and metonymy thus tends to leave poetry as prediscursive, pre-rational, and pre-realistic, so that it takes other complicating elements (additional tropes) to account for poetry's metaphorical nature as post-metonymic. To see poetry as a literal return to—or as an original beginning in—the pre-discursive state of metaphor is to fail to do justice to its sophisticated nature. Now it is true that the twofold scheme furnishes a distinct place for poetry, however romantically irrationalist it may be, while the fourfold scheme may seem to tie poetry to other discourse as being similarly tropological. But the latter scheme permits any distinction between poetry and other discourse to reflect the duplicitous relation poetry has to metaphor.

Although the ironic is seen by White as the final trope for
all discourse, it is different for literature from what it is for
non-literature in that it permits literature an illusionary return
to metaphor under a show of identity that comes out of a full
sense of difference as the essential principle behind words.
Non-literary discourse may well attain the reflexive air of self-
consciousness which irony permits, but in literature such a reflexive self-consciousness becomes a precise verbal device which
momentarily alters the nature of our perception of language,
reopening us to a vision of verbal identity, though it requires
us to hold it as an illusion only. Consequently I object—in White
as well as Jakobson—to the use of terms like *similitude* or *analogy* to characterize metaphor as if they were interchangeable
with *identity*. It is my point that the special character of the
poetic device which achieves the show of identity is marked by
its distinction from similitude or analogy, since either of the
latter two terms reminds us of the commitment of language to
difference.   I recall John Crowe Ranson's important claim
that the fully earned metaphor finds itself only where similarity
and analogy end, where utter identity is achieved, achieved in
the teeth of language's differential habits.[13]   According to this
view, similarity and analogy both acknowledge the wide range
of differences between the two items being compared because
of—perhaps—only a single common element or structure. The
poet's task is precisely to move from such similarities or analogies as non-poetry affords us, to the illusionary miracle—in
violation of language habits—which shows us the two as utterly
become one (except that, as the poem may also remind us, our
metonymic memory knows better).

We can say, then, what the peculiarly poetic illusion is:
that there is in the poem the collapse of verbal difference into
the receptive capacity of a corporealized word which has a-
chieved its fullness as a spatialized entity. It is an attempt to
use language to return it and us to the primal identity which
metaphor alone affords. But it is an ironic attempt which
acknowledges that the world of linguistic difference is not
only the world from which it springs but also one that, though
paradoxically, coexists even in the illusionary metaphor itself,
denying the metaphor even as that metaphor affirms itself.

This duplicitous relationship between the identity and difference of originally distinct linguistic entities is like that which I have some time ago noted (or rather noted Shakespeare as noting)[14] between us and our mirror image. The image in the mirror, as our double, seems to match our reality with its own, except that, as an illusion, it is without substance and not ourselves at all. Further, I saw the magical nature of glass as permitting the unsubstantiality of the mirror image to open outward—through the mirror become a window—onto a separate reality of its own. In a recent essay, Geoffrey Hartman finds a similar double that yet has its own life in the mirror—"the specular name"—and defines literature by its unique "nominating" capacity to establish a paradoxical sense of its reality and to create a language to speak it.[15]

The mirror plays a major self-referential role in Jan van Eyck's famous wedding portrait of Arnolfini and his wife. In the painting, hanging on the far wall behind the couple being married, a mirror re-reflects the scene already being mirrored in the picture. In that second-order reflection, we can make out the artist himself seated before the couple and painting the picture we are looking at, thereby corroborating visually the statement he has written on the painting, which testifies to his witnessing of the marriage: "Johannes de eyck *fuit hic.*" There are here several orders of illusion and reality, of art and life, being collapsed into an identity for all the differences that are mutely acknowledged. They thus reveal the several kinds of paradoxical relationships I have been observing in literary language.

As with poetic metaphor, whatever reality the illusion persuades us to confer upon that double in the mirror, we must remind ourselves that the mirror never stops being an illusion even if—like van Eyck—the artist also was here, breaking through his created reality to our living reality. So too, despite his ironic reflexivity that puts us off, the poet asserts his presence and with it the presence of his poem; and he means—at least momentarily—to overwhelm our anti-metaphorical skepticism with such presence. Confronted by his fully charged literary work, for the occasion we become—for all our metaphysical disclaimers—magic-worshippers once again.

NOTES

[1] I of course do not mean to suggest that these movements were primarily motivated by the desire to counter any aspect of the New-Critical orthodoxy or, in some cases, that they were even aware of the New Criticism as a movement to be countered. But I would argue that the effect of these movements, seen from this end of recent critical history, was to undo the several aspects of what we think of as New-Critical doctrine.

Perhaps I should make explicit at the outset my intention to limit my use of the term "literature" to *"poesis"* in the Aristotelian sense of self-conscious fiction-making. Hence my use of the term "poetry" or even "poems" (with no reference to verse, of course) as a synonym for it. If, then, I am defining "literature" at its narrowest point, I am defining "poetry" at is broadest.

[2] See, for example, my treatment of the poems by Ben Johnson and John Donne in *Theory of Criticism: A Tradition and its System* (Baltimore, Md.: The Johns Hopkins Univ. Press, 1976), pp. 234-240. In it I try to demonstrate the poem's capacity, by its own verbal nature, to collapse the distance which it acknowledges.

[3] Just about any work in Brooks' early career will serve my purpose here (with perhaps *The Well Wrought Urn* [New York: Reynal and Hitchcock, 1947] my best example), while the discussion of irony in de Man's influential essay, "The Rhetoric of Temporality," in *Interpretation: Theory and Practice*, ed. Charles S. Singleton (Baltimore: Johns Hopkins Univ. Press, 1969), pp. 173-209, furnishes the most obvious contrast.

[4] This is to use, for a moment, the language of Harold Bloom, who has been showing some signs—despite his vast difference from them in emphasis—of becoming their ally.

[5] Such deviations do not, of course, refer to anything as superficial as "poetic diction." Rather, in the tradition of Russian and Prague School Formalism and the New Criticism, these are seen as "dislocations" or

"defamiliarizations" in the semantics or syntactics of language, breaking in upon our normal responses to discourse in order to promote a special fictional or aesthetic function.

[6] Fish, "How Ordinary is Ordinary Language?" *New Literary History*, 5 (1973), pp. 41-54, and recently, "Normal Circumstances, Literal Language, Direct Speech Acts, the Ordinary, the Everyday, the Obvious, What Goes Without Saying, and Other Special Cases," *Critical Inquiry*, 4 (1978), pp. 625-644.

[7] Originally in *Metahistory: The Historical Imagination in Nineteenth-Century Europe* (Baltimore: Johns Hopkins Univ. Press, 1973), especially "Introduction: The Poetics of History"; but more carefully and persuasively in "Introduction: Tropology, Discourse, and the Modes of Human Consciousness," *Tropics of Discourse* (Baltimore: Johns Hopkins Univ. Press, 1978). The term "swerve" is of course borrowed from Bloom.

[8] E. D. Hirsch, Jr., to the contrary, argues that there *is* synonymity in discourse, and—since for him literature exists within "the continuum of discourse" without a "special nature" to separate it from that continuum—synonymity can exist in poetry and non-poetry alike *(The Aims of Interpretation* [Univ. of Chicago Press, 1976], especially Chapter 4 and 8). It should be noted that his argument for synonymity is one I am quite prepared to accept for all discourse in which the satisfaction of minimal criteria of meaning is all that operates in the selection of words. But this very argument leaves open the place for a discourse (if it can be shown to exist) in which the maximal exploitation of the potentialites of words precludes the possibility of synonymity. And this would move us again toward separating literature from other discourse, though Hirsch would obviously have to hold back.

[9] It is thus that I have argued elsewhere for the paradoxical term, *micro-langue*, as a label for this verbal creation. See *Theory of Criticism*, p. 188: "Like all the other generic and minimal elements, the *langue* has been violated to the point that the *parole* appears to have become its own *langue*, a system of which it is the only spoken representation. In effect it becomes its own *micro-langue*, the only *langue* that speaks, the only *parole* that is its own system—the true concrete universal. Not that it is literally incompatible with the existing *langue* of which it is a *parole*, but that the *langue* cannot account for what this particular speech act has performed."

¹⁰For the following discussion, see the introductory chapter to *Tropics of Discourse* (note 7, above).

¹¹In a recent essay ("The Epistemology of Metaphor," *Critical Inquiry*, 5 [1978], pp. 13-30), Paul de Man shows an interest in making common cause with those like White who see figuration as a discursive necessity which, at the epistemological level, breaks down our attempts to put up barriers between poetry and philosophy as kinds of discourse.

¹²I trace the common early romantic fascination with the "fortunate fall" from innocence to experience in both man and culture in Chapter 6 ("William Wordsworth and the *Felix Culpa*") of *The Classic Vision: The Retreat from Extremity in Modern Literature* (Baltimore: Johns Hopkins Univ. Press, 1971), especially pp. 153-57.

¹³The passage occurs in "Poetry: a Note in Ontology," *The World's Body* (New York: Scribner's, 1938), pp. 139-40. He finds a special "miraculism" in the poem "when the poet discovers by analogy an identity between objects which is partial, though it should be considerable, and proceeds to an identification which is complete. It is to be contrasted with the simile, which says 'as if' or 'like,' and is scrupulous to keep the identification partial." Ransom blunts my point a bit by speaking of "partial identification" when I would prefer "similarity" (with its implication that the one moment or area of likeness is surrounded by moments or areas of difference), reserving "identification" for the completeness which the poet has forced. Still, Ransom makes the point tellingly for us even now.

¹⁴See *A Window to Criticism: Shakespeare's Sonnets and Modern Poetics* (Princeton: Princeton Univ. Press, 1964).

¹⁵"Psychoanalysis: The French Connection," his introductory essay to the English Institute volume on psychoanalysis and literature, *Psychoanalysis and the Question of the Text: Selected Essays from the English Institute, 1976-77*, New Series, No. 2 (Baltimore: Johns Hopkins Univ. Press, 1978). Hartman derives his notion of the "specular name" from the "mirror phase" of Lacan, seeking as he does (yet while escaping differentiation) a linguistic equivalent for Lacan's prelinguistic moment of identity in the image.

SANTAYANA'S POETICS OF BELIEF

by
Nathan A. Scott, Jr.

It is a kind of total grandeur at the end,
. . . .
Total grandeur of a total edifice,
Chosen by an inquisitor of structures. . . .
—Wallace Stevens, "To an Old Philosopher in Rome"

Among the great masters in this century of the philosophic vocation—James, Whitehead, Dewey, Husserl, Wittgenstein, Heidegger—there is perhaps none whose legacy is today so indifferently valued as is George Santayana's. Nor does the inappreciation that generally marks the prevailing view of his work represent a development that has only just gradually come to pass in the years since his death in Rome in the early autumn of 1952: on the contrary, throughout his entire career, though he was always far from being ignored, he constantly faced an intellectual community, particularly in the United States, that reserved sympathies for him that were very imperfect indeed. The "intense masculinity" (as, I believe, Santayana himself somewhere phrases it) of his own Harvard mentor, William James, was slightly offended by a certain mandarinism and "moribund Latinity" it descried in the young Santayana, offended enough for James to have convinced himself that the early work of his protégé did in fact express what he called "the perfection of rottenness." And something like James's animus (which in his case, to be sure, was mingled with affection) was persistently a part of the response Santayana was offered during his lifetime on the American scene.

The themes of the philosophical disputation that he aroused in the sixty years of his publishing career (from his debut in 1890, with his first major essay in *Mind*, to the appearance in 1951 of his last book, *Dominations and Powers*) are, of course, long since familiar. Many of his contemporaries were not in the first instance easily to be convinced that he was even properly to be regarded as a philosopher at all. Is not this chap who writes so prettily, who takes so manifest a delight in the various gestures his diction and syntax can be made to perform, really a sort of dandy, an *élégant* more fascinated with the pirouettes of his own rhetoric than with the exactions of rigorous analysis? So it was that the impeachment went with numerous pedants who, like their kind generally, supposed that seriousness of thought bears some necessary relation to circuitousness and obscurity. Is he not rather a poet than a philosopher? And, assuredly, the members of his own academic guild in advancing this suggestion were not intending praise.

Moreover, throughout the central period of his working career—the period, let us say, extending from 1905 (when the first volumes of *The Life of Reason* were issued) to 1940 (the year in which the fourth volume of *Realms of Being* appeared)—Santayana's basic conception of philosophy was very much at odds with the reigning doctrines. Viewing the life of culture from the standpoint of a generous democracy that accorded an almost equal weight to religion and art and science and the counsels of common sense, he felt the philosopher's obligation to be that of building a synoptic vision of the human situation that renders an appropriate justice to all the great ways of man's reckoning with his experience. But most of his immediate contemporaries, having liberated themselves from what they conceived to be the vaporousness of German Idealism, were taking it for granted that, now in this late time, the one legitimate role for philosophy is that of extending scientific procedure into every nook and cranny of human life; and such a man as Santayana, who appeared to regard the symbolic forms of science as having no more privileged an ontological status than the symbolic forms of religious faith, struck them as being little more than a professional obscurantist. Whereas by the late 1930's his younger contemporaries, as they began to be stirred up by the new excitements brought onto the Anglo-American scene by the spokesmen for the Vienna Circle, were deciding that philosophy is a procedure of linguistic sanitation, and thus to them Santayana's manifest lack of concern for this whole program made him appear a sort of late Victorian belle-lettrist whose only interest lay in the curious example he presented of a *fin de siècle* Catholic who had lost his faith but who remained a *fin de siècle* Catholic.

Nor did his American confreres ever quite forgive Santayana for the critical assessments he permitted himself of the country that was his host through most of the years from 1872 (when his father brought him from Avila to Boston to take up residence with his mother and the children of her first marriage) to 1912, when he resigned his Harvard professorship for a European life of study and writing. The stringent appraisal he presented in his novel *The Last Puritan* of the distortions of feeling and conscience bequeathed a type of American character by the Puritan tradition, the thrusts he directed at the airy mysticism of the Transcendentalists, his gentle raillery of the pensive and ineffectual agnosticism of our high culture, the ironies he bestowed on "the heartiness of American ways, the feminine gush and the masculine go"—none of this represented anything more severe than the judgments people like Cabot Lodge and Trumbull Stickney and William Vaughn Moody amongst his early Harvard friends would themselves have been inclined to express. And, indeed, the phrase forming the title of one of Santayana's most famous essays, "the genteel tradition," was immediately picked up in the 1930's and converted by Vernon Parrington and Malcolm Cowley and scores of others into far more of a pejorative then he had ever intended it to be. But *he* was a foreigner, and not an Englishman or a Frenchman but a Spaniard: so his estimate of the American condition, for all its cogency and lack of malice, was felt to represent an egregious condescension, and the impertinence of this "dainty unassimilated man" (as the classicist Paul Shorey spoke of him) was unpardonable. So, though such a figure as Dewey was offered garlands and testimonials on his seventieth and eightieth and eighty-fifth and ninetieth birthdays and though Santayana "outlived the conventional three score and ten by nearly another score, and many of his contemporaries received public congratulations from their sixty-fifth birthdays on,"[1] there was never any occasion during his long span (as Horace Kallen remarked at the time of the hundredth anniversary of his birth) when a decent tribute was paid this great old Lucretian by those whose philosophical tradition he had so greatly dignified. Yet, as he said when he was not far from passing into the ninth decade of his life—with no doubt the bemused smile of one who knew how questionable was his status as a European—"it is as an American writer that I must be counted, if I am counted at all."[2]

But now this man—who was christened Jorge Agustín Nicolás Ruiz de Santayana y Borrás on January 1, 1864, in the parish church of San Marcos in Madrid and whose remains are buried in the *Tomba degli Spagnuoli* of the Verano cemetery in Rome but whose formative years were shaped under American auspices—is virtually unremembered and unspoken of in our intellectual life, despite all that he *added* to our native inheritance: it is a strange and unfortunate circumstance, this inaptitude that we have for practicing the art of anamnesis.

The strangest anomaly, however, that we face in the history of Santayana's reputation is that it is precisely the element of the most genuine profundity in his thought which has occasioned the most firmly dismissive charges of "defiant electicism."[3] For it is his way of combining a thoroughgoing materialism with a kind of chastened transcendentalism (which he was as eager to distinguish from Emersonian romanticism as from the more classic forms of Idealism descending from Kant) that constitutes the special signature of his genius, and yet it is just his hospitality toward these divergent perspectives that has proved most irritating.

But, whatever may be the verdict of his critics, Santayana himself, in his ripe maturity, wanted very emphatically to insist that the real ground of his thought is to be found nowhere else than in his materialsim. "My philosophy," he said, "is not an academic opinion adopted because academic tendencies seemed . . . to favour it. I care very little whether, at any moment, academic tendencies favour one unncecessary opinion or another. I ask myself only what are the fundamental presuppositions that I cannot live without making. And I find that they are summed up in the word materialism."[4] Yet Santayana's materialism hardly proposes any sort of systematic cosmology, and nothing could be more alien to its true import than so quintessentially materialistic a dictum as that which Hobbes lays down in Chapter XLVI of the *Leviathan*, when he says: 'The universe, that is, the whole mass of all things that are, is corporeal, that is to say, body, and hath the dimensions of magnitude, namely length, breadth, and depth . . . and that which is not body is no part of the universe: and because the universe is all, that which is no part of it is nothing, and consequently nowhere." Indeed, wherever one turns amongst the key statements of his career, whether to *The Life of Reason* or to *Scepticism and Animal Faith* or to *Realms of Being*, Santayana's profession of materialism, far from being inspired by scientific precept and far from claiming that matter and reality are coextensive, would appear to be saying nothing other than that the supporting matrix of the human enterprise formed by all the coherences and continuities of the natural order represents an absolutely recalcitrant kind of otherness which can in no way be thought to be called into being by any creative act of the human spirit itself. He conceives the controlling principle of matter or existence to be the principle of "substance," since substance is that which "actualizes and limits the manifestations of every essence that figures in nature or appears before the mind."[5] And the account in *Realms of Being* of the "presumable properties" of substance makes a nice example of his dialectical powers at full stretch, but the doctrine of substance does, at bottom, want to assert nothing more than the primacy of that aboriginal world which primitive experience and common sense confront "as the condition of mind" and as that which makes us know that "mind . . . [is not] the condition of nature."[6] Man does not dwell, in other words, as Santayana wants to say, in his own brainpan but, rather, in the presence of a world which, in respect to the human agent, is *wholly other:* he is its witness, not its creator: it is to nothing more than this that his materialism comes down in the end, and to conceive it otherwise is to misconceive it.

Santayana's account of the human situation goes on, however, to insist on the dark inscrutability of that order of things *out there* with which we have our daily commerce. His German contemporary Edmund Husserl, to be sure, was launching his whole project of phenomenology with the contention that things are nothing other than what they are as "things of experience" and that the inexperienceable is beyond the domain of both thought and discourse. But to the great innovator at Freiburg Santayana would have been inclined to say, "When I rub my eyes and look at things candidly, it seems evident to me that they stubbornly refuse to be sucked into the immediacies of actual experience." And it was in this conviction that a cardinal premise of his thought was deeply rooted.

That there is a natural world by which we are surrounded and which is peopled with myriad things and creatures—this Santayana took to be a necessary postulate of that "animal faith" which the venture of living requires of us all. And he considered it to be the task of philosophy not so much to justify this assumption as to advertise its presumptiveness, and thus to keep steadily before us the essentially fideistic basis on which all our transactions with the world are conducted. But, though animal faith must take it for granted *that* the circumambient world has a genuinely real status in the realm of being, *what* the various things and creatures of our experience are, in the absolute specificity of their actual existence—this, as Santayana insists, remains forever hidden. The only "givens" that human intelligence has at hand are its apprehensions of this and that, what he calls "essences." Yet these data which are immediately present to consciousness are powerless to authenticate their own factuality, and thus Santayana finds himself driven to his skeptical conclusion, that "nothing given exists."[7]

Santayana's "essence" is not, of course, as he frequently found it necessary to insist, merely another version of the Platonic Idea, for Platonism, as he reminds us, materializes the Idea into a supernatural power capable of acting causatively upon the natural order. In his own vision of things, however, an essence, since it does not "exist," lacks any sort of material efficacy. It is simply the indelible impression that a particular fact, that a particular chunk of reality, scores upon the mind (RB, 155-57). Indeed, Santayana's doctrine of essence is not unlike Gerard Manley Hopkins's doctrine of "inscape." Hopkins considered all things to be "upheld by instress,"[8] and by "instress" he meant that power and drive of Being which keeps each created thing from scattering and dissolving, that ontological energy wherewith a bird or a flower or a cloud in the sky is *assembled* into the given *Gestalt* which it constitutes and made to be what it is—rather than another thing. Whereas a thing's "inscape" is just the pattern or form which its instress rivets upon the alert witness. And Santayana's essence is, basically, Hopkins's inscape: it is just that elementary *haecceitas,* that radical particularity, which is felt in *this* "red wheelbarrow glazed with rain water," in *this* girl's face when it is touched by the slanting rays of the afternoon sun, in *this* limestone landscape with its "murmur/ Of underground streams" —when any one of these things manages so to penetrate (in Coleridge's phrase) "the film of familiarity and selfish solicitude" as to command upon itself a heedful gaze of the mind:

> Whatsoever existing fact we may think we encounter, there will be obvious features distinguishing that alleged fact from any dissimilar fact and from nothing. All such features, discernible in sense, thought, or fancy, are essences; and the realm of essence which they compose is simply the catalogue, infinitely extenisble, of all characters logically distinct and ideally possible.[9]

The essence, however, in Santayana's conception, is not what traditional empiricism speaks of as sense-datum, for, though his materialism requires him to regard it as indeed an awareness of *something* and as thus bringing us tidings of the real, it is not so much an affair of mere unorganized sensory impression as it is a kind of symbolic form which intuition *posits* and which henceforth serves as something like a sign or portent of a certain feature of reality. So, since it is not actually intermingled with that which it exemplifies but stands rather only in a sort of parallel relation to it (RB, 134), he insists that an essence may not be considered to "exist": it is an expression of nothing more than that capacity of the human spirit to reach intentively beyond itself toward its environing world, that capacity which (in his transcendentalist idiom) Santayana speaks of as "spirit."

Yet, however "theoretic" the realm of essence may be, its periphery defines the limit beyond which, in Santayana's sence of things, there is no possibility of extending our cognizance of the world. Which is to say that the realm of the essences offers us our one mode of fathoming that generative order of reality which he calls "the realm of matter," So, to all intents and purposes, we dwell actually in "the realm of spirit"—which is not, as he conceived it, any sort of ghostly heterocosm but simply that region of endeavor in which we seek to organize and integrate our experience by way of religion and science and philosophy and literature and the arts.

And, of course, the life of spirit reaches out, eagerly and yearn-
ingly, toward that most elusive of all the Realms of Being—
namely, "the realm of truth." But essences are the only earnest
of reality we can ever win, and since they do not "exist" and
therefore tell no tales about what is *actually* the case, Santayana's account of truth, perhaps expectably, is as elusive as the
thing itself. For all the abhorrence he felt for the fundamental
world-view of American pragmatism, he was, to be sure, occasionally inclined toward a kind of pragmatic view of our situation
as one in which, by way of our dealings with essences, we dream
awake and our "dreams are kept relevant to . . . [their] environment . . . only by the external control exercised over them by
Punishment, when the acompanying conduct brings ruin, or by
Agreement, when it brings prosperity."[10] On other occasions,
however, he seems to have been inclined to think of truth as
constituted of those essences that find real embodiment in
existence—though, since we have immediate contact only with
the essence itself and are never therefore able strictly to verify
its relation to actuality, he, in accord with his basic premises,
considered *knowledge* to be assumptive, a matter of "animal
faith" that the data present to the mind are indeed indicative
of existing states of affairs (SAF, 179). Yet one feels that,
finally, the doctrine of truth that Santayana's skepticism found
most congenial is nowhere more suggestively and poignantly
adumbrated than in the concluding sentence of the Epilogue
of his novel *The Last Puritan*, which says: "After life is over
and the world has gone up in smoke, what realities might the
spirit in us still call its own without illusion save the form of
those very illusions which have made up our story?"

Nor did he want even in the slightest degree to exempt
his own philosophy from the kind of unillusioned stringency
expressed in this concluding sentence of *The Last Puritan*.
At a certain point he imagines himself being interrogated about
the truth-claims he would make in behalf of his own reflections; he says:

> A rationalistic reader might . . . ask: "Is there no truth within
> your realm of essence? Are not unity and distinctness present in
> all essences, and is it not true to say so? And all that you your-
> self have written, here and elsewhere, about essence, is it not
> true." No, I reply, it is not true, nor meant to be true. It is a

grammatical or possibly a poetical construction having, like mathematics or theology, a certain internal vitality and interest; but in the direction of truth-finding, such constructions are merely instrumental like any language or any telescope. A man may fall into an error in grammar or in calculation. This is a fault in the practice of his art, at bottom a moral defect, a defect in attention, diligence, and capacity: and in my dialectic I have doubtless often clouded my terms with useless or disturbing allusions. But when consistently and conscientiously worked out and stripped to their fighting weight, my propositions will be logically necessary, being deducible from the definitions or intuitions of the chosen terms, and especially of this chosen term "essence" itself. But logic is only logic: and the systems of relation discoverable amongst essences do not constitute truths, but only other more comprehensive essences, within which the related essences figure as parts. (RB, 418-19)

We are compassed about, then, by the four realms of matter, essence, spirit, and truth. And though, in the order of experience, it is the realm of essence which claims primacy, in the ontological order it is the realm of matter which is the truly aboriginal and generative dimension of reality. But in relation to this region of things we see through a glass darkly and face, for all its pomp and circumstance, unfathomable mystery. "The light of the spirit which shines in the darkness cannot see the primeval darkness which begat it and which it dispels" (RB, 249). Indeed, Santayana's vision of the human situation is more than a little touched by a sense of what Martin Heidegger called *Geworfenheit,* by a sense of our having been "thrown" into a world which is not of our own making and which in its sheer givenness, in its sheer thereness, confronts us with a contingency so absolute that we find ourselves staring at "dark abysses before which intelligence must be silent, for fear of going mad."[11] The world in its various concrete aspects is, to be sure, easily perceptible: yet "what is most plain to sense is most puzzling to reason . . . and what is intelligible to reason at one level . . . may become arbitrary and obscure to a reason that . . . asks deeper questions."[12] "The aim of intelligence is to know things as they are."[13] But it finds the universe with which it undertakes to treat to be "a conjunction of things mutually irrelevant, a chapter of accidents, a medley improvised here and now for no reason, to the exclusion of myriad other forces which, so far as their ideal structure is concerned, might have been performed just as well."[14] Ours, in short, is a world that simply cannot be brought to heel and that evokes a great *o altitudo!* of astonishment, as we find ourselves (in a metaphor of Pascal that Santayana could easily have appropriated) "in a vast sphere, ever drifting in uncertainty," where "to attach ourselves to any point and to fasten to it" is to find it wavering and slipping past us and vanishing forever. "This," says the *Pensées,* "is our natural condition, and yet most contrary to our inclination; we burn with desire to find solid ground and an ultimate sure foundation whereon to build a tower reaching to the Infinite. But our whole groundwork cracks, and the earth opens to abysses"[15]—abysses, says Santayana, "before which intelligence must be silent."

Yet, absurd as the world appears to be in the inexplicableness of its sheer factuality, we are nevertheless in thousands of ways dependent upon it for health and sustenance. We need air to breathe and space in which to abide and the nourishment of food and drink and the countless other bounties with which nature ministers to our frailty and makes our sojourning on the earth supportable. And thus, for all the recalcitrancy of the material universe, it would be, as Santayana wants to urge, a foolish mistake for us to permit ourselves any great aversion from the realm of matter, for, were we to hold it in contempt, "it would not be merely ashes or dust that we should be despising, but all natural existence in its abysmal past and in its indefinite fertility; and it would be, not some philosopher's sorry notion of matter that we should be denying, but the reality of our animal being . . ." (RB, 190). Indeed, as he insists, if reverence is to be offered anything at all, it ought to be directed not toward "ideal objects" but toward "the realm of matter only" (RB, 191), since, opaque and mysterious though it may be, it is that which chastens and corrects us, which preserves and protects us, and which with its far horizons grants us a place in which to dwell.

Now the form in which Santayana conceives this *pietas* to find its proper expression he frequently speaks of as "pure intuition"—which may not be the happiest locution, since it can suggest what is really contrary to the final drift of his basic meaning: namely, that it is a kind of angelism, the delights of something like a Platonic heaven, at which "spirit" aims. But in *Scepticism and Animal Faith* (Chapter XXVI) he speaks of "discernment of spirit" as an affair of "attention" and "wakefulness"—which is no doubt a language more apt, for this is indeed the kind of response that, in his sense of things, a true piety will make toward the world which is at hand: "we may say that for the mind there is a single avenue to essence, namely attention" (RB, 15). But even when he speaks in this connection of "intuition," he does not mean any sort of "divination, or a miraculous way of discovering that which sense and intellect cannot disclose. On the contrary," as he is careful to say, "by intuition I mean direct and obvious possession of the apparent" (RB, 646). Or, as it might be somewhat differently put, by intuition or wakefulness of attention he means nothing other than a heedful openness toward all the things of earth as, in their concrete particularity, they take on the dimension of *presence*: he means the kind of openness that wants, in Richard Hovey's phrase, to "have business with the grass."

Spirit—"the light which lighteth every man that cometh into the world"—is, of course, for Santayana the name and nature of *humanitas,* of what (had he ever produced an anthropology) he would have declared to be the distinctively human thing itself. And it is simply that capacity for self-transcendence which enables the human creature to hail or salute its world and to be so awake to the furniture of existence as to discern the "inscapes" of its various items. Indeed, "the exercise of sight as distinguished from blindness" (SAF, 273), the act whereby we "greet" and pay heed to the things of earth, is precisely that which Santayana considers to be the central act of the human spirit, for it constitutes the agency by means of which "essences are transposed into appearances and things into objects of belief" and both "are raised to a strange actuality in thought" (SAF, 274). But intuition or wakefulness of attention is not merely an affair of simple awareness, for it is laden with what he (rather obscurely) calls "intent." And by intent he means that leap of animal faith whereby "spirit," though dealing always with essences which do not "exist," nevertheless *posits* a relation between the "given" (essence) and that which is not given (the existing thing)—and not only posits such a relation but holds it to be "true," in the manner of a symbolic form. What intent achieves, in other words, is a grasp of things which is "not true literally, as the fond spirit imagines when it takes some given picture, summary, synthetic, and poetical, for the essence of the world; but true as language may be true, symbolically, pragmatically, and for the range of human experience in that habitat and at that stage in its history" (RB, 350).

It is in such terms that Santayana renders the life of spirit, and thus his whole system of reflection represents the truly human mode of being as one involving a very strict kind of receptivity and alertness to the stars of heaven and the winds of earth, to the fowls of the air and the beasts of the field, to mountains and plains, to nights and days, to the high and exalted and the low and downtrodden—indeed, to all the myriad forms of the world that presses in upon us. And, as he suggests, it is only by way of such vigilance and wakefulness of attention that we may escape the grosser forms of egotism and win through to that capaciousness and clarity of vision belonging to "the life of reason."

Nor should it go unremarked that it is just in this connection that Santayana wants to record what it is that he finds irresistibly appealing in the figure of Christ. For spirit "claims nothing, posits nothing, and is nothing in its own eyes, but empties itself completely"[16] into that which it contemplates, and it is precisely this readiness for *kenosis*, this *disponibilité*, that he considers to be "one of the [chief] beauties in the idea of Christ":

> in spite of his absolute holiness, or because of it, he shows a spontaneous sympathy, shocking to the Pharisee, with many non-religious sides of life, with little children, with birds and flowers, with common people, with beggars, with sinners, with sufferers of all sorts, even with devils. This is one of the proofs that natural spirit, not indoctrinated or canalised, was speaking in him.[17]

And it is, indeed, in the breadth of his sympathies and his quick responsiveness to every slightest bid for his attention that comes from the world about him that Santayana finds also a sort of proof of the fullness of Christ's humanity.

The kind of punctiliousness of attention that marks the life of spirit in its purest modes is, however, a moral achievement by no means easily realized, and, in a manner strikingly reminiscent of Pascal's anatomy of the various forms of *divertissement,* Santayana discriminates the several types of "distraction." "By distraction," he says, "I understand the alien force that drags the spirit away from the spontaneous exercise of its liberty, and holds it down to the rack of care, doubt, pain, hatred, and vice. And I will distinguish the chief agencies in this distraction, after the picturesque manner of Christian wisdom, as the Flesh, the World, and the Devil" (RB, 673).

In regard to the carnal passions, it is not, of course, any kind of sour asceticism that Santayana wants to espouse, for he knows that the flesh, forming as it does "the raw material of human nature," cannot be simply discarded and that, indeed, the fleshy inpulses, if merely gagged and repressed, will take their revenge, often in cruel and devastating ways. Yet he does want to lay down the necessity of taming and transmuting them in such a fashion that they will warm rather than anarchize the affections, so that spirit may not be distracted from its true vocation.

Nor does he want to preach any fanatical doctrine of contempt for the world, since he takes it for granted that the charms and delights of the world—comfort and security and favorable repute—are well enough, taken simply in and of themselves: "spirit does not come from or demand another world, or reject any form of life as unworthy. It is ready to participate in any undertaking and to rejoice in every achievement" (RB, 708). And for him the principle of worldliness stands not for a sober accommodation to the material requirements of earthly life but rather for the kind of entanglement in the cares and trivialities of the quotidian realm that hobbles and restricts the full range of sympathy that spirit might otherwise have for the whole panaroma of existence. Which is to say that the worldling's self-preoccupation leads to a certain tragic desuetude of attention: he smokes "his excellent cigar with a calm sense that there is nothing in the world better than what he does" (RB, 711), and the tax that is levied against him for his philistinism is a very great poverty, the poverty of insentience and dullness and ennui.

And, as for the devil, Santayana says that he takes this personage to stand for "any enemy of spirit that is internal to spirit [itself]" (RB, 719)—which makes bedevilment the subtlest and most insidious of all the snares we face. Its tempting power arises out of the strange situation in which spirit finds itself, of being committed to the intuition of essences that have no status in existence other than that which animal faith posits and of being, therefore, peculiarly susceptible to a kind of monarchism, to the dream of omniscience. It seems that "either we can know nothing, because confined to our passing dream, or we can know nothing because there is nothing but our passing dream to be known" (RB, 727)—and, when the dream of omniscience has taken hold, it is the second alternative that will be embraced, spirit then imagining itself to be absolutely free and absolutely creative. But when spirit in this way denies its dependence on the ancestral order of nature, it is at the point of closing itself in upon itself, of forfeiting precisely that attentive openness toward the circumambient world which is its distinctive genius: its pride in its own creativeness is by way of leading it to assert its essential infinity—and this way madness lies, the kind of madness that Lucifer prepares.

The flesh, the world, and the devil, then—these three—are the great agents of "distraction." But, insofar as the spirit can be preserved from its threefold enemy, it will then proceed to do the work which it is man's special vocation to do, of building up that "ideal," symbolic universe (of science and poetry and art and religion and metaphysics) which results from the play of the mind on the vast domain of quiddities which is called "the realm of essence." The human situation, as Santayana conceives it, is one of our being situated in a universe which is neither spirit nor spirit's vision of it: so he calls it "the realm of matter." And the vocation of spirit, after keeping for itself a proper piety in recognizing its dependence on this universe, is to *comment* upon it. But the world on which this commentary is made remains forever dark and hidden: "its powers germinate underground, and only its foliage and flowers emerge into clear light."[18] Indeed, its very existence is no more than a postulate of animal faith, for the only terms available to any exploration of it are the essences which belong to an ontological realm wholly other than that generative order of nature which they characterize. Matter, in other words, is absolutely transcendent, for it "is always more and other than the essence which it exemplifies at any point. . . . We may enjoy it, we may enact it, but we cannot conceive it; not because our intellect by accident is inadequate, but because existence . . . is intrinsically absurd . . ." (RB, 218-19). Yet, though we find ourselves enveloped by darkness, we, since we are creatures of spirit, have it as our destiny to try to illumine the darkness—by giving the most careful heed to all the various impressions (or essences) that are scored upon the mind, by, as we trust, the world *out there* and by using this material as the basis for a symbolic transformation of the dazzling darkness into those fabrics of meaning that are posited by science and poetry and religion and art.

Santayana was, of course, reluctant to advance any claim about the veridical capacities of these fabrics of meaning, since they are all wrought out of nothing more than our experience of essences. True, he was prepared occasionally to suggest that the terms of the natural sciences—as compared, say, with those of mythology—are comprised of essences which "are the fruit of a better focussed, more chastened, and more prolonged attention turned upon what actually occurs" (SAF, 177) and that, therefore, however much faith may be entailed in living by science, "not to live by it is folly."[19] But though, at the level of practice, experience gives a certain urgency to the essences with which physics and biochemistry deal, he was not inclined, finally, to concede that they give us any real "information" about existence: they and all other sciences represent "only a claim . . . put forth, a part of that unfathomable compulsion by force of which we live and hold our painted world together."[20] And it was with a similar agnosticism that Santayana was disposed to respond to any depositions regarding the cognitive import of poetry and the arts and religion, for, in his estimate of things, none of these has any "standing ground in fact": like science, they represent only spirit's attempt at lighting a candle in the dark. Yet, if he ever paid any attention to a brash little manifesto called *Language, Truth and Logic* issued in 1936 by a bright young Englishman named A. J. Ayer, he must surely have felt it to express a particularly repellent kind of coarseness in its relegation of poetic and religious discourse to the province of "nonsense." For Santayana conceived the poetic and the religious imagination to be deeply a part of "the life of reason." Religion and poetry, to be sure, provide us with no information about things (about the realm of "matter")—though (as Santayana would have wanted to say to Mr. Ayer) in this respect, strictly speaking, they are no more impotent than science; but, as he felt, they do hold up "those large ideas tinctured with passion, those supersensible forms shrouded in awe, in which alone a mind of great sweep and vitality can find its congenial objects."[21] Both, as he proposed in his famous formula, "are identical in essence and differ merely in the way in which they are attached to practical affairs. Poetry is called religion when it intervenes in life, and religion, when it merely supervenes upon life, is seen to be nothing but poetry."[22]

For Santayana a very troublesome kind of mischief begins to be made, however, when (as Matthew Arnold put it) religion materializes itself in the fact, in the supposed fact, when it attaches its emotion to the fact[23]—and the same mischief will be made by science and by poetry whenever they in their way forget the virtuality of their perspectives and seek to impute to spirit the authority of matter by claiming to enunciate something like "absolute truth." What the scientist and the artist need to remember no less than the expositor of sacred mysteries is that "in so far as spirit takes the form of intelligence and of the love of truth . . . it must assume the presence of an alien universe and must humbly explore its ways, bowing to the strong wind of mutation, the better to endure and to profit by that prevailing stress" (RB, 398). Indeed, spirit is by way of being betrayed when its devotees forget that all their fashionings are but imaginative projections and then seek to materialize them "in the supposed fact." To try thus to convert spirit into matter is merely to compound illusion with illusion:

> Mind was not created for the sake of discovering the absolute truth. The absolute truth has its own intangible reality, and scorns to be known. The function of mind is rather to increase the wealth of the universe in the spiritual dimension, by adding appearance to substance . . . and by creating all those . . . perspectives, and those emotions of wonder, adventure, curiosity, and laughter which omniscience would exclude. (RB, xiii)

"The light of the spirit which shines in the darkness cannot see the primeval darkness which begat it," but by the deepest necessities of its own nature, spirit is driven to form by processes of *poiesis* such structures of vision and belief as will permit it to dwell amidst the environing darkness in sanity and peace. These structures—what we call science and religion and poetry and art—are, of course, grounded in essences which are "the native grammar of the mind," and thus they are not so much "maps" of reality as they are ventures of the imagination at a systematic deciphering of a world which everywhere outruns all our systems of figuration and which asks us therefore not to insist that things are just as we represent them but to say rather of our various schematisms that *something* of the sort may be the case.

So, then, the late Henry Aiken was surely right in suggesting that Santayana "is best understood as a . . . philosopher of symbolic forms,"[24] for this is certainly the field of his most fundamental interest, and thus he deserves to be regarded as one of the great forerunners of what may well turn out to be the decisive enterprise in the intellectual life of our period. But though his idioms made an easily negotiable currency of exchange for the generation of Whitehead and Cassirer, they are no doubt not so readily usable in the age of Roland Barthes and Algirdas Greimas and Gérard Genette. And if one wants summarily to account for what it is in our present situation that makes Santayana's system seem unnegotiable, one must say that the New Men are bent on hypostatizing "spirit," in a way that would to him have appeared to represent a very strange sort of astigmatism indeed.

The names just mentioned, of Barthes and Greimas and Genette, are cited merely as emblems of that French movement which we speak of (in the loose way in which all "movements" are spoken of) as Structuralism and which, as it has drifted onto the Anglo-American scene over the past decade, has increasingly demanded recognition as the reigning accountant now of the *problématique* of symbolic forms. And what perhaps most chiefly distinguishes the present time from that of Santayana is that, whereas then (for such people as Ernst Cassirer and Wilbur Marshall Urban and Susanne Langer) it was natural to think of the great symbolic forms as structures wherewith human subjectivity constitutes and organizes its experience, the new dispensation regards them as merely a function of certain governing codes or systems of language and social usage.

Contemporary reflection (Jacques Derrida, Michel Foucault, Tzvetan Todorov, Julia Kristeva) takes it as its *absolute* presupposition that the symbolic order so absolutely precedes *le signifiant* that its work (*parole*), however elaborate it may be, must be regarded as but a fragmentary expression of the *langue* from which it issues. Indeed, a part of what is anomalous in the whole scheme is that its stress on *le signifiant* is caluclated very greatly to devalue the signifier, for the *absolute* presupposition says that, however conveniently first-person verbs may function as a category of reference to the human individual as an agent of certain vocal and bodily acts, the transcendental subject of traditional humanism is in point of fact an invented fiction quite without any substantial non-linguistic reality. The real situation, in other words, is that the "I" is simply a linguistically encoded stereotype emanating from the cultural matrix by which it was formed—and thus, in the terms of the familiar Saussurean distinction, since *parole* is but an epiphenomenon of *langue,* the truly decisive cultural fact is not the creative power of the autonomous self but the impersonal system of language-structures which shapes and authenticates all human utterance. So it is that "man is dissolved . . . into little more than . . . a speaking pronoun, fixed indecisively in the eternal, ongoing rush of discourse,"[25] one who instead of being the impresario of his language is its slave. And, given this assassination of the subject, the poetries and religions and sciences that he might himself have been thought to have created are seen rather to be merely diverse materializations of that vast superstructure defining the nature and range of linguisticality (and thus of thought and feeling) in a particular cultural situation.

Moreover, trapped as we are within the order of *langue,* it is assumed that nothing could be more misguided than the search after some transitive relation that symbolic forms bear to *le signifié*: so tyrannously, indeed, does this assumption prevail that the symbolic order is itself conceived to be coextensive with all of reality, and nothing is more irritating for the strategists of the *nouvelle critique* than some attempt at resurrecting a metaphysics of "presence," at reviving the notion that univocal substances extrinsic to the symbolic order do in fact exist. For, of course, the new theorists have been taught by Saussure that, even were it analytically possible to isolate *le signifié* as an object of inquiry, it would be found, inevitably and in the nature of the case, to be itself simply another sign-system, since any accessibility it could have to the mind would necessarily be a consequence of its having been organized and constituted by some *signifiant*. So, as it is taken for granted, the symbolic order—that environing superstructure which precedes all particular acts of symbolization—*is* reality, and thus each "text" that we confront, whether it be a poem or a scientific theorem or a theological proposition or a ritual of sport or a style of courtship or a mode of burying the dead, makes reference to nothing other than that system of *intertextualité* that forms the grid through which it asks to be read and correlatively placed with respect to the other texts to which it is adjacently related. And, therefore, a hermeneutic of culture will entail at bottom an effort of *découpage,* an attempt at cutting through the various epiphenomena of poetry and religion and art and science to the fundamental linguistic codes by which mind is decisively controlled.

True, traditional humanism (whether by way of the Greeks or of such modern guides as Herder and von Humboldt and Coleridge and Nietzsche) considers *langue* in all its manifestations—poetic, scientific, religious—to be a foremost case of that creativity wherewith the human spirit gives pattern and order to the multifariousness of experience. But, in these late days of our misery, our present overseers are not inclined to traffic with a "myth of origins": so eager are they to establish the primacy and the exteriority of the symbolic order with respect to *le signifiant* that any attempt at going back behind it to its source in the radical freedom of creative intelligence is deemed a sterile kind of philosophastry. And thus, as the doctrine of imagination is relegated to the discard, a strange anomaly emerges, of what Santayana took to be an expression of "spirit" being so hypostatized now that, far from being thought of as a result of that immanent power of self-transcendence whereby man constitutes his world, it begins to appear as a structure separate from and standing over against him, as indeed coextensive with reality itself.

We ought not to find it surprising, then, given the climate in which humanistic studies must presently be practiced, that, apart from the occasional reference that glances at his influence on Wallace Stevens, the name of Santayana is rarely mentioned today. For the fundamental terms for the author of *Realms of Being* are spirit *and* matter, and the linchpin of his whole concept of the realm of essence is a very large and robust doctrine of the imagination. Yet, despite the velocity with which the winds of change sweep across the contemporary landscape, particularly in the field of literary criticism, the principles ultimately controlling the intellectual life are essentially conservative, and we are therefore doubtless always mistaken when we are quick to conclude that the legacy of so magisterial a thinker as Santayana has been suddenly rendered passé by one or another shift of the *Zeitgeist.* So, as we are seeking today new bearings in theory of interpretation, it may not be unprofitable to turn to major figures of the recent past who are currently neglected, for the sake of appropriating the kind of interrogation of our present moment that they would seem to propose; and, amongst these, Santayana is surely one—and Wilbur Marshall Urban is another— whose testimony, when reconsidered, may have the effect of cross-questioning us into new clarity about the tangled issues facing criticism in our period.

He always stubbornly refused, of course, any pansymbolism of the sort unembarrassedly embraced by his young German contemporary Ernst Cassirer. In Cassirer's view, the world of symbolic forms stands as "an autonomous creation of the spirit"; "the question of what, apart from these . . . [forms] , constitutes absolute reality," as he felt, presents us with "an intellectual phantasm."[26]   And, thus regarding the search for what may be the relation between symbolic forms and "a self-subsistent world of 'things'" to be misconceived, he forswore any real interest in the issues of ontology.   But this was not Santayana's way, since Lockean though he was in his conviction of the ultimate impenetrability of "matter," he never relaxed his assurance that the great symbolic forms do nonetheless make reference to the realm of matter—that is, to the world *out there.* For, despite the absolute transcendence of the essential interiority of things with respect to human intelligence, they do make their impact in the form of the myriad impressions that they leave as their residue in the mind, and our highest vocation is to keep the strictest possible alertness to these intuitions—and to comment upon them, as we do by way of our science and literature and art and religion.

True, we can have no certain assurance that the commentary we produce embraces the essential truth, since the mind's transactions are, all of them, restricted to essences, but, by a venture of "animal faith," we wager that we are not altogether misled by the best acts of attention we perform before the great pageantry of the world.   And, indeed, our having a "world" at all is a consequence simply of our paying the most careful kind of heed to the "inscapes" of things and to the way in which they bring (as Heidegger would say) "what presences to presence."[27]   For the mind not to be focused on the various external influences that are brought to bear upon it and for it not to undertake to build into systems of symbolic forms the various transcripts of reality that the essences convey to us is for it to dwell amidst nothing more than a wilderness of its own contriving.   It is, in short, our intuitions of essences and our ordering of these intuitions into the large designs of science and art and religion that give us structures of belief whereby the whole welter of existence can be transformed into what is truly a "world."

For Santayana, however, the imagination is by no means an agency of pure formation that takes reality to be a cliché requiring annulment or redemption, by way of some heterocosmic alternative to the existing world.   Indeed, he is quite unprepared to accord (in Henry James's phrase) any "obstinate finality" to consciousness or to endorse the injunction of Emerson's Orphic poet to "build therefore your own world."   He does not, in other words, conceive the imagination to possess anything like the aseity that the old doctors of Catholic theology attributed to the Godhead, since, in his sense of things, the principle of ultimacy is to be found only in the Realm of Matter—which constitutes, therefore, that to which the imagination is accountable and to which it owes its final obedience. Indeed, far from being entitled to claim any sort of absolute freedom, the imagination finds itself bidden to reckon with, to be *wakeful* before, that-which-is-at-hand.   And thus no symbolic form, however elaborately intricate it may be, can be accorded value by reason of the "reality" it has in its own right or can be assumed to have an intelligibility of a purely intransitive kind. For the languages of the symbolic imagination bring "what presences to presence." "Saying and Being," as Heidegger puts it, "word and thing, belong to each other in a veiled way, a way which

. . . is not to be thought out to the end."[28]   And Santayana would have wanted to render a similar judgment, given his impatience with the notion that the great symbolic forms present us with closed systems of signification that signify nothing extrinsic to themselves: the degree to which they approximate the things of "matter" may be resolvable only in the terms of animal faith, but they aim at least at some fairly decent ostensiveness—and thus they are betrayed if their intent is taken merely to be self-reflexive.

Those strategists, however, who, under the influence of contemporary Structuralism, are charting out a new program for the philosophy of symbolic forms register a great disinclination to make room for what Jacques Derrida calles a "transcendental and privileged signified."[29]   Roland Barthes insists, for example, that in the world of the literary imagination language is misconceived altogether if it be thought to involve any kind of reference to "a social, emotional, or poetic 'reality' which pre-exists it, and which it . . . [seeks to] express."[30] Or, again, Michel Foucault even more stringently asserts the "radical intransitivity" of poetic language—which, as he says, "has no other law than that of affirming . . . its own precipitous existence; and so there is nothing for it to do but to curve back in a perpetual return upon itself, as if its discourse could have no other content that the expression of its own form . . . ."[31]   And it is a similar testimony that is being voiced today by the other leading representatives of the *nouvelle critique* and by their increasingly numerous American discipleship.

So, given Santayana's high doctrine of imagination—of man as the creator of forms—and given his "faith" that these forms do really speak of the world of which we are members, his basic outlook is one that, when juxtaposed against the canons being pressed upon us by the new *avant-garde*, will surely underscore, by reason of its sharp difference from current orthodoxy, what is most truly fundamental in the assumptions on the basis of which the contemporary movement proposes to reconstruct not only theory of literature but also our way of thinking generally about symbolic forms. This, one suspects, is the chief merit of our undertaking now to remember Santayana's legacy: it is not that a man of his time may be expected to speak in some immediately direct way to the generation of Derrida and Foucault but, rather, that, by making a return to one of the great saints of modern humanism and by confronting the salient antithesis between his testimony and that of the reigning wisdom, we may see more precisely the kind of basic decision that has been made by those in our own period who want to interpret what is at stake in the work which is done by the *animal symbolicum*. And, indeed, this is a juxtaposition that cannot fail to alert us in a newly vivid way to how great is the retreat being arranged by those who seek today to define what it is that man does with his world, for to contemplate their testimony from the perspective of a Santayana is to be reminded that, on their accounting, he does nothing with it at all: he simply accedes to being puppetized by antecedent linguistic codes whose constituent terms refer only to one another and not at all to the circumambient world.

Now it is clear, of course, given the special kind of parochialism generally represented by Continental intellectuals, that the Frenchmen so much in vogue at the moment have never bothered to consult the literature produced by the Anglo-American formalism of a generation ago, and the American epigones of European Structuralism are just now so eager to distance themselves from the New Criticism that they are busily forgetting the inheritance bequeathed them by Cleanth Brooks and Allen Tate and W. K. Wimsatt and the people of their time. But, again, as it would seem, the art of anamnesis very much needs to be freshly cultivated, for the question immediately brought to the fore by our juxtaposition of Santayana and the luminaries of recent Structuralism, as to whether the principal modalities of the symbolic imagination (and, most particularly, the great forms of literary art) do indeed make reference to anything beyond themselves—this is the question that was being deeply pondered on the American scene in the period when the New Criticism was at full tide.

The New Critics were not, of course, interested in redeeming mimeticist doctrine, by way of any version of it at all resembling its primitive or classical forms. For they knew that, in our own late post-Kantian time, the grammar of modern intelligence requires us to think of man as dwelling most immediately not in a world of Things but in a world of symbolic forms.[32]   Indeed, so far were they from wanting to resurrect

for literary theory any simple imitationism that their anxious
concern for what was called the "autonomy" of the verbal
arts frequently led them to give the impression that they were
proposing to sunder the poem *qua* poem from any and all ex-
tramural attachments. It is, as they tended to argue, a structure
whose constituent terms behave not ostensively or semantically
but reflexively and syntatically, for, however much they may
appear by reason of their currency in conventional usage to have
some referential bearing on the world of common experience,
they do in fact, once they are drawn into the poetic organism,
immediately begin to fuse into one another and to gather new
meanings that are a function only of the interrelationships
whereby they are knitted together into the total pattern that
forms the unity of the poem. The terms and "statements"
comprising a literary work do not, in other words, refer
to anything extrinsic to the work itself but refer, rather, most
essentially to one another and thus form an independent system
whose organic unity has the effect of shutting off the language
of the poem from the "buzzing, blooming confusion" of "the
ordinary universe."   So it was that Brooks and Ransom and
Blackmur and Tate conceived (in René Wellek's phrase) "the
mode of existence of a literary work of art."

Yet, for all the apparent inordinacy with which this poetic
fenced literature off from the existential world, its major ex-
ponents retained a considerable eagerness to accord an important ontological import to the verbal arts and wanted very much
to insist that they represent one of the great ways of reckoning
with What Is. For, as it was maintained, though the forms of
statement employed by the literary imagination do not yield
predications of the sort advanced by scientific discourse, nevertheless that pattern of thrust and counterthrust which constitutes the fundamental "tension" and "irony" of poetic art
does, in its rich complexity, so fully reflect the complexity of the
human world that the poem, closed system though it may be,
does at last in analogical fashion prove to be a simulacrum of
reality. In short, the poem presents itself as something like
"a world enclosed by endlessly faceted mirrors, reflecting and
re-reflecting images," but "mirrors [that] somehow become
windows opening again upon our everyday world"[33] and grant-
ing us an access to it so fresh and full that we find ourselves,
as it were for the first time, in possession of "the world's body."

It was in such terms, by way of a by no means simple dialectic, that the New Criticism sought at once to honor the autonomy of the symbolic forms created by the literary imagination and to avow their power to illumine and comment on the instant facts of "the ordinary universe." No doubt the poetic designed to meet this dual purpose represented some incoherence: as one of the strictest arbiters of the whole movement says, the poem "cannot be partly closed, partly open":[34] consistency requires that it be one or the other. Yet the inconsistency in the poetics of the New Criticism represented nothing other than an attempt at dealing candidly with the actualities of that literature on which it was focused—such texts as "The Canonization," *The Tempest*, the Immortality "Ode," *Pride and Prejudice, The Possessed, The Waste Land,* "Among School Children," *Ulysses,* and *Doctor Faustus.*

The New Criticism could, of course, accord an ontological import to literary art because it harbored no skepticism at all about the objective existence of the poem *qua* poem. In its impatience with "intentional fallacies," its refusal "to locate the *subject* of a text beyond its particular verbal organizations,"[35] and in its sense of the executive role played by the linguistic medium in the creative process, the school of Blackmur and Brooks and Wimsatt may have been intending, in something like the manner of recent Structuralism, that "man the author . . . [should be] unceremoniously deposed."[36] And in this regard certainly this was a poetic requiring to be adjudged highly questionable from the perspective of a Santayana. But at least it never doubted the stoutly perduring thinginess and iconicity of verbal art, and thus, for all its obsession with the autonomy of the literary work, it never ceased to try to reckon with the ways in which the poem may be an instrument of mediation whereby we are given a kind of genuine insight into the essential realities of human existence.

At our present juncture, however, the *nouvelle critique* offers us little more than "a lesson in how to subvert the specificity of literature,"[37] for it is bent on reducing man himself and all the great forms of the symbolic imagination to the status of being simply functions of the linguistic codes and systems that rule us. The language of the poem, we are told, only doubles back on itself and thence on to the language of other poems to which it is related by the logic of *intertextualité*, and thence on to that system of signification of which the poem is merely an epiphenomenon. Which means, therefore, that the function of the literary economy "is not to communicate an objective, external meaning which exists prior to the system but only to create a functioning equilibrium, a movement of signification."[38] The "presence" of the poem, in other words, is displaced by *langue*, and the essence of the poem is to be found simply in the significatory process itself, not in what it signifies.

So, as we are reminded by our new guides, the literary experience is bound to be filled with emptiness and disappointment, for, however much the work of art may seem to promise mediation of the "world," this pledge will at last be found to be spurious, mired as the poem is in a relational universe of linguisticality by which it is ultimately and inevitably devoured. In short, all *tropiques* and *pôles* of the literary universe are *tristes*, since they must all be finally descried to lead into nothing more than "signs" and never into what Santayana's mythography calls "matter." And thus, since the figurative impluse leads nowhere beyond sheer figuration itself and since literary art is therefore quite blind with respect to "the ordinary universe," what Derrida calls "the interpretation of interpretations"—which must necessarily claim the paramount interest of the new *avant-garde*— becomes a strange carnival[39] involving something like the dancing of a jig on the grave of both literature and criticism. Hayden White's summary of it is splendidly comprehensive and concise; he says:

> To see through the figurative to the literal meaning of any effort to seize experience in language is impossible, among other reasons, because there is no "perception" by which "reality" can be distinguished from its various linguistic figurations and the relative truth-content of competing figurations discerned. There is *only figuration.* . . . Being, itself, is absurd. Therefore there is no "meaning," only the ghostly ballet of alternative "meanings" which various modes of figuration provide. We are indentured to an endless series of metaphorical translations from one universe of figuratively provided meaning to another. And they are all equally figurative.[40]

Recent theory of symbolic forms, at least as it is being

carried forward within the literary community, signalizes, then, the advent of a strange, new mood that surely deserves to be very carefully pondered. For what it would seem to express on the part of the curators of *litterae humaniores* is an intention to assert the essential emptiness of the verbal arts. Within the terms of Saussure's dualities of *le signifiant* and *le signifié*, of *parole* and *langue*, we are assured by such authorities as Jacques Derrida and Roland Barthes and Michel Foucault and Paul de Man that the distance between human subjectivity and the world of "things" is so unbridgeable that, as a consequence, all our "signifiers" are without any "signified" and that our gestures in the direction of *parole* are therefore fated to figure forth nothing more than that system of norms and rules constituting the *langue* off which they ricochet. In short, *écriture* is utterly "worldless," being fashioned of "cercles immense/ Dans le néant";[41] and thus it brings us to something like a *degré zéro*, where there is only "the ghostly ballet . . . of figuration"—dancing about the Void. Such is the verdict we are given.

So it is clear, indeed, that the protocols of Santayana's system do not offer an easily negotiable medium of exchange in the context of contemporary reflection on the symbolic process. For, despite all his resolutely skeptical commitments, he conceived man's place to be at a point of juncture between "spirit" and "matter": he took it for granted, therefore, that any theory of meaning must embrace *both* dimensions, that it must entail a semantics as well as a semiotics, and the positing of figuration itself as the sole object of figuration would have struck him as being what it surely is, a radically absurd hypostatization of "spirit" alone. Santayana does not, of course, from within the terms of his own thought offer any semantic refutation of the theory of symbolic forms currently in vogue, but the whole drift of his vision, when we undertake today to recover it, may, by its sharp divergence from the reigning doctrine, have the effect of newly putting us in mind of how drastic is the new hermeticism. And it may also bring us to the threshold of a new *decision*, as to whether or not we shall give our suffrage to a poetic that does, at bottom, contend for the essential worthlessness of literary art.

To read Roland Barthes on Racinian tragedy or Gérard

Genette on Proust or Tzvetan Todorov on *Les Liaisons dangereuses* or Michel Foucault on Raymond Roussel is no doubt to be somewhat dazzled, and a little intimidated, by the brilliance of inventiveness and wit that marks their discourse, for they and numerous others of their general party are—let us freely admit it—consummately resourceful performers. But, having duly acknowledged what there may be of ingenuity and even wizardry in the *esprit* brought onto the contemporary scene by the *nouvelle critique,* the question ought not then to be evaded as to whether this is a movement whose doctrine is calculated to support or to subvert what needs to be called (banquet phrase though it may be) the fundamental humanistic enterprise—of exhibiting wherein the work of the literary imagination illumines and helps us to reckon with our fears and hopes, our loves and hates, our deceptions and our self-deceptions, our finitude and our capacity to touch the fringes of eternity. And if it appears that a given poetic, with whatever cleverness it may be espoused, not only abdicates from this whole range of discrimination but positively disavows even its possibility for critical discourse, then, as it would seem, it simply deserves what the poet of the *Commedia* spoke of as *il gran rifuto* ("the great refusal").

One occasionally hears today nervous declarations about the "crisis" that has overtaken contemporary criticism, and no doubt ours is a period in which the condition of criticism deserves to be so conceived. But it may need to be remembered that "crisis" speaks not merely of a bothersome situation of difficulty but of a situation in which the occasion has arisen for *deciding* whether a given state of things should continue to prevail or should be modified or terminated. And, indeed, if the legacy of a Santayana offers us any kind of tonic just now, perhaps it is one that chiefly consists in a certain invitation that legacy conveys from the Old Philosopher in Rome, who, from "that Platonic heaven to which the circumstances of time are wholly irrelevant,"[42] may be thought to look down upon us with the "smile of Parmenides"[43] on his face, gently voicing an entreaty that we simply decide whether or not in the last analysis we shall cast our vote for the enterprising anti-humanism that presently bids for our allegiance.

NOTES

[1]Horace Kallen, "The Laughing Philosopher," *The Journal of Philosophy,* 51 (January 1964), 19.

[2]George Santayana, "Apologia Pro Mente Sua," in *The Philosophy of George Santayana,* ed. Paul Arthur Schilpp (Evanston: Northwestern Univ. Press, 1940), p. 603.

[3]The phrase is Charles Hartshorne's, but, though his term makes a convenient umbrella for much of the inconsistency with which Santayana has been taxed, the particular meanings with which it is freighted in Professor Hartshorne's use are not at issue in my appropriation of it: see his "Santayana's Defiant Eclecticism," in *Journal of Philosophy,* 51 (January 1964), 35-44.

[4]"Apologia Pro Mente Sua," pp. 504-05.

[5]George Santayana, *Realms of Being* (New York: Charles Scribner's Sons, 1942), p. 206, hereafter abbreviated as RB.

[6]George Santayana, *Reason in Common Sense* (New York: Charles Scribner's Sons, 1905), p. 104.

[7]See George Santayana, *Scepticism and Animal Faith* (New York: Charles Scribner's Sons, 1923), Chapter VII, hereafter abbreviated as SAF.

[8]Humphry House and Graham Storey, eds. *The Journal and Papers of Gerard Manley Hopkins* (London: Oxford Univ. Press, 1959), p. 127.

[9]George Santayana, "A General Confession," in *The Philosophy of George Santayana,* pp. 28-29.

[10]"A General Confession," p. 14.

[11] George Santayana, "Ultimate Religion," in *Obiter Scripta*, ed. Justus Buchler and Benjamin Schwartz (New York: Charles Scribner's Sons, 1936), p. 290.

[12] George Santayana, "Literal and Symbolic Knowledge," in *Obiter Scripta*, p. 128.

[13] "Literal and Symbolic Knowledge," p. 108.

[14] George Santayana, *Soliloquies in England* (London: Constable, 1922), p. 142.

[15] Blaise Pascal, *Pensées*, trans. William Finlayson Trotter, from the ed. of the text prepared by Léon Brunschvicg (London: J. M. Dent and Sons, 1908), pp. 19-20.

[16] George Santayana, *Platonism and the Spiritual Life* (New York: Charles Scribner's Sons, 1946), p. 81.

[17] George Santayana, *The Idea of Christ in the Gospels* (New York: Charles Scribner's Sons, 1946), p. 251.

[18] John Herman Randall, Jr., "The Latent Idealism of a Materialist," in *The Journal of Philosophy*, 28 (November 1931), 648.

[19] George Santayana, *The Life of Reason; or, The Phases of Human Progress* (New York: Charles Scribner's Sons, 1954), p. 490.

[20] *The Life of Reason*, p. 489.

[21] George Santayana, *Interpretations of Poetry and Religion* (New York: Harper and Bros., 1957), p. 6.

[22] *Interpretations of Poetry and Religion*, p. v.

[23] See Matthew Arnold, "The Study of Poetry," in *Essays in Criticism*, Second Series (New York: Macmillan, 1896), p. 1: "Our religion has materialised itself in the fact, in the supposed fact; it has attached its emotion to the fact, and now the fact is failing it."

[24] Henry David Aiken, *Reason and Conduct: New Bearings in Moral Philosophy* (New York: Alfred A. Knopf, 1962), p. 348.

[25] Edward W. Said, *Beginnings: Intention and Method* (New York: Basic Books, 1975), p. 287.

[26] Ernst Cassirer, *The Philosophy of Symbolic Forms*, I, trans. Ralph Manheim (New Haven: Yale Univ. Press, 1953), p. 111.

[27] Martin Heidegger, *On the Way to Language*, trans. Peter D. Hertz and Joan Stambaugh (New York: Harper and Row, 1971), p. 155.

[28] *On the Way to Language*, p. 155.

[29] Jacques Derrida, "Structure, Sign, and Play in the Discourse of the Human Sciences," in *The Languages of Criticism and the Sciences of Man: The Structuralist Controversy*, ed. Richard Macksey and Eugenio Donato (Baltimore: Johns Hopkins Univ. Press, 1970), p. 250.

[30] Roland Barthes, "Science versus Literature," in *Structuralism: A Reader*, ed. Michael Lane (London: Cape, 1970), p. 411.

[31] Michel Foucault, *The Order of Things: An Archaeology of the Human Sciences* (New York: Vintage, 1973), p. 300.

[32] Even the most bilious scold of the New Criticism and the most intrepid defender of mimeticist theory, the late Ronald Crane, when he undertook in his Alexander Lectures at the University of Toronto (*The Languages of Criticism and the Structure of Poetry* [Toronto: Univ. of Toronto Press, 1953]) to specify the nature of the object which the poem imitates, declared it to be something "internal and hence strictly 'poetic' in the sense that it exists only as the intelligible and moving pattern of incidents, states of feeling, or images which the poet has constructed in the sequence of his words by analogy with some pattern of human experience such as men have either known or believed possible, or at least thought of as something that ought to be" (p. 56). Which was in effect for Crane to forswear any merely "representationalist" view of literary art as an affair of copying or reproducing what is already *out there*.

[33] Murray Krieger, "After the New Criticism," *The Massachusetts Review*, 4 (Autumn 1962), 188.

[34] Murray Krieger, *The Tragic Vision* (Chicago: Univ. of Chicago Press, 1960), p. 236.

[35]Leo Bersani, "From Bachelard to Barthes," in *Issues in Contemporary Literary Criticism,* ed. Gregory T. Polletta (Boston: Little, Brown and Co., 1973), p. 92.

[36]Edward Said, *"Abecedarium Culturae:* Structuralism, Absence, Writing," in *Modern French Criticism: From Proust and Valéry to Structuralism,* ed. John K. Simon (Chicago: Univ. of Chicago Press, 1972), p. 371.

[37]Geoffrey Hartman, *Beyond Formalism* (New Haven: Yale Univ. Press, 1970), p. xi.

[38]Roland Barthes, *Essais critiques* (Paris: Seuil, 1964), p. 156.

[39]The term is Hayden White's: see his "The Absurdist Moment in Contemporary Literary Theory," *Contemporary Literature,* 17 (Summer 1976), 401.

[40]"The Absurdist Moment," p. 402.

[41]Pierre Emmanuel, "Plus silencieux que le silence," in *Chansons du dé à coudre* (Paris: Egloff, 1947), p. 55.

[42]John Herman Randall, Jr., *The Making of the Modern Mind* (Boston: Houghton Mifflin, 1940), p. vii.

[43]Early in 1948 Thomas N. Munson, S. J., sent to Santayana the M.A. thesis he had done many years before on his thought. And in his letter of reply, in the course of trying to sort out the various confusions he felt Fr. Munson's essay reflected, he spoke of how deeply affected he was in his formative years by a passage in Plato's *Parmenides* "about 'ideas' of filth, rubbish, etc., which the moralistic young Socrates recoils from as not beautiful, making Parmenides smile. That smile of Parmenides," he said, "made me think." See *The Letters of George Santayana,* ed. Daniel Cory (New York: Charles Scribner's Sons, 1955), p. 373.

LITERATURE AS ASSERTIONS

by

Gerald Graff

Nobody denies that literary works contain propositions about various real-life subjects. But literary theorists for some time have disagreed about whether these propositions are to be viewed as genuine *statements*. A distinguished line of theorists—going back to Kant—argues that literature (and more generally, art) invests its propositions with a kind of immunity, that propositions stated or implied in literary works, even those which appear to make general claims about human experience, are not meant to be taken as serious assertions. Literary propositions do not make the kind of truth-claims, it is said, for which they might be liable if they occurred in non-literary forms of discourse. According to this view, the statements in literary works are pretended or fictive statements, and therefore the question of their truth or adequacy to life should not arise. One distinguished theorist, for example, Richard Ohmann, says that "there is a perfectly clean cognitive break between literature—poems, plays, novels, jokes, fairy tales, fantasies, etc.—and discourses that are not literature. Literary works are discourses with the usual illocutionary rules suspended. If you like, they are acts without consequences of the usual sort, sayings liberated from the usual burdens of social bond and responsibility."[1] A second theorist, Barbara Herrnstein Smith, concedes that a poem (or other literary work) *can* often be used to make a genuine statement, as for instance when one selects a greeting card because the sentiments expressed by its verses happen really to convey what one wishes to say. But Smith goes on to argue that "insofar as they are offered and recognized as statements in a poem," that is, insofar as they are treated *as literature*, such sentiments must be seen as fictive or pretended rather than real assertions.[2] In a third instance, Martin Steinmann and Robert Brown argue that "if we know the rules constituting" fictional discourse, we recognize that an utterance in a literary work "is not a commitment but a pretense of one."[3]

On the other hand, a number of recent theorists (myself among them) dissent from this anti-assertionist view, as it may be called.[4]   John Searle maintains that "serious illocutionary intentions" can "be conveyed by the pretended illocutions of literary fictions." Conceding that many of the propositions in literary works are pretended illocutionary acts, Searle holds that such pretended acts may themselves be used to make serious statements: "serious (i.e., non-fictional) speech acts can be conveyed by fictional texts, even though the conveyed speech act is not represented in the text. Almost any important work of fiction conveys a 'message' or 'messages' which are conveyed *by* the text but are not *in* the text."[5]   On the other hand, such non-fictional messages sometimes do appear *in* the text, as in the case of the opening sentence of *Anna Kerenina,* which seriously asserts that "All happy families resemble one another, but each unhappy family is unhappy in its own way."[6]   E. D. Hirsch makes the point even more succinctly: "Fiction has value beyond the pleasure it gives only because it presents something that is not fiction."[7]

The anti-assertionists argue that because literature is a species of fictional discourse, any commitments that may appear to be made in it are necessarily pretended rather than serious. They concede that utterances in literary works may be *used* to make serious commitments, but only by taking them out of the work and thus divorcing them from their literary use. When we read a text as literature we necessarily treat its propositions as pretended, fictive, hypothetical, and thus without liability for claims of truth. The assertionists, in countering this view, do not deny that literature often makes use of fictive discourse, but they go on to hold that one important use of such discourse is to assert "messages" which ask to be taken seriously as statements about real states of affairs. The point at issue, then, is how far the principle of fictionality is to be taken. Consider the following passage from Céline's *Journey to the End of the Night:* "It's no good the rest of us striving: we slip, stumble, over-balance into the alcohol which preserves both the living and the dead, we get nowhere. It's been proved."[8]   The anti-assertionists presumably would argue that the sentiments expressed here have the same fictive status as propositions in Céline's novel about characters, settings, and actions. He might point out that these sentiments are spoken by a character—the first-person narrator of the novel—but he would hold that even were they spoken by an authorial narrator they would still have the status of fictive statements. Even if it could be shown that Céline endorsed the view of life expressed by these statements, the fact that they appear in a work of literature obliges us to suspend their normal illocutionary force. For the assertionist, by contrast, there is nothing in the nature of literature that obliges us to treat Céline's propositions as non-assertions. Of course if it could be shown that other elements of the novel call into question the adequacy of these propositions—as might be the case if scenes could be adduced which seem to suggest that there *is* some point, after all, in "the rest of us striving"—then the assertionist could concede that the original propositions should not be accepted at face value. But he would argue that in such a case, the message of the work would simply be more complex: it would be a message implied *by* the text, arising dialectically out of a clash of different messages, and would not appear *in* the text. Insofar as the text is a "serious" work of literature (an important stipulation, to which we will return), such messages ask to be received as genuine statements. The reader, that is, is asked to *believe* in their truth, or at least to *take them seriously* as statements which might be true. Their adequacy or applicability to real life, whether as historical descriptions, moral judgments, or philosophical generalizations, is not a question to be waived merely because they appear in a work of literature.

The question arises whether it might be possible to reconcile these opposing theories. One could argue that they are actually concerned with different aspects of literature and therefore are not really in disagreement. The anti-assertional view, one could hold, is concerned primarily with what we have come to call the "intrinsic" aspect of a literary work, its internal coherence as a self-contained universe of discourse which can be enjoyed or studied without posing the question of its adequacy as a representation of something external—just as sentences can be looked at in terms of their grammatical and syntactical well-formedness without respect to whether they happen to be true or false. The assertional view, it may be said, is concerned with the "extrinsic" question of how the literary work relates to the worlds of morality, society, and history. Both kinds of critical attention are justifiable and thus complementary; each has its eye on a different object, so that any quarrel thought to exist between the two is a pseudo-quarrel.

Much though there is to be said for this kind of attempted accommodation, it works only up to a point. For finally these two views are not concerned with different aspects of literature. They are concerned with the single question of how readers are supposed to take those statements, or ostensible statements, which both parties concede are present at some level in literary works, and they offer conflicting and incompatible answers to this question. Confronted by the same literary work, these two views propose entirely different models of proper response. The one maintains that the beliefs and values reflected by the work must be taken as pretended commitments, the other that these beliefs and values (assuming agreement by the two sides on what they are) make genuine truth claims and thus demand to be taken seriously by the reader. The problem is not merely hypothetical: we read Milton, Lawrence, or Céline, and wonder how seriously we must take the author's view of life in order to appreciate his work. Are we to suspend this sort of interest as a non-esthetic irrelevance, or is such suspension merely patronizing? We encounter students who think they detect racism or sexism in literary works; do we accept such criticisms as relevant to literature or not? The question need not of course be settled in an either-or way, either by flatly rejecting or accepting the work on ideological grounds alone. The question is not whether the statements made by the work are the *only* things that matter but whether they are at least *among* the things that matter. If one view holds they are and the other denies it, both views can't be right.

To this last point it may be objected that no one way of responding to a work of literature, after all, is "right." Yet we do normally expect responses to literary works by qualified readers to share some degree of common ground. We assume there are minimal conditions which everybody's experience of a given work will fulfill, and when these are not fulfilled we are reluctant to concede that the work has successfully been "read" at all. If a student comes away from *Moby-Dick* convinced that Starbuck is the author's norm because he gives Ahab sound commercial advice, one would be obliged to tell him that he had—as we say—missed the point of the book. We assume that in this respect literary works are like jokes, having a "point" (or points) that can be "got" or "missed" to a greater or lesser degree. We are not dissuaded from this assumption by knowing that the point or points of a literary work are seldom easy to summarize in so many words (but neither for that matter, is the point of a good many jokes) and that what the point actually is may be highly debatable. The proponents of the opposing views I have been summarizing could easily agree that the student just mentioned above had missed the point of *Moby-Dick*, and there is no reason why they might not also agree on what that point is, or how it could be more successfully formulated. Where they would begin to disagree would be over the question of what sort of thing that "point" is, how it is to be taken. And this brings us back to the difficulty with which we started.

The difficulty is, how do we *know* how the point of a literary work is to be taken? By what process does one determine that the usual illocutionary rules are suspended, or not suspended, when it comes to dealing with literature? Literary theory is more abundant in strongly worded pronouncements[9] deciding the matter one way or the other than in examinations of the grounds on which any pronouncements can be based. Common sense may seem to dictate that we need only *look* at specific literary works, confident that pure induction will yield the answers we want about how these works mean. But this procedure is not much help, since the problem to be solved is precisely what it is we mean by "looking" in this context, which is to say, how are literary works to be looked at? Since no anti-assertionist theorist denies that propositions having the ostensible *form* of assertions do often appear in literary works, simply to adduce the presence of a number of such propositions in specific works does nothing to refute the theoretical claim that literature as such makes no assertions. One could adduce any number of seemingly asserted propositons from literary works, but the anti-assertionist will be unperturbed by this "evidence," which for him begs the question. For he is not denying that ostensibly asserted propositions occur in literary works, but rather that these propositions are genuinely asserted.

Adopting another strategy (one I myself have used frequently), one could point out that the anti-assertionist position often derives from an extraliterary ethical or political belief about the nature of assertion. That is, his resistance to permitting literary works to be read as making assertions comes not from any notion that it is not *possible* for such works to be read that way—he concedes, in fact that many people do read them this way; it comes rather from the conviction that literary works *ought* not be read as making assertions, that if they are read that way we give encouragement to a philistine or reactionary view of culture. In other words, what is often at issue for the anti-assertionist is the fear that literature will be degraded to the purely utilitarian level to which a practical and commercial society reduces all objects. (It is no accident that anti-assertionism arose historically at the moment when the practical-commercial society triumphed.) By defining literature as immune to assertions, anti-assertionist theory both protects literature from instrumentalism and even puts it forth as an antidote to instrumentalism, the latter strategy being one of the most common ways in which anti-assertionist theory recovers and redefines a moral and political purpose for literature. To the degree to which anti-assertionism is animated by some such ethical or political logic as I have just described, we can see that it has shifted the focus of the debate from the nature of literature as such to the way the nature of literature will have to be conceived if certain bad cultural consequences are to be avoided. This move is vulnerable to criticism, then, on the ground that (1) it has not been clearly demonstrated that attributing assertions to literature really does necessarily promote the kind of bad instrumentalism that worries the anti-assertionist; and (2) even if it could be shown that attributing assertions to literature does necessarily promote bad instrumentalism, that would not be a compelling reason for denying that literary works make assertions. The fact that a practice may have bad consequences is not a reason for denying that the fact occurs, or supposing that we can prevent its occurence.

To attack the arbitrariness, or wrongness, or irrelevance of the ethical or political assumptions that often underlie the anti-assertionist theory does not, however, take us very far toward answering the original question: how do we know how propositional elements in literary works are to be taken? A promising beginning, I think, is afforded by approaches such as structuralism, speech act theory, and "institutional" theory of art, approaches which consider the problem to be one of *convention*. Communication between writers and readers is seen by these approaches to depend on tacit contracts, the understanding of which is entailed in the acquisition of linguistic and literary competence. Such a view helps to demystify questions about literary meaning by viewing meaning not as a mysterious essence but as a function of human institutional behavior, behavior theoretically open to empirical investigation. The anti-assertionist arguments I quoted above are in each case grounded in an appeal to convention:[10] they hold that literary convention calls for the suspension of the usual illocutionary rules governing assertions. The assertionist counterargument appeals equally to convention but conceives it differently. How can one decide which view presents the convention accurately?

It may be useful to look at non-literary occasions in which the usual illocutionary rules governing assertions *are* suspended and inquire how it is we are able to tell the suspension is in force. Speech act theory suggests that we determine whether an illocutionary act counts as seriously performed or not by noting whether certain conventionally established "felicity conditions" have been fulfilled. A person cannot be said to have performed the illocutionary act of promising if it is well known that he has no power to carry out his promise. The sentence "I now pronounce you man and wife" sounds like an act of marrying somebody, but it counts as such only if spoken under special circumstances by an accredited official. In other words, the semantic properties of an utterance are *in themselves* not sufficient to tell the hearer or reader whether the utterance has been used to perform an illocutionary act. We need to know what an utterance is being used to do in a particular situation in order to understand in any adequate way what it means.

Suppose, for example, I am on different occasions called an insulting name, once by a personal enemy, once by a close friend. In the first instance, I have reason to suspect the insult is seriously meant, that an illocutionary act of "insulting" has taken place. In the second instance, I take the remark as a pretended insult which actually "performs" a gesture of affection.

Since both the words and even the intonation in the two cases may be identical, the differences in illocutionary force can only be inferred from the situation. Knowledge of analogous situations in which epithets have functioned either as insults or as badinage provides a set of precedents for guessing what is intended in such cases. But it is easy to imagine a third situation (being called the name by somebody one does not know, or by a friend with a reputation for irascibility, or a friend one has recently offended) in which it would be difficult to decide for sure whether the insult were intended seriously or not.[11] The relevant point here is that utterances do not acquire functionally determinate meanings until they are used to *do* something in specific situations; being seriously meant or pretended are instances of such use. Thus propositions do not become *assertions* until used by somebody, under appropriate conditions, for the purpose of asserting that such-and-such is the case.

To say that literature is a discourse with the usual illocutionary rules suspended, then, is to imply that utterances in literature are rather like mock-insulting epithets spoken by a friend. We are not to take them as doing the work, bearing the freight of serious assertion, that they could and do perform under real-life circumstances. Presumably, the propositions in literature have other uses besides assertion—to exhibit turns of consciousness, to move the emotions, to try out ways of viewing the world to which neither writer nor reader need be absolutely committed. Just as my understanding of the conventions of friendly badinage prevented me from taking my friend's epithet as the performance of a serious insult, so (it is implicitly claimed) a comparable convention prevents competent readers of literature from taking literary propositions as genuinely asserted. This, at any rate, I take to be the implicit logic of theories which argue that literary propositions are protected from the responsibility of real assertions. But there are problems with this view.

It is true that we have conventions for distinguishing between pretended and seriously committed illocutionary acts. But in everyday situations, we do not know *in advance* which convention may be actualized. That is, in these situations, we have to have *reasons* for deciding whether a given act is probably pretended or serious: So-and-so is a good friend and thus would never say something like that to me unless he were joking; or, So-and-so is a habitual kidder and sometimes goes too far; or, So-and-so dislikes Such-and-such's habit of insulting people and thus must want me to see he is parodying it. Now to say that in literature the usual illocutionary rules are suspended is to say that in literature we do not need such reasons for inferring pretense or seriousness, since literary convention decrees that we have no choice. Again, it is important to recall that this view aims to cover not merely narrative propositions about, say, settings or characters' actions, but also any larger general claims ("messages") which may be stated or implied as exemplified by the narrative. There is according to anti-assertionist theory no breaking out of the limited liability imposed by the convention that deems literature to be fiction; presumably (to follow out the apparent logic of this view), even if a writer sets out deliberately to violate this convention by actually *saying* something in a literary work, he cannot succeed. Either he succeeds in creating a work of literature, in which case his work (as literature) can make no statement, or he succeeds in making a statement, in which case his work is not literature.

This strong view might be supported if it could be shown that competent readers of literature *do* operate according to the convention put forward. But one of the better recent treatments of literary convention, Jonathan Culler's in *Structuralist Poetics,* suggests they do not. Culler's testimony is all the more pertinent, since he himself seems to endorse what he takes to be the structuralist view "that literature is something other than a statement about the world,"[12] and he thinks of his account of literary convention as confirming this view. That it may not actually confirm it, however, is suggested by Culler's discussion of the convention or "rule of significance," which dictates that to read a work as literature is to read it "as expressing a significant attitude to some problem concerning man and/or his relation to the universe."[13] "Reading a poem," Culler says (and his observation would seem to hold for other genres as well) "is a process of finding ways to grant it significance and importance, and in that process we call upon a variety of operations which have come to form part of the institution of poetry."[14] If reading a text as literature is, among other things, a process of finding ways to grant it "significance and importance," "a significant attitude to some problem concerning man and/or his relation to the universe," does this not call into question the view that to read literature as literature we have to refrain from attributing any statements to it? What after all is a "significant attitude" to problems of man and his relation to the universe if not at the very least a statement that there are such problems? That "significance" for Culler himself can equal some kind of statement is seen, for example, in his observation that "if all else failed, we could read a sequence of words with no apparent order as signifying absurdity or chaos and then, by giving it an allegorical relation to the world, take it as a statement about the incoherence and absurdity of our own languages."[15] What Culler means, however, is that such statements in literature function merely as organizing principles ("myths"), and not as theories about the world, as they would be if uttered as part of a "communicative project."[16] Why, though, would such an organizing principle need to be "significant and important" unless readers were supposed to take it seriously as a statement about the world? If it were merely a matter of furnishing an arbitrary conceptual scaffolding on which to build the work, why would not trivial propositions ("Human beings drink water.") do the job? As I point out elsewhere,[17] Culler, despite himself, grants serious theoretical status to a literary view of life when dealing with Flaubert's work.

In an intriguing application of the convention of significance, Culler takes up the problems posed by so-called "found poetry." It seems that almost any verbal expression can be made to count as poetry if presented in such a manner as to invite readers to apply specifically poetic conventions to it.[18] Thus the most banal news item presented in the right format (in a book of verse, or arranged typographically to resemble verse) will be recognized as a poem, though not necessarily a good or great poem. Such a news item will acquire significances in the transformation it had not seemed to posses before by virtue of the convention of significance. The more banal the item, in fact, the more readily will it lend itself to being read in terms of one kind of significance, appearing as an allegory of the banality of modern life.

What is especially worth noting here is that the process of

converting the news item into literature in this case involves us in *adding* the element of statement, not in subtracting it. Literary theorists have been so intent on distinguishing literary from non-literary discourse by proving that it possesses a special freedom from assertion that they have hardly considered the possibility that the reverse is true: that literature differentiates itself from other modes not by refraining from assertion but by making a stronger, more universalizable kind of assertion, that it is *hyper*-assertive rather than *non*-assertive. We do not attribute "significance" in Culler's sense to "natural" utterances. When we overhear the neighboring couple quarreling on the back stairs, for example, we "read" their remarks very differently from the way we would if we encountered their dialogue in a serious novel, where we would look for thematic links between this episode and the rest of the novel and implications relevant to the world of experience.[19] We might, of course, regard the real-life quarrel as "significant" in a *symptomatic* way of many things, e.g., the imminent likelihood of a divorce, the deterioration of the nuclear family, the need for better apartment insulation, and so forth. But this kind of interpreting differs from the kind we do in construing literary significance, for our object in the latter case is the discovery of an author's rhetorical purpose. Real-life conversations differ from novelistic ones in that they are not arranged by any author for any rhetorical purpose; they are free to be random and pointless in a way novelistic conversations are not. Literary conversations are expected to illustrate some point, and when a work comes along in which they fail to do so (e.g., *Tristram Shandy* or Ionesco's *The Bald Soprano*), we begin to look for the point of their not illustrating a point. Real-life talk does not convey a message the way literary talk does, though individual speeches convey messages. The messages conveyed by individual speeches do not exemplify any larger illustrative message, as do the speeches in a literary work. Thus to say that a real-life quarrel exemplifies the breakdown of human communication is different from interpreting a quarrel in a literary work in this fashion. Only in the second instance could one claim to describe a meaning communicated by another person.

The potential of a text to be read thematically (as exemplifying an intended general point or message) may finally, then, have more to do with determining whether we read it as a literary work than the presence in it of fictionality. Such a view would explain why non-fictional works such as *The Gulag Archipelago* are accorded literary status in a way that fully fictional works like the James Bond novels are not. It would also explain why it is often difficult to determine whether or not certain works of history and sociology (Gibbon's *Decline and Fall of the Roman Empire*; Oscar Lewis' *The Children of Sanchez*) should be classed as literature. Many works of literature contain no fiction whatsoever, and much fictional narrative is not literature, as has been pointed out by Mary Louise Pratt, who draws on William Labov's studies of "natural narrative," in *Toward a Speech Act Theory of Literary Discourse*. On the other hand, it is also true that certain literary genres—didactic lyrics, most notably—cannot be said to invite a thematic reading, since their messages are directly asserted and not exemplified by any action.[20] Thus one cannot go so far as to argue that thematic exemplification (through application of the convention of significance) is *the* defining principle of literature. Didactic lyrics differentiate themselves from non-literary discourse by other means, by the use of verse, for example, or certain rhetorical figures. But of course these works too are not immune from assertions.

How is a text's "potential to be read thematically" to be assessed, especially if virtually any text, when presented in a format conventionally recognized as literary (e.g., in verse), seems to have this potential? Consider once more the case of the news item. A trained reader guesses that such an item set up typographically as verse is meant to be read as literature, hence as thematically significant, since his training enables him to see that kind of typographical arrangement as a clue to the presence of that kind of authorial purpose. It does not follow that any text can be turned into literature by the mere fact that somebody looks at it that way, however. Suppose you were to publish a complicated thematic interpretation of, say, a daily gossip column. Most readers would assume you intended a parody of pretentious or overingenious literary analysis. Successful critical parodies, which are based on such works as *Winnie-the-Pooh*, "Thirty Days Hath September," and *The Chicago Telephone Directory*,[21] exploit the fact that the convention of significance cannot be applied to all texts. Parodists, that is, take for granted their readers' secure confidence that nobody could be serious in ascribing to such texts any profound thematic purposes.

On the other hand, distinctions between "serious" and other genres are far from fixed or clear-cut. Contemporary experimental writers have persistently reminded us of that fact by making a systematic project of conquering the latent resistance of certain kinds of linguistic raw material (e.g., slang, obscurity, dialect, jargon, scientific and technical argot, and so forth) to be used for literary purposes. Nobody today is surprised when poets violate what was once considered proper "poetic diction" by incorporating prosaic styles into poetry. In another kind of genre-shift, critics have recently begun taking detective fiction more seriously as literature, often by reading it as a form of epistemological inquiry. It is possible to imagine an analysis of the James Bond novels as deep statements about the amorality of modern life that would not be taken as a parody, though it might not convince anybody either. Whatever the case, such genre-reclassifications reinforce my point: in order for a text to make the crossover from the "pure entertainment" category to that of "serious literature," it is necessary that readers begin to exploit whatever potential these texts may have to be thematized as significant statements.

I have mentioned that all texts (or all events, for that matter) have a kind of *symptomatic* potential, as it may be called, to be seen as significant, but that this potential has nothing to do with our reading them as literature, since what we are thematizing in a literary work is something which has already been thematized by the purposive decision of the author. But cases arise frequently in which it is difficult or impossible to tell whether a text's significance is symptomatic or purposive, which is to say, whether the deep thematic meanings we apprehend in the text are part of its rhetorical purpose or not. Some critics of intentionalism have argued that it is irrelevant whether the meanings we apprehend are intended by the author or not, but this view does not seem to me to square with the actual behavior of readers, who in fact worry a good deal about whether or not they are connecting with the author's purposes. If we were to learn that an apparent hieroglyphic found on a rock had actually been created by natural erosion, we would stop treating it as a hieroglyphic.[22] It would no longer be seen as a text or as readable at all. Though "extrinsic" information drawn from biography, social history, and interviews with the author is never conclusive evidence for an interpretation, we are unsettled when such information contradicts or fails to confirm our hunches.

Texts which harbor any large degree of unconscious meaning pose the most acute problems in this respect, both of classification and evaluation. Are Poe's tales, for example, profound explorations of the depths of the psyche or are they lightweight thrillers which happen to be rich hunting-ground for psychoanalysts? There is room for disagreement, but Poe's literary status may turn on the degree to which the depth-meanings which are attributed to his work are intended, if unconsciously.[23] That it may not ever be possible to say whether they are shows that it is not only difficult to pin down the meaning of a literary work—a fact well enough known—but that it may be difficult even to determine the relevance of looking for meaning. We cannot always be sure that a particular text invites the kind of thematization called for by the convention of significance. But the fact that we do not always know whether the convention applies to a text does not make it any less authoritative.

To see what these generalizations may mean in practice, let us try to apply them to Joyce's *Ulysses*. Richard Ellmann takes the central theme of *Ulysses* to be that "casual kindness overcomes unconscionable power. Stephen's charge against Mulligan is that Mulligan is brutal and cruel; Molly's complaint against Boylan is again on the score of brutality, of animal sensuality without feeling. Bloom is allowed to formulate the theme of the book, though in comic circumstances, when he defends love to the Cyclops, and defines it meekly but deftly as 'the opposite of hatred.' It is opposite also to chauvinism and force."[24] Note that Ellmann's formulation—which is not unlike what could be found in countless critical essays—commits Joyce to a number of beliefs and values. If one argued that all commitments in a literary work are by convention only pretended, these beliefs and values would have to be pretended commitments. But this argument, as I hope it is by now clear, is arbitrary. There is no evidence that readers actually observe such a convention; Ellmann, who surely qualifies as a competent reader, does not observe it. He assumes that Joyce is expressing a certain view of the world and that this view matters both to Joyce and to his reader.

How far must the reader, then, commit himself to the commitment of the author? Or, to put it another way, to what degree will the reader's inability to accept the commitments of the author affect his judgment of the work? Such a question cannot be answered with a simple formula, since readers are capable of imaginative appreciation of widely divergent, perhaps even mutually contradictory, views of the world. But this capacity operates within certain limits. Few readers would not find their response to *Ulysses* tempered or at least altered if Joyce had made it his point to show unconscionable power, brutality, and cruelty *justly* triumphing over love and kindness. The reader of *Ulysses* is asked to believe in a vast number of propositions about the real world in order to read the book sympathetically, beliefs not only about morality but about history and psychology as well. Many of these beliefs are so universally taken for granted that doing without them is practically inconceivable, and therefore it is difficult to recognize that in accepting them we are trafficking in "beliefs" at all. Yet to imagine a situation in which we learned these beliefs were false is to discover how important it is to assume them. Suppose that we were somehow to learn that no such place as Dublin really ever existed, or that the type of society Joyce depicts there—which includes such things as modern transportation and communication systems, modern political and economic organizations, and a diverse group of social and national types—never existed in anything like the fashion in which Joyce presents them. Suppose too that we were to learn that human beings have never acted according to the patterns of thought and motive Joyce presents, that is to say, out of lust, greed, pride, curiosity, and so forth. Though Joyce, like any novelist, takes liberties with historical, social, and psychological truth, he does not assume that the reader's sense of this truth can be suspended.

Many of the beliefs we need to entertain in order to read *Ulysses* are *presupposed* rather than asserted explicitly. They "go without saying," so to speak, as do perhaps most of the beliefs to which authors and readers commit themselves. The specific content of what can be left to go without saying, what can be taken for granted as already understood and accepted by readers and thus need not be asserted explicitly, varies from period to period and culture to culture. Thus the degree to which literary artists may need to make their commitments explicit varies with the period and the culture, and the conventions of expression in different periods and cultures will be affected by this variation in the degree to which explicit foregrounding of assumptions is necessary. These conventions will also be affected by the prevailing attitudes in a culture toward explicit or implicit communication. In the modern period, an interesting contradiction has arisen, for while on the one hand the diminished supply of the cultural givens that create a consensus between readers and writers forces writers to become more "ideological" and aggressively schematic, on the other hand a strongly suspicious attitude toward aggressively ideological, schematic expression encourages writers to conceal or mute their commitments. I have argued elsewhere that contrary to a popular view, modern literature tends to be more rather than less didactic than earlier literature, in part because the beliefs which earlier writers could assume they could presuppose as cultural givens in their readers now have to be made explicit. But at the same time, these beliefs cannot be made too explicit lest the work be found guilty of serving as instrumental discourse. One response to this dilemma is to make one's meanings so complex that they cannot easily be formulated in terms of any simple message.

The very complexity of the thematic meaning of a work like *Ulysses* inspires skepticism about the possibility and the propriety of thematic readings. What this scepticism ignores is that when thematic assertions become complex, ambiguous, contradictory, plural, and even indeterminate, they do not cease to be assertions. One may argue—with some justice— that *Ulysses* dramatizes the un-thematizable irrationality of experience. But to dramatize the un-thematizable irrationality of experience is still to thematize that experience in terms of assertions. I am aware that no self-respecting New Critic—to say nothing of a post-structuralist—will allow me to get away with that claim. "No," it will be objected, "here is where any assertional view of literature must break down: for 'dramatizing' experience, which is what literature specializes in doing, is not at all the same as making statements 'about' experience. The enormous difference between abstractly generalizing about experience and *presenting* it is what your view ignores." With this objection, however, the anti-assertionist strategy has changed its ground. Up to now, the key argument has been that literary propositions are pretended assertions, utterances in which the usual illocutionary rules are suspended. This argument implicitly conceded that the unit-meanings, as we may term them, of a literary work are propositions. The objection I have just mentioned goes further, arguing that it is incorrect to talk about literary meanings as an affair of propositions at all.

Again, a good way to counter this objection is to look at the way actual readers behave, and in this case we can consult relevant studies of the reading process. It is true that not much information about specifically literary reading exists, the bulk of the data being about the dynamics of reading in general. Though one may seem to be begging the question to apply this information to literary experience, it is worth while examining it to see where it may lead. Fortunately for my purposes, E. D. Hirsch, in *The Philosophy of Composition,* has summarized much of the available research on the reading process. According to Hirsch's abstract of this research, the reader of a text must project a sense of the whole even as he experiences the text part by part. One perceives the work "all at once" at the same time as one encounters it as a linear sequence. "In order to perceive something all at once," Hirsch observes, "though it passes through our attention system bit by bit, we need to have a consolidating function that supplements our attention-monitor. We need a perceptual depository able to store perceived but not yet organized items and to keep them available on demand."[25] Psycholinguists call this depository "long-term" (as opposed to short-term) memory. Long-term memory receives what has already faded from the reader's immediate conscious awareness and must be fished up, in William James's figure (as quoted by Hirsch) "from a reservoir in which, with countless other objects, it lay buried and lost from view."[26] Its counterpart, short-term memory, stores impressions of which we are still immediately aware. For example, my reference to William James's fishing metaphor will still at this moment be present to my reader's immediate awareness (short-term memory), since he encountered it in the previous sentence. But a page or two hence, it will have faded into his long-term memory of my essay, where it will repose (one hopes) available to be recalled

if I should later on need to refer back to it (as it happens, I
will not). There is a well known short story by Jorge Luis
Borges entitled "Funes the Memorious," whose protagonist
has so capacious a short-term memory that he is virtually incapable of abstract thought. We would all be so incapacitated
if our long-term memory did not relieve us of the burden of
the immediate experience flowing in on us and permit us to
stop thinking of it.

What is significant for my purpose here is the finding
that the nature of what is processed by the reader of a text
is modified as it passes from short term to long-term memory.
In order to understand a discourse, it seems we must be able
to forget a good deal of it, to forget selectively. What we recol-
lect of what we have read is not particular details so much as
that schematic sense of the whole we projected in order to make
sense of the details. Experiments repeatedly prove that readers
recall meanings much more sucessfully than they recall the
specific lexical and syntactic forms in which the meanings were
expressed, which is to say that our recollection of abstract
content exceeds our recollection of the formal means by which
that content is conveyed. Hirsch relates the 1894 findings of
Binet and Henri, who reported that "when children were asked
to recall short, eleven word passages, they *could* remember the
syntactic and lexical form of the utterances; but, when asked
to read longer passages of sixty to eighty-six words, they remembered the meaning accurately but not the form."[27]   In the
light of later confirmations of these results, it may be reasonable
to conclude that "after a linguistic clause has been processed
[i.e., after it has passed from short-term to long-term memory],
it is stored in a nonlinguistic, nonsequential form," which is
to say, as a conceptual schema.[28]   According to Johnson-Laird,
"all forms of syntactic structure are normally lost to memory
within a few seconds. . . . No one knows how meaning is represented within memory, but there is no evidence to show that
any form of syntactic structure is directly involved."[29]

If I understand these findings correctly, they challenge
some of the cherished assumptions of literary theorists and
teachers. If it is true that we tend to detach meanings from
syntax when we store them in our momory, then the sacred
doctrine that form and content are inseparable in literature

would seem to need qualification. And the so-called "heresy of paraphrase," which several generations now of critics have been seeking to expunge, begins to appear not as a heresy but as a normal and unavoidable aspect of the reading process. Of course it may be objected that what holds in general for the reading process does not necessarily hold for the reading of literature, and it can be argued that literature is a special case in which meaning cannot be detached from syntax, content from form, without serious impoverishment. For some literary texts, perhaps, if not for all, these arguments would be reasonable. In *The Aims of Interpretation,* where Hirsch argues that meaning may be independent of surface structure, he exempts some literary works whose meaning seems to be language—constituted.[30] It need not follow from psycholinguistic research that surface linguistic features are never effective in the experience of reading literature, much less that it makes no difference how literary meanings are conveyed as long as the writer's message gets across. Nevertheless, one need not go to the extreme of holding that nothing but the message matters in order to argue that literary theorists have overemphasized the degree to which messages are tied to the forms in which they are embodied and have underrated the importance of abstract schematization in the process of making sense of literature.

One theorist who has studied the literary reading process seems to me to give support to this view. Teun A. Van Dijk, writing on "Cognitive Processing of Literary Discourse," states that "a hearer or reader . . . gradually constructs a *conceptual representation* of the text in memory. Thus the variety of 'surface structural,' e.g., morphological and syntactic information in the text is 'translated' or 'transformed' into meanings which are cognitively represented in terms of 'concepts.'"[31] I do not take Van Dijk to be saying that readers of literature simply substitute abstract schemas for literary scenes or poetic stanzas, as if to say that we read novels and poems by translating them into essays. He implies rather that though thematic concepts to some degree displace the more concrete level of literary detail, they also help us store and retrieve this level of detail, for we tend to store in long term memory those details which are particularly relevant to the concepts we have formed. In this respect, abstract concepts are not in *competition* with the scenes, actions, stanzas, and the syntactic and structural forms of a literary work, for they assist the reader in retaining these things. Thus an answer becomes possible to those who object that propositional views of literature ignore literature's "dramatic" nature; one can reply that it is through propositional understanding that the dramatic materials of literary works are retained in memory and are made intelligible. We should not be asked to choose between the propositional and the presentational.

Van Dijk would seem to be moving in the direction of such a view when he observes that "in literary processing more than in other kinds of communication, cognitive comprehension, storage, rehearsal, and memory (and reproduction, i.e., telling about it), is geared toward the assignment of *relevance* of *salient* detail."[32] This is not to suggest that readers recall nothing except what they can appropriate conceptually, for to widely varying degrees, readers recall conceptually "irrelevant" materials. Van Dijk terms this kind of recall "incidental memory."[33] But as a rule, readers retain best what they have been able to process conceptually. It is not a question of the reader's translating the concreteness of scenes and sections into an abstract idea, but of making use of the idea to retain a sense of the scenes and actions themselves in their interconnection.

I submit the above arguments are confirmeed more than discredited by the most extensive account of the experience of reading literature that has so far been provided, that by Wolfgang Iser in his two books, *The Implied Reader* and *The Act of Reading*. At first sight this claim may seem improbable, since Iser repeatedly insists in these works on the discrepancy between the reader's grasp of abstract concepts and his experience of the dynamic process of the literary text unfolding in time. Rather like the early Stanley Fish of the theory of "affective stylistics," Iser tends to view the temporal flow of the text as resistant to and subversive of all efforts to conceptualize the text by means of abstract ideas. Indeed, this very resistance of the process of temporality to abstract conceptualization is for Iser central to the meaning of literary works such as *Tom Jones*, which he reads as exemplifying the "gulf between the rigid confines of principle and the endless fluidity of human experience." One might object, however, that to experience the temporal flow of *Tom Jones* as an instance of the gulf

between abstract principle and the fluidity of experience is itself
to experience the work as an idea as well as a temporal process—
or, more precisely, it is to experience the temporal process
of the work *as itself implicated in a set of ideas.* Iser's model
of the reading experience, then, depends more heavily on the
application of thematic ideas to the text than Iser allows. John
Reichert has acutely pointed out this dependence in his review
of *The Act of Reading:*

> A peculiar feature of *The Act of Reading,* given its stress on
> the discovery of the meanings of novels, is its initial exposé of
> the "traditional expository style of interpretation" whereby
> the work is "reduced" to a "single 'hidden' meaning" (p. 10).
> Iser makes use of James's "The Figure in the Carpet" to discredit
> such reductions, but proceeds to enunciate the story's meaning:
> "that meaning is no longer an object to be defined, but is an
> effect to be experienced" (p. 10). Indeed, Iser tells us the 'hid-
> den meaning' of every text he discusses, and he may be read not
> as having discredited traditional interpretation but as having
> lent it theoretical substance. While he insists on the difference
> between "image" and "discourse," the fact remains that we must
> fall into discourse when we start to discuss a work. Like Iser,
> we come up with general propositions to account for the fic-
> tional "world" we have discovered and assume them to repre-
> sent the novelist's ideas about the world we live in.[34]

I would add only two things to this excellent statement: first,
that one need not subscribe to the view that literary works
can be reduced to "a single hidden meaning" in order to defend "the traditional expository style of interpretation" as I
have been doing here and as Reichert does above. There are,
after all, no countable *units* of meaning, so that the notion of
a "single" meaning is meaningless on the face of it. An interpreter who expounds a set of meanings in a text does not pretend to exhaust all its meanings; he simply claims that those
he is expounding are there and presumably are important. Second, I would argue that "we must fall into discourse" not only
when we "start to discuss a work," but even before that, when
we start to read it.

Reading any complex literary work is rather like a filing
operation in which one must find conceptual "filing drawers"

for an immense stream of detail. Ellmann's paraphrase, quoted a moment ago, may stand for a mental "drawer" labelled "kindness vs. power." It is but one of the many such drawers the reader must be able to open up in order to assimilate successive events in *Ulysses* effectively. Usually, a formulation like Ellmann's takes shape only gradually, after many revisions, readjustments, and corrections. Thus the contrast between kindness and power is instanced as early as the opening encounter between Stephen and Mulligan, but the relevance of this scene to that contrast is likely to occur to the reader only in retrospect, and he may be forced to discard an earlier thematic construction of the scene. When one construction fails to fit—fails to help process further detail—we discard it or set it aside temporarily and try out others. There may be whole episodes for which a reader cannot be sure he has found the correct conceptual drawer—or *a* correct one, since there may be several. We can lose the thread for long stretches without total breakdown as long as we recover it within a reasonable time. The average critical paraphrase gives little sense of this step-by-step process of reading in all its unruliness, and of course it should not be expected to give such a sense. But this mistaken expectation may be at the root of much of the resistance against recognizing the importance of conceptualization in the process. If we mistakenly expect a paraphrase to be equivalent to the meaning it partially abstracts, we will naturally end up rejecting the possibility of paraphrasing meaning.

If the foregoing arguments have any merit, they ought to have relevance to the teaching of literature. Many students who have no difficulty comprehending literary works on the level of action and story are unable to perform the operations required to make conceptual sense of action and story. This failure to process literature conceptually leads to imporverishment of emotional response as well. All but the most receptive students of literature have difficulty performing the thematizing operations that come so easily to the practiced teacher and critic. If the problem of the degree of belief required by a work of its reader arises only intermittently in the classroom, this is because many students fail to arrive at the stage of conceptualization that would enable the question of their engagement with the author's outlook to become an issue. The student whose papers are repeatedly marked down for failing to go beyond plot-summary has usually not learned to produce the conceptual propositions that organize the dramatic materials. Not only do his grades suffer, his responses to literature are constricted.

Nobody wants to deprive readers of the pleasure of reading *Guliver's Travels* or *Moby-Dick* as pure adventure yarns. And one can concede that the use of literature as an object of classroom analysis runs the risk of placing too much emphasis on thematic reading and on the ability to verbalize it in a highly conscious way. As the university and the school become practically the only places where literature is taken seriously, various diffuse resentments against overintellectualization—resentments long present in our culture—are turned against classroom procedures. One can frequently sympathize with the student who feels oppressed by what looks to him like an arbitrary and pedantic demand that he discover Hidden Meaning and Symbolism in every work, who finally concludes that critical analysis is a kind of game, the goal of which is to "read into" the work meanings that are not there. Other students learn to play this game all too well and become either enthusiasts or cynics before their time. The psychology of student revulsion against overinterpretation seems to me to have more than a little in common with that of sophisticated efforts to theorize the propositional element out of literary experience. Both hostile reactions arise from exposure to the wrong kind of thematic reading, which is either farfetched and wrong or else fails to acknowledge sufficiently that there is more to any literary work than its thematic message. Such reactions are understandable enough, but they create a false dilemma, putting thematic reading into an unnecessary competition with appreciation and experience. The student (or layman) conceives of reading for pleasure and reading for meaning as incompatible activities. The literary theorist conceives experiencing literature as incompatible with entertaining conceptual statements. Ideally, learning how to thematize a literary work should enhance the experiential pleasure, not compete with it.

Everybody who has learned to read literature successfully has acquired the trick of thematization and knows how to use it to enhance rather than limit experiental pleasure. Perhaps if this trick came as easily to most students as it does to pro-

fessional critics and teachers, there would be more to be said
for efforts to discourage the "message hunting" mode of reading. But it is questionable tactics to warn a student against the
abuses of message hunting if locating any kind of message in a
literary work is precisely what he has not learned how to do.
Perhaps at one time, students had to be cured of the habit of
making glib appropriations of literature; this is no longer the
case—most students are uncertain what to say or think about
literature at all. The critic or teacher who exhorts his students
not to hunt for messages is a bit like a millionaire who exhorts
poor people not to be overly concerned about material prosperity. The real challenge of literature teaching is not to get
students to stop hunting for messages, but to show them how
to hunt for messages in a fashion that is not simply coarse
and crude. To argue as if the choice in dealing with literature
were between messages or no messages, instead of between
crude and complex messages, contradicts what is known about
the experience of reading and makes the teacher's job harder.

To be sure, "what is known about the experience of reading" is as yet not much, especially as regards these problems of
belief in literature. Furthermore, even if a great deal more were
known, and empirical evidence supporting my argument were
conclusive, there would still be plenty of ground for objection.
One could always object that even though it may be true that
readers obey the convention of significance by thematizing
literary works, they *ought* not to do so. One could go on to
try to modify the convention, to install a new convention according to which literary works would be read as immune from
any liability to assertion. In a sense, recent literary theories
which would have us believe that this latter convention is already
in effect, and perhaps always has been, may be seen either as
wishful thinking or as attempts at "behavior modification."
In any case, the grounds of this theoretical impulse are often
ethical, springing from the deep-seated feeling that there is
something demeaning about propositional modes of discourse
and therefore that literary communication is degraded insofar
as it is associated with these modes.

I have discussed elsewhere some of the reasons for this
feeling and shall not go into them here, except to say that the
moral opposition to assertion would not have become so in-

fluential in literary criticism had it not been reinforced (one might even say, inspired) by an impressive body of literature which itself sets out to frustrate efforts to reduce it to an assertion. Assertion, conceptual appropriation of any kind, is identified with the predatory utilitarianisms of commerical effort, technological domination, advertising and propaganda, abstract moralism, and the processing and consumption of commodities. Assertion-making is viewed as a kind of "packaging" of thought and feeling, as the rhetorical complement of the acquisitive spirit. But these efforts have not succeeded in making literature less propositional and assertive, and it is hard to see how they could succeed without cancelling both their own seriousness and their critical thrust. If anything, such literature has had to become *more* propositional and assertive than its predecessors, for exposing the corruptions of packaged discourse and its cultural correlatives requires making assertions, even though these assertions may be directed against the making of assertions. The anti-assertionist stance is despite itself a means of asserting, and therfore one must not take its theoretical claims literally.

To summarize, then, there are two arguments for rejecting the anti-assertionist view and accepting the claim that literary works make assertions. Briefly put, the arguments are that authors intend assertions and readers can scarcely help looking for them. Authors intend to make assertions whenever they set out to write "serious" works. Even when an author attempts to undermine or negate all assertions—as frequently is the case with modern authors—that very enterprise involves him in making or presupposing assertions to which he commits himself. Readers, for their part, can scarcely help formulating assertions, in the form of thematic propositions, in making sense of literary works, and in practice readers are balked when these thematic propositions are greatly at variance with their own beliefs about the world. Whether writing and reading literary works as discourses with something to say is a form of behavior that could be altered is difficult to judge. But it is what we have long done and what we continue to do.

NOTES

[1] Richard Ohmann, "Speech, Literature, and the Space Between," *New Literary History*, IV, no. 1 (Autumn, 1972), p. 53.

[2] Barbara Herrnstein Smith, "Poetry as Fiction," *New Literary History*, II, no 2. (Winter, 1971), p. 271.

[3] Robert L. Brown, Jr. and Martin Steinmann, Jr., "Native Readers of Fiction: A Speech-Act and Genre-Rule Approach to Defining Literature," *What Is Literature?* Paul Hernadi, ed. (Bloomington: Indiana University Press, 1978), p. 149. Brown and Steinmann add: "Briefly, to take a discourse as fictional is, as other writers have observed, to take it as an utterance act that pretends to be, but is not, a propositional act and an illocutionary act as well. In performing an utterance act, the speaker or writer pretends to refer to things, to predicate properties or relations of them, and to perform an illocutionary act, but he does not really do so. And *pretend* is the key word" (p. 148).

[4] *In Poetic Statement and Critical Dogma* (Evanston: Northwestern University Press, 1970), I used the term "antipropositional" to describe this kind of theory. But "anti-assertionist" is technically more precise. Some theorists, however, are fairly described as antipropositional as well as anti-assertionist.

[5] John R. Searle, "The Logical Status of Fictional Discourse," *New Literary History*, VI, no 2. (Winter, 1975), p. 332. For Searle, the "essential rule" is that "the maker of an assertion commits himself to the truth of the expressed proposition" (p. 322). In arguing that "serious speech acts" are conveyed by literature, Searle does not restrict the range of these acts to assertions alone but includes others such as warnings, pleadings, scoldings, and so forth. Presumably, he would agree with J. L. Austin's point that though such speech acts do not themselves constitute assertions ("constatives" in Austin's vocabulary), they nevertheless *imply* or *pre-*

suppose assertions. (See Austin, *How to Do Things With Words,* ed. J. O. Urmson [New York: Oxford University Press, 1965], p. 100.) Ohmann, Smith, and others who use speech act theory in literary criticism have neglected the implications of this point: from the fact that an utterance *does* something, we should not infer that it does not also *say* something.

[6] *Ibid.,* p. 332.

[7] E. D. Hirsch, *The Aims of Interpretation* (Chicago: University of Chicago Press, 1976), p. 157.

[8] Louis-Ferdinand Céline, *Journey to the End of the Night,* trans. John H. P. Marks (New York: New Directions, 1960), p. 330.

[9] For example, in *Poetic Statement and Critical Dogma,* I find myself claiming that "the poet, regardless of what type of poet he is, . . . cannot help saying something about the human situation in general, cannot avoid incurring the risks of assertion" (p. 25). Perhaps so, but how did I *know* that? On what grounds could such a claim be defended? I would no longer hold that a poet "cannot avoid" making assertions, though I would question the likely importance and value of a poem that avoided making them.

[10] Smith, for example, writes that "when we read the text of a poem or hear it read aloud, our response to it as a linguistic structure is governed by quite special conventions, and it is the understanding that these conventions are operating that distinguishes the poem as a verbal artwork from natural discourse" ("Poetry as Fiction," p. 267).

[11] The utterer of the epithet might *himself* be unsure whether or to what degree he intends it as a serious insult, or he might half-intend it as such while half-intending it as a mere gesture. Theorists of intention have not, so far as I know, devoted much attention to the problems posed by blurred or ambivalent kinds of intentions—kinds which are increasingly important in a fluid social world where the proprieties are not clearly defined. Jacques Derrida exploits this difficulty in his critique of Searle's implicitly intentionalist view of meaning (see his essay, "Limited Inc abc . . ." trans. Samuel Weber, *Glyph,* 2 [1977], pp. 215-6). But Derrida is content to revel in the presumed duplicity and indeterminacy of all intentions rather than make the careful distinctions that seem to me to be needed.

[12]Jonathan Culler, *Structuralist Poetics: Structuralism, Linguistics, and the Study of Literature* (Ithaca: Cornell University Press, 1975), p. 130. For the argument of this section, as for much else in this paper, I am indebteded to my colleague Martha Woodmansee. See her forthcoming critique of literary-critical uses of speech act theory in *Centrum*.

[13]*Ibid.*, p. 115.

[14]*Ibid.*, p. 175.

[15]*Ibid.*, p. 138. See also his comment that "if a poem seems utterly banal it is possible to take banality of statement as a statement about banality and hence to derive a suggestion that poetry can go no further than language . . ." (p. 177). Culler is here talking about the convention "that poems are significant if they can be read as reflections on or explorations of the problems of poetry itself." For a poem to say, in effect, "This poem is about its own language," or "This poem cannot be about anything outside language" is to make a statement.

[16]*Ibid.*, p. 146.

[17]See my discussion of Culler's *Flaubert: the Uses of Uncertainty* in *Literature Against Itself: Literary Ideas in Modern Society* (Chicago: University of Chicago Press, 1979), pp. 152-67.

[18]Culler, *Structuralist Poetics,* pp. 161-62.

[19]I am indebted for this illustration to an unpublished paper by Marilyn Cooper of the University of Minnesota.

[20]Some (not all) anti-assertionists argue that even didactic works like Pope's *Essay on Man* and *Essay on Criticism* must be read as spoken not by the poet but by a *persona* distinct from him. This view is probably less widespread today than it was in the heyday of the New Criticism, but it still resurfaces from time to time, especially in the classroom. The problem with this view is that it rests on nothing but an *a priori* assertion about the nature of poetry or literature. If, as in the case of Pope, there appears to be no evident discrepancy between the views and attitudes advanced directly by the speaker of the poem and the author, it is difficult to see what is gained by insisting that these views and attitudes be ascribed to the speaker, not the poet. There are many poems, of course, in which there does appear to be such a discrepancy, and in these cases

the distinction between poet and *persona* is necessary. But erected into a general rule alleged to cover *all* poetry, the doctrine that it is always a *persona* who speaks, never the poet, is transparently a last-ditch strategy designed to avoid having to treat poetry as a form of statement.

[21]My references are, successively, to Frederick Crews, *The Pooh-Perplex* (New York: E. P. Dutton & Co., 1963); Theodore Spenser, "How to Criticise a Poem (In the Manner of Certain Contemporary Critics)," *Inquiry & Expression: A College Reader,* ed. Harold C. Martin and Richard Ohmann (New York: Holt, Rinehart & Winston, 1961), pp. 489-92; W. B. Scott, "The Problem of Tragedy," *Chicago Letter and Other Parodies* (Ann Arbor: Ardis Publishers, 1978), pp. 13-16.

[22]Michael Hancher makes this point in "Sermons in Stones," *Centrum,* II, no 1 (Spring, 1974), pp. 78-86.

[23]See above, n. 11.

[24]Richard Ellmann, *James Joyce* (New York: Oxford University Press, 1959), p. 390.

[25]E. D. Hirsch, *The Philosophy of Composition* (Chicago: University of Chicago Press, 1977), p. 110.

[26]*Ibid.*

[27]*Ibid.*, p. 122.

[28]*Ibid.*

[29]*Ibid.*, pp. 122-3.

[30]E. D. Hirsch, *The Aims of Interpretation,* p. 51: "the issue is not whether the forms of the mother tongue sometimes constrain forms of thought, but whether they always necessarily do so." Hirsch argues (in the essay "Stylistics and Synonymity") for the former position.

[31]Teun A. Van Dijk, "Cognitive Processing of Literary Discourse," *Poetics Today,* I, no. 1 (Autumn, 1979), p. 145. Van Dijk, however, seems to espouse a version of the "anti-assertional" view when he says, "the poem is produced, read and understood as a speech act which need not have the usual 'practical' pragmatic func-

tions, such as [real] assertion, question, threat, or promise in our every-day conversation, but may have only or primarily a *ritual* function" (p. 151). He does not elaborate, except to add that "this specific pragmatic function of literature as a kind of ritual speech act is further specified by the socio-cultural context . . ." (p. 152). But what evidence is there that in our specific "socio-cultural context" literature *has* been accorded a "ritual" rather than an assertive function?

[32]*Ibid.*, p. 157.

[33]*Ibid.*

[34]John Reichert, review of Wolfgang Iser, *The Act of Reading: A Theory of Aesthetic Response, Philosophy and Literature*, 4, no. 1 (Spring, 1980), p. 132. The above quotation from *The Act of Reading* is taken from Reichert's review.

THE BOOK OF DECONSTRUCTIVE CRITICISM

by
Vincent B. Leitch

> The classifier of methodologies can look back only with nostalgia
> at the simplicity of his problems in the limited warfare among New
> Critics, biographical and historical scholars, new-humanists, neo-
> Aristotelians, and old-style Freudians and Marxists. Much more
> confusing these days are the challenges not only to critical method
> but to the very assumption that there is an object or language for
> criticism.

Introduction: Writing the History of Modern Literary Criticism

Pretext (I)

As I look once again at these words from a recent book advertisement, I realize that I'm witnessing the formation of a history. In this confident sketch I discover, among other things, that
the Neo-Humanism of the 1920s, the New Criticism of the 1930s
and 1940s, and the Neo-Aristotelianism of the 1950s constitute—
from the perspective of the American literary critic of the late
1970s—rather simple fare. Past the simpler days of former times
looms the present nightmare that threatens "critical method,"
that doubts the existence of the literary "object," and that questions the status of critical "language" itself. Appropriately, the
"only" response now proper to the grand old warfare of earlier
critics is "nostalgia." Present-day critics, who heroically endure
the current disarray of threatening (non)methodologies, are depicted later in the advertisement as responding fittingly with
"bafflement." And finally the offending critical methodologies
are identified in the sketch: " structuralisms, post-structuralisms,
and phenomenologies." With self-consciously provocative words,
the advertisement sums up the overall current state of criticism
and theory as "probably one of the most complex situations in
the history of literary criticism."

The historiographical strategy underlying this advertising narrative is a conventional literary structure: the contentious factions of past history are, in retrospect, much simpler to account for than the camps of combatants in present times. While the mood in this plot changes predictably from nostalgia to confusion, the theatrical imagery remains steadfastly military. And the unnamed persona, who tells this quasi-pastoral sketch, exhibits similar steadfastness against the "largely continental" hoard of contemporary confusers.

What is beguiling about this sales pitch on *Directions for Criticism* (1977), edited by Murray Krieger and L. S. Dembo, is precisely its seductive use of the ancient pastoral mode. Actually, many recent accounts of the critical scene rely on one version or another of this effective narrative pattern. Although arbitrary, reliance on this mode is perhaps unavoidable. Present-day critics apparently cannot altogether escape this easy network of narrative elements.   Why, though, could not the book on contemporary American literary criticism and theory be written as— say—a picaresque adventure?

Pretext (II)

The history of literary criticism in the 1960s and 1970s is currently being written.   In one version it is a tale in the comic mode about the fall and rise of old methodologies as they withstand and encompass the energetic critiques made by irreverent homegrown riffraff and foreign vagabonds.   In another version it appears as a tragic story of the terrible destruction of formerly triumphant schools at the hands of righteous visionaries from French shores. Yet other accounts, we know, are nostalgic versions of the pastoral. Surprisingly, there is no version in the romance mode.

Insofar as the deeds and adventures of contemporary theoreticians seem an extravagant fiction, remote from the ordinary life of scholar-teachers, this story, overlaid with fantastic episodes and spontaneous battles, resembles a romance.   And the widespread quest for a set of mysterious goals, interrupted with entertaining, if aimless, digressions, seems to seek of its own volition the pattern of romance.   Most decisively, the intrusions of the ensemble of bemused narrators of the story into the narrative itself constitute the strongest indications of the courtly mode in operation.

Pretext (III)

As a part of the overall romance of our age, the story of deconstruction in my account consists of a series of texts that assume different forms. I start with a chronicle. In the fall of 1966 a Conference at The Johns Hopkins University investigated "The Languages of Criticism and the Sciences of Man," disclosing not only that the phenomenological criticism of Geneva was miraculously thriving but also that the magical structuralism of Paris was likely to sweep the virgin realm. (Not without significance, the Conference skirted older American specialties like Neo-Humanism, New Criticism and Neo-Aristotelianism.) By the time the proceedings were published in 1970, however, it was evident that the flower of structuralism had not taken root as imagined in the early prophecies. Instead, its many persistent opponents crowded out structuralism and emerged triumphant in the new daylight. Thereupon a sweltering evening of exotic descents and wayward journeys ensued after which the visionary post-structuralist criticism named *deconstruction* bloomed in radiant fullness. Three of the finest critics in America buried their old critical wands and successfully devoted themselves to the new—Paul de Man, J. Hillis Miller and Joseph N. Riddel. They were not alone for long. Preeminent among the new mysterious forms of criticism in the 1970s, deconstruction seemed to constitute, alternately, a nihilistic ungraspable threat and an outright enlivening challenge. In both cases, this criticism appeared as a wondrous and strange creation in obscure harmony with an age of actual anti-matter and black astral absences.

The critical landscape for American critics in the 1960s and 1970s resembled an overgrown forest. Phenomenology, structuralism, post-structuralism, semiotics, reception aesthetics and deconstruction sprang to life to clutter the terrain. They flourished, often changing form and intention as suddenly as any mythical forest creature. In less that two decades, another age had dawned: a brave new world.

Chapter I. The Concepts behind the Theory

Abstracts of Five Concepts

Textuality.   Language is the (prison)house of being; it is constitutive of reality so that it has no actual—but only supposed—origin.   Our world is text, irreducibly.   Nothing stands behind.   Originally and at once, language is both "referential" since it signifies literal reality and "rhetorical" since it constructs fictions through figures.

Intertextuality.   Every text emerges out of a textual tradition.   In actuality, countless sources, influences and epochs—both hidden and revealed, spoken and written—are interwoven into language itself.   The very syntax and lexicon in the system of language carry the work of innumerable and often unnameable precursors.   Consequently, the lineage of any text quickly approaches an impasse in the inevitable labyrinth of intertextual connections and combinations.

Freeplay.   Any given word has a number of possible meanings as well as substitutions, displacements and differences.   And any given string of words, therefore, has an extensive range of potential meanings.   As a result, any text can generate an (almost) infinite set of statements of possible meaning.   Such semantic freeplay is paralleled by the freeplay of structures that any given text could be made to produce.

Structurality.   As a system of signs, language operates by phonological, syntactic and semantic rules.   Such rules are commonly thought to be universal laws or inherent structures.   Since all accounts and descriptions of systems are given in language (sign codes), they are not simply referential.   Structures are necessarily fictions—interpretations.   Consequently, structuration takes precedence over any particular structures.

Differance.   A word (signifier) stands for a thing, a feeling or a thought (referent).   The signifier is not the actual referent.   They are *different*.   The signifier is one thing and the referent an *other*.   Since it stands for or in place of the referent, the signifier indicates the actual absence of the referent.   The signifier marks a *postponement* or *deferment* in as much as it momentarily takes the place of the referent. In short, words suggest the *presence* of an entity but actually mark its *absence*. Written with black ink on white paper, the word "library" is clearly not the object itself. Words work by an enigmatic functioning of presence/absence, difference/deferment, other/postponement. A neologism designates this working of the sign—"differance."

(Since any given word is in question, any word—to show its differance but necessity—may for convenience be written, then crossed out, and kept with both it and the deletion: this strategy indicates the equivocal status of the word. To cross out yet keep a word in this way is to put it "under erasure.")

Commentary on the Concepts, or the Ethics of Deconstruction

Textuality. Conceived as simply referential, language is undermined by textuality, that is, by the absence of actual extralinguistic origin and by the play of rhetorical figures. Since the signifier's relation to the referent is both direct and fictitious, all reading practiced as though language were only referential is misreading. Referentiality requires "misreading." Yet to foreground self-consciously and actively the play of rhetorical fiction with referentiality is to perform misreading of a higher order.

Intertextuality. Working always within a given textual tradition, each writer proceeds to incorporate some parts and destroy others of the rich order of discourse. However, the presence of unconscious or unintended sources and unrealized influences or affinities, when combined with the deliberately chosen materials, creates a labyrinthine configuration of intertextuality, rendering any later critic's catalogue of borrowed pieces or chart of accumulated layers a fragment of the text's genealogy. Critical reading experiences an impasse created by the infinite interplay of texts that are always already engraved in the system of discourse.

Freeplay. The semantic fields of words multiply exponentially in the chain of words constituting a text so that the possible meanings of a text are limitless. (The task of traditional criticism is endless.) Just as any univocal word, concept, trope, structure, form or truth exists through the obvious suppression of freeplay, so any valorized reading of a text falsifies literary experience by restraining freeplay.

Structurality. Any set of data or facts can be structured in a number of ways. Theories, models and laws—empirical or otherwise—are got-up assemblages. The process of reifying such structures creates privileged products through limiting the range of possible structures and denying the force of structuration itself.

Differance. Just now, as I sit in my university office, I write "my library." Two things are obvious. First, those nine letters themselves are different from or other than my books or shelves at home. Second, the two words, while they evoke in my mind the presence of the library, really mark its absence; it's at home, not here. I have deferred or postponed producing the actual library; instead I wrote nine letters to summon up this book collection. The lesson of differ*a*nce: signs work by an enigmatic functioning of presence/absence, difference/deferment, other/postponement.

To apply differ*a*nce to the most important signs in the Western critical tradition—for instance, Meaning, Self, Consciousness—is to uncover crucial absences of presence. The forever deferred other (the "trace") is at the core of our metaphysics. Five telling applications: (1) the sovereign Self of the critic or the author; (2) the Truth of any text; (3) the Meaning of a key word or text; (4) the Structure of a text; (5) the Genealogy of literary history. Here is the absence of presence five times and the subversion of classical metaphysics.

Chapter II. The Strategies of Deconstruction

Note: On Method (1)

To subvert without pity the obvious and stubborn referentiality behind a word or figure, or to undermine a reified idea or structure is to do deconstruction. A deconstruction carefully demonstrates the absence of literal nonlinguistic origin, the slippery operation of the freeplay of semantic and/or structural substitution, and the functioning of differance. All texts can be deconstructed: all texts can be shown to be at once referential and fictive and at the same time to be based on the play of absence and presence.

A deconstruction can itself be deconstructed. This reversal results from the unrelenting and insistent operations of freeplay and differance. Yet each demystified reading, each self-conscious interpretation, each deconstruction clarifies, though the number of such potential clarifications is (nearly) infinite.

In practice, a deconstruction follows the movement in a text from the referentiality of the literal to the play of fiction; it forgrounds the enigmatic flights of stable meaning and presence; and it self-consciously charts a host of (mis)readings. In effect, deconstruction systematically demonstrates the impossibility of single or literal interpretations.

A deconstruction may recover from the text itself evidence of pre-existent deconstruction. In other words, it may show the text to admit its own complex transitions from referentiality to the play of fiction. In this case, deconstruction is more discovery than production. Since a text may embody its own deconstruction, it suggests that the writer anticipates the critic while allowing the possibility that the writer is mystified or not fully conscious of his deconstruction. In no case, though, is a text undeconstructible.

Naturally, deconstruction occurs in poetic practice as well as in critical work. When a poet deconstructs other writers, her text becomes partially deconstructed intertext. One way or another, all texts are "unreadable" not merely because of semantic or structural freeplay and differance, but because of intricate patterns of deliberate and unconscious intertextuality. A deconstruction, then, shows the text resolutely refusing to offer any privileged reading; in fact, potential readings approach infinity. Embodying almost infinite possibilities for interpretation, texts in the vision of deconstructive criticism appear as ineffably rich palimpsests inscribed with countless layers of heterogeneous textual materials.

Note: On Method (II)

The exact place where the critic locates a displacement in a text from the referential to the rhetorical, or from the univocal to the field of freeplay, or from presence to absence constitutes invariably the site of a philosophic or thematic opposition. Disclosing such a crevice, the critic systematically and tenaciously inverts the opposition to reveal the actual hierarchical nature of the dichotomous terms. At this point he or she steadfastly disallows any reconstitution or sublimation of these opposing terms. This strategic inversion and stubborn exposé produce an unexpected gap and force the emergence of a new concept, which nameless mark neither neutralizes nor reforms the old opposition. Rather, it functions as a disorganizing structural force that invisibly inhabits the opposition like the unconscious of Freud which secretly dwells amidst the subconscious and conscious domains of each person's psyche. The aim of the deconstructive critic is to produce such *undecidables* and to track their operations throughout the text. In this work the critic does not trace literary theme since the new concept is always subtracted from, then added to theme.

The *double science* of deconstructive criticism consists of deliberately *inverting* conventional thematic oppositions and *marking* the mysterious and disorienting play of hitherto invisible concepts that reside, unnamed, in the gap between opposing terms. In this double gesture, deconstruction avoids simply neutralising thematic oppositions or simply reconstituting them; in other words, deconstruction resists the inclusion of the new concept into the old dichotomy. Yet, since deconstructive criticism works within language, it cannot escape such reappropriation; finally its productions, in turn, fall prey to further deconstruction.

Advertisement for the Notes

For the classifier of methodologies, deconstructive criticism clearly transgresses the limits established by traditional criticism. It does not reproduce or recreate through the effaced doubling of commentary or interpretation the conscious or intentional meaning made by the writer in interaction with her world and time. Since there is nothing beyond the text, deconstruction works always from the inside. Yet this formalism is not interpretation or commentary inscribed by critics who serve as transparent mediums—purveyors of truth; it is joyous production of hidden and mirage-like semiological structures that reveal the radical and prolific play of differance in texts. Deconstruction is the free, systematic and painstaking practice of "erasure" and the "double science." As such, it employs new critical vocabularies, conceptualizations and procedures: it produces new forms of method and language for criticism.

Chapter III. Jacques Derrida: The Master in the Academy

An Essay on the Early History of Deconstruction

When Jacques Derrida presented his "Structure, Sign, and Play in the Discourse of the Human Sciences" at The Johns Hopkins University Conference in October 1966, he unobtrusively produced a rupture in the history of present-day literary criticism and theory. In this first foray of deconstructive criticism in America, Derrida deconstituted the structuralist strategies of Claude Lévi-Strauss, creating not only a devastating assault on structuralism but also a plot for the deconstructive project of the future. In the present essay this Conference presentation serves as *the* inaugural event in the history of contemporary deconstructive criticism.

I

In Derrida's account, the project of deconstruction begins in an earlier epoch when the *structurality* of structure and the *textuality* of texts were initially conceived.

> The event I called a rupture . . . would presumably have come about when the structurality of structure had to begin to be thought. . . . From then on it became necessary to think the law which governed, as it were, the desire for the center in the constitution of structure and the process of signification prescribing its displacements and its substitutions. . . . From then on it was probably necessary to begin to think that there was no center, that the center could not be thought in the form of a being-

present, that the center had no natural locus, that *it was not a fixed locus but a function,* a sort of non-locus in which *an infinite number of sign-substitutions came into play.* This moment was that in which language invaded the universal problematic; that in which, in the absence of a center or origin, *everything became discourse . . .* that is to say, when everything became a system where the central signified, the original or transcendental signified, is *never absolutely present outside a system of differences.* The absence of the transcendental signified *extends the domain and the interplay of signification ad infinitum* [my italics] .[1]

This passage serves as a chartering document because it discloses forcefully, if rather briefly, the dramatic operations of textuality, freeplay, structurality, differance and deconstruction itself. Explaining how "everything became discourse," Derrida uncovers the play of signification—the infinite number of sign-substitutions at play in texts. In addition, his radical analysis of the classical concept "center" not only liberates all structures but also celebrates "center" as a structural force or function free to serve countless hermeneutic roles. And he introduces the disruptive movements of differance by focusing our attention on the startling absence in the system of language of any central or transcendental signified. Denying any presence to an original referent beyond the play of language, Derrida insists on the destruction of the traditional concept of the sign.[2] In decentering the classical structure "center" as well as in destroying the old concept "sign," Derrida unveils the powerful deconstructive method at work.

The epoch of deconstruction starts, in Derrida's account, when Nietzsche, Freud and Heidegger call into question and destroy the metaphysical concepts of being, truth, consciousness, self, identity and presence. Quite openly, Derrida carries out his project in the intertextual aftermath of these three revolutionary forefathers. At the same time, his writings frequently show him breaking away from this modern deconstructive tradition: "It was within concepts inherited from metaphysics that Nietzsche, Freud, and Heidegger worked, for example. Since these concepts are not elements or atoms and since they are taken from a syntax and a system, every particular borrowing drags along with it the whole of metaphysics. This is what allows these destroyers to destroy each other reciprocally . . ." (251). In the (prison)house of language no text is undeconstructible—not even those by Nietzsche, Freud, Heidegger and

Derrida. Despite differences, Derrida, like these earlier deconstructers, destroys the old metaphysics, though he appears more rigorous and systematic in his project than all forerunners.

The affirmative yet anxious mood displayed at the close of "Structure, Sign, and Play" is perhaps only slightly less interesting than the conceptual framework. On the one hand, Derrida criticizes Lévi-Strauss's "sad, *negative,* nostalgic, guilty, Rousseauist facet of the thinking of freeplay" and praises "the Nietzschean *affirmation*—the joyous affirmation of the freeplay of the world and without truth, without origin . . ." (264). On the other hand, Derrida, as he envisions the birth of the coming brave new world, admits that he himself is one of those who "turn their eyes away in the face of the as yet unnameable which is proclaiming itself and which can do so, as is necessary whenever a birth is in the offing, only under the species of the nonspecies, in the formless, mute, infant, and terrifying form of monstrosity" (265).

II

The development of deconstruction comes quickly after 1966. In the next year Derrida dramatically launches his project with three texts: (1) *La voix et le phénomène: introduction au problème du signe dans la phénoménologie de Husserl*—essentially a deconstruction of phenomenology; (2) *De la grammatologie*—primarily a model deconstruction of Rousseau's *Essay on the Origin of Languages,* as well as a manifesto of deconstructive theory; and (3) *L'écriture et la différence*—a collection of eleven essays, including the historic "Structure, Sign, and Play."[3] Since most of the deconstructive criticism practiced by others in the 1960s and early 1970s takes its lead from these three books, the year 1967 is the *annus mirablis* of the school. Five years later Derrida published three more books: (1) *La dissémination*—a collection of four essays presenting three influential extended textual deconstructions;[4] (2) *Positions*—a gathering of revealing interviews;[5] and (3) *Marges de la philosophie*—a collection of ten essays, including the earlier groundbreaking essay "La différance" (1968).[6] Along with *Glas* (1974), a Joycean deconstruction of Hegel and Genet, and many (as yet) uncollected essays, Derrida's early outpourings serve as *the* library of deconstructive criticism.[7]

The single most influential book in the dawning history of the deconstructive school is *Of Grammatology* because it offers the earliest detailed exposition of the theories and strategies of deconstruction and because it renders a full and telling deconstructive reading of a text. What can only be inferred from "Structure, Sign, and Play" is made manifest in the *Grammatology*. In particular, although Derrida inverts and marks a crucial "undecidable" in the Conference presentation and later in the Husserl critique, not until the *Grammatology* does he present a complete deconstruction of this hitherto unnamed new concept—the *supplement*. Tracing the mysterious operations of this repressed motif in Lévi-Strauss and Husserl, as well as in Rousseau, Derrida effectively establishes the contemporary era of deconstruction.

As Derrida points out, many artists and philosophers throughout history posit or employ the opposition "nature/culture." According to the traditional account, archaic man, living in an innocent and blissful state of nature, comes upon a danger or insufficiency of some sort, bringing about a need for community. In the evolution of man from nature into society, the latter stage of existence is pictured as an addition to the original happy state of nature. In other words, culture supplements nature. Before too long culture comes to take the place of nature. Culture, then, functions as a *supplement* in two ways: (1) it adds on and (2) it substitutes. Moreover, it is potentially both detrimental and beneficial. Significantly, this structure of the nature/culture opposition repeats itself in other traditional oppositions: for example, health/disease, purity/contamination, good/evil, object/representation and speech/writing. Temporal priority distinguishes the first term in each pair; the second entity comes as a supplement to the first. In the case of speech/writing, for instance, the conventional explanation relates how writing comes late in the history of man, arriving as a double-edged supplement that offers gains and losses to man. Traditionally, the first term in each opposition constitutes the priviledged or better state or entity: nature over culture.

Derrida shows that the *structure of supplementarity* resem-

bles the structure of differance: "The same is here called supplement, another name for differance."[8] In effect, Derrida argues
that nature untouched by the force of supplementarity has no
truth-value. There is no original unsupplemented nature—only
a desire for it or a myth creating it. The absence of presence
in the sign "nature" erases and overturns this metaphysically
pure concept. Inverting the nature/culture opposition, Derrida
marks the emergence of the undecidable (the *supplement*),
tracing its pervasive operations throughout the text of Rousseau
and others. The effect is to deconstruct nature and culture,
showing that culture does not supplement nature but rather
that nature is *always already* a supplemented entity.

Midway in his analysis of the *supplement* in Rousseau, Derrida offers a provocative summation of his understanding of
supplementarity:

> Thus supplementarity makes possible all that constitutes the
> property of man: speech, society, passion, etc. But what is this
> property of man? On the one hand, it is that of which the possi-
> bility must be thought before man, and outside of him. Man
> allows himself to be announced to himself after the fact of supple-
> mentarity, which is thus not an attribute—accidental or essential
> —of man. For on the other hand, supplementarity, which *is
> nothing*, neither a presence nor an absence, is neither a substance
> nor an essence of man. It is precisely the play of presence and
> absence, the opening of this play that no metaphysical or ontologi-
> cal concept can comprehend. *(Grammatology,* p. 244)

Supplementarity is the condition of humanity. Or, more precisely, the operation of the supplement is a precondition of man.
Thus, all that man is is constituted by the force of supplementarity. There is no question of choice here. Needless to say,
supplementarity is neither a touchable substance nor a tangible
presence; it is not a thing. Yet the supplement is not characterized by absence, obviously. Outside the grasp of classical
metaphysics and ontology, the supplement is a special form
of differance, which operates, invisible and unnamed, in the
texts of philosophers and poets. This undecidable escapes
appropriation into the binary oppositions of philosophy and
literature, yet it dwells amidst the oppositions, resisting and
disorganizing them while refusing inclusion as a third term.

In Derrida's text, the supplement appears as a nonsynony-
mic substitution of differance: "no concept overlaps with any
other. . . ."[9] To a large extent, the early history of deconstruction consists of Derrida's relentless search for and discovery of
the many forces of differance in the Western tradition. Some
other names of differance (other undecidables), produced by
Derrida's later deconstructions, include *dissemination, entame,
gramme, greffe, hymen, iterability, parergon, pharmakon, re-
serve, spacing* and *trace.*

III

In the decade after Derrida launched deconstructive criticism, his three early works and selected others were translated
into English and widely discussed in America. At the 1977 convention of the Modern Language Association, for example,
there were more than a dozen presentations on deconstruction.
In the same year, The Johns Hopkins University initiated a serial
publication (named *Glyph*) devoted to articles analyzing and
practicing "textuality." And in 1977 a heated debate over deconstruction flared up among major critics in the pages of
Critical Inquiry.

Significantly, the first issue of *Glyph* contained an article
and the second a monograph by Derrida.[10] The wider context
of these works is revealing: latter-day deconstructers, displaying highly individualized versions of the method, self-consciously deconstruct, disseminate and displace the master. Needless
to say, the history of deconstruction can turn out no other
way. Indeed, my own history of the history, while inscribing
the supplement and engraving differance, produces an extravagant fictional displacement and remote substitution. There
was never any question of choice in this adventure.

Chapter IV. Paul de Man: The New Rhetorician

An Essay on the Later History of Deconstruction

Since 1966 Paul de Man has written roughly two dozen
essays, placing nine of these in the collection *Blindness and
Insight: Essays in the Rhetoric of Contemporary Criticism*

(1971) and twelve of these in *Allegories of Reading* (1979). Over the course of a dozen years de Man developed a complex thematics of deconstruction. Centrally important for the experience and understanding of his critical ideas are his various conceptions of language and rhetoric. "My tentative generalizations," proclaims de Man in the Foreword to *Blindness and Insight,* "are not aimed toward a theory of criticism but toward literary language in general."[11]   In a more recent study, published in 1977, he indicates in the conclusion that his emphasis continues upon language rather than theories of criticism or ontology: "The main point of the reading has been to show that the resulting predicament is linguistic rather than ontological or hermeneutic," and indeed the specific purpose of this essay is ultimately to demonstrate a profound "discontinuity between two rhetorical codes."[12]

* * * * *

The most lucid and direct expression of de Man's fundamental notions about language and rhetoric emerges in a conference presentation on Nietzsche's theory of rhetoric (1973), where we learn that Nietzsche shifts the study of rhetoric from methods of persuasion and eloquence to the prior theory of figures and tropes. About Nietzsche's formulation that "Tropes are not something that can be added or subtracted from language at will; they are its truest nature," we discover:

> . . . the straightforward affirmation that *the paradigmatic structure of language is rhetorical* rather than representational or expressive of a referential, proper meaning . . . marks *a full reversal of the established priorities* which traditionally root the authority of language in its adequation to an extralinguistic referent or meaning, rather than in the intralinguistic resources of figures [my italics].[13]

Nietzsche presents a categorical rupture in the theory of language, starting a new historical epoch in which language is first consciously conceived of as always at once and originarily figural or rhetorical, rather than referential or representational. No primitive unrhetorical language exists. As the distinctive feature of language, rhetoricity necessarily undermines truth and "opens up vertiginous possibilities of referential aberration."[14]   Thus the linguistic sign is the site of an ambivalent and problematic relation between referential and figural meaning, which brings into question thematic interpretation and encourages rhetorical reading.   The revisionary project of criticism, therefore, is to create a nonthematic figural criticism—a new rhetoric.

The continuous elaboration of "rhetoricity" leads to the incorporation of enriching materials from contemporary speech act and grammatical theory.   De Man aligns "constative language" with rhetorical persuasion and referentiality, and he correlates "performative language" with rhetorical devices and figurality.[15]   The chain of oppositions in his consciousness becomes clearer now: typical polarities include substance/action, reference/figure, meaning/(vertiginous) aberration, persuasion/trope, constative/performative, referentiality/rhetoricity. When he first introduces grammar into this chain in 1973, de Man observes: "To distinguish the epistemology of grammar from the epistemology of rhetoric is a redoubtable task" ("SR," 28-29).   Indeed, the later work bears out this point.   Although not (yet) completely accommodated to the theory of rhetoricity, grammar in recent reading experiences reaches tentative formulation.   Seemingly, grammar interrupts the reference/rhetoric polarity and creates the very possibility of figurality: "The divergence between grammar and referential meaning is what we call the figural dimensions of language."[16]   Rather than a displacement of rhetoric by grammar in the chain of oppositions, a triad composed of grammar/rhetoric/reference enters the chain; the implication is that "the logic of grammar generates texts only in the absence of referential meaning . . ."("PAR," 669). The addition of grammar to the theory of rhetoric is crucial because it produces an altered conception of the text: all texts now necessarily consist of *grammatical*, rhetorical and referential strata.   Since each stratum may and frequently does have divisions within itself, the rendition of a text in any particular reading approaches the extravagant limits of vertigo.

Implicitly, the expanded conception of the rhetoricity of language embodies operative notions of freeplay, structurality and textuality. Only lately, though, has the experience of textuality apparently displaced the residual presence in the text of the intentionality of language as well as the intentions of the author. Here is an early formulation of textuality derived from Nietzsche's rhetoric:

> The wisdom of the text is self-destructive . . . , but this self destruction is infinitely displaced in a series of successive rhetorical reversals which, by the endless repetition of the same figure, keep it suspended between truth and the death of this truth. A threat of immediate destruction, stating itself as a figure of speech, thus becomes the permanent repetition of this threat. ["NTR," 43]

The states of "suspension" and "repetition" announce the impossibility of reading—the necessary unreadability of texts. A more extreme version of textuality emerges when reading Rousseau's autobiographical works:

> Far from seeing language as an instrument in the service of a psychic energy [i.e., intentionality], the possibility now arises that the entire construction of drives, substitutions, repressions, and representations is the aberrant, metaphorical correlative of *the absolute randomness of language,* prior to any figuration or meaning [my brackets and italics; "PR," 44].

In this later tentative conception of textuality, it is the generating force of grammar, which is a precondition of rhetoric and reference, that seems to produce an "absolute randomness of language," displacing the author and intentionality from the text. This radical concept of textuality is grounded ultimately in the relentless and machine-like processes of grammar.

Since all formulations of rhetoricity apply to language in general, it appears inevitable that literature assume no priority over criticism. The precise way to make this point is to say: literary language is characterized by rhetoricity and, accordingly, any language in *any* text is "literary" to the extent that it is rhetorical. "Literature as well as criticism—*the difference between them being delusive*—are condemned (or privileged) to be forever the most rigorous, and consequently, the most unreliable language . . ." (my italics, "SR," 33; see "PAR," 650). Any prior or absolute distinction between literature and criticism partakes of delusion because "The criterion of literary specificity does not depend on the greater or lesser discursiveness of the mode but on the degree of consistent 'rhetoricity' of the language" (*BI,* 137n).

* * * * *

Establishing the rhetorical nature of language (its "literariness"), de Man is enabled to conceptualize his experience of unreadability into a theory of misreading. The elucidation of the nature of misreading is at the heart of his deconstructive thematics: "we reach the conclusion that the determining characteristic of literary language is indeed figurality, in the somewhat wider sense of rhetoricity, but that, far from constituting an objective basis for literary study, *rhetoric implies the presistent threat of misreading*" (my italics).[17] We can put this perhaps more directly: "the specificity of literary language resides in the possibility of misreading and misinterpretation" ("LL," 184). In other words, if it ruled out or refused all misreading whatsoever, a text would not be literary. A text is literary to the extent that it permits and encourages misreadings. As a consequence, any criticism that tries to achieve "controlled" or "correct" readings is obviously deluded.

Because misreading is a necessary and inevitable constituent of literary criticism, the history of criticism constitutes itself as a systematic narrative of error. Rousseau and Nietzsche, to give just two cases, have been misread throughout critical history: "the established tradition of Rousseau interpretation," in particular, "stands in dire need of deconstruction" (*BI,* 139). Here we have the grounds for a new critical project: to revise the traditions of Rousseau and Nietzsche interpretation, which is what de Man in his series of essays on these writers is carefully doing. Straightforwardly, de Man generalizes his overall conception of misreading as he considers Nietzsche: "Perhaps we have not yet begun to read him properly. In the case of major authors, this is never a simple task. *There are likely to be long periods of continual misinterpretation.*" And "As long as we are not sufficiently aware of this, we risk to produce the wrong kind of misreading. For *there can be more or less valid misreadings . . .*" (my italics; "NTR," 49-50). If misreading is a constituent of "literary" texts, then, paradoxically, the extent or range of misreadings of a text certify its literariness. Indeed,

"By a good misreading, I mean a text that produces another text which can itself be shown to be an interesting misreading, a text which engenders additional texts" ("NTR," 51). To sum up, all interpretation, given the rhetoricity of language, is misreading; when a text is densely rhetorical, it will generate numerous misreadings. Any critical reading that aims to contain the inevitable misreadings itself affirms the inevitability of misreading in spite of its very desire to circumscribe the random play of grammatical structures and the vertiginous aberrations of rhetorical figures. Necessarily, the critical interpretations of an author or of a text exist in the mode of error.

This theory of misreading is applicable in all cases, though thus far de Man's demonstrations have been mainly with various critics in his early essays and primarily with Rousseau and Nietzsche in his later studies. For these latter authors themselves the operation of the misreading phenomenon is likewise inevitable. Of Rousseau, we discover: "Just as any other reader, he is bound to misread his text. . . . The error is not within the reader; language itself dissociates the cognition from the act *Die Sprache verspricht* . . ." ("PAR," 675). In short, any reading by an author (as well as by a critic) is ultimately unable to control or delimit the text. The phenomenon of misreading can never be contained or erased.

One recurrent manifestation or version of misreading is of particular interest to de Man during the late 1960s and early 1970s. Through examination of selected major critics, he reveals for us that each of these critics unwittingly manifests a discrepancy between his explicit theories of literature and his actual interpretations. Paradoxically, these critics "seem to thrive on it and owe their best insights to the assumptions these insights disprove" (*BI,* ix). This "blindness/insight" pattern is "a constitutive characteristic of literary language in general" (*BI, ix*). The basic point is that both literary and critical texts exhibit the misreading experience. Texts are unreadable for both the author and the critic of the text. Neither author nor critic can *read* his own or anyone else's text.

When it is observed that "There is no need to deconstruct Rousseau; the established tradition of Rousseau interpretation, however, stands in dire need of deconstruction" (*BI,* 139), the implication is that Rousseau himself is enlightened. "On the question of rhetoric, on the nature of figural language, Rousseau was not deluded and said what he meant to say" (*BI*, 135). We can, though, refine this formulation in light of later reading experiences. Given the random operation of grammar as a determining element of the rhetoricity of language, the possibility of the author's *total* enlightment or control is relinquished: "Just as any other reader, he [Rousseau] is *bound* to misread his text . . ." ("PAR," 675). In the deconstructive thematics the conception of the text as self-deconstructive ultimately subsumes the phenomenon of the author as self-deconstructer: "A literary text simultaneously asserts and denies the authority of its own rhetorical mode. . . . Poetic writing is the most advanced and refined mode of deconstruction . . ." ("SR," 32).[18] In essence, *literary* texts deconstruct themselves; they are always already deconstructed whether the author realizes it or not. Each author, as we would expect, exhibits individual degrees of understanding and awareness about the unsettling rhetoricity of language.[19]   Nevertheless, an author is finally never free to hem in the randomness of grammar, the play of figures, and the semantic richness of reference.

*   *   *   *   *

Since 1966 Paul de Man has deconstructed texts by Rousseau, by Nietzsche, and by their critical interpreters as well as texts by literary critics and by theoreticians, including such authors as Lukács, Binswanger, Poulet, Blanchot and Derrida. As he carries out this work, de Man formulates a thematics of deconstruction from his developing consciousness of *rhetoricity* and *misreading,* which themselves reflect his experiences of textuality, play, structurality and aberrant *sign*ification. In his writings, de Man articulates ideas *while* he reads texts; consequently, his critical theories are for the most part embedded deeply in his various works. He offers no programmatic statement or essay about his deconstructive thematics.[20]

For de Man the deconstructive critic is never outside or beyond textuality; criticism is inherently an "intrinsic" activity. Within the litearary text all interpretation is misinterpretation. And de Man does not exclude his own work from such an impasse; he accounts for this phenomenon of *aporia* in his general economy of misreading. All deconstructions insist on performing that which cannot be performed—reading texts. Deconstructive criticism "persists in performing what it has shown to be impossible to do. As such, we can call it an allegory" ("PAR," 674; see "TG," 554-55). Indeed, my own history of the history of deconstruction relies ultimately on an allegorical figure: the formalist essay on Derrida and the phenomenological one on de Man consist each of twelve paragraphs and ten notes, divided into three discrete parts, and deployed in the mode of temporal narratives, symmetrically unfolding assembled histories grounded fundamentally in synecdoche. "All rhetorical structures, whether we call them metaphor, metonymy, chiasmus, metalepsis, hypallagus or whatever, are based on substitutive reversals, and it seems unlikely that one more such reversal over and above the ones that have already taken place would suffice to restore things to their proper order" ("NTR," 41).

Conclusion. Writing the History of Deconstructive Criticism

A Review of "The Book of Deconstructive Criticism"

"The Book of Deconstructive Criticism" offers the reader a short introductory history of deconstruction by summarizing the theories and methods of the school and by focusing briefly upon the contributions of two leading deconstructers—Jacques Derrida and Paul de Man. In the margins, so to speak, the "Book" questions the various processes of narrating history. For those critics uninformed about deconstructive criticism, this text is a useful starting point but for the initiated the book has less to recommend it. Nothing new is contributed to the school itself or to the critique of the school.

The main limitation of the study is that it leaves out altogether the very obvious contributions of J. Hillis Miller and Joseph N. Riddel, not to mention several others. This omission would be roughly equivalent to writing the history of Romantic Poetry in England by centering exclusively on Coleridge and Wordsworth, offering no discussion at all of Byron and Keats. Arother, though perhaps less disturbing, limitation is the absence of any consideration of the opposition to deconstruction. It's as though all the recent reviews and debates didn't take place.

Finally, the book never actually comes to grips with the problematics of history writing, preferring to remain self-consciously diffident and coy, even though it openly raises these issues itself.

The task of writing the history of deconstruction is certainly worth doing. At best the present study is a small step in that direction. This book is too obviously clever and willfully incomplete. It is characterized by hyperbole and ellipsis, not—as the author thinks—by synecdoche.

Letter of Response to the "Review of 'The Book of Deconstructive Criticism' "

The review of "The Book of Deconstructive Criticism" misses the major issue entirely insofar as it fails to take the study to task for what it presents incorrectly as fact, stressing instead historical materials it does not even cover. For the question is, "Does the history have the facts right?" The answer is, "Frequently not."

Take, for example, the following factual statement about deconstructive criticism: "It does not reproduce or recreate through the effaced doubling of commentary or interpretation the conscious or intentional meaning made by the writer in interaction with her world and time" (chap. II, sec 3). Aside from the "hip" writing style, this depiction is in error. Deconstruction produces a host of interpretations of a text, some of which recreate meanings intended by the writer. Referentiality, after all, is as inescapable as textuality. What deconstruction actually does is to worry the epistemological certainty of such readings.

Essentially, "The Book of Deconstructive Criticism" reifies Derrida's and de Man's concepts. No doubt, it will successfully serve to swell the growing ranks of would-be deconstructers and to arm the anxious platoons of hostile detractors through metonymic substitution.

Afterword: Writing "The Book of Deconstructive Criticism"

Like many other academic critics, I have spent most of my writing life turning out proposals, critiques, abstracts, notes, commentaries, essays, advertisements, reviews and letters of response. While writing "The Book of Deconstructive Criticism," I employed the genres with which university critics are most familiar and, in so doing, I recapitulated my own history as a writer. Insofar as this work is like a montage in a chic film or a carousel ride in a remote ground of play, it seems light-hearted and extravagant, yet it is—after all—thoroughly conventional.

The genre of the journal article presents us overly confining limits; it needs to be threatened. The project of deconstructing the literary essay is a redoubtable task for the romance of our age. One day we shall not, I hope, look back only with nostalgia at the simplicity of the old essay given us by creative fathers; we shall, I trust, joyously affirm our new forms of expression and our independence from the long dead.[21]

* * * * *

POSTSCRIPT:

HERMENEUTICS, SEMIOTICS AND DECONSTRUCTION

In the history of contemporary deconstruction the great year is unquestionably 1967 when Jacques Derrida, the main figure in the movement, published his *Of Grammatology, Speech and Phenomena* and *Writing and Difference.* Among other things, these texts show Derrida unleashing powerful critiques of phenomenology and structuralism. Saussure and Lévi-Strauss, like Husserl and later Heidegger, come in for startling and subversive reassessment. At the same time Nietzsche and Freud undergo inchoate revaluation and emerge in a new and positive light. As deconstruction spreads during the late 1960s and early 1970s in France, England and America, the Derridean critiques of structuralism and phenomenology take on canonical status while the improved stocks of psychoanalysis and Nietzsche studies continue to attract further energetic investigation.

By 1972, when Derrida published *Positions, Margins of Philosophy* and *Dissemination,* deconstruction had attained widespread, often reluctant, recognition as the newest avant-garde intellectual movement in France and America. It remained steadfastly post-structuralist and post-phenomenological. And it seemed still Freudian and decidedly Nietzschean. In France it was vaguely Marxist, although not in Derrida's hands; in America, it was non-Marxist, if not silently anti-Marxist.

As these developments unfolded, structuralism itself was being absorbed by semiology or, if you prefer, semiotics. By the middle 1970s it became clear that semiotics was a global discipline, a new mega-science, with ambitions Faustian enough to encompass not only the fine arts and social sciences but also several areas of the natural and physical sciences.

Meanwhile, hermeneutics, long ago cast as a minor branch of biblical studies, expanded its purview, reaching out to take in all manner and means of interpretive activity and theory. No doubt, Heidegger's dramatic shifting of hermeneutic theory from epistemological to ontological grounds (from *Verstehen* to *Verstehen* as a function of *Sein*) facilitated this transformation and expansion of hermeneutics. If I were to play the prophet, I would predict a new flourishing of research into general hermeneutics.

What will be interesting to see in all this "progress" is how semiotics and hermeneutics cut up and divide the ground. At certain fundamental points they, of course, share similar interests and goals. (The problematic of language is a crucial case in point.) One wonders if, in the distant future, semiotics will remain structuralist at heart while hermeneutics will preserve its methodological ties with phenomenology? We cannot know. Semiotics may encompass hermeneutics. Or vice versa. Or they may be defunct like alchemy.

In any case, deconstruction could be absorbed by either or both of these transdisciplines. Possibly a generation from now deconstruction will register as a minor, perverse offshoot of a large enterprise.

But what is deconstruction? Does it, like semiotics and hermeneutics, possess an object or field of objects for study? Does it practice or favor identifiable methods and goals of inquiry? The answers must be *yes* and *no*. One mode of deconstruction—an apparently constricted and utilitarian one—focuses on texts, on ways of reading texts and tracking textual signification. We might fancifully indentify such a practice as "deconstructive hermeneutics." In addition, we can uncover certain instances of a "deconstructive semiotics," that is, of a practice of marking a priori modes or grounds of textual organization and signification. Yet such slick conjoinings of deconstruction with hermeneutics or with semiotics seem willfully paradoxical. After all, deconstruction, vaguely at the outset and more forcefully now, envisions itself in fundamental, if opaque, opposition to the arts and sciences of hermeneutics and semiotics.

In an interview published in March, 1977 in *Digraphe* Derrida characterizes deconstruction, saying:

> mais la déconstruction n'est pas une opération critique, le critique est son objet; la déconstruction porte toujours, à un moment ou à un autre, sur la confiance faite à l'instance critique, critico-théorique c'est-à-dire décidante, à la possibilité ultime du décidable; la déconstruction est déconstruction de la dogmatique critique. . . .

> (but deconstruction is not a critical operation, the critical is its object; deconstruction always bears, at one moment or another, on the confidence given the critical, critico-theoretical, that is to say, deciding authority, the ultimate possibility of the decidable; deconstruction is deconstruction of critical dogmatics. . . .)

What strikes me here is Derrida's little phrase « à un moment ou à un autre» (at one moment or another)! Sooner or later, you see, deconstruction turns on any critical reading or theoretical construction. When a decision is made, when authority emerges, when theory or criticism operate, then deconstruction questions. . . . It looks at every or any boundary, frame, margin, inscription, border. It examines the instances of decision: it investigates deciding authority. As soon as it does so, it becomes subversive. Mainly, it exhibits over and over how all borders, rules, concepts, structures—how all creations and constructions—suppress primordial difference in favor of dubious identity. To uncover the infinite varieties of such suppressions constitutes the dominant project of Derridean deconstruction.

When deconstruction looks at semiotics, it immediately takes up the theory of the sign. It questions the self-identity of signifier and signified and the self-presence of the speaking voice and the written sign. Derrida's work on Saussure and Lévi-Strauss early sets this pattern.

When deconstruction considers hermeneutics, it again problematizes the concept of the sign as well as a number of other notions. A deconstructive inquiry into hermeneutics or into semiotics would focus on fundamental ideas of language, self, author, reader, text, interpretation, history, meaning, context and critical writing. Other topics could obviously be added to the list.

Ultimately, deconstruction effects a striking revision of traditional thinking. Being (*Sein*) becomes the deconstructed self, the text becomes a field of differential traces, interpretation an activity of exploding meaning beyond truth toward joyous dissemination, and critical discourse a deviating and differentiating process of troping. Stability gives way to vertigo; identities to differences; unities to multiplicities; the center to infinite centers (or to no privileged centers); ontology to philosophy of language; epistemology to rhetoric; mysticism to demystification; intimacy to space; presence to absence; literature to textuality; the full to the empty (or overfull); *alethia* to *free play*; correctness to errancy; hermeneutics and semiotics to de-construction; the One to—not the Many—but the Infinite. In this transformation, hermeneutics and semiotics—as self-assured sciences, as useful arts of exegesis, or as deliberate textual cartographics—appear to be approachable dreams disguising impossible wishes.

In the late 1970s American deconstruction starts to fear its "progress" and success. There is worry that deconstruction is becoming predictable and rigidified—that it is now a method. The recipe for Derridean deconstruction is: take any traditional concept or established formulation, invert its set of hierarchical terms, and subject them to fragmentation via an insistent principle of difference. After unhinging the elements in any structure or textual system toward radical free play, stand back and sift the rubble for hidden or unexpected formations. Tout these special findings as outlawed truths. (Hence the infamous *supplement* of the *Grammatology*.) Mix all of this work with dashes of erotic lyricism and with apocalyptic intimations. Packaged within this quick codification—this easy parody—lies a rigid formulation of deconstruction as well as an anxious realization of the present crisis of deconstruction. No longer busy being born, deconstruction is busy dying. Or so it seems just now.

On the horizon of deconstruction looms a new stage now being born. It could spread further—to semiotics and hermeneutics. Let me call it the "Era of the Libidinous Critical Text." Up till now the textual surface of the *critical* work has been largely undisturbed. However dense and speculative, the critical text comes to us nicely coherent, carefully developed and altogether unified. Invariably, it unfolds along an orderly temporal line, which is to say it plies the narrative path. Even the most structuralist of studies, the most spatial and synchronic of inquiries, presents itself as a chronological story. It is somehow emplotted. This undisturbed state of affairs cannot long continue. The critical text is beginning to break up. Everything we have learned about literary textuality forces itself upon critical textuality. We can expect that the new essay on *Finnegans Wake* or the *Cantos* will itself be paronomasial and chaotic. (At the same time it may have a mythic understructure.) The borders between the literary text and the critical text are giving way. And metatexts on critical texts are springing up everywhere. The critical object and its modes of analysis are shifting—as the "nature" and force of textuality come clearer. Significantly, the quest for meaning, a function of desire, is erupting into or giving way to an indistinct *desiring analytics*. Faintly, criticism is becoming libidinal: a self-indulgent, yet earnest, joy of reading and writing.

I suppose our orderly paradigm of the universe, the last in a succession of world pictures, is ending now. Older modes of explanation—whether providential or scientific, whether predicated on a master plan or an enriched model of cause-effect—seem at an end. Even the more recent field-theory and eco-system paradigms appear inadequate. Randomization and chance appear the most fit maps. Our texts, literary, critical and otherwise, proclaim a new era. Our disciplines, including semiotics and hermeneutics, seem last-ditch efforts to institute and protect order and meaning. It is no surprise that the Soviet Union continues as a leader in semiotic studies and that traditional religious scholarship still champions hermeneutics, say what you will. But the epoch of order and meaning is being forced to face the coming era of discontinuity and desiring activity. I expect that semiotics and hermeneutics, as disciplines, will grow and grow as conditions "worsen." They represent the last "best" hope of a passing epoch. I also imagine that both disciplines will be transformed by isolated visionaries to accommodate the monstrous coming era. This way hope lies.

NOTES

[1] "Structure, Sign and Play in the Discourse of the Human Sciences," *The Languages of Criticism and the Sciences of Man: The Structuralist Controversy*, ed. Richard Macksey and Eugenio Donato (Baltimore: The Johns Hopkins Univ. Press, 1970), p. 249. Hereafter page numbers will be cited in parentheses in my text.

[2] Derrida develops the theory of "differance" in "La différance," *Bulletin de la société française de philosophie*, 62 (July-Sept. 1968), 73-101; published also in *Théorie d'ensemble* (Paris: Seuil, 1968). Available in English as "Differance" in Derrida's *Speech and Phenomena: And Other Essays on Husserl's Theory of Signs,* trans. David B. Allison (Evanston: Northwestern Univ. Press, 1973), pp. 129-60.

In his work on the sign, Derrida builds on the earlier insights of

Saussure, who conceived of the "sign" as having an acoustic element (signifier) and a conceptual component (signified). Dismantling Saussure's phonocentrism, Derrida inserts the written mark (*graphie*) in place of Saussure's acoustic element (*phonè*). In other words, Derrida introduces the force of differance into the signifier, thereby subjecting the sign to the operations of textuality.

[3] This text is available in English—Alan Bass, trans., *Writing and Difference* (Chicago: Univ. of Chicago Press, 1978).

[4] The three deconstructive readings in *La dissémination* (Paris: Seuil, 1972) are of Plato's *Phaedrus* in "La pharmacie de Platon," pp. 69-197; of Mallarmé's "Mimique" in "La double séance," pp. 199-317; and of Philippe Soller's *Nombres* in "la dissémination," pp. 319-407. Available in English as *Dissemination,* trans. Barbara Johnson (Chicago: Univ. of Chicago Press, 1981).

[5] Some of this material was early in English—*Diacritics,* 2 (Winter 1972), 35-43; and *Diacritics,* 3 (Spring 1973), 33-46. My own "Note: On Method (II)" is based partly on observations expressed in the first interview published by *Diacritics.*

[6] Available in English as *Margins of Philosophy,* trans. Alan Bass (Chicago: Univ. of Chicago Press, 1982). Some of the essays were earlier available in translation, including " '*Ousia*' and '*Grammé*': A Note to a Footnote in *Being and Time,*" trans. Edward S. Casey in *Phenomenology in Perspective,* ed. F. J. Smith (The Hague: Martinus Nijhoff, 1970), pp. 54-93; "The Ends of Man," trans. E. Morot-Sir, W. C. Piersol, H. L. Dreyfus, and B. Reid in *Language and Human Nature,* ed. Paul Kurtz (St. Louis: Warren H. Green, 1971), pp. 180-206; "Differance," trans. David B. Allison in *Speech and Phenomena;* "White Mythology: Metaphor in the Text of Philosophy," trans. F. C. T. Moore in *New Literary History,* 6 (Autumn 1974), 5-74; "The Supplement of Copula: Philosophy *Before* Linguistics," trans. James Creech and Josué Harari in *Georgia Review,* 30 (Fall 1976), 527-64; and "Signature Event Context," trans. Samuel Weber and Jeffrey Mehlman in *Glyph,* 1 (1977), 172-97.

[7] For a discussion of *Glas* see Geoffrey H. Hartman, *Georgia Review,* 29 (Winter 1975), 759-97, and *Georgia Review,* 30 (Spring 1976), 169-204; and Gayatri Chakravorty Spivak, *Diacritics,* 7 (Fall 1977), 22-43. Although it is not possible to list here all of Derrida's uncollected works, I would like to mention for the English reader his revealing essay on the "textual psychoanalysts" Nicholas Abraham and Maria Torok—"Fors," trans. Bar-

bara Johnson in *Georgia Review*, 31 (Spring 1977), 64-116.

[8] *Of Grammatology*, trans. Gayatri Chakravorty Spivak (Baltimore: The Johns Hopkins Univ. Press, 1976), p. 150. See also "Structure, Sign, and Play," pp. 260-61; "Interview I," *Diacritics* (1972), 36; "Differance," p. 142; and *Grammatology*, p. 314. (It should be noted that Spivak provides a comprehensive introduction to Derrida's work in her "Translator's Preface," pp. ix-lxxxvii.)

[9] "Interview II," *Diacritics* (1973), 41. For later remarks on supplementarity see Derrida's *L'archéologie du frivole*, which serves as a preface to Condillac's *Essai sur l'origine des connaissances humaines* (Paris: Galilée, 1973), pp. 68-70.

[10] Derrida's monograph—titled *Limited Inc* and published in *Glyph*, 2 (1977), 162-254—is a reply to a critique by John R. Searle, which was published in *Glyph*, I (1977). Basically, Derrida here deconstructs "speech act theory."

Among other reasons, *Limited Inc* is interesting because Derrida comments here and there about his own method of reading and analysis; for example: "I do not 'concentrate' . . . either exclusively or primarily on those points that appear to be most 'important,' 'central,' 'crucial.' Rather, I deconcentrate, and it is the secondary, eccentric, lateral, marginal, parasitic, borderline cases which are 'important' to me . . ." (180). The limits of such reading and analysis are discussed by Derrida in "Spurs: Nietzsche's Styles," trans. Barbara Harlow in *Éperons/Sproni/Spurs/Sporen*, intro. by Stefano Agosti (Venice: Corbo e Fiore Editori, 1976), pp. 95-107.

[11] *Blindness and Insight* (New York: Oxford Univ. Press, 1971), p. viii. Hereafter this book is designated *BI* and page numbers are cited in parentheses in my text.

[12] "The Purloined Ribbon," *Glyph*, I (1977), 45, 46. Hereafter this essay is labelled "PR" and page numbers are given in parentheses in my text.

In his "The Epistemology of Metaphor," *Critical Inquiry*, 5 (Autumn 1978), de Man continues this work on "language" and "rhetoric."

[13] "Nietzsche's Theory of Rhetoric," *Symposium*, 28 (Spring 1974), 35. Hereafter abreviated "NTR" with page numbers cited in parentheses.

A somewhat similar argument about Rousseau's theory of rhetoric is developed in Paul de Man, "Theory of Metaphor in Rousseau's *Second Discourse*," in *Romanticism: Vistas, Instances, Continuities*, ed. David Thorburn and Geoffrey Hartman (Ithaca: Cornell Univ. Press, 1973), pp. 83-114.

[14] Paul de Man, "Semiology and Rhetoric," *Diacritics*, 3 (Fall 1973), 30. Hereafter cited with pages numbers as "SR."

[15] See, for example, de Man's "Action and Identity in Nietzsche," *Yale French Studies*, 52 (1975), 28-29, and his "The Purloined Ribbon," 45—where he discusses the limitations of speech act theory.

[16] "Political Allegory in Rousseau," *Critical Inquiry*, 2 (Summer 1976), 669. Hereafter abbreviated "PAR." See also "The Purloined Ribbon," 44-46.

[17] Paul de Man, "Literature and Language: A Commentary," *New Literary History*, 4 (Autumn 1972), 188. Hereafter abbreviated "LL."

On the concept of "unreadability" see Paul de Man, "The Timid God: A Reading of Rousseau's *Profession de foi du vicaire savoyard*," *Georgia Review*, 29 (Fall 1975), 558. Hereafter designated "TG."

[18] See also Paul de Man, "Genesis and Genealogy in Nietzsche's *The Birth of Tragedy*," *Diacritics*, 2 (Winter 1972), 52.

[19] For de Man the congnitive elements of literary texts rest in the language, not in the author. The issue, therefore, of whether the author is or is not blinded by language is, in a limited sense, irelevant. To the extent that a literary text reveals and acknowledges the rhetoricity of its mode, it affirms the inevitability of its misreading. "It knows and asserts that it will be misunderstood. It tells the story, the allegory of its misunderstanding . . ." (*Blindness and Insight*, p. 136).

To the degree that a literary text renders in a diachronic structure the facts of its own rhetoricity, it is *allegorical* (*Blindness and Insight*, pp. 135-36). (De Man's concept of allegory is developed at length in "The Rhetoric of Temporality," in *Interpretation: Theory and Practice*, ed.

Charles S. Singleton [Baltimore: The Johns Hopkins Press, 1969], pp. 173-209.) The texts of Nietzsche and Rousseau are particularly allegorical, in the special sense of this term. "If we read Nietzsche with the rhetorical awareness provided by his own theory of rhetoric we find that the general structure of his work resembles the endlessly repeated gesture of the artist. . . . What seems to be more difficult to admit is that *this allegory of errors is the very model of philosophical rigor*" (my italics; "Nietzsche's Theory of Rhetoric," 45). And "Rousseau's fictional as well as his discursive writings are *allegories of (non)signification or of unreadability,* allegories of the deconstruction and the reintroduction of metaphorical models" (my italics; "Political Allegory in Rousseau," 659).

See also Paul de Man, "Proust et l'allégorie de la lecture," in *Movements Premiers: Études critiques offertes à Georges Poulet* (Paris: José Corti, 1972), pp. 231-50, esp. pp. 244-50.

[20]My "Note: On Method (I)" roughly approximates de Man's *reading strategies.* To the extent that the "Note" suggests a rigorous application of "differance," it falsifies de Man's method, for he never—as far as I know—mentions differance, though he is very attentive to the play of difference in its many forms.. From a strategic point of view, de Man's theory of *sign*ification (grammar/rhetoric/reference) functions, like differance, as a decentering force in the work of textual deconstruction.

(Although de Man concerns himself with intertextuality, he generally focuses on critical responses to and readings of texts rather than on the influences of forerunners or the supposed (pre)determining extrinsic forces operating upon texts.)

[21]I was enabled to complete this work by the grant of a fellowship in 1978 from The School of Criticism and Theory at the University of California, Irvine. I am grateful to Murray Krieger and Geoffrey Hartman for assistance and advice.

H. D.'S SCENE OF WRITING—
POETRY AS (AND) ANALYSIS*

by
Joseph Riddel

Thoth, Hermes, the stylus,
the palette, the pen, the quill endure

though our books are a floor
of smouldering ash under our feet . . .
(H. D., *Trilogy*)

She herself is the writing.
(H. D., *Helen in Egypt*)

I did know that I must keep faith
with something, I called it writing,
write, write or die . . .
(H. D., *Hermetic Definition*)

I

Freud locates the beginning of analysis (might we extend it to literary criticism? even poetry?) in the legendary problematic of Moses' stutter; that is, in the necessity for translation, but a translation that can never quite correct a textual distortion it aggravates. In that curious reconstruction of a certain "history" that became his own allegory of modern crisis, *Moses and Monotheism,* Freud provides history itself with a most deci-

*I would like to thank Mrs. John Schaffner, representative for the H. D. estate, and the Collection of American Literature, Beinecke Rare Book and Manuscript Library, Yale University, for permission to quote from unpublished manuscripts.

sive origin, by excavating what has been forgotten and/or repressed. His reconstruction, however, has the effect of doubling
and retextualizing the "origin," implicating it in the question
mark of all writing, in the cursive traces of the alphabet. We are
not, here, at the beginning of culture, but at the "moment" of
cultural dispersal, or its division of a division, where in the Freudian projection, the polytheistic and monotheistic "families" have
their origin in the tangle of a "father" whose role is always more
decisive than clear. In the Freudian history, polytheistic culture
is characterizing by "hieroglyphic picture writing" and monotheism by the problematic of representation signified by a prohibi-
tion of images or representations of the deity. Hence monotheism is allied with a history of "phonetic" writing, the "fix-
ation by writing" of an "event" which is itself already an interpretation, maintained in the "oral tradition." This "text," which
has displaced an "event" only to reveal the irreducible textuality
of the "event," is never the hand of a single author, but is already a diacritical text. And though Freud is addressing here
the particular texts that make up the "history of King David"
and the "scribes of Moses," what he has to say locates the origin
in a text that has no depth but two faces: "Two distinct forces,
diametrically opposed to each other, have left their traces on it."[1]

The two "forces" characterize a surface of a palimpsest, or
a multiple of surfaces, that make up the illusion of depth: the
one working a transformation which falsifies the text (itself
already a transcription) "in accord with secret tendencies," the
other anxious to conserve the mystery of the text's original relation with the event. The two effect a distortion, simultaneously
grounding and erasing the ground of the text. Thus Freud's remarkable elision of historical textuality and dream-work:

> . . . almost everywhere there can be found striking omissions, dis-
> turbing repetitions, palpable contradictions, signs of things the
> communication of which was never intended. The distortion
> of a text is not unlike a murder. The difficulty lies not in the
> execution of the deed but in the doing away with the traces.
> One could wish to give the word 'distortion' the double mean-
> ing to which it has a right, although it is no longer used in this
> sense. It should mean not only 'to change the appearance of,'
> but also 'to wrench apart,' 'to put in another place.' That is why
> in so many textual distortions we may count on finding the sup-

pressed and abnegated material hidden away somewhere, though in an altered shape and torn out of its original connection. (*Moses,* p. 52)

The question of textuality is inextricable from the Oedipal crossing, from a murder whose traces will not be erased but which are never anything more than traces of other distortions. Freud's text is already allegorized in his writings as the "family romance," and therefore already marked by the double face: 1. is it the interpretation of an event? or 2. an interpretation of interpretation? A murder in two senses? Is it the clarification of a tangle and the re-inscription of it? A complex! Or an image that is neither a pictorial representation nor an abstract description, but a weave of two diametrically opposed kinds of writing? The "family romance" is an analytical machine which can never be extricated from nor given priority or privilege to the subject matter it allegedly addresses or re-presents. This distortion, then, cannot be the sole product of the analytical text, or the translation, but is integral to the very notion of a primary text—whether that primary text is thought of as poetic (literary) or historical. What we call "modern" or even Romantic literature has been the cunning recuperation of an "analysis" that has always been marked in literature as the Oedipal crossroads, the scene of interpretation that is not only a murder but a strategically shoddy covering up of its traces. This crossing has taken the place of the "origin," proving finally to be the only mark of origin—the sign of the beginning as distortion or maiming, and of writing as a strange, wayward walking, or as the bridging of an abyss that indelibly marks the abyss as the vertiginous meaning. A chiasmus signifying a catachresis.

I have argued elsewhere, following Gilles Deleuze,[2] that Pound's theory of the Image (Imagisme) was in itself a kind of anti-logos or "literary machine," producing and disseminating in the fictions of stylistic objectivity and *mot juste* a theory of translation as creative distortion, a double writing. If the primoridal text or event is already literary, already cultural (an interpretation) and not natural, literature is never at the origin, nor even proximate to a nature, but the text in which nature appears. Nature as presence, therefore, does not precede what "properly" represents its appearance as text. The so-called self-reflexive quality of modern literature is never an hermetic self-mirroring but an inevitable reworking of its own mimetic illusion, hence a maiming or distortion, a doubling and fraying of representation. If H. D. was, as Pound called her, the model "Imagiste," she was also one of those who quickly defined the limits of Imagism as a doctrinaire theory of style. Her own poetry reworked the notion of the Image, as surely as Pound reworked it in Vorticism and in the *Cantos,* in a way to indicate that a "presentation" which precedes "representation" (to recall Pound's terminology) is the gounding of poetry in its own textual complications—in the double movement of a text that tries at the same time to maintain the illusion of its fidelity to an external event or to nature and to falsify the event, thus marking its textuality. The Image in this sense is an analytical scene.

Pound called the poetic Image (which included the "complex" of images, and hence the whole poem) "interpretative metaphor," and without any sense of contradiction, he overlayed the metaphor of the organic poem with the metaphor of the electrical circuit or system of transferences (see, for example, his own compilation in essay form of Ernest Fenollosa's notes on the Ideogram, "The Chinese Written Character as a Medium for Poetry"). The Image as translation (or better, as transcription and hence reinscription) could only effect a distortion, a script, producing a poem that could never be whole, could never totalize or remythologize the texts it appropriated. The coincidence between the interpretation and any uninterpreted event that might have preceded and given rise to it (the event whose textuality is forgotten) remains as problematic as it does in Nietzsche. The interpretation is inextricable from the "tangle" of the origin. Like the mystery of the Oedipal crossing, there is never any pure reality to be recuperated. Or to put it another way, the "family romance" could only have originated at a crossroads of two texts which never meet; it does not define Oedipus's genealogy, a repressed family line that might properly account for his birth, but inserts itself belatedly as the mark primordially disrupting or fraying that line. The "family romance" is both a complex and a question mark, that which precludes the unfolding of a sentence or the closing of a narrative. It is a poem that originarily opens poetry.

II

In the early 1930's, H. D. became an analysand of Freud, participating in two rather brief sessions, broken by a year's hiatus. Appropriately, the analysis was never finished, if indeed analysis can ever be said to close, though at the time its termination did not seem desired by either, but the result of historical circumstances. A decade later, during a most intense period of World War II, H. D. began to write poetry in what was to become known as her late, post-Imagist style, long poems of which the first and perhaps greatest is *The Walls Do Not Fall*, the first third of *Trilogy* (once called *War Trilogy*, and including as its second and third parts, *Tribute to the Angels* and *The Flowering of the Rod*).[3] She also began a kind of memoir, later entitled *Tribute to Freud*, reflecting on the period of her analysis. The *Tribute* was not published until 1956, and then, in 1974, it was republished posthumously by Norman Holmes Pearson in a text that included not only "Writing on the Wall" (as it had once been called) but also "Advent," a diary-like series of notes which she called a "gloss" on the meditation (*Tribute*, p. viii). The two texts do not exactly duplicate one another, though there are common themes, but compose a sort of palimpsest of supplementary reflections. Far from being either a simple diary or an autobiographical recounting of notes of the analysis, "Advent" is as literary a text as "Writing on the Wall"—made up of intertextual overlays, the one extending the other in often unexpected ways, dispersing rather than unifying the crucial dreams (the reference dreams, as it were) that form the material for the two analysts.

Tribute to Freud, like the analysis it pursues, is a hieroglyph of the analytic scene, but no less the allegorization of that scene as a poetic space. That poetic space, therefore, has at least two authors, and two analysts, and dialogically projects itself as a "writing on the wall," a writing that is at the same time an overwriting or transformation of writing. "Advent" names a beginning that has already begun, not in an experience that is accessible through dream analysis, but in the reconstructive activity of analysis itself, including all its deformations. Little wonder, then, that H. D. recalls the analysis as a kind of restoration, of the "house" (and family), a rememorization of her earlier life that displaces the "house" with a "Cathedral." For the

Cathedral becomes her figure of the scene of analysis: "We are all haunted houses," she reflects in "Advent," and the "house in some indescribable way depends on father-mother" (*Tribute*, p.146). Yet, she has been dreaming of a Cathedral, and it is the Cathedral, not the house, that is "all important," because inside the "Cathedral we find regeneration or reintegration. This room [Freud's office] is the Cathedral": "The house is home, the house is the Cathedral. He wanted me to feel at home here" (*Tribute*, p. 146). Here the "uncanny" would not threaten.

The scene of reconstruction is a sanctuary within a space (a metaphor within a metaphor) like a crypt within a house, and Freud's study, filled with Etruscan and Egyptian artefacts, is like a Cathedral reduplicating a mausoleum, a pyramid. Like Hegel's figure of the pyramid as the form of representation, as the alphabet, Freud's house/Cathedral is the only space where reconstruction can take place. It consists of signs, memory objects but also artefacts antedating all personal memory. H. D. recalls one of Freud's objects in particular, a "broken wood dog" (sign of Osiris?), a "toy from a tomb in Egypt," which reminds her of Freud's dog Yoti and his daughter Anna's Wulf. The analysis has also been a kind of rememorization, hence re-entombment, since the reuniting of signs, the reconstruction of the family, not only suggests the father's death but the whole series of displacements uncovered by an analysis of the "family romance," by an analysis whose instrument or paradigm is the "family romance": "Yes (I repeated), the Cathedral of my dream was Sigmund Freud. 'No,' he said, 'not me—but analysis'" (*Tribute*, pp. 146-47). Freud, the Professor, the Father-surrogate, is only another name of the father, as analytical origin.

His "house," therefore, which reduplicates her childhood house, is a scene of analysis, where the forces of reconstruction and distortion are simultaneously at play. For reconstruction (whether it suggests recuperation of a forgotten or repressed memory or a mimetic repetition of some earlier state) is not separable from de-construction, since the process of reworking involves not only a distortion but a re-marking of the distortion. The Cathedral of "analysis" marks itself as a "dream," and the dream is already an image-substitution and distortion in need of analysis. Like Freud's "uncanny" (*das Unheimlich*) the imaginary or poetic reconstruction of the house involves a distortion or change of context, a mixing of the homelike and unhomelike, a breaking of context. The analytical scene must, therefore, double or put into question the dream's navel and the house's father. If as Freud says, the Cathedral is analysis, the father/ Professor/analyst is never its center but the sign of its center-lessness, of two forces at work.

At the very beginning of "Writing on the Wall," H. D. re-capitulates the break in time, marked by Freud' death and the war, that lies between her analysis and the "quest" to recover what the analysis had unveiled, the "house" or "family." Yet, her text can only reconstruct the analysis which, far from restor-ing her family, had doubled her anxiety about her own participa-tion in its disintegration. Freud, already the ambivalent substi-tute of her own Father, a Professor, marks the breach of time— Freud who had "brought the past into the present," who had broken the notion of time's depth, but by advocating a kind of elliptical repetition/distortion which forever deferred any think-ing of analysis as making possible the repetition of the same. The war now doubly marks Freud's death as the death not only of the father but of the analyst, the ambivalence of analysis itself. It is another sign of the uncanny desire to restore the home, of a history that is, unlike Freud's in *Moses and Monotheism,* without a hero. The war is a "cataract." And H. D. recalls that when she was in analysis, analyst and analysand together had "touched lightly on some of the more abstruse transcendental problems . . . but we related them to the familiar family-complex" (*Tribute,* pp. 13-14).

Now, in her dream of a "memory" she must recapitulate what is latent and even repressed of the pre-war (WW I) memory, the ambivalences of the "family-complex" itself. For in her re-construction the deconstructive element of the "romance," itself both an allegory and an analytical instrument, becomes more evi-dent, like her "bell-jar" dream or the palimpsest she recognizes to be the layered text of her life. As a writer, she interprets her memories by the use of mythological and literary parallels, but these texts are not unambiguous. Nor are her memories uncon-taminated by the dreamwork, by being reworked in terms of a literate consciousness. Like the heroine of her late long poem *Helen in Egypt, "She herself is writing,"* but the "she" no longer has a place. She is always other, like a character in one of the images of her dream, a substitute for a substitute. Her dreams are always already structured like a text.

Freud was at work on the early essays of *Moses and Mono-*

theism during the period of H. D.'s analysis, and she alludes to its significance in her *Tribute:*

> it was in the desert that Moses raised the standard, the old *T* or Tau-cross of Thoth of the Egyptians. The Professor had been working on a continuation of his 'Moses, the Egyptian' theme, though we had not actually discussed this when I had my 'real' dream of the Egyptian princess. The professor asked me then if I were the child Miriam who in the Doré picture [the "illustrated Doré Bible" pictures titled *Moses in the Bulrushes*] had stood, half-hidden in the river reeds, watching over the new-born child who was to become leader of a captive people and founder of a new religion, Miriam? Mignon? (p. 108)

Earlier, they had discussed the Egyptian theme and the Doré illustration as "hieroglyph" links in her "Princess" dream, the most clearly defined of all her dreams. She had, as she recalls, discussed with Freud "a few real dreams, some intermediate dreams that contained real imagery or whose 'hieroglyph' linked with authentic images and some quaint, trivial mocking dreams" *(Tribute,* p. 36). Though she can characterize dreams along a scale from "real" and "authentic" to "trivial' (in *The Walls Do Not Fall* she reflects that "gods have been smashed before// and idols and their secret is stored/ in man's very speech,// in the trivial or/ the real dream . . ." [*Trilogy*, p. 15]), a dream unveils nothing outside of a chain of associations with other dreams. Nor can it be interpreted without being reworked in another dream, so that the authentic and real are already textual in origin. Thus Thoth's mark of the physician and of writing is appropriate to Freud and his Moses theme, though the cross of Thoth identified by H. D. with her "serpent-and-this-tle" dream (to which I return later) is a sign of writing the significance of which awaits later associations.

The Princess dream, therefore, is worked through both Freud's and the Biblical text, and more particularly through the illustrations of the Doré Bible, until it becomes a multi-layered Image of Miriam/Isis, of the Princess who retrieves the child from the waters (or restores fragments into a figural whole, restores Osiris), thereby becoming the true "founder of a new religion" *(Tribute,* pp. 36-37). As H. D. continues, "any dabbler with the theories of psychoanalysis" can read this dream in the

frame of the "family-complex," and she recalls her own anxie-
ties when as a little girl she would bring her doll to her father's
study, contesting with her more martially accoutered brother
for the attention of the *"Father,* aloof, distant, the provider,
the protector—but a little un-get-at-able, a little too far away
and giant-like in proportion," unlike the *"Mother"* who signified "a virgin" *(Tribute,* p. 38). If one reads the language of ego-
psychology (here, the Oedipal or castration dream as Freud
would call it) in the language of mythology, and hence as the
interpretation of interpretation, the "family triangle," as H. D.
calls it, comes to signify not simply a child's anxiety but, as
Freud himself hinted, a crisis of analysis. As Freud reads the
recollection, the "doll" is the "symbol of the dream" itself,
which projects a desire for the restoration of a family circle or
triangle, a triangle that has been squared or opened—hence the
dream-wish of analysis, or poetic reconstruction, to restore
some fragmented whole underscores the question of a fragment and the desire for totalization. If one follows out this
marking of the play in the analytic scene, where the analysis
becomes a double scene of maintaining (or restoring) and reworking (maiming) the text, he may conclude that it doubles
as a dream of poetry itself in H. D.'s mythology.

The "doll" may very well be a symbol of castration, as
any "dabbler" in Freud must acknowledge, and hence the sign
of a daughter's doubled restoration/displacement of the father/
brother. A phallic symbol, then? the sign of the writer's maimed
authority? of a tangled genealogy, whose doubled origin of
father/mother the writer desires to recuperate? hence, the ambivalent movement of the stylus which restores and tears? (Some
caution is surely necessary here. In an essay published almost
a decade ago, I alluded to H. D.'s concern in the *Tribute* for
the status of the woman writer, "wingless Niké" as she emble-
matizes that role, who must appropriate a "stylus," the sign
of writing represented for her by the objects of the Professor's
study.[4] This has been interpreted rather unkindly by at least
one [female] critic as a typical chauvinist attribution of penis-
envy to H. D., though I was cautious in the essay about distinguishing phallus [the signifier, substitute] from penis [the
object, the signified] in terms more or less Lacanian. The
essay, any way one wants to take it, was not only not psychoanalytic in its project, but was directed against ego-psychology.

If the essay is seriously flawed, it now seems to me that the problem issues from its reliance on a phenomenological language, particularly its stress on reconstruction of the authorial *cogito*. But far from opposing women and men writers, it argued in effect that the writer must always be figured as the woman, as the sign of the other, possessor of a stylus that is irreducibly a substitute. William Carlos Williams dramatizes the indispensable woman in *Paterson* and elsewhere, and numerous other male writers mythicize what they call the feminine self which lends the power of origin to their style. The stylus never belongs originally but is a sign of broken immediateness. Nietzsche, in Derrida's deconstruction of his deconstructive writing, identifies the woman with "styles" or the irreducible multiplicity and disseminating power of language, in contrast to any metaphysical notion of style and self-identity.[5] The deployment of sexual language for writing was metaphorical before it became referential or political.)

The phallus or stylus, here identified with the child's gift, is in Freud's sense the uncanny sign of a castration in which writing is always implicated, if writing is thought of in the classical sense of a proper representation or substitute for presence and a restoration of meaning. The "doll" as "symbol of the dream" is a poem/gift, and the poem is analytical, not expressive. To read H. D. here, recounting her and Freud's mutual analysis of the Princess dream, is not to confront a crisis in H. D.'s early life so much as to confront the crisis of writing and hence of representation and authority, the problematic identity of the author. Castration fear, as post-structural interpreters of Freud make evident, is never neurosis manifest in the simple perception of an absence, but a complication of perception itself which indelibly poses a question of absence and what represents absence. The dream of the Princess who restores Moses, of the daughter who gives birth to the male child, the "founder of a new religion," is the dream of recuperating the "family complex" as a scene of interpretation, where the Father's role is unambiguous. But the restoration can never be complete, nor simple, since analysis always uncovers the "complex" or tangle of the origin, and hence of the father's role. The "house" turns out to be the Cathedral, and the Father already represented by an intermediary, the physician who is both poet and analyst. Moreover, the "founder of a new religion," like Moses, has had to be born again, saved, as it were, by translation. And H. D. is quick to note that Freud called his disciple and translator, Marie Bonapart, the "Princess," the "obvious mother-symbol" (*Tribute*, p. 39).

Analysis as restoration involves a double movement of castration (which can never be perceived, just as the woman signifies a phallus that is never seen and therefore never properly represented, even by a surrogate)—hence castration involves at once a maiming and a restoration of sorts, since it is the sign of both the father and the son, of the tangle of father and son, as much as it is a sign of women. Or as Derrida says, castration is just what never has occurred. Throughout this text of H. D.'s Freud speculates on the poet's compulsion to identify: 1. with her mother, 2. her father, 3. her brother, and 4. with surrogates for each, one of which the text makes clear, is Freud himself, the Professor who now stands ambivalently for her own Father/Professor, a mathematician and astronomer, seeker of origins whose sign was his office sanctuary and his library. Her father is identified with a "study . . . lined with books," a room otherwise decorated with but one picture and adorned with a "white owl under a bell-jar" and a human skull (*Tribute*, pp. 19-34). She recalls his authoritative reign over this "quiet place" where he worked, at a desk marked by a "paper-weight that shows the room repeated in various dimensions" (*Tribute*, p. 34). She remembers him writing "rows on rows of numbers, but I could then scarcely distinguish the shape of a number from a letter" (*Tribute*, p. 19). H. D. thinks of this hermetic, tomb-like space, as a deathly scene, an en-closure of scientific self-reflexivity. Just as his triangular or pyramidal paper-weight reflects repetitiously the room as a closed cosmos, the father derives his authority from a kind of interpretation based on the ideal of representation, of the book to the cosmos. It is a strangely narcissistic study, in contrast to Freud's, which has fewer "volumes" and is dominated by his own writing and the signs of its dissemination through the work of disciples, interpreters, translators: "compilations of his followers, disciples, and pseudo-disciples and imitators," which open the room's three-dimensional gathering of past, present, and future into "another time-element," the "fourth-dimensional" (*Tribute*, p. 23). Freud's study, indeed, textualized the Professor, who is signified not only by his library and the interpretations which

It is the woman, then, who saves or gives birth (a second or belated birth) to the "founder of a new religion," by the force of her heterogeneity, her ambivalent role that obscures not only the origin of the child (like Freud's Moses) but provides it with a genealogical fiction. The woman is a text for H. D. as she is for both Freud and Nietzsche—not a proper displacement or representation but a spurring, signifying force. Just as Freud is a Moses for H. D., the new religion of "analysis" (emblematized by the Cathedral) is sustained only by a textuality that both dissimulates hiding a mystery and distorts or wrenches the simulacrum, so as to open interpretation. All the women in Freud's life—Anna, Marie Bonapart, H. D. herself among them—become for H. D. the fecund multiplicity of his utterance, the virulence and the cure of writing. The woman, then, is the doubled center of the Freudian scene, the sign of the always displaced center of the Freudian scene of analysis. She is not an alternative to the father, but uncanny, the sign of a translation that does not reproduce presence or meaning but disperses meanings, like a text. She is the sign, as Derrida says of Nietzsche's woman, of a castration that does not take place: the woman whose dream/gift (like the doll the young H. D. brought to her father) bears all the double meaning Derrida attributes to the *pharmakon,* of a giving that must take, a gift that is also a poison, that undoes the opposition between simple differences or between that which appears and that which remains hidden, as in the classical notion of a writing that unveils or presents truth. The tainted (and for some chauvinist) vocabulary, which we have borrowed directly from H. D. and from Freud, can never itself have any direct reference to sexual politics; for H. D.'s poetics, like her dream, appropriates Freud's "family romance" or "family-complex" and restores those metaphors which have gone awry, which no longer promise the closure of analysis and the restoration of the "house," but open a reading. And for H. D., the poem is a reading, and hence a scene of analysis, an uncanny yet homelike place of a double movement, the equivocal play of restoration and distortion dis-played by the intertextuality of every text. A home away from home.

III

Over the last two decades of her life, H. D. was heavily

committed to what might be called her autobiographical project. If her meditations on analysis turn out to be an analysis of her analysis which renewed her poetic energies, and *Trilogy* is the poetic complement of "Writing on the Wall," *Tribute* is also an anomalous chapter in a sequence of narratives (many of which remain in unpublished manuscripts in the Beinecke Library collection) that attempt a reconstruction of her own ancestry. *Bid Me To Live,* her more or less official, if barely fictionalized, autobiography, is one of the few published chapters of an extended and incomplete family romance. One of the manuscripts, *End of Torment*, is an elegaic reminiscence on the odyssey of Pound's late life, and a testimony of her enduring love: "To recall Ezra," she writes, is "to recall my father"; "To recall my father is to recall the cold, blazing intelligence of my 'last attachment' of the war-years of London." Other texts, projected or completed, were to form a series collectively entitled *The Gift.* Notes on this series, to which *Bid Me To Live* (once called *Madrigal*) and *End of Torment* are supplementary, suggest that *Tribute to Freud* is a kind of discourse on her method of restoration. The texts of *The Gift* are made possible by analysis, reconstructions of the Doolittle family history in what she calls the form of a "Greek novel," one chapter of which was to be called *White Rose and Red,* a fictional reminiscence on the Pre—Raphaelite Brotherhood. (If this manuscript is extant I have not seen it.) H. D.'s only connection with the Rossetti circle was, as she notes, the kind of arbitrary association uncovered by analysis, and literally by writing, the uncovering of a kind of repetition made possible by the discovery in one life of a single element or sign from the other. Each reconstruction of her "life" (whether her own, or that of her parents or grandparents) is composed out of a "child's alphabet chart," which guarantees that her contemporary life has been some kind of repetition of the earlier. A daughter of Helen, born in Bethlehem, she is, like Helen of *Helen in Egypt, "the writing."* What she calls her "psychical communication" with the Rossetti circle, then, reaches back also to the Dante circle, and is translated into a contemporary link through the William Morris tripod table on which she writes. Norman Pearson had remarked in his introduction to the *Tribute* that "H. D. as a girl sometimes thought of William Morris as a spiritual father" (p. xii), and she sometimes fantasized herself as an Elizabeth Siddal, receiving messages through the Morris table, itself already a surviving sign of the oracle of Delphi whose tripod put her in contact with the "ABC" of writing.

The "Tripod," as one might expect, is excavated once more in the *Tribute*, a "shadow" at the uncertain center of the central dream or hieroglyph that gives its name to the text itself, "Writing on the Wall." There, in the picture on the wall which H. D. fancied she saw as a dream writing in a room on the island of Corfu in 1920, and which she recounted to Freud as the primary symptom for analysis, the central image is the "shadow"—not a shadow on light but a shadow on which a dim light showed, the silhouette, she queries, of a "dead brother? lost friend?" Freud translated her dream as a "desire for union with [her] mother" (*Tribute*, p. 44), but only after she translated the silhouette into a "design," a "neat trick, a shortcut, a pun, a sort of joke": "For the three-legged lamp-stand in the miscellaneous clutter on the wash-stand is none other than our old friend, the tripod of classic Delphi . . . this venerable object of the cult of the sun god, symbol of poetry and prophecy" (*Tribute*, p. 46). The tripod "symptom" is at once the most venerable and most common, yet abnormal of symbols, the sign of the sign itself, a "hieroglyph" that demands reading, both translation and interpretation. For what the oracle reveals (always indirectly) at Delphi is never simple; as H. D. recalls, the Delphic utterance is always rendered through the "Pythoness" who attends the sacred place. What is revealed at Delphi is, like a "writing on the wall," made up of signs of overlayed texts.

H. D. seems to acknowledge the ninety-third fragment of Heraclitus: "The lord [or master] whose oracle is at Delphi: he does not speak, he does not conceal, he makes [or gives] signs." Modern critical scholarship has begun to extricate the problematic of this fragment from the metaphysical readings which have suppressed the question of the sign, which read the oracle's sign as *alētheia*. For the problematic of the oracle, as Clémence Ramnoux has argued, lies precisely in the impossibility of clarifying the oracle's utterance without posing another question, the *si*, of deciding that it means this *if*, or that *if*—hence of dividing the utterance, of deciding whether the sign might mean this or that under certain conditions (*if*) when the sign is *undecidable*. This also takes the form of hypothesizing a privileged reader or interpreter, one who believes or has faith that the word can never deceive. But this poses the further question of the obscurity of the sign, as against the clarity of speech, therefore underwriting the *"double sens"* of every oracular signature. The oracle does not reveal (or speak), nor does it deceive (or conceal), but in making signs it discourses; or as Ramnoux reads it: "The signs of the world and my discourse conceal and say exactly the same thing," say by concealing, conceal by saying.[6] To put one's trust in a translator of this "double sense" is to see the translation as privileged, as a language that renders the concealed, a common privilege accorded the poet and poetry. But the poet as translator, the woman as translation, does not reveal; she discourses in the double sense of the image or sign. The discourse (or translation) divides the utterance not only from any origin but from itself: the sign of the oracle was originally free floating or disseminated, that is, translated, textualized as a writing of an unheard voice.

The understanding of H. D.'s poetics—and in a sense the thrust of poetic modernism—must be situated in this problematic of the oracular sign and in the question of style (or styles), of the hieroglyph, of dream-writing. Like the metaphysical readings of Heraclitus, which give us a decidable either/or reading yet acknowledge that the oracle's wisdom exceeds the limits of human understanding, H. D.'s poetics has been interpreted in terms of prophecy or mystical revelations, as an archeological uncovering of the secrets concealed in ancient words or texts. (One example would be Robert Duncan's projected H. D. book.) Norman Pearson writes in his introduction to the posthumously published *Hermetic Definition*, "Like many Freudians, she became quasi-Jungian and could bring the cabala, astrology, magic, Christianity, classical and Egyptian mythology, and personal experience into a joint sense of Ancient Wisdom" (p. vi). The cabala, however, and we have only to witness Harold Bloom's appropriation of it, is not necessarily a mystical text of revelations or even a Dream Book, but only a machine for interpretation, and hence for misprision. That is, it works its own distortions or reworks the hieroglyph. H. D.'s alleged Jungianism, and mysticism, is the issue of a blind or idealized reading of her texts which ignores her own problematizing of the image, her own deployment of the text as an analytic. The play between deconstruction and reconstruction in both her poems and prose characterizes (literally and figuratively) this problematic. If for her a poem affirms by *feeling* "the meaning that words hide," that words are "anagrams, cryptograms,/ little boxes, conditioned// to hatch butterflies," their revelation is never direct or simple; the poem always remains "jottings on a margin,/ indecipherable palimpsest scribbled over // with too many contradictory emotions" (*Trilogy,* pp. 53, 42). The image is never congruent with its origin, its origin never evident outside of the images doubling or distorting, and hence dispersing, it. The unconscious is not a reservoir of some untapped truth, but a chaos:

> Depth of the sub-conscious spews forth
> too many incongruent monsters
>
> and fixed indigestible matter
> such as shell, pearl; imagery
>
> done to death; perilous ascent,
> ridiculous descent; rhyme, jingle,
>
> overworked assonance, nonsense,
> juxtaposition of words for words' sake,
>
> without meaning, undefined . . .
> (*Trilogy,* p. 44)

The poem originates in a place (or a scene) of extraordinary heterogeneity, and proceeds not by opening or unconcealing, but by layering. Yet, it can never reconstruct an original model, let alone a simple origin, or recuperate some original whole, since any notion of the origin (as represented, say, in the "family-complex" by the home) is already only one of the images. Reconstruction involves reading/writing, translation and distortion. Every poem reveals its own operation, or describes its own sense, therefore, because it conceals by revealing, reveals by concealing. A passage in *The Flowering of the Rod* says it with concise ambivalence:

> And no one will ever know
> whether the picture he saw clearly
>
> as in a mirror was pre-determined

by his discipline and study

of old lore and by his innate capacity
for transcribing and translating

the difficult secret symbols
. . . .
no one will ever know

whether it was a sort of spiritual optical-illusion,
or whether he looked down the deep deep-well

of the so-far unknown
depths of pre-history . . .
(*Trilogy*, p. 165)

She is probably allegorizing Freud here, as the Magus to whom she is a Mary, but the allusion is of little matter. Freud and/or Pound. In the *Tribute,* the central dreams—the Princess dreams and the "Writing on the Wall"—signify the same question, since they have no bottom, no origin in a single event, but originate in what is already a hieroglyph or maimed text. They begin, as at Delphi or at the writing desk, in a double reading/writing of the sign:

> *Signet*—as from sign, a mark, token, proof; signet—the privy seal, a seal; signet-ring—a ring with a signet or private seal; sign-manuel—the royal signature, usually a mention of the sovereign's name. (I have used my initials H. D. consistently as my writing signet or sign-manuel, though it is only, at this moment, as I checked up on the work 'signet' in my Chambers' English Dictionary that I realized that my writing signature has anything remotely suggesting sovereignty or the royal manner.) Sign again—a word, gesture, symbol, or mark, intended to signify something else. Sign again—(medical) a symptom, (astronomical) one of the twelve parts of the Zodiac.
>
> (*Tribute*, p. 66)

H. D.'s "writing on the wall" dream is never interpreted, except as a question of the sign, which must always be read in "two ways or in more than two ways," read as translation: either as the "suppressed desire for 'signs and wonders'" and hence as the "suppressed desire to be a Prophetess" (like the "Pythoness of Delphi," whom she identifies with her companion *Bryher*); or as mere illustrations or representations, images borrowed from an actual dream to *"echo"* an idea (*Tribute*, p. 51). Yet this last is not simple representation or expression but something like a dreamwork which reworks a repression, thus protecting against a "freak" idea or "dangerous symptom." Poetry need not be identified with neurosis, but it is never immediate, and always a distortion or reworking of other images. Poetry, like Freud's "complex," is Mosaic. One may desire to read it, like a dream, as containing one symbol which determines all the others, like the "sun" of her hieroglyphic "Writing on the Wall," but no sign can be extricated as central or singular in itself. It can only be "read," and this involves another, just as there are always two readers in the scene of analysis (*Tribute*, p. 56).

It is significant, then, that the "Writing on the Wall" dream or daydream is read in conjunction with an even earlier, childhood dream, which she calls her "serpent and thistle" dream— a vision or picture of an "alter-shaped block of stone," divided in two by a rough curved line, a stone cut mark: "In one half or section, there was a serpent, roughly carved; it was conventionally coiled with head erect; on the other side, there was a roughly incised, naturalistic yet conventionally drawn thistle" (*Tribute*, p. 64). Ezra Pound had helped her interpret this dream, with the assistance of reference books and concordances from his parents' library, which he used much as one would employ a Dream Book. Pound called it a "flashback in time or a prevision of some future" that concerned Asklepois, child of Apollo, patron of healers, whose sign, the serpent, is a symbol of both death and resurrection. But Pound could not account for the "thistle," except as an ornament, and H. D. was never able to recall seeing the two in combination other than in her dream; except for one instance, a small Hellenistic signet-ring she discovered one day in 1911 at the Louvre. The thistle comes to remind her of a spear, a sign she interprets years later to signify an absence, like the figure of Wingless Victory or Nike A-pteros Freud shows her: "'She is perfect,' he said, *'only she has lost her spear'*" (*Tribute*, p. 69).

Now the two dreams, two hieroglyphs, fold over one another. Another of Freud's objects, an ivory Indian figure of a seated Vishnu surrounded and covered by a dome of serpents, recalls the Corfu dream, the "Writing on the Wall," or more particularly the most enigmatic and abstract signs of that writing: "a half-*S,* which might have recalled the scroll pattern of the inverted *S* or incomplete question mark in the picture series on the wall" (*Tribute,* p. 67). H. D. does eventually translate or interpret these signs, but not with the help of Pound's Dream Book. Rather, more in the spirit of Freud's rebus, the dream as code instead of the dream as symbol. But the reading turns out to be a radical reworking, an uncovering of what she calls the "common property of the whole," the "universal language" of the dream which man spoke "as at the beginning of time" (*Tribute,* p. 71). What she deciphers as a hieroglyph is reworked as a hieroglyph, a single word that is originally heterogeneous. That word is any one of the names for Freud himself—the Professor, the Cathedral, in a word (cursively), Sigmund:

> My serpent-and-thistle motive, for instance, or *Leitmotiv,* I had almost written. It was a sign, a symbol certainly . . . My serpent and thistle—what did it remind me of? There was Aaron's rod, of course, which when flung into the ground turned into a living reptile. Reptile? Aaron's rod, if I am not mistaken, was originally the staff of Moses. There was Moses in the bulrushes, 'our' dream and 'our' Princess. There was the ground, cursed by God because Adam and Eve had eaten the Fruit of the Tree. Henceforth, it would bring forth thorns and thistles—thorns, thistles, the words conjure up the same scene, the barren, unproductive waste or desert. *Do men gather grapes of thorns, or figs of thistles?* Another question, another question mark, a half-*S,* the other way round, *S* for seal, symbol, serpent certainly, signet, Sigmund.
>
> *Sigmund,* the singing voice; no, it is Siegmund really, the victorious mouth or voice or utterance. There was Victory, our sign on the wall, our hieroglyph, our writing. (*Tribute,* pp. 87-88)

"Our writing"—a question of signs, signs as (question) marks. Like the recollection of Bergasse (Freud's street, a hill and a path, a design, she writes, crowned by *acanthus,* the prickly plant, the thistle). It was H. D., we recall, who alone had been able to re-member serpent and thistle ("Thy rod and thy staff"), emblems of the most radical incongruence, yet emblems of Freud and herself, of analyst and poet, in a dream

which antedated her analysis by decades. But this singular combination will not yield to a "Freudian" reading, to the symbol
serpent or the symbol thistle, the spear and the spearless, male
and female. H. D. has momentarily excavated a site, only to discover that what is at its center is uncanny, an undoing of the emblem of the "family" as some archetypal and original moment.
For the serpent, as in Nietzsche, is language, language as the
mark, the sign, the question. And the thistle is the double sign
of the phallus, of the undecidable, the mark of a writing as a castration that never occurred. Neither presence nor absence nor
the sign of presence or absence, it is the signifier of the signifier—
the stylus, both the mark and the origin of the mark, the sign of
writing as dissemination.

"Our hieroglyph"—"Put H. D. in the place of Sigmund
Freud" (*Tribute,* p. 74), she had proposed, imagining the possibility of turning upside down the "hourglass" of vulgar time,
of the poet displacing the analyst who had proclaimed the poets'
firstness. The translator speaks by translation, in an *Alcestis*-
like economy of writing, in the theft that is writing. *"Stop
thief,"* she exclaims, in yet another leitmotiv of the *Tribute.*
Thoth and Hermes, those names of writing, are no less names
of Freud. But Isis is also the name of the writer, the re-member-
er. Only the poet has style, is both the writer and the writing,
serpent and thistle, the irreducible double. Only the poet remembers this curious combination, as an uncanny double inscription on a rock, the double mark of which the only name
is *signet.* An uncanny marriage: "There are dreams or sequences
of dreams that follow a line like a graph or a map or show a
jagged triangular pattern, like a crack on a bowl that shows
the bowl or vase may at any moment fall to pieces" (*Tribute,*
p. 93). Similarly a poem, which reflects its own operations.
It cannot mirror its own whole-ness, but only its distortive
reworking. It is not sincere (sin-cere, that is, without the wax
that might cover over the flaw or the crack), but a golden bowl,
like Henry James', that is always already flawed. H. D.'s signature repeats the sign of the poet, the serpent of the text, its
question, doubly marked by a thistle or stylus which both writes
and is written, is and is not, like a phallus. Let her (who is
the *"writing"*) have the last words: "She asks the question.
Each verse of the lyric is a question or a series of questions. Do
you know the Land? Do you know the House? Do you know
the Mountain?/ *Kennst du den Berg und seinen Wolkensteg?/*

'Do you know the mountain and its cloud-bridge?'' is an awkward enough translation but the idea of mountain and bridge is so very suitable to this whole *translation* of the Professor and our work together. *Steg* really means a plank; *foot-bridge* is the more accurate rendering. It is not a bridge for a great crowd of people, and it is a bridge flung, as it were, across the abyss, not built and hammered and constructed. There is plenty of psychoanalytic building and constructing: . . . We are dealing with the realm of fantasy and imagination, flung across the abyss, and these are the poet's lines" (*Tribute,* p. 108).[7]

NOTES

[1]*Moses and Monotheism*, trans. by Katherine Jones (New York: Vintage, 1967), p. 52. Hereafter cited in text as *Moses.*

[2]"Pound and the Decentered Image," *Georgia Review*, 29 (Fall 1975), 565-91. Deleuze's argument is most forcefully put in "Antilogos, or the Literary Machine," chapter VIII of his revised and expanded *Proust and Signs*, trans. by Richard Howard (New York: Braziller, 1972).

[3]Quotations from H. D.'s work, hereafter cited in the text, are from the following texts: *Trilogy* (New York: New Directions, 1973); *Tribute to Freud* (Boston: Godline, 1974), hereafter *Tribute; Helen in Egypt*, introd. by Horace Gregory (New York: New Directions, 1961); and *Hermetic Definition* (New York: New Directions, 1972).

[4]"H. D. and the Poetics of 'Spiritual Realism'," *Contemporary Literature*, 10 (Autumn 1969), 447-73;

[5]Derrida, *Éperons*, introd. by Stefano Agosti (Venezia: Corbo e Fiore, n.d.). Hereafter cited as *Spurs*, the English translation of this long essay which is produced in this text along with translations of the essay into German and Italian. The essay is subtitled, "Les Styles de Nietzsche," and is an extensively revised and expanded version of an earlier essay which was first called "The Problem of Style" or "The Question of Style" ("La

Question du style'').

[6] Clémence Ramnoux, *Héreclite, ou L'Homme entre les choses et les mots* (Paris: Societé d'edition "Les Belle lettres," 1968), pp. 302-04.

[7] Would a concluding footnote be a "postscript" overthrowing a poet's "last words"? Eugenio Donato, in an essay called "The Idioms of the *Text*," *Glyph* 2 (Baltimore: The Johns Hopkins University Press, 1977), exploring the complicated significance of the "dialogue" in Heidegger, remarks on the etymological accident that throws together in German the notion of translation (*Übersetzung*) and the figure of the abyss or *abime*. He cites Grimm on the multiple sense of translation—as transformation, metamorphosis, jumping over, hyperbole—and refers to his example: " '*den Abgrund ubersetzen*,' hence to jump over an abyss or a groundless space" (p. 6). A translation may abridge an abyss, (abridge indeed by bridging), but only by becoming the form or symbol of the abyss, as Jacques Derrida has revealed of Heidegger's metaphorics. The translation or poem erases any notion of an original being or text. Not so incidentally, Donato's essay later turns to a text of Flaubert, where the figure of the Cathedral, like that we saw earlier in H. D.'s emblem for Freud's study/scene, is the sign of the belatedness, the memorial signature, of writing; testament to an unrecoverable past and an unrealizable future.

* * * *

POSTSCRIPT:

IN OTHER WORDS

There is a certain inevitability to the postscript, since it marks not some aftering but only the limit of any "first" or "last" word. Did H. D. have the "last" word, even in the passage I quoted, a translation and a discourse on translation? A carrying over and an attempt to bridge over the artifices of such a bridge? H. D. lingers upon the question of the bridge and the abyss. Which is artifice? Which produces the need of the other? Does the bridge overcome the abyss or mark it? Is not the bridge, to use another's question, the form of the abyss, "in other words"?[1] Re:versely.

The editor requests that I provide a "context" for my reading of H. D.'s text. A "theory" perhaps, since my essay is a "reading" of a text and not the extrapolation from it of a theoretical statement or a set of theoretical assertions. Indeed, he seems to ask, why this resistance to "theory" in an essay commissioned for a collection on "theory"? Why this rendering of H. D.'s text as at once theoretical and atheoretical? Is H. D. a theorist of modernism or a tributary of Freud? What is in question here is precisely the status of her text, and in turn of poetry. A question of translation, as she aptly puts it. And as a question of translation, a problematic that is inscribed at the epicenters of contemporary criticism.

One would like to make appeal, at least at this new juncture, to Jacques Derrida's extraordinary meditation on "method," or on the "Pas," that is the "Pas de méthode," a phrase that includes at once the suggestion of the "methodical step" and the "no method," the im*pli*cation that one cannot at any particular moment of the text decide whether the text proceeds in an orderly fashion or is already adrift, off course, and therefore cannot disentangle the methodical from its aberrance.[2] Or perhaps, because of the apparent status of this text, appeal to Paul de Man's question about autobiography and its seeming referential mode.[3] After all, H. D. offers us more than a pretext that she is re-membering an analysand's "experience," even if the reconstruction has to take the form of a certain fictionlized transference, and even if the documentary form includes two texts or two versions. Is the text, then, autobiographical? A remembrance or a reading of Freud? An analysis (hers? theirs?) of her dreams? or a narrative of analysis? Of dreams as analysis? Or is it, perhaps, a kind of quest romance, a poetic reflection upon the myths of poetic creation?

Interpretation and translation obviously play crucial roles in this reflection, particularly since the search for origins poses at its very beginning a question of analysis and of method. Questions, perhaps, which perpetuate speculation by precluding its closure or resolution, and thus which fracture the dream of speculation or self-referentiality, of a text which could be at the same time methodical and a discourse on its method or a poem which could be at the same time a representation and a meta-commentary on poetics. I placed a great deal of emphasis on the moment in "Writing on the Wall" when H. D. announced that she and Freud would employ the metaphor of the "family complex" to reflect on "metaphysical" issues. Among those issues is the status of the metaphor itself, the family complex or "family romance" being already derived from literature or myth to stand as an emblem for some law of origins, a genealogy of history as well as of a psychic life. For Freud, then, the "family romance" is not only a figure which represents the order of history, the regulation of succession and restoration, but it is a figure in the employ of the analyst. Both a figure of analysis and for analysis.

The metaphor of the "family romance" inscribes, in a multiple of senses, its own doubleness. Derived from myth for use as an analytical model, the figure is reinscribed into literature by criticism either as a structural paradigm (e.g., for revealing the "genealogical" structure of narrative) or as a regulative trope (e.g., Harold Bloom's theory of influence and intertextuality). It becomes both the theme and form of a certain temporal mode which theorists now want to set in opposition to the privileged "spatial" form of lyric. But it is not simply a figure of opposition or antithesis, of history as opposed to universality, since it bears within itself an irreducible difference (or even, *différance*): it is a figure of figure, of the chiasmus or crossing, a figure which erases and marks a problem of representation (and of naming) even as it promises some kind of orderly if deferred restoration, some kind of corrected genealogy. The prefigured story of the Oedipal crossroads, then, inscribes the doubleness of literature: the dream of a corrected line, a restored genealogy, and a clarified perception, even as it introduces the critical riddle or fate of interpretation. The metaphor, thus, indexes literature and criticism in a way that suggests not only literature's inevitable impurity (or ultimate failure to achieve self-reflexiveness) but indicates its hermeneutic "stairway of surprise" (Emerson).

H. D. came to Freud, then, not simply as a poet to her analyst, to endure the satisfactions of some strange adoption, but as one aware of the original and originary critical (or is it diacritical?) nature of poetry. Whenever Freud, for instance, indulges in the clichés of Freudianism, suggesting for example that she wanted "to be a boy" and a hero like Moses (TF, 120) and therefore not only wanted to displace her brother so as to be the son who would displace the father but wanted to identify with her companion Bryher (who in Freud's terms is *"only a boy,"* though H. D. envisioned her in association with the "Pythoness of Delphi," the detached translator of Images, as we have seen)—whenever Freud reduces his own hermeneutical detachment into a protective repetition of his "theory" (becoming increasingly literal or allegorical), H. D. reintroduces the fact that they have been at work upon a "hieroglyph," whether "Our hieroglyph" (TF, 88) or a "hieroglyph of the unconscious" (TF, 93). The thrust of this analysis, this search for poetic origins, is not, however, simply a resistance to the patriarch of analysis, nor can it be simply construed as the opposing of poetry to analysis, of a matriarchal art to a patriarchal science (no more than it is, as some would want to read it, an argument like Graves' in support of a matriarchal tradition in poetry which supersedes the patriarchal western tradition). When H. D. reflects that Freud's probings tunnel deep but uncover only a "scene or picture from those [deep] realms" and that this "clearest fountain-head of highest truth" is irreducibly an *"illuminated manuscript,* and has its place in that category among books and manuscripts" where "books and the people merge in this world of fantasy and imagination," she reinscribes the origin into the false depth of a palimpsest, or better, a library. Her poet is therefore neither sexual nor an asexual figure, but a "figure," like the "Pythoness of Delphi," or perhaps, like Isis (the restorer) and Thoth (the physician, translator, thief). And the origin is a "text," not in the material or colloquial sense of that word, but in the sense of an irreducibly figural or doubled "being," of an origin that is always already displaced, of a poetic "truth" that begins in repetition (re:petition).

Freud's calling H. D. "translation" (in the cancelled passage, alas) is not gratuitous, then, although she manages at once to erase the designation and to turn it against his authoritarian, or fatherly, implication. In the first place, translation involves at least a double operation: a re-membering of the dismembered and dispersed (Isis), and a theft that signifies an incorrigible displacement (Thoth). It at once rehearses the primary sense of a fall, loss, dispersal of some original language, and exposes the possibility that such an historical figure, both promising and prefiguring a future restoration, is, as Nietzsche argued, the very work of language itself and not some "truth" it represents or expresses. The legend of Moses' stutter includes, albeit eccentrically, the death of the father, even as Nietzsche indicated that getting rid of God would necessitate the getting rid of grammar, or grammatology. Moses' stutter is already a figure for translation as criticism. And what is translation?

"What is translation?" Derrida asks in his long footnote, "on" translation, to "Living On," an essay ostensibly of literary criticism.[4] The footnote also bears a title, "Border Lines," itself already a translation of "Journal de bord" or an untranslatable phrase that includes, as he advises his translator, the double sense of "shipboard journal" and "journal on *bord,*" the latter sense being further untranslatable in that *bord* may imply either edge or ship, either margin or voyage, the double sense of an absolute demarcation and a space which regulates the legal crossing of boundaries or frontiers. The entire situation of this "foot"-note that should ground the text but sets it afloat, of this border that invades the text it edges, thus erasing edges or contaminating (like a bordello?) those marginal demarcations which allow us to order the hierarchy of texts, of this meditation on translation which is to instruct a translator on the economy and limits of translation (especially ironic since the essay and its note on translation are first to appear in English, and hence as Derrida points out, in the note's fourth language, its first paragraph having been written in a French that employs both Greek and German terms)—this ship of misrule is a di-version that names the irreducible diversion of all notes, those always already "origins" of the "text." Or should one say the *foot*note is Oedipal? There are many questions which Derrida's note poses, and one is the pose of the note, its posture as ground and margin, particularly since its message to the translator (of both texts) includes the double bind that he must translate his instructions on translation, and *after,* one assumes, he has translated the *primary* text. The note has problematized every primary term, and left as primary the already freighted and derived notion of translation.

Readers of Derrida, not to say of the poets, of H. D., then, should be wary of what this privileging of "translation" instigates. First, there are his seemingly direct or cognitive statements, such as the remark that there are always two notions of translation, the normative one that suggests an orderly transfer of meaning, or signifieds, through an efficient displacement of signs, or more precisely, of signifiers, and the disseminative (in the Derridean non-sense of *dissémination*) function which implies a radical displacement and a fracturing of meaning (which does not support the classical sense of slippage as the movement away from an original or unitary meaning, but suggests instead a movement that is indeterminate because any determination of original meaning is already doubled). Derrida, in short, must attack the question poetically, in an essay on poets who have above all else poetically insisted on the primacy of the question. And the question of translation, of "living on" or even carrying on and over, of continuity and genealogy, is a question of "death." Of that "border" (how often "he," the personified death, has appeared as a boarder, producing edginess) where the "system" of orderly displacement must take place. That "margin" which Derrida often calls "text," itself already a figure and hence a translation and a "breaking" of what the metaphysicians call "Being" or "presence."[5] A text includes death, includes translation, just as it includes a ciphered and deceptive account of its own origin; just as a text, always already derived (de:rived) is never its material or scriptive form, never that simple translation which some call representation and others expression.

When Derrida says, then, that "One never writes either in one's own language or in a foreign language,"[6] he reiterates the re:iterative economy of translation: "This is my starting point: no meaning can be determined out of context, but no context permits saturation. . . . When a text quotes and re-quotes, with or without quotation marks, when it is written on the brink, you start, or indeed have already started, to lose your footing."[7] Derrida's riving of contexts, his "con-ning" of them, his de-control of reading, has become a sort of scandal for the Anglo-American metaphysics of taboo. But not for the poets who, Freud after all had said, were "there" before us. "There"? Where? At the translative beginning of (the fiction of) the origin. At (or about) the "text." "What is translation?" Derrida writes, "Here economy. To write in a *telegraphic* style, for the sake of economy."[8] If poetry is the economy, the tele-graphic, of dream, of what is dream the economy?

Of poetry, H. D. and other poets seems to say; that is, dream is originarily poetic and critique.

It is not the nature of a "truth" that is translated or conveyed across some limit which H. D. thinks of when she thinks of poetry, on the model of psychoanalysis, as tapping the "springs" of a "deep" and accumulated "human consciousness." That "consciousness" of Freud's can only be prefigured as irreducibly metaphorical or diacritical, or as a "spring" of images (at least two languages) sealed up or blocked; so that to tap the spring one had to clear the blockage. But clearing the blockage does not simply release a present or immediate language. It involves a translation, writing, and reading. There is an "economy" involved, and H. D. underscores the pertinence of this metaphor (TF, 82-83). The analysand (or patient) is responsible for digging up the suppressed material, itself already figural, and the analyst is responsible for the "system" or economy of translation which can read the *"hieroglyph of the unconscious"* (TF, 93). Consciousness is irreducibly textual, and more precisely, intertextual, not only in the sense of a tropological relation between earlier and later texts (or in analysis, between the marks of some early primal trauma and its later and repeated occurrence or re-mark), but in the sense that every text is made up of a heterogeneity of textual elements and hence a con-text that cannot be saturated. Poetry, then, translates by breaking contexts.[9]

At the point in "Writing on the Wall," where H. D. turns to the Goethe poem and hence to the question of translation I quoted at the end of the essay, her sense of poetry as an originally doubled notion of recuperation/translation becomes an unresolvable contradiction that only poetry itself can bridge over. Goethe's poem, beginning "Kennst du das Land . . ." signifies the mother language of his consciousness (or unconscious), a metaphorical "Haus" made up like Freud's study of the artefacts of all human culture. But if Freud is at home here in (if his home is) this archeological site, where the repressed has been returned, H. D. has come from another land and has "brought nothing with me." Freud's study, like Goethe's poem, signifies "the tradition of an unbroken family" (TF, 97), and seems to promise a continuity or succession, but H. D.'s is the mother tongue of Poe who can only speak of the emptying out of the "Holy Land" of the "Psyche," and of some problematic and deferred unity, some crypt to be opened. Where Freud's judgment is more rooted in the encumbered past, H. D.'s "Intuition" is swifter, she claims, and "challenges the Professor, though not in words" (TF, 99). This contest of "question and answer" as a play between analysis and poetry, (between philosophy and poetry, as it were) is dramatized as a play between German and American, old and new world thought, a play which prefigures all "beginnings" in the Janus-like opposition of a translation that carries over and a translation that displaces and defers. Just as Goethe's poem raises problems for his translator, it raises questions about translation, about the continuity of a journey from a known "Land" to an unknown. Thus, H. D. notes, the poem is poised upon the abyss between question and answer, or poised upon its own curious signs which H. D. thinks of as "question marks" or reversed "S's," those serpents of language which mark its double nature, which signify that it is not simply a bridge between two worlds, a bridge over the abyss, but the sign of the abyss as well. It is in this abyss, this "land" of the psyche which is language, that H. D. locates the origins (or better, beginnings which displace origins) of poetry, the translated/translating thing itself, like the "Penelope's web" she is weaving (an instrument as well for unweaving). Poetry, then, is at once a re-weaving of earlier poems (an anthology of myths and texts) and an unweaving, a deferral, like Penelope's, that seems to make way for the return of the father yet marks the artifice of his restitution. Like Penelope in Stevens' "The World as Meditation," poetry seems to signify a return, a restoration, but what returns is uncertain, like a figure (a sun?) coming "constantly so near," but never fully arriving, like a figure that is re-membered because it is "never forgotten." The "never forgotten" signifies the status of the "remembered," of the "re" which precedes its members.

The figur-ology of *Tribute to Freud*, which would authorize yet bridge over the displacement of the father, which would substitute the child for the father, but also for the mother, which implicates sexuality in textuality, folds into the double figure of the dream-text the question of death and translation, of the substitutive mechanism itself. It is a figuration, as it were, of the poem as body-image and as figural ground, doubly bound to the task of signifying the moment, as H. D. puts it, "an exact moment," when "the boat slipped into enchantment" or when "'crossing the line'" (she is writing here of the metaphoric theme of a story which for her is the story of story) occurs, as in the moment in which a poet/poem appropriates/ translates. The remembrance of this story of story takes place in a sequence in which H. D. recalls the perils of travel between the wars, or during which she meditates upon the poetics of displacement, of having no "room," let along a "Haus" like Freud and Goethe. One might exaggerate to call this an allegory of American writing, or simply of writing in general, of reading, as it were, only in borrowed books. Of writing always already in at least two languages, the poetic and the critical.

NOTES

[1] Readers of Derrida will connect the question to "deconstruction," and will recall that "in other words" is the iterated phrase—an inaugural refrain, if one will pardon the contradiction—at the beginning of his "Living On," *Deconstruction and Criticism* (New York: Seabury, 1979), pp. 75-176. esp. p. 75, an essay to which I will return in a moment for its crucial reflections on "translation," "quotation," and even "reflection." In that repetition of "in other words," as Derrida points out, there is a sliding that does not put the phrase in "other words," so that the effect is to make it sound "like a quotation." Such is the problem of this "commentary"—on which text?

[2] "Pas," *Gramma,* nos. 3/4 (1976), 111-215.

[3] *Allegories of Reading* (New Haven, Conn.: Yale Univ. Press, 1979), p. 278.

[4] *Deconstruction and Criticism* (see note 1). The footnote "Border Lines" runs along the entire lower edge of the lengthy "primary" text, a text which, one *notes,* puts in question the very notion of a *primary text* or indicates that the phrase is already an oxymoron. That *note* will be my primary concern in a moment.

[5] Rodolphe Gasché is writing a series of essays, of which "Deconstruction as Criticism," *Glyph* 6 (Baltimore: Johns Hopkins Univ. Press, 1979), pp. 177-215, is one of the earliest in print, that takes up the problematics of deconstruction, including the question of Derrida's play upon concepts like "text," a word he detaches from the colloquial, literal, or empirical usage and reinscribes as a "transcendental concept," in this instance as a continuation of Heidegger's non-reflexive meditations on the question of "being."

[6] *Deconstruction and Criticism*, p. 101n.

[7] *Deconstruction and Criticism*, pp. 81-82. The two texts, essay and note, repeatedly engage in a commentary not only on other texts (literary?) but on the question of commentary, and hence cross and recross the boundaries which would discreetly maintain a hierarchy of texts and commentaries. This breaching of boundaries and frontiers stages the question of quotation, citation, commentary, translation, etc., both as strategy and a commentary on strategy. Thus it is a problem to determine the status of what appears to be a meta-commentary or ontological statements such as the one I have just quoted, a quotation which might have been extended, by the way, to include its next sentence: "You lose sight of any line or demarcation between a text and what is outside it."

[8] *Deconstruction and Criticism*, p. 77n. Much of Derrida's recent writing has touched upon this "economical" yet pleonastic notion of "translation." See, for example, "The *Retrait* of Metaphor," trans. in *Enclitic*, II, no. 2 (Fall 1978), 5-33.

[9] See Harold Bloom, *Wallace Stevens, The Poems of Our Climate* (Ithaca, N. Y.: Cornell Univ. Press, 1977), *passim.*, on the poetics of "breaking." Though Bloom poses the question in a psychological as opposed to a deconstructive way, his notion of revisionary tropology bears within its own economy a deconstructive phase, just as his theory of "influence" and "misprision" includes a problematics of "translation."

RETRIEVING HEIDEGGER'S DE-STRUCTION:
A Response to Barbara Johnson

by

William V. Spanos

"Levelling is not the action of one individual but a reflective-game in the hand of an abstract power."

Soren Kierkegaard, *Two Ages*

I

In her essay "Nothing Fails Like Success," Barbara John-son's defense of deconstructive criticism betrays the "blindness of its insight" of virtually all the practitioners of this method deriving from the authority of Jacques Derrida: she *overlooks*, that is, the fact that deconstruction, as articulated and prac-ticed by Derrida himself, has its source in and constitutes a *re-vision* (not deconstruction) of Heidegger's *destruction* of the metaphysical tradition. This oversight, the result, above all, of archivalizing Derrida's Nietzschean text, making it the original Book of the deconstructed Word, as it were, not only precludes or at least minimizes an adequate defense against the counter-critique of conservative traditional humanist critics like Meyer Abrams, Wayne Booth, Gerald Graff, and Dennis Donaghue, but also, and more important, against the critique of those politically radical critics like Edward Said, John Brenk-man, Paul Bové, and Jonathan Arac, who accuse deconstruction "of not living up to its own claims of radicality." That is to say, this oversight succeeds in making deconstruction not simply susceptible to institutionalization, but also, if inadvertently, an instrument legitimating the spirit of the technological "age of the world picture" and the consumer society that spirit elaborates. In the following all-too-brief remarks, I intend to explore some important aspects of this critical oversight. I want to suggest by such a disclosure that the Heideggerian destruction is more capable than deconstruction, not simply of a more adequate "defense" against the charge of relativism made in traditional humanistic criticism, but also of a more effective critique of the "binary logic" of mastery—"culture [or] anarchy." In short, the Heideggerian destruction is more amenable to the literary, cultural, and socio-political adversary purposes of the de-centered postmodern counter-memory.

Since I cannot assume that my readers, both humanists and, especially, deconstructors, are conversant with Heidegger's *Destruktion,* or, at any rate, with its differential relationship to deconstruction, I will "begin" for the sake of orientation by recalling Heidegger's definition in the introduction of *Being and Time* which the oversight of the deconstructors forgets:

> If the question of Being is to achieve clarity regarding its own history, a loosening of the sclerotic tradition and a dissolving of the concealments produced by it is necessary. We understand this task as the de-struction of the traditional content of ancient ontology which is to be carried out along the *guidelines of the question of Being.* This de-struction is based upon the original experience on which the first and subsequently guiding determinations of Being were gained.
>
> This demonstration of the provenance of the fundamental ontological concepts, as the investigation which displays their "birth certificate," has nothing to do with a pernicious relativizing of ontological standpoints. The de-struction has just as little the *negative* sense of disburdening ourselves of the ontological tradition. On the contrary, it should stake out the positive possibilities of the tradition, and that always means to fix its *boundaries.* These are factually given with the specific formulation of the question and the prescribed demarcation of the possible field of investigation. Negatively, the de-struction is not even related to the past; its criticism concerns "today" and the dominant way we treat the history of ontology, whether it be conceived as the history of opinions, ideas, or problems. However, the de-struction does not wish to bury the past in nullity; it has a positive intent. Its negative function remains tacit and indirect. . . .
>
> In accord with the positive tendency of the de-struction the

question must first be asked whether and to what extent in the
course of the history of ontology in general the interpretation of
Being has been thematically connected with the phenomenon
of Time. We must also ask whether the range of problems concerning Temporality which necessarily belongs here was fundamentally worked out or could have been.[1]

What should be marked, above all, in this passage, is that the
"beginning" that Heidegger wants to retrieve is not an absolute origin as it seems to be understood both by his deconstructive critics and his humanist disciples. It is, rather, as the "existential analytic" of *Being and Time* bears witness, a temporality grounded in Nothing (the absence of presence), that disseminates differences, of which language (words as opposed to
the Word) is the bearer.

II

The primary function of deconstructive criticism is to
demystify the privileged binary logic inscribed in the metaphysical rhetoric of the logocentric tradition: to expose the
mise-en-abîme between signifier and signified, the groundless
ground of mimesis or re-presentation; ie. to show that language is
not Adamic, does not "name" (bring to presence) the object it
intends, but "doubles" or "supplements" and thus always defers
it. More specifically, Derrida and especially others like Paul de
Man, J. Hillis Miller, Joseph Riddel, Eugenio Donato, and Barbara Johnson, who practice deconstructive criticism, assume
from the beginning that *all* texts, past and present, no matter
what they attempt to signify, deconstruct themselves, that is,
are, by the very nature of writing, replete with aporias that
transgress and undermine the intended totalization of logocentric discourse. In Derrida's rhetoric, they are subject to the
"play of difference," to the "movement of supplementarity"
of writing.

> If totalization no longer has any meaning, it is not because the
> infiniteness of a field cannot be covered by a finite glance or
> a finite discourse, but because the nature of the field—that is,
> language—excludes totalization. This field is in effect that of
> *play*, that is to say, a field of infinite substitutions only because it

is finite, that is to say, because instead of being an inexhaustible field, as in the classical hypothesis, instead of being too large, there is something missing from it: a center which arrests and grounds the play of substitutions. One could say . . . that the movement of play, permitted by the lack or absence of a center or origin, is the movement of *supplementarity*. One cannot determine the center and exhaust totalization.[2]

The writer, no matter who he is or when he writes, can therefore never say what he wishes to say (*vouloir dire*). Thus the essential function of the interpreter is not, as it is for traditional critics, to interpret the writer's intention, but to discover the blindness of his logocentric insight:

> The writer writes *in* a language and *in* a logic [the binary logic of logocentrism] whose proper system, laws, and life his discourse by definition cannot dominate absolutely. He uses them only by letting himself, after a certain fashion and up to a certain point, be governed by the system. And reading must always aim at a certain relationship, unperceived by the writer, between what he commands and what he does not command of the patterns of the language that he uses.[3]

Though the classical or humanistic effort to represent the "conscious, voluntary intentional relationship that the writer institutes in his exchange with the history to which he belongs" is necessary to guard against the possibility of "say[ing] almost anything" about the text,[4] such traditionalist "doubling commentary," devoid of any awareness of the duplicity of writing, closes off rather than opens up a reading—and only reveals its deferring supplementarity, its "undecidability," to the ironic deconstructive reader of the commentary:

> . . . if reading must not be content with doubling the text, it cannot legitimately transgress the text towards something other than it, towards a referent (a reality that is metaphysical, historical, psychological, etc.) or towards a signified outside the text whose content could take place, could have taken place outside of language, that is to say in the sense that we give here to that word, outside of writing in general. That is why the methodological considerations that we risk applying here to an example [Rousseau] are closely dependent on general propositions that we have elaborated above; as regards the absence of the referent or the transcendental sig-

nified. *There is nothing outside the text* [there is no outside-text; *il n'y a pas de hors-texte*] .[5]

This is, of course, hardly an adequate summary of an immensely complex and brilliantly articulated methodology of reading. But it is enough to suggest what is both valuable and problematic about it from the point of view of the Heideggerian destruction. To the degree that it reminds us of what the humanistic tradition exists finally to make us forget—of the unbridgeable abyss between words and between words and their referents, of the groundlessness of the privileged metaphysical discourse, i.e., that language does not "name" the earth, but fictionalizes and defers it and thus that language as (objective *Truth*) constitutes a violence against the earth—the Derridean deconstruction is useful to criticism as a theory of reading which is simultaneously a socio-political activity or counter-*praxis*. That is, it is capable of thematizing the logocentric language of representation, of awakening us to the power inscribed in and hidden by the "structurality" of traditional metaphysical humanistic binary discourse. But, unlike the Heideggerian destruction, its refusal of intentionality or, what is the same theory, its insistence on the autonomy of the text (its "textuality")—*il n'y a pas de hors-texte*—and the consequent interpretive imperative that "our reading must be instrinsic and remain within the text"[6]—tends both in theory and in practice, especially by Derrida's academic disciples, to dehistoricize both the text and the reading process. Instead, deconstruction pursues the secondary purpose of demystification, the purely negative ironic process of disclosing the unintended (or intended) aporias that "always already" breach all writing—literary or veridical— whatever its *occasion.* Although, as Ms. Johnson says, deconstruction "at its best . . . undoes the very comforts of mastery and consensus that underlie the illusion that objectivity is situated somewhere outside the self," this insistence on the purely writerly nature of writing, this failure to acknowledge that writing, however misunderstood and mystified its essence, has consequences in the world, minimizes, if it does not preclude, precisely what the Heideggerian destructive (which is also to say, "pro-jective") mode takes to be the first stage of the hermeneutic process. This destructive mode invites an opening out of its horizonal focus on the question of being, in accordance with its disclosive imperative to take into consideration the cultural, economic, and socio-political *sites* along the continuum of being, those sites, that is, which are the archeological concerns of such critical theorists as Antonio Gramsci, Theodor Adorno, Max Horkheimer, Michel Foucault, Edward Said, and other "worldly" critics of Enlightenment logic and its hegemonic institutional elaborations. I mean the study of "affiliation," as Edward Said calls it, the exposure of the usually invisible "network of peculiarly cultural associations . . . between forms, statements, and other aesthetic elaborations on the one hand, and, on the other, institutions, agencies, classes, and fairly amorphous social forces:"

> . . . affiliation [in contrast with homology and filiation, which "so far as humanists are concerned have created the homogeneously utopian domain of texts connected serially, seamlessly, immediately only with other texts"] is what enables a text to maintain itself as a text and thus is covered by a range of circumstances: status of the author, historical moment, conditions of publication, diffusion and reception, values drawn upon, values and ideas assumed, a framework of consensually held tacit assumptions, presumed background, and so on and on. In the second place, to study affiliation is to study and recreate the bonds between texts and world, bonds which specialization and the institutions of literature have all but completely effaced. Every text is an act of will to some extent, but what has not been very much studied [and deconstruction tends to overlook] is the degree to which—and the specific cultural space by which—texts are made permissable. To recreate the affiliative network is therefore to make visible, to give materiality back to, the strands holding the text to the society that produced it. In the third place, affiliation releases a text from its isolation, and imposes upon the scholar or critic the presentational problem of historically re-creating or re-constructing the possibilities out of which the text arose. Here is the place for intentional analysis, and for the effort to place a text in homological, dialogical or antithetical relationship with other texts, classes, institutions, etc.[7]

To be more specific, in freeing the signifier from the transcendental signified that, according to Derrida, remains vistigially in Heidegger's understanding of language, the Derridean revision of the destruction minimizes the potential to disclose and analyze not only the hidden violence that informs the logocentric

text, but also, and more important, the particular historical, cultural, and socio-political sources, nature, affiliations, and effects
of this violence at every site on the continuum of being. I say
this despite or, indeed, because of the fact that Derridean deconstruction wilfully denies the question of being, the question
of the temporality, the historicity of being, as *hors texte.* Thus
it cannot, on the basis of this methodological emphasis, differentiate between and situate the kinds of cultural/social/poli-
tical power authorized or legitmated by, say, Plato's *Republic,*
Hegel's *Phenomenology of Spirit,* or Bentham's *Panopticon;*
Aristotle's *Poetics,* Samuel Johnson's *Prefaces to Shakespeare,* or Percy Lubbock's *The Craft of Fiction.* In so far as
the Heideggerian destruction acknowledges that texts (language) are "the house of being," i.e. make a difference in the
shaping of a world, it can be appropriated to locate historically and to discriminate, acutely and in detail, between, say,
the prophesy/fulfillment structure (and rhetoric) of *The Aeneid,*
which discloses its formal and thematic complicity with the di-
vinely sanctioned Augustan imperialism; the well-made narrative
plot of Fielding's *Tom Jones,* which, in sublimating accident,
affiliates itself with the formative disciplinary goals of the
deistically sanctioned and empirically oriented humanism of the
Enlightenment; and the recollective or re-presentational narrative structure of the essentially sane and normal, "disinterested,"
observer in Joseph Conrad's *The Heart of Darkness,* which,
in rationalizing its excesses, mystifies, normalizes and legitimates the hegemonic purposes of Western (British) capitalistic
colonialism. Because of its commitment to the textuality of
texts—the absolute absence of presence in the signifier—the
deconstructive mode, on the other hand, must of necessity
bypass such affiliations between text and world and such historical discriminations between economies of power, in favor of
its primary purpose: to disclose the transgressions—the plays
of difference that characterize all writing—against the impulse
of logocentrism to totalize. This methodological refusal to
encounter language as the temporal "house of being," not,
as Ms. Johnson says, "an over-simplified understanding of certain aspects of deconstructive theory," lies behind the current
institutionalization of deconstruction, its failure in practice
to cross over the boundary line of literary criticism into the
economic and socio-political sites it hedges. In other words,
this theoretical necessity renders deconstructive criticism, like

the New Criticism it ostensibly repudiates, an academic *discipline* rather than a historical interdisciplinary activity capable of "analyzing its institutional underpinnings, and economic and social relations with the world."

III

Further, or perhaps, another way of putting this, the deconstructive mode, precisely because of its theoretical commitment to the autonomy of the text, and within this commitment, to the idea of difference as *textual difference*, tends to be a negative hermeneutic activity. This is not only because it is, despite J. Hillis Miller's easy rhetorical manoeuver to disarm the objectivist critique,[8] parasitic on canonized host texts, but also, and more importantly, because, in translating its possibilities into the empty, free-floating realm of rhetoric and textuality, it undermines the will to *praxis:* thinking, that is, gets dissociated from doing. For Heidegger, we recall, the destruction is intended to retrieve *(Wiederholen)* the question of being (or rather be-*ing*) from the oblivion to which a sclerotic metaphysical thinking has relegated it, in order to "free" human being—*"especially* . . . that understanding (and its possible development) which is rooted in the proper Being of Dasein—the ontological understanding"—from the "world in which it is" and the "tradition"—the various but supplementary semiotic systems inscribed in the cultural Memory—in which it is "ensnared." In reifying or spatializing time, this tradition, which perceives *meta-ta-physica*, "deprives Dasein of its leadership in questioning and choosing."[9] Though Heidegger himself was reluctant to explore this intention fully, the destruction is intended to activate an opening of the horizon of understanding or, rather, of understanding to horizonality, to include the "worldliness" of the world: a liberating awareness or remembrance that the prison house of logocentrism exists not only at the site of metaphysical thought *per se,* but, because language is the house of being, all along the continuum of being from culture through economics to socio-politics. The destruction is not a nihilistic activity of thought that neutralizes its active force. Rather, it is, paradoxically, a positive or projective interpretive activity in which thinking (theory) *is* doing-in-the-world *(praxis).* The disclosure of the origins of the fundamental ontological concepts, we recall,

> has nothing to do with a pernicious relativizing of ontological
> standpoints. The destruction has just as little the *negative* sense
> of disburdening ourselves of the ontological tradition. On the con-
> trary, it should stake out the positive possibilities of the tradi-
> tion. . . . Negatively, the de-struction is not even related to the
> past: *its criticism concerns "today" and the dominant way we
> read the history of ontology, whether it is conceived as the history
> of opinions, ideas, or problems.* However, the destruction does
> not wish to bury the past in nullity; it has a *positive* intent. Its
> negative function remains tacit and indirect. [My emphasis, ex-
> cept for the single italicized words.]

The Heideggerian destruction, thus understood as a re-
membering of what a recollective metaphysics forgets, is both
a historical and a dialogic project in the sense that, as the etymology itself suggests, it is simultaneously de-structive and pro-
jective. Like Foucault's and Said's "archeological" projects,
it activates critical consciousness of the varieties of cultural and
socio-political power that the supplementary *epistémès* of
the ontotheological tradition have concealed in their discourses.
But in de-stroying (destructuring) the intended totalized structures and the circular geo-metry of these panoptic discourses, the
destruction also dis-closes, activates, and nourishes the will
to *praxis.* That is, in breaching the panoptically inscribed structures of the ontotheological tradition, it opens up and remembers
the question of being as it was originally posed: as a question of
the be-*ing* of being. More specifically—and in order to address,
if not to disarm the objection made by Derrida that the retrieval of the *Seinsfrage* is a recuperation of metaphysics, the destruction retrieves from the traditional understanding of Being
as Identity (the One, the Unmoved Mover, Causality, etc.)
the *temporality* of being, a being, that is, "grounded," not in
Something but in nothing, in absence, in which presence is infinitely deferred and in which, therefore, temporality disperses
Sameness, disseminates or makes (the) difference. The retrieval
of the *Seinsfrage,* in short, is the retrieval of the ec-centricity,
the ex-orbitance or, in Heidegger's preferred word, the "care"-
provoking err-ancy of being.

As I have said, the destruction of the tradition inscribed
in canonical texts retrieves the idea of language as the "house
of being." Understood as I think Heidegger insists that it should

be, this means that, in retrieving the be-ing of being from the meta-physical tradition, the destruction also retrieves the idea of language as *words* from the re-collective tradition of the *Word*. (Derrida, of course, criticizes Heidegger's phenomenology as a vestigial continuation of the logocentric tradition in the degree to which it continues to privilege speech [*parole*] as the agent of recuperating or re-presenting presence. If, however, Heidegger's phenomenological retrieval of the *logos* as speech [*legein*] is understood as an acknowledgement of dispersal [difference] as its primordial condition, this criticism is defused.) Thus destroyed, this problematic phrase discloses a function of textual interpretation that is quite different from that usually inferred. It not only activates, as in Foucault and Said, the possibility of recognizing and defusing the power and authority of metaphysical discourse and the affiliated semiotic elaborations of a civil society grounded in a logocentric measure. It also opens up, as I shall suggest, the possibility of a discourse capable of rewriting—and rebuilding—the *polis* on the groundless ground of a differential measure that, emerging from its occasion, allows men and women to "dwell poetically" in the "rift" occasioned by the strife that temporality activates between world and earth.[10]

For Derrida and his followers, deconstructive criticism, on the other hand, is in essence a negative, indeed, a nihilistic critical movement. To put it briefly and all too reductively, in absolutely separating language (writing) from the world outside to which it putatively refers, it precludes, of necessity, admitting the question of language to be simultaneously a question of being, in favor of observing, pointing to and delighting in the spectacle of the play of difference at the scene of writing. Derrida's appropriation of Heidegger's notion of the ontological difference (that "Being" is not *a* being [*Seiende*] as it has been understood throughout the ontotheological tradition, but be-*ing* [*Sein*]), translates the difference of being into the levelled-out space of the textual *différance*.[11] This suggests that deconstructive criticism understands the dismantling process not, as in Heidegger, to be an opening up and releasement of that which metaphysical thinking closes off and forgets, but a disclosure of the false base of canonical logocentric texts. In other words, deconstructive reading remembers the supplementarity, the doubling, of all writing, and thus the duplicity, the absolute undecideability, of all written texts, but not the pro-jective possibilities of being.   Although deconstruction, like destruction, calls into question the privileged status of the dominant philosophical discourse, it also "liberates" man from the prisonhouse of language into an essentially *similar* nihilistic world. At best, as in Derrida, it activates the

> Nietzschean affirmation, that is the joyous affirmation of the play of the world and of the innocence of becoming, the affirmation of a world of signs without fault, without truth, and without origin, which is offered to an active interpretation. *This affirmation thus determines the non-center otherwise than as a loss of center.*   And it plays without security.   For there is a *sure* play: that which is limited to the *substitution* of *given* and *existing, present,* pieces.   In absolute chance, affirmation also surrenders itself to *genetic* indetermination, to the *seminal* adventure of the trace.[12]

At worst, however, as Ms. Johnson herself admits, it becomes, as in an increasing number of Derrida's belated followers, a purely formal—and comfortable—activity of exegesis, virtually devoid of real awareness of the abyss—the uncertain temporal realm of radical difference or otherness—over which this interpretive activity dances.   It is true, of course, that Ms. Johnson criticizes the tendency of recent deconstructive critics to transform this exegetical activity into an assured methodology and recalls them to the Nietzschean/Derridean affirmation of uncertainty:

> Much has been made of the fact that "knowledge" cannot be taken for granted.   But perhaps rather than simply questioning the nature of knowledge, we should today re-evaluate the static, inert concept we have always had of ignorance.   Ignorance, far more than knowledge, is what can never be taken for granted. If I perceive my ignorance as a gap in knowledge, instead of as an imperative that changes the very nature of what I think I know, then I do not truly experience my ignorance.   The surprise of otherness [difference] is that moment when a new form is suddenly activated as an imperative.   If the deconstructive impulse is to retain its vital, subversive power, we must therefore become ignorant of it again and again.

But this imperative, finally, cannot answer "the critique of deconstruction, which accuses it of not living up to its own claims of radicality, of working with too limited a notion of textuality, of applying its critical energy only within an institutional structure that it does not question and therefore confirms." For, it seems to me, it is precisely this *purely* negative stance before the text—this restriction of deconstructive criticism to the exposure of the mastering impulse behind the binary logic of logocentrism, for the sake of affirming ignorance (undecideability)—that not only blinds itself to the "negative capability," the projective possibilities, disclosed by the Heideggerian destruction, but also ends in the metamorphosis of ignorance into empty formalism. Limiting the function of deconstruction to calling into question the "exclusive" either/or of logocentric logic, in other words, all too easily and despite protestations to the contrary, ends, as Kierkegaard reminds us, in the futile hovering "logic" of the neither/nor, in a willed will-lessness that transforms the projective measure disclosed by the destruction—the measure which is the measure of man's occasion—into the certain, regulative, empty, and finally timeless methodology of "unmastered irony."[13]

In thus reducing the signifiers emerging from and addressing *different* historical/cultural situations to a timeless intertextual (ironic) text, deconstructive criticism ironically betrays its affiliation with the disinterested—and indifferent—"inclusive" formalism of the New Criticism and Structuralism[14] which it is one of its avowed purposes to repudiate. The deconstructive reader, like the New Critic and Structuralist, becomes a distanced observer of the "scene of textuality"[15] or, in Kierkegaard's term, an aesthete who perceives the text from the infinitely negative distance of the ironic mode. With his levelling gaze, he, too, like his adversaries, refines all writing, in Derrida's own phrase, into "free-floating" texts. All texts thus become the *same* text. It all becomes one, as it were. In thus curiously coercing difference into identity, deconstructive criticism paradoxically traps itself in precisely what it would call into question with its deconstruction of the tradition of presence. Despite its intentions, it becomes, in tendency at least, the obverse face of the same coin: a negative violence that mirrors the positive violence of metaphysical speculation. It is not, therefore, as Ms. Johnson asserts, the institutional success of

deconstructive criticism that, as an increasing number of examples in standard academic journals testify, has rendered it
a self-replicating, predictable, indifferent, and self-defeating
professional activity that confirms the institution it would
call into question. It is, rather, its methodological failure, inherent, I submit, in Derrida's project, to sit-uate the text in
the world. To put it another way, this failure—this successful desituation of language into the "scene of writing"—accounts
not only for the academic domestication of deconstruction—
the divestment of its original adversary purpose: to interrogate
the humanistic impulse to *reduce* language, history, society,
culture, to the Same—but also for its transformation into an
indifferent instrument that affiliates itself with, indeed legitimates, the institutions that the humanistic discourse authorizes
and elaborates.

Understood from the perspective of the Heideggerian destruction, the deconstructive project that dominates the "advanced criticism" of our time reminds us of Kierkegaard's recognition that the "present [Hegelian] age of reflection" is positively capable of producing the illusion among its intellectuals
that, as speculative thinkers, they are active adversaries of the
dominant culture and of the power structures that lie behind it:

> A passionate, tumultuous age wants to *overthrow everything, set
> aside everything.* An age that is revolutionary but also reflect-
> ing and devoid of passion changes the expression of power into a
> *dialectical tour de force: it lets everything remain but subtly
> drains the meaning out of it; rather than culminating in an up-
> rising, it exhausts the inner actuality of relations in a tension of
> reflection that lets everything remain and yet has transformed
> the whole of existence into an equivocation that in its facticity
> is—while entirely privately a dialectical fraud interpolates a secret
> way of reading—that it is not.*[16]

As a form of "reflection," or as Edward Said has aptly characterized it, an intellectual activity "dominated by the spirit of refinement,"[17] the deconstructive "play" of mind becomes, paradoxically, perilously like an exemplary instance of this kind
of passionless revolutionary thinking, which transforms the
inner impulse to revolt against the old order into an infinitely
negative and ineffectual play of dialectics. Further, in empty-

ing out the "inner actuality of relations in a tension of reflection that lets everything [power] remain," it becomes perilously similar, again in Kierkegaard's terms, to the garrulous "chatter" of a wit industry that ultimately, if unwittingly, validates and serves the levelling hegemonic socio-political purposes of the "present age."

NOTES

[1] Martin Heidegger, "Introduction: The Exposition of the Question of the Meaning of Being," *Being and Time,* tr. Joan Stambaugh in *Basic Writings,* ed. Joseph Farrell Krell (New York: Harper & Row, 1977), pp. 67-68.

[2] Jacques Derrida, "Structure, Sign, and Play in the Discourse of the Human Sciences," *Writing and Difference,* tr. Alan Bass (Chicago: University of Chicago Press, 1978), p. 289.

[3] Jacques Derrida, *Of Grammatology,* tr. Gayatri Spivak (Baltimore: The Johns Hopkins University Press, 1976), p. 158. For Paul de Man, of course, creative writing, unlike commentary about it, is self-consciously demystified from the start and exists to deconstruct the mystified *expectations* of the logocentric reader. "The Rhetoric of Blindness: Jacques Derrida's Reading of Rousseau," *Blindness and Insight: Essays in the Rhetoric of Contemporary Criticism* (New York: Oxford University Press, 1971), pp. 102-4.

[4] Jacques Derrida, *Of Grammatology,* p. 158.

[5] Jacques Derrida, *Of Grammatology,* p. 158.

[6] Jacques Derrida, *Of Grammatology,* p. 159.

[7] Edward Said, "Reflections on Recent American 'Left' Literary Criticism," *The Problems of Reading in Contemporary American Criticism: A Symposium, Boundary* 2, Vol. VIII (Fall 1979), p. 27.

[8] J. Hillis Miller, "The Critic as Host," in Harold Bloom, Paul de Man,

Jacques Derrida, Geoffrey Hartman, J. Hillis Miller, *Deconstruction and Criticism* (New York: The Seabury Press, 1979), pp. 217-53.

[9]Martin Heidegger, "Introduction: The Exposition of the Question of the Meaning of Being," *Basic Writings*, pp. 65-6.

[10]I have conflated several essays of the later Heidegger in this last sentence, above all, "The Origin of the Work of Art," ". . . Poetically Man Dwells . . .," and "Building Dwelling Thinking," in *Poetry, Language, Thought,* tr. Albert Hofstadter (New York: Harper & Row, 1971). The meaning of a measure which is "the measure of its occasion" is implicit in the etymological roots of "occasion," immediately from *occasus* ("to fall," "to drop," as in the setting of heavenly bodies; and "to fall," "to perish," "to die," as in *de casibus virorum illustrium*—"of the fall of great men"). An interpretive activity which is the measure of its occasion, then, is not a constraining, masterful and transcendent "geometry" having its ultimate model in the Platonic *mousiké* of the spheres. It is not, to appropriate Yeats's rhetoric in "Sailing to Byzantium," the "Oriental" measure of a golden bird singing "of what is past, passing, or to come" from the infinitely negative distance of eternity, but rather the measure of "Those dying generations—at their song," a measure that acknowledges man's "mortal dress" as the *case*. It is, in other words, the measure of "being-in-the-world," of *Da-sein* (being there) "caught" in that which passes. As Heidegger puts it in an essay on Hölderlin's poetry, it is the decentered or ec-centric measure of mortality, of dwelling on this earth in the context of mortality: "In poetry the taking of measure occurs. To write poetry is measure-taking, understood in the strict sense of the word, by which man first receives the measure for the breadth of his being. Man is mortal. He is called mortal because he can die. To be able to die means: to be capable of death as death. Only man dies—and indeed, continually, so long as he stays on this earth, so long as he dwells. His dwelling, however, rests on the poetic. Hölderlin sees the nature of the 'poetic' in the taking of the measure by which the measure-taking of human being is accomplished." ". . . Poetically Man Dwells. . .," pp. 221-222. It is, finally, a "westering" measure, for another etymological root of "occasion" is, of course, the cognate *occidere* (which "means" both "to fall," especially "to set," as in the case of the "movement" of the sun; and "to die," "to perish" from the present participle of which [*occidens*] the English word "Occident" comes). See my essay, "Postmodern Literature and the Hermeneutic Crisis," *Union Seminary Quarterly Review*, Vol. XXXIV (Winter 1979), pp. 119-31.

¹¹A full treatment of the difficult distinction between "ontological difference" and *différance* would invoke, above all, Martin Heidegger, *Identity and Difference,* tr. Joan Stambaugh (New York: Harper & Row, 1979), supplemented by the analysis of Temporality in *Being and Time;* and Jacques Derrida, "Differance," in *Speech and Phenomena and Other Essays on Husserl's Theory of Signs,* tr. David B. Allison (Evanston, Ill.: Northwestern University Press 1973), pp. 129-60, supplemented by the discussion of the "trace" and *différance* scattered throughout *Of Grammatology* and the essays in *Writing and Difference.*

¹²Jacques Derrida, "Structure, Sign, and Play in the Discourse of the Human Sciences," p. 292.

¹³Soren Kierkegaard, *The Concept of Irony,* tr. Lee M. Capel (Bloomington: University of Indiana Press, 1971), pp. 336-42. See also my essay, "Heidegger, Kierkegaard, and the Hermeneutic Circle: Towards a Postmodern Theory of Interpretation as Dis-closure," in *Martin Heidegger and The Question of Literature,* ed. William V. Spanos (Bloomington: University of Indiana Press, 1979), pp. 115-48.

¹⁴I am referring, of course, to I. A. Richards's (and Cleanth Brooks's) distinction between two general types of poetry, that which leaves out the opposite and discordant differential qualities of an experience, *excluding* them from the poem (the poetry of the "objective" imagination) and that which *includes* them (the poetry of the ironic imagination): "The structure of these two kinds of experiences are different and the difference is not one of subject but of the relation *inter se* of the several impulses active in the experience. A poem of the first group is built out of sets of impulses which run parallel, which have the same direction. In a poem of the second group the most obvious feature is the extraordinary heterogeneity of the distinguishable impulses. But they are more than heterogeneous, they are opposed. They are such that in ordinary, non-poetic non-imaginative experience, one or other set would be supposed to give as it might appear freer development to the others. The difference comes out clearly if we consider how comparatively unstable poems of the first kind are. They will not bear an ironic contemplation. . . . Irony in this sense consists in the bringing in of the opposite, the complementary impulses; that is why poetry which is exposed to it is not of the highest order, and why irony itself is so constantly a characteristic of poetry which is." Quoted in Cleanth Brooks, *Modern Poetry and the Tradition* (New York: Oxford University Press, 1965), p. 41.

[15]See Edward Said, "Reflections on Recent 'Left' Criticism," pp. 16-18.

[16]Soren Kierkegaard, *Two Ages: The Age of Revolution and the Present Age: A Literary Review,* ed. and tr. Howard V. Hong and Edna H. Hong (Princeton: Princeton University Press, 1978), p. 77. I am indebted to my editorial colleague Paul Bové for bringing this passage to my attention.

[17]Edward Said, "Reflection on Recent 'Left' Criticism," p. 20.

THEOLOGY AND LOGOLOGY IN VICTORIAN LITERATURE*

by
J. Hillis Miller

> All destructive discourses and all their analogues are trapped in a sort of circle. This circle is unique. It describes the form of the relationship between the history of metaphysics and the destruction of the history of metaphysics. *There is no sense* in doing without the concepts of metaphysics in order to attack metaphysics. We have no language—no syntax and no lexicon—which is alien to this history; we cannot utter a single destructive proposition which has not already slipped into the form, the logic, and the implicit propositions of precisely what it seems to contest. (Jacques Derrida)

> Men make their own history, but they do not make it just as they please; they do not make it under circumstances chosen by themselves, but under circumstances directly encountered, given and transmitted from the past. The tradition of all the dead generations weighs like a nightmare on the brain of the living. And just when they seem engaged in revolutionizing themselves and things, in creating something that has never yet existed, precisely in such periods of revolutionary crisis they anxiously conjure up the spirits of the past to their service and borrow from them names, battle cries and costumes in order to present the new scene of world history in this time-honored disguise and this borrowed language. (Karl Marx)

All interpretation, according to Nietzsche, is misinterpretation, the misappropriation of the traces of the past for some present purpose. Nevertheless, there is a difference, in scale at least, between the act of interpretation necessary to sustain large historical generalizations and that necessary to the reading of a single text or even the totality of works by a single author.

My own work has been primarily of the latter kind. It seems likely to become even more exclusively so, though of course I know that one cannot take even the first step in the reading of a single text without making historical and literary-historical assumptions. Even so, I have puzzled a bit about the contribution I might make to this symposium.[1] In the end it has seemed that I might best try to raise the question of how one aspect of Victorian "counter-culture," in this case religious doubt, scepticism, or unbelief, entered into the intimate texture of important literary works of the Victorian period, even into those apparently affirming the official culture, that is, some form of Christianity.

Everyone who has studied nineteenth-century England knows of the wide range of religious conviction, or lack of it, represented in the period, from Roman Catholicism and High Church Anglicanism at one extreme through Evangelicalism, to various forms of Broad Church adherence to Christianity, to the Nonconformists, and finally to various sorts of liberals, modernists, humanists, agnostics, and outright atheists. The best studies of the important examples of these religious positions have of course recognized the complexity in the religious commitments of a Newman, a Browning, a Dickens, a Leslie Stephen. Noel Annan has magisterially identified the recurrent pattern in Victorian culture of early Evangelical upbringing followed by a loss of faith and a commitment to some form of agnostic humanism, but with the ethical patterns of Evangelicalism still remaining firm, as in the case of George Eliot or of so many others.

In spite of their recognition of this complexity, however, critics and intellectual historians have sometimes tended to pigeon-hole individual figures. Each has been thought of as representing one more or less unified religious position, the Scottish Catholicism of Gerard Manley Hopkins, the agnosticism of Huxley, the Feuerbachianism of George Eliot, and so on. Or the complexity of an individual figure has been seen as diachronic rather than synchronic. In the latter case the individual is represented as passing through a series of distinct stages of faith or unfaith, each in itself a unified and unequivocal position. An example of this perhaps inevitable pigeon-holing is the organization of the valuable new handbook, *Victorian*

Prose: A Guide to Research. In this book, along with the separate sections on Newman, Arnold, Pater, Ruskin, and the rest of the major figures, there are sections on "The Oxford Movement: 1833-45," on "The Victorian Churches" (with subsections on "Church of England," "Nonconformists," and "Roman Catholics"), and on to "The Unbelievers" (Federick Harrison, Thomas Henry Huxley, John Morely, and Leslie Stephen).

This kind of organization, however necessary in a book of this sort, is misleading. It tends to imply that the quarrel among various forms of belief and unbelief was fought between individuals and sects, each with a well-defined and coherent position. Complexities in a given thinker are likely to be condemned as "inconsistencies" or "contradictions," as has often been the case, for example, in the abundant secondary literature on Matthew Arnold's religious writings. In fact, however, as I shall argue (it is the central point of this brief paper), the battle among various forms of belief and unbelief was fought within each individual mind, or, more precisely, within each individual text.

In a celebrated letter to W. M. Baillie of January 4, 1883, Gerard Manley Hopkins develops a theory that in classical literature, for example Greek tragedy, the overt narrative meaning may be matched by a covert sequence of figures or allusions constituting what he calls an "underthought." This will be an "echo or shadow of the overthought, something like canons and repetitions in music, treated in a different manner, . . . an undercurrent of thought governing the choice of images used." "My thought," says Hopkins, "is that in any lyric passage of the tragic poets . . . there are—usually, I will not say always, it is not likely—two strains of thought running together and like counterpointed; the overthought that which everybody, editors, see . . . and which might for instance be abridged or paraphrased . . . the other, the underthought, conveyed chiefly in the choice of metaphors etc. used and often only half realized by the poet himself. It might be possible to extend Hopkins' insight hypothetically to all literary texts and to suppose that each may have its underthought, a submerged counterpoint to its manifest meaning, more or less opposed to that meaning. In Victorian England the "counter-culture" was present within the characteristic expressions of the official culture as a covert "counter-thought," a subversion not from the outside but from within.   On the other hand, even the most extreme expressions of the "counter-culture," for example the deliberately provocative atheism of Swinburne, tend by an inevitable law to contain within themselves, as *their* counter-thought, exactly that system of concepts, figures, and myths which they are most concerned to reject.

I propose to test this hypothesis briefly in a few salient examples, chosen rather arbitrarily to represent a spectrum from fervent commitment to one form of Christianity to defiant rejection of Christiantiy.   My hypothesis could only be genuinely tested by a full and intimate interpretation of the writers in question, something impossible to do in such a brief paper. In fact, one major desideratum in the study of Victorian literature and culture is a reinterpretation of major texts, an interpretation not governed by disabling presuppositions about the way texts have meaning.   One such presupposition expecially relevant here is the notion that a literary work has, or ought to have, a single, verifiable, unambiguous "meaning."   The exegete who would undertake this difficult but necessary enterprise would find himself with an embarrassment of riches, since there is not one important Victorian writer who does not turn out to be another variation on my theme.   In each some version of Christian-Platonic metaphysics is co-present with its undermining deconstruction.   In fact I should say that a test of the importance of a writer, in the Victorian or any other age, is the presence together of the metaphysical system and its subversion.   Only a writer who has not thought out his premises far enough to encounter the latent presence within them of their apparent opposite does not subvert himself in this way.

My examples are Carlyle, George Eliot, Swinburne, and Gerard Manley Hopkins.   After discussing each briefly, I shall try to draw a few tentative conclusion suggesting why it is that every distinguished literary text of the Victorian period turns out when examined closely to contain within itself both its manifest religious position (whether "official" or "counter") and the opposing position.   In each case, the counter-culture is entangled within the official culture and undermines it from within, or, contrariwise, the counter-culture is unable to free itself from what it rejects and is forced to restate the old faith in spite of itself.

Carlyle's life and writings are a paradigmatic model in nineteenth-century English literature of the attempt to maintain the basic structure of the Christian faith without its essential dogmatic elements, such as the belief that the Bible is the single Scripture or the belief that Jesus was the Messiah. If some Victorians, like John Stuart Mill or George Eliot, develop a positivistic, even openly atheistical, faith to replace a lost supernaturalism, and if others, like Newman and Hopkins, go back to Roman Catholicism in order to preserve their endangered belief, others, of whom Carlyle was perhaps the most influential, develop some form of secular religion, or, as Carlyle called it, "natural supernaturalism." This enterprise is a continuation of Romanticism, or at least of one essential aspect of Romanticism. Such a secularized supernaturalism maintains in new forms the images, metaphors, concepts, and narrative patterns or "myths" of Christianity or of the Platonic idealism which is such a basic ingredient of post-Augustinian Christianity. Carlyle's natural supernaturalism differs from Christianity, however, in believing that these metaphors, concepts, and myths can be transformed, the old wine poured into new bottles, without being destroyed. As opposed to Christianity, with its notion of a single revelation and a single set of religious symbols and observances, Carlyle believes that all symbolic systems are inadequate to the divine reality, hiding it as much as revealing it. They quickly become fixed and dead, almost as soon as they are established, worn out old clothes which must be discarded, to be replaced by newly woven symbolic tissues, products of a fresh inspiration, in a never-ending sequence of creation followed by obsolescence, destruction, and a further creation again.

As subsequent literary and cultural history has suggested, Carlyle's attempt to naturalize supernaturalism was unstable. Like all contradictions or oxymorons, it expresses rather an unfulfilled yearning than a realized fact. It is difficult to change so much of a system of thought and belief without suggesting, whether one wishes to do so or not, that the whole structure may be a man-made fiction, not something based on eternal truth. That profound psychologist, Friedrich Nietzsche, felt that the rhetorical fervor with which Carlyle proclaimed his new secular faith betrayed his unfaith, the hollowness of his "Everlasting Yea." Carlyle was, said Nietzsche in *Twilight of the Idols,* an example of "pessimism as a poorly digested dinner *(Pessimismus als zurückgetretenes Mittagessen)."* He was "a man of strong words and attitudes, a rhetor from *need,* constantly lured by the craving for a strong faith, and the feeling of his incapacity for it. . . . The craving for a strong faith is no proof of a strong faith, but quite the contrary. . . . At bottom, Carlyle is an English atheist who makes it a point of honor not to be one" (Kaufman trans.).

Ultimately destructive of the traditional faith Carlyle wanted to maintain in a new form are Carlyle's ultra-Protestant idea that every man can be his own priest or poet and his idea that each system of thought or belief, with its embodying symbols, is valid for no more than a time, since all such systems are fictions, "supreme fictions" as Wallace Stevens was to call them. Each is inadequate to the mystery it is meant to express, a veil as well as a revelation, and therefore it needs to be changed frequently. To take it as permanently valid is idolatry. It is only a step from this to that moment in Stevens' "The Comedian as the Letter C" when the whole fabric of occidental concepts, symbols, and mythological figures vanishes at once: "Exit the whole/Shebang." To shift the attention, as Carlyle consistently does, from what is received in inspiration to the prophet, poet, statesman, or other hero who receives the inspiration, to shift attention from the content of a doctrine to its form, from meaning to language, is inevitably to imply that there is a radically inventive or constructive aspect of the hero's work. To see his work in this way is to see him as perhaps indeed no more than a maker of supreme fictions, as, like Carlyle himself, an atheist who makes it a point of honor not to be one.

Nietzsche may be cited again for his insight into the paradoxical structure of George Eliot's thought. She attempts to maintain the Evangelical virtues of self-sacrificing commitment to duty and a strong habit of fellow-feeling for one's neighbors in the absence of belief in the Christian God who had been the traditional basis for those virtues. In *Twilight of the Idols* Nietzsche speaks of those who "are rid of the Christian God and now believe all the more firmly that they must cling to Christian morality. This is an English consistency; we do not wish to hold it against little moralistic females à la Eliot. . . . We others hold otherwise. When one gives up the Christian faith, one pulls the right to Christian morality out from under one's feet. This morality is by no means self-evident: this point has to be exhibited again and again, despite the English flatheads *(den enlischen Flachköpfen zum Trotz).* Christianity is a system, a *whole* view of things thought out together. By breaking one main concept out of it, the faith in God, one breaks the whole: nothing necessary remains in one's hands. Christianity presupposes that man does not know, *cannot* know, what is good for him, what evil: he believes in God, who alone knows it. Christian morality is a command; its origin is transcendent; it is beyond all criticism; all right to criticism; it has truth only if God is the truth—it stands and falls with faith in God" (Kaufman trans.).

This seems to me an accurate judgment of one aspect of George Eliot. I should like, however, to affirm a counter truth. Insofar as George Eliot does in fact reaffirm the Christian morality in her novels, she inevitably drags in with that morality Christian metaphysics also. She affirms the existence of that transcendent deity who is precisely what she is determined to do without. I say "insofar as" because both the morality and the "ontology" of George Eliot's later novels are complex. In *Middlemarch* and *Daniel Deronda,* for example, the deconstructive effort of interpretation, based on a recognition of the role of language, especially figurative language, in shaping human convictions, extends beyond the undermining of belief in the basic metaphysical assumptions of origin, ending, and teleological movement between origin and ending. It ultimately also recognizes, however implicitly, that, as Nietzsche says, when belief in a transcendent deity vanishes a new kind of morality must replace the old. In Eliot's early work, however, for example in *Adam Bede,* there is a more straightforward attempt to maintain the peculiarly precarious Feuerbachian poise which says, in effect, "All the affirmations of Christianity are true, but not as the believers believe."

This attempt makes *Adam Bede* throughout a deliberately ambiguous text. It is intended to be taken in one way by the credulous and in another way by those who know that God, as Feuerbach defines him, "as the epitome of all realities or perfections is nothing other than a compendious summary devised for the benefit of the limited individual, an epitome of the generic human qualities distributed among men, in the self-realization of the species in the course of world history." "Theology," says Feuerbach in another place, "is anthropology, that is, in the object of religion which we call *Theos* in Greek and *Gott* in German, nothing but the essence of man is expressed." It accomplishes nothing, however, to affirm one's mastery over words in this way, Humpty-Dumpty-like, and so to say that the word "God" really means "man." The theological words, of which the word "man" is also to be sure an example, form a system which is stronger than the intention of any writer. The result is that certain key passages in *Adam Bede* vibrate before the reader's eyes like one of those Gestaltist diagrams which may be seen as duck or rabbit, or as inside out or outside in. The entire system of Christian metaphysics insinuates itself willy-nilly into George Eliot's expression of the Feuerbachian version of the counter-culture. It forces her to say both what she means to say and its tranquilly orthodox opposite.

An example of this is a passage in Chapter XLV where she says, "God . . . manifest[s] himself by our silent feeling, and make[s] his love felt through ours." Another example is four widely spaced echoing passages in Chapters III, XX, XXXIII, and L. Each of these asserts that there is a divine ocean of love which is the transcendent basis of individual human love and experienced in it. The divine ocean is also glimpsed in experiences of religious worship and in responses to nature and to works of art. "[I]t seems to be a far-off mighty love that has come near to us, and made speech for itself there," says the narrator of Adam's love for Hetty in Chapter XXXIII, and in Chapter III the narrator affirms that "Our caresses, our tender words, our still rapture under the influence of autumn sunsets, or pillared vistas, or calm majestic statues, or Beethoven symphonies, all bring with them the consciousness that they are mere waves and ripples in an unfathomable ocean of love and beauty; our emotion in its keenest moment passes from expression into silence, our love at its highest flood rushes beyond its object, and loses itself in the sense of divine mystery. Only in the almost unnoticeable words of qualification, "it seems to be," "consciousness that," "sense of," does George

Eliot's Feuerbachianism, fully developed at the time she wrote these words, appear on the surface as a gentle ripple to disturb her reaffirmation of certain central concepts and metaphors of just that aspect of the official culture she was in her translations of Strauss and Feuerbach most concerned to counter.

Swinburne seems to fit perfectly that description Walter Pater gives of what he calls, speaking especially of William Morris, "aesthetic poetry." Pater means by that term what we should today call "Pre-Raphaelite poetry." "Greek poetry," says Pater, "medieval or modern poetry, projects, above the realities of its time, a world in which the forms of things are transfigured. Of that transfigured world this new poetry takes possession, and sublimates beyond it another still fainter and more spectral, which is literally an artificial or 'earthly paradise.' It is a finer ideal, extracted from what in relation to any actual world is already an ideal. Like some strange flowering after date, it renews on a more delicate type the poetry of a past age, but must not be confounded with it. The secret of this enjoyment of it is that inversion of home-sickness known to some, that incurable thirst for the sense of escape, which no actual form of life satisfies, no poetry even, if it be merely simple and spontaneous" (213-214).

A poetry building itself not even on the "abolishing," to use Mallarmé's word, of physical nature, but on a further refinment or sublimation of a previous poetry which had already performed that effacement of the solid and earthly, a poetry metaleptically based on an earlier poetry and so annihilating any substantial presence or present within itself, perversely hungry not for home but for an ever more impalpable exile— Swinburne's version of "aesthetic poetry," so defined, and his greatness as a poet, take the form of an ability to use words as independent powers, powers liberated from their referential ties to "reality." Words, in Swinburne's hands, are like tones for the musician or colors for the painter. They can be repeated, modulated, and combined with other words to form new melodies or new chromatic sequences. To hazard a dangerous comparison between several arts, one might say that the effect of Swinburne's poetry is something like that of two artists whom he greatly admired, J. M. W. Turner in painting and Richard Wagner in music. If one adds to this creation of a self-sufficient realm of words in Swinburne's poetry the fact that the conceptual content of this poetry often takes the form of violent denunciations of Christianity, it would seem that Swinburne is an unusually pure example of what might be meant by "Victorian counter-culture" in its religious dimension. Moreover, in his notorious life and in the sado-masochistic aspects of his poetry he would seem to be also an example of other aspects of Victorian counter-culture.

When one turns to the most salient examples of his defiant rejection of Christianity, however, for instance in the celebrated chorus of *Atalanta in Calydon* where he speaks of "the supreme evil, God," one finds not atheism at all but a language heavy with the conceptual terms, the metaphors, and the narrative patterns of Graeco-Roman literature and the Bible. John Ruskin called *Atalanta in Calydon* 'The grandest thing ever yet done by a youth—though he is a demonic youth." According to W. B. Yeats's name as an initiate of The Order of the Golden Dawn, however, "Demon est Deus Inversus." To put a minus sign instead of a plus sign before the elements of western culture is not to liberate oneself from them but to remain entirely bound within their net. To define God as the supreme evil is as much an act of homage and belief as to define him as the supreme good. Far from establishing the subversive attitudes of a counter-culture or the dangerous freedom of a purely "aesthetic" poetry, Swinburne, one might argue, is as traditional as Job or Aeschylus, for example in these lines near the end of that famous chorus:

> Because thou hast bent thy lightnings as a bow,
>   And loosed the hours like arrows; and let fall
> Sins and wild words and many a wingèd woe
>   And wars among us, and one end of all;
> Because thou hast made the thunder, and thy feet
>   Are as a rushing water when the skies
> Break, but thy face as an exceeding heat
>   And flames of fire the eyelids of thine eyes;
> Because thou art over all who are over us;
>   Because thy name is life and our name death;
> Because thou art cruel and men are piteous,
>   And our hands labour and thine hand scattereth;
> Lo, with hearts rent on knees made tremulous,

> Lo, with ephemeral lips and casual breath,
>   At least we witness of thee ere we die
> That these things are not otherwise, but thus;
>   That each man in his heart sigheth, and saith,
>   That all men even as I,
> All we are against thee, against thee, O God most high.

(11. 1174-1192)

The religious thought of Gerard Manley Hopkins is centered on an ultimately acentering analogy: the parellelism between the structure of language and the structure of the creation in relation to the creator.   The most obvoius way in which this analogy appears is in the systematic and of course the wholly orthodox use of a metaphor drawn from language to describe the relation of the world to God.   Christ, the second person of the Trinity, is the Logos, the word or utterance of God.   The world with all its multitude of creatures, including man, is created in the name of Christ, modelled on Christ, just as all the multiplicity of words in a language might be considered as the product of an increasingly elaborate differentiation of a primal word, an ur-word. "God's utterance of himself in himself," writes Hopkins in his commentary on the *Spiritual Exercises* of St. Ignatius, "is God the Word, outside himself is this world.   This world then is word, expression, news of God.   Therefore its end, its purpose, its purport, its meaning, is God and its life or work to name and praise him."   Nature is the "Word and Image" of God, and "All things therefore are charged with love, are charged with God and if we know how to touch them give off sparks and take fire, yield drops and flow, ring and tell of him." Each creature is like a separate word or name in a language.   Just as all words in a language may be thought of as having derived by a principle of phonemic division and subdivision from a single original word and therefore as all saying versions of the same thing, so each creature speaks in its own way the name of God, in whose name it has been created.   Christ the Word is the creative principle by means of which all things came into being.   He is therefore also the avenue by which things may return to God the Father.   He is the primal speaker who spoke by means of what Hopkins calls, in *The Wreck of the Deutschland,* the "arch and original breath" (1. 194).   This rhythm of exhalation and inhalation, of speech and echoing answer, is the systole and diastole of the creation.

The structure of language is, then, the vehicle of a metaphor which is the irreplaceable means by which Hopkins expresses his conception of God in his relation to the creation. One might say that his theological terminology is logocentric. Language itself, however, is also a primary theme in Hopkins' writing, not only in the brilliant etymological speculations in the early diaries or in the early essay on words, but also in the mature poetry itself, for example, in "That Nature is a Heraclitean Fire and of the Comfort of the Ressurection," and in "I wake and feel the fell of dark, not day." The theme of language is most elaborately developed in Hopkins' masterpiece, *The Wreck of the Deutschland*. This motif runs all through *The Wreck*, not just as a metaphor but as a theme treated directly, for itself.

If the overthought of *The Wreck* is the salvation of the tall nun and the poet's corresponding experience, in madrigal echo, of a renewed inspiration or breath of God's grace the underthought of the poem is language itself. The poem, like so many romantic and post-romantic poems, has as one of its themes its own possibility of being. Hopkins's insight into the nature of language is a complex matter, but here, as in other areas of thought, he had the insight of genius. The remarkable quality of his speculations about language, particularly the language of poetry, is suggested by the admiring interest in them of a present-day linguist like Roman Jakobsen. The center around which Hopkins' linguistic speculations revolve, the unsettling intuition which they approach toward and withdraw from, is the exact opposite of his theological insight. It is the notion that there is no primal word, that the divisions of language have always already occurred as soon as there is language at all. If this is so, there is no word for the Word, only displaced metaphors of it. In the word lists in Hopkins's early onomatopoeic etymological speculations, each list goes back to an ur-gesture, action, or sound. In each case this is an act of division, marking striking, or cutting. Here are examples of these lists: "grind, gride, gird, grit, groat, grate, greet," "flick, fleck, flake," "skim, scum, squama, scale, keel," "shear, shred, potsherd, shard." Of the first list Hopkins says, "Original meaning to *strike, rub*, particularly *together.*" Of the second list, *"Flick* means to touch or strike lightly as with the end of a whip, a finger, etc. *To fleck* is the next tone above flick, still meaning to touch or strike lightly (and leave a mark of the touch or stroke) but in a broader less slight manner. Hence substantively a *fleck* is a piece of light, colour, substance etc. looking as though shaped or produced by such touches. *Flake* is a broad and decided *fleck*, a thin plate of something, the tone above it. Their connection is more clearly seen in the applications of the words to natural objects than in explanation.'' The third list involves the notion of "the topmost flake what [sic] may be skimmed from the surface of a thing," and the fouth list is of words playing variations on the act of division, as "the *ploughshare* [is] that which divides the soil." For Hopkins, "the onomatopoetic theory has not had a fair chance," and all these word lists lead back to an original sound or sound-producing act of differentiation. For Hopkins, as for modern linguistics, the beginning is diacritical.

The dramatic climax of *The Wreck of the Deutschland* is also the climax of its treatment of the theme of language. Its dramatic climax is the tall nun's saying the name of Christ and thereby being saved, transformed into Christ at the moment of her death. The linguistic climax is the implicit recognition, in stanzas 22 and 28, that there is no way of speaking of this theological mystery except in a cascade of metaphors whose proliferation confesses to the fact that there is no literal word for the Word. Stanza 22 presents a chain of words for the act of sign-making, the marking of the nun with the stigmata which sign her with the seal of sacrifice, of "resignation":

>   Five! the finding and sake
>   And cipher of suffering Christ.
>   Mark, the mark is of man's make
>   And the word of it Sacrificed.
>   But he scores it in scarlet himself on his own bespoken,
>   Before-time-taken, dearest prizèd and priced—
>   Stigma, signal, cinquefoil token
>   For lettering of the lamb's fleece, ruddying of the rose-flake[.]

In stanza 28 the syntactical control of the poet breaks down, as well as his ability to find a single adequate literal name for "it," the apparition of Christ to the nun, walking towards her on the water in the moment of her salvation:

>   But how shall I . . . make me room there:

Reach me a . . . Fancy, come faster—
Strike you the sight of it? look at it loom there,
Thing that she . . . there then! the Master,
Ipse, the only one, Christ, King, Head . . .

Rather than being in happy correspondence, Hopkins' theological thought and its linguistic underthought are at cross-purposes. They have a structure of chiasmus. The theological thought depends on the notion of an initial unity which has been divided or fragmented and so could conceivably be reunified. The linguistic underthought depends on the notion of an initial bifurcation which could not by any conceivable series of linguistic transformations, such as those which make up the basic poetic strategies of Hopkins' verse, reach back to any primal word. There is no such word. Hopkins' linguistic underthought subverts his Catholic overthought. A particularly deconstructive form of counter-cultural insight is present not as the enemy without but as the enemy within, entwined in the intimate texture of his language.[2]

I shall try in conclusion to identify one or two small consequences which follow from what has been said so far. One has already been formulated in my epigraph from Jacques Derrida. The counter-culture has no instruments with which to attack the official culture but those drawn from the twenty-five-hundred year old official culture. For this reason, the counter-culture turns out regularly and inevitably, in spite of itself, to be another version of what it attempts to destroy.

A second consequence is a recognition of the irreducible plurality of any cultural expression, such as a literary text. This plurality does not result from confusion on the part of the author, his inability to get his thoughts straight or to say what he means. Nor does it result from some remediable error or willful overcomplication of things on the part of the interpreter, though a new definition of the relation between reader and text would emerge from the problems I have been discussing. No, the plurality of meanings in each literary text, the presence of an underthought inextricably interwoven with each overthought, a counter-culture within each culture, arises from an intrinsic necessity of the literary texts themselves, insofar as they depend, as all texts in our language do, on conceptual terms, metaphors, and narrative patterns drawn from the finite reservoir of such elements in our Western family of languages. The counter-culture has always been present within the official culture, waiting to be brought out into the open in new ways by the George Eliots, Swinburnes, and Wildes of each new generation. Anti-Platonism was already present within the dialogues of Plato, not something added later by Plato's antagonists.

The final consequence of what I have said is a notion of history—of literary history, of cultural history, or of history as such—different from the familiar paradigm of a series of self-enclosed "epochs," each with its own intrinsic set of forms, its own "world picture." Not that there is no such thing as history, in the sense of intrinsic differences between epoch and epoch, country and country, individual and individual, text and text. Each text, person, country, and epoch are indeed different from one another, as no two signatures from the same hand are identical, no two copies of a text the same, no two performances of a play exactly congruent. The concepts of difference, of signature, of history are in fact integral elements within the cultural remains, such as literary texts, which they are used to investigate. Like the other elements, they must be solicited, interrogated. A more adequate concept of history must add to the notion of difference the notion of repetition. The problematic of repetition balances the problematic of difference, in an unstable equilibrium or oscillation. The writings and other cultural artifacts of the Victorians appear, in the light of these modes of interpretation, as latecomers in a long line of repetitions with a difference of concepts, figures of speech, and myths going back to Plato and the Bible, and behind them to their antecedents.[3] These elements contain within themselves the genetic possibility of both thought and underthought, both cultures and counter-cultures, in inexhaustible, though not unbounded, permutation.

NOTES

[1] This was first presented to a symposium on Victorian "counter-culture."

[2] As in the last two lines of "That Nature is a Heraclitean Fire": "This Jack, joke, poor potsherd, patch, matchwood, immortal diamond,/ Is immortal diamond" (11. 23-24), where the tautology reveals the failure of the language of the poem to correspond to the spiritual transformation it describes.

[3] Compare the admirable opening of Pater's *Plato and Platonism* (London: Macmillan, 1893), so definitive a qualification, before the fact, of A. N. Whitehead's celebrated dictum that all Western history is a footnote to Plato: "Plato's acievement may well seem an absolutely fresh thing in the morning of the mind's history. Yet in truth the world Plato had entered into was already almost weary of philosophical debate, bewildered by the oppositions of sects, the claims of rival schools. Language and the processes of thought were already become sophisticated, the very air he breathed sickly with off-cast speculative atoms. . . . Some of the results of patient earlier thinkers, even then dead and gone, are of the structure of his philosophy. They are everywhere in it, not as the stray carved corner of some older edifice, to be found here or there amid the new, but rather like minute relics of earlier organic life in the very stone he builds with. The central and most intimate principles of his teaching challenge us to go back beyond them, not merely to his own immediate, somewhat enigmatic master—to Socrates, who survives chiefly in his pages—but to various precedent schools of speculative thought, in Greece, in Ionia, in Italy; beyond these into that age of poetry, in which the first efforts of philosophic apprehension had hardly understood themselves; beyond that unconscious philosophy, again, to certain constitutional tendences, persusasions, forecasts of the intellect itself, such as had given birth, it would seem, to thoughts akin to Plato's in the older civilisations of India and of Egypt, as they still exercise their authority over ourselves" (pp. 2-3). In this exemplary rejection of any notion of origin or of originality, each text refers to some still earlier text, that to still another, and so on. Moreover, "influence" is not a matter of conscious borrowing, but something that, like a disease, in fact like "influenza," insinuates itself into the air we breathe, or something that is present, whether or not we know it or wish it, in the intimate texture of our material, in the words we must use to speak

or write at all. If we are another footnote to Plato, Plato was himself already a footnote to still earlier footnotes, in an endless chain of footnotes to footnotes, with nowhere a primary text as such.

PART TWO

Mediation and Reading

TRANSACTING MY "GOOD-MORROW" OR, BRING BACK THE VANISHED CRITIC

by

Norman N. Holland

To transact: to act across or through, to manage or conduct (as business or affairs). Transactive criticism, then, a criticism that explicitly takes as its base the critic's transaction of the text. To be sure, all criticism rests on the relation the critic establishes with the text, but few critics acknowledge their transacting *explicitly.* Most adopt a convention: they are talking about something "out there" and everyone would perceive that something the same way. Therefore one can promote a critical "I" into a cultural "we."

Other critics turn the subject-verb relationship of critic transacting poem into one or another of the magical nouns that have lately been translated from France: "textuality," "problematic," "aporia," "valorization," for example, or potent adjectives like "cataleptic," "polyptotic," or (more mercifully) "intertextual." Inanimate objects become the subjects for verbs that require animate subjects: I read, for example, of "the ways in which any literary work's consciousness of its own status as language necessarily affects its meanings, or even its way of meaning." Somewhere in there, I suppose, is a person who is conscious both of the work and its status as language and who makes it mean accordingly through the transformations pointed to by modern (that is, post-Saussurean) linguists. Somewhere, in short, there is a person transacting that work, but his trans-action is reified and he himself whisked away as by a magician's wand. And we have gotten quite used to this trick. You probably scarcely noticed my earlier phrasing, "a criticism that explicitly takes as its base the critic's transaction of the text." I say, bring that vanished, banished critic back!

So here I am, and here is a text for me to transact, Donne's "The Good-Morrow."

> I wonder by my troth, what thou and I
> Did, till we loved? Were we not weaned till then,
> But sucked on country pleasures, childishly?
> Or snorted we in the seven sleepers' den?
> 'Twas so. But this, all pleasures fancies be.
> If ever any beauty I did see,
> Which I desired, and got, 'twas but a dream of thee.
>
> And now good morrow to our waking souls,
> Which watch not one another out of fear:
> For love all love of other sights controls,
> And makes one little room an everywhere.
> Let sea-discoverers to new worlds have gone.
> Let maps to other, worlds on worlds have shown.
> Let us possess one world: each hath one, and is one.
>
> My face in thine eye, thine in mine appears,
> And true plain hearts do in the faces rest.
> Where can we find two better hemispheres
> Without sharp North, without declining West?
> Whatever dies was not mixed equally.
> If our two loves be one, or thou and I
> Love so alike that none do slacken, none can die.[1]

Forgive me my jargon, but I find the coincidence between Donne's first stanza and the psychoanalytic description of infancy so striking I need to say Donne is describing his two lovers as "oral" infants. That is, they are not yet weaned. They suck. They sleep in a timeless sleep. Psychoanalysts even have a special term for this combination; they call it the "oral triad,"[2] a combination of three wishes: to be suckled, to sleep, but also to experience that special feeling of yielding, falling, relaxing, and being merged into something larger that we sometimes feel just before sleep even as adults. Analysts think of this feeling as a sensation of not being separated from the source of gratification, of there being no real division between you and the thing you desire, as though you were incorporated in it. Thus, Donne describes himself as hallucinating gratification or, more exactly, as not distinguishing between real gratification of desire ("got," as he says) and "a dream of thee," of the gratifying person. But that was before the actual presence of the loved, gratifying person: except for "this, *all* pleasures fancies be." All pleasures are fantasies compared to union with his beloved.

For me, the seemingly extra phrase, "by my troth," establishes this theme in the first line. "Troth": the Indo-European root means to be firm, solid, steadfast, as in *tree* or *truce* or *truth*. He swears by the firmness with which the lovers are bound together. Yet the strongest images for that firmness he brings from a time prior to their love: "the seven sleepers' den" that every editor glozes; "country pleasures, childishly"—I picture a village idiot from *Monty Python*, as well (of course) as the bawdy pun. The strongest sounds, too, image their pre-love state: "sucked" and "snorted," bodily verbs that contrast with the abstract language of "pleasures," "beauty," "desire," or "dream," that closes the stanza. These are "fancies" yet they seem more real to me than the abstract "loved" to which they are compared.

For me, stanza two breaks with the dreamy, infantile sleeping of the first stanza. The lovers wake and watch, not guardedly as a sentinel might keep watch, but because love overrules "all love of other sights," any desire to look elsewhere. I read Donne as re-creating the "troth," the bond, that makes this love as firm as that of a child for its nurturing mother, that "makes one little room an everywhere." That one gratifying relationship simply *is* the world of infancy, all of it.

In the first stanza Donne withdrew from a time that was not the time of his love. In the second, he withdraws from a space that is not the space of his love. He re-creates the total fusion of the suckling, the symbiosis we know in infancy, "a feeling of an indissoluble bond, of being one with the external world as a whole," as Freud noted. Such a one-ness, Freud said, "an infant at the breast" feels, or the mystic who has an "oceanic feeling associated with religion" (as in Donne's later poetry), or "a man who is in love," who will therefore declare "against all the evidence of his senses . . . that 'I' and 'you' are one, and is prepared to behave as if it were a fact."[3] Yet despite what seems to me a remarkable coincidence of Donne's fancy with Freud's insight, Donne can image that overwhelming relationship only by what it is not. In the second stanza as in the first, the images I find most vivid are those that describe the non-love, the elsewhere: "sea-discoverers," "new worlds," "maps," "worlds on worlds."

Even so, in what I think is the highest tension of the poem, he ends stanza two by describing being in love as both having the world of the other and being a world to that other. Then he collapses his gigantic geographical metaphor into the tiny reflection of each lover's face in the other's eye. As the faces are in the eyes, so the hearts are in the faces. These miniscule worlds embody "hearts," as the third stanza moves to body from the second stanza's "souls," hearts that are "true" (like "troth") and "plain" (whose sound and root is the same as a geometric "plane"). These "hemispheres" refer most directly to the lovers' eyes, but also, I think, to the breasts implicit in the first stanza and I recall, too, Aristophanes' myth in the *Symposium* of men and women as halves of a sphere. Again, Donne's images become vivid as he describes what the lovers' hemispheres do *not* have, "sharp North" or "declining West," a painful lack of heart or a depressing loss of the sun. They are "plane."

Donne returns to abstract language—this time from al-chemy—as he describes the lovers' aspiration: never to "die" (and I think of the three possible meanings of "die" in Ren-aissance poetry: physical death, having an orgasm, dying into resurrection). These lovers will be immortal even in the tension of their desire: "none do slacken." They will be two, yet so per-fectly balanced as to share the immortality of the alchemical One—or so Donne hopes. Logic, science, and abstract thought image his wish. In effect, he wants to re-create the symbiotic union of mother and infant (*in* + *fans*, unspeaking) in a per-fect abstract balancing of two adult and articulate lovers.

As I read them, then, the poem's three stanzas move from past through present to future. In each stanza, however, the concrete language (to the extent any of this language seems con-crete) describes the elsewhere, the time or space that is *not* the lovers' time or space. In the same way, I find myself moving from the solid, earthy humanity of "sucked" or "snorted" to an abstract, intellectual balance in the last three lines. Indeed, it is so abstract there is no telling whether the lover spoken to is male or female. The only clues to gendered relationships occur in the weaning and sucking of the first stanza.

As I read it, this is a poem defining the here by the elsewhere. Donne has substituted an intellectual balance, in which lovers only look at one another (although there is that "die"), for a physical, fleshy fusion like that of a mother holding and nursing a sleepy, dreaming baby. Paradoxically, just as that relationship is unequal, the mother giving into the baby's mouth, so the relationship Donne envisages at the end is unequal: he is doing all the talking. In making things come out of his mouth, however, he becomes an opposite to the mother or the baby. Again, I feel reading this poem is trying to discover one relationship, but expending all my energy in the opposite to that relationship.

So far, I have been (in the inaccurate phrasing of our professional vocabulary) "talking about the poem itself." I can also, however, read this poem as saying something about John Donne, even though I believe in the critical principle that one cannot equate the *persona* speaking the poem with the actual poet, at least not in any direct sense. That is, I cannot show that Donne did in fact have a lover to whom he made this rather contrived declaration. I feel quite comfortable, however, associating Donne with the poem by assuming that this *persona* represents an aspect of Donne's life style, even if not his life history. In that sense, I read the intellectual game of this poem (and indeed all of Donne's work) as if he were making up for the loss of a child's oneness with a nurturing other.

I have another association, Dr. Johnson's well-known phrase for the metaphysical style: "The most heterogeneous ideas are yoked by violence together." Here Donne actively yokes together legends and geography and alchemy and his love. The yoking, I feel, substitutes for a primitive but more human union rejected in the first stanza. Activity—loving so that none do slacken—will substitute for the unintellectual, sucking, snoring dependency of child on mother. In this emancipation, Donne achieves a witty, Renaissance version of a medieval *contemptus mundi:* by loving you, I can give up the world.

But these were not my first associations when I looked back

at this poem. In fact, at first I did not respond at all to the text-as-text, but to a memory: Douglas Bush's course in Renaissance poetry which I took in graduate school in the early 1950's. I remembered how important Donne's poetry was for us, then, at the height of the academic vogue for the metaphysicals: Herbert, Vaughan, Marvell, Crashaw, but above all, Donne, whose poems so lent themselves to that untangling and unfolding at which we proto-professors were becoming skilled. We—I— read the Romantics in the light of the metaphysicals and found them wanting. They were guilty of "dissociation of sensibility," that dread disease, the divorce of thought and emotion, diagnosed by T. S. Eliot, while the metaphysicals, he informed us, could "feel their thought as immediately as the odour of a rose."

We also read the then moderns in the light of the metaphysicals, prizing the intricacies of Pound, Stevens, Auden, Thomas, but above all, Eliot. They, in their turn, seemed to have written to be read just exactly the way we were reading them, relating one image to another to form themes, unifying those themes until we had arrived at a way of articulating a unity in the whole experience of the poem. These readings toward organic unity seemed to me an extremely rigorous, almost scientific way of reading, and I expected them to cumulate into an intense, disciplined knowledge of particular texts, writers, and eras. I thought—and still think—we had discovered something new under the sun, a more precise way of reading than any seen before in the history of literature. Aspiring to it, we graduate students wrote heavily intellectual, thirty-page explications of particular poems and stories, the more obscure and difficult the better.

If I continue associating, I read this poem (and its popularity in the 1950's anthologies for freshmen and sophomore introductions to literature) as saying something political about our attitudes toward literature then. "The Good-Morrow" is not only a prime subject of the New Criticism, but its emblem. Just as the poem substitutes cleverness for childishness, we explicators were substituting close, exact reading for an earlier, impressionistic relation to literature that seemed false or childish, an elitist posturing and showing off. We were discovering a new world, a rigorous map of reading, something really new in literary studies, something "true plain" that would be a place for people displaced from an older literary style. That is, we were opening literature for a new, larger college population that did not have, as prior cohorts had had, a valued acquaintance with literature during school years or even before. We were democratizing or, more exactly, "meritocratizing" high culture by grounding it on rational, evidenced interpretations equally available to all, regardless of tradition or upbringing. Earlier generations might have sucked on literary pleasures childishly. Not us. We and our students would possess that world by true, plain intellectual work. By paying attention to "point of view," "irony," or "tensions," we would achieve a deeper understanding of literature. We would show up the gushy enthusiasms of high school teachers or the pretensions of reviewers in the middlebrow press.

As it turned out, of course, we ended up doing all the talking ourselves, as Donne does in this poem. We might have read his necessary failure to achieve perfect equality as an omen for our own democratizing. The professors remained experts, and the students remained, well, students. There was something of a rebirth, to be sure, a new mixing of literary intelligence and availability, but today it has slackened, and something else is taking its place.

In the literary imagination of the eighties, I think we are very busy reacting against the New Criticism's threat of doneness (no pun intended). So many of us were asking the same questions of poems. "What is that word doing there?" "Why did the poet use this phrase and not some other?" So many of us were using the same methods, converging details to a thematic center, there was bound to be a great deal of overlap in our conclusions. To be sure, if one examined a dozen or more readings of, say, "Dover Beach" closely, the seeming unanimity evaporated as it became clear that different critics emphasized different themes, different meanings of a word, or different kinds of structure. Nevertheless, it often seemed to me in the fifties and sixties as though literature had become a closing universe. That is, a critic doing thematic analysis tended to treat the poem as a problem to be solved. Interpretations would accumulate until a consensus among skilled critics came into being, at that point there would be a kind of official interpretation of a given text, a solution to the problem, it would be "done," and the professors, like an army of ants, would march on to the next text until they had nibbled it away, too, and so on and on.

I see three ways our imagination of literature in the 80's is moving away from that closure. The first had already come in the 50's and 60's from a change in the poetic tradition itself. Re-reading this poem, I thought of the transition from so-called "modern" poetry to so-called "post-modern"—both terms equally temporary, I suppose. Our two major schools of poetry in the 50's and 60's, no matter how much they differed in other ways, led to a re-personalizing of poetry. Lowell's and Ginsberg's writing both respond to quite different kinds of reading from Donne's or Eliot's. I "get" one of their poems by paying more attention to the moment in the poem, less to the themes that connect moment to moment. I can still do explication, but it runs against the grain, leading to an uncomfortable disappointment between explicator and poem. I came to feel another kind of response was called for, an intense sensing of the particular rather than a situating of the particular within the unity of the whole.

Something similar was happening in fiction and drama and film. Beckett, Ionesco, Robbe-Grillet, or a host of others were replacing the tidy unities of the well-made novel and the well-made play and the well-made film with discontinuities. Rather like conceptual sculpture in the 60's, we were being asked to consider our relation to the work of art rather than the work of art as a separate entity "out there." All our makers of imaginative literature were asking us to turn away from abstract, problem-solving thought about literary works. All wanted us to open up to something strange and uncanny.

Some critics took up this demand on their own. That is, a second way to get beyond the closure threatened by our notions of right readings of an established text is by restoring a sense of play to the act of reading. This has happened in the seventies. I am thinking of the *jouissance* of which, say, Lacan speaks, a serious play like those games Huizinga describes in *Homo Ludens*. Earlier, the structuralists had begun to ask questions like those of the old New Critics, but, since no one could quite agree as to what structuralism was, structuralism evolved into a logical game. Derridean deconstructivism is even more explicitly a game, in which the critic, by sensing one position, stands it on its head, then pivots round himself, does a somersault or two and, with an enigmatic bow, vanishes, leaving us charmed but also mystified by his very demystification.

This kind of critical wit asks for the critic's imagination and creativity instead of a more ponderous skill at solving problems of explication. In that way, it opens up the closure that the New Criticism threatened in the hands of the professoriat. Yet these new methods pretend to the same impersonality that explication did. The somersaults become simply words tumbling over one another, for deconstructivism and semiotics claim to be games without players—mere linguistic moves that take place as words do tricks with words. Their jumps and skips are all in a safety net of language—much as the last three lines of "The Good-Morrow" speak of love in alchemical propositions.

If we use these highly intellectual strategies in teaching and criticism, we can reach those literents (usually graduate students in elite universities) who like to play those linguistic and philosophical games. But I do not think these abstract acrobatics will help us reach literents with more familiar human concerns: emotions, the body, and one's deeper human relationships with lovers and kin. For that reason I prefer another criticism of the late 70's that provides a third way out of the closure the New Critics threatened, a way that offers something important to our teaching.

The New Critics aspired to a cumulation of expert critical explications that would yield a (for a while) final reading of a work, much as in the sciences a cumulation of thought and experiment leads to temporarily final interpretations of events. What the New Criticism could not account for, however, was the variability of readings even among experts. That variability, however, should have come as no surprise to psychoanalysts or psychoanalytic critics, for it is an experience familiar to every analyst and every analysand that a person's "professional" views and skills function within the total psychic economy of that individual.

Identity theory (as originated by Heinz Lichtenstein)

offered a way of conceptualizing the individuality of that individual much more precisely.[4]   Following Lichtenstein, I can conceptualize the dialectic of sameness and difference, of change and continuity, that make up an individual.   I can understand how the "I" who reads this poem reads it in "I's" particular way.   I can do so by understanding my actions as variations on the theme of "me."   You can infer the theme of "me" by seeing what persists against all the changes in my life.   You can understand each new action as a creative variation on the persisting "me."   That theme may or may not be something intrinsic in my being.   At the very least, however, it is a theme which you or someone else can infer and thereby conceptualize a continuity in all my actions from the time when I was the "oral" infant of the first stanza to the moment when this critic is writing this sentence.

By this theme-and-variations concept of identity, it becomes possible to trace an individual style through writing and reading and relate it to the whole life of the person and to do so quite precisely.   The question is no longer *whether* a person's interpretation reflects his personality.   We have gone beyond that.   We have already begun to answer *how* this or that interpretation is related to this or that person's character.[5]   This was—and, to a large extent, still is—something new under the sun.   We now know something about the reading and writing of literature we did not know before, namely, that it is not a separate cognitive or imaginative faculty.   Rather, we can understand someone's literary activity as a variation within a theme-and-variations picture of everything that person has done.

We can go even further, tracing my reading of the poem in more detail.   Specifically, you can read for the defenses, expectations, fantasies, and transformations, D-E-F-T, the DEFT through which I have read the poem.[6]   You can read what I have written for the expectations I brought to the poem, my knowledge of Donne and Renaissance poetry, obviously, but more deeply, the curious minglings of hope and skepticism I characteristically bring to any new experience.   You can read in what I have written the defenses by which I shaped the poem into something congenial (in Hazlitt's sense, something that fits my *genius*, the born "me").   You can see, for example, how I have persistently intellectualized the poem, working out Donne's analogies, instead of, say, emphasizing the sounds of the poem as a poet would. You can understand the particular fantasies I have brought to the poem (my wishes and fears about loving and eyes and breasts). You can also see how I have used my characteristic defenses (intellectualization, for example) to transform those fantasies and make the poem into a coherent, meaningful experience ("a poem defining the here by the elsewhere").

What I have just sketched is a theoretical framework, a psychological understanding of what people customarily do with literature. So far, it is value free. At least it shares the neutrality on literary values of any psychological proposition.

This psychological description does not urge critics to turn from "objectivity" to "subjectivity." Neither should you think of what I have written about this poem as either "subjective" or "objective." Those words are highly misleading in our literary context, for they presuppose that one can divide an objective part of one's relation to a literary text from a subjective part—a manifest impossibility.

For example, as a psychoanalytic critic, I read the poem's opening stanza in terms of Freud's discussion of the "oceanic feeling" of early infancy. As a purely literary critic, I felt the need to justify Donne's seemingly extraneous phrase, "by my troth," and I used etymology to do so. Both readings mingle supposedly "objective" elements like psychoanalytic theory or etymology with "subjective" concerns, my interest in infancy or my choosing to talk about the word "troth" but not the word "country." Obviously, what I am doing is neither simply objective nor simply subjective. I am using "objective" knowledge in the service of "subjective" wishes. Since it is false to lift "objective" elements out of the net of "subjective" needs, we would do well to chuck those confusing terms and seek a fuller way of exploring a person's transaction of a poem. "Fuller," I think, means acknowledging that when I experience a poem I must have established some kind of relationship to it and when I talk about "The Good-Morrow" I am talking not about the poem as it exists in some realm of Platonic ideas, but about that relationship. I may be psychoanalytic or etymological, intellectual or emotional, associative or explicating, but

I can describe my relation to the poem in far more detail than the mere labels, "objective" and "subjective," permit. Further, I can understand my reading as a function of my identity. I read this poem the way I do because I am the person I am.

I can, of course, direct my relationship with the poem toward interrelating all its details around a centering theme—that would be the critical tradition I learned and admired in the 1950's. I can equally well, however, use the poem as a way of hypothesizing about John Donne the man. I can also treat the poem as a parable of the state of criticism in 1982.

All these and many more are possible relationships with "The Good-Morrow." It is when I come to choose among them, valuing one more or less than another that I turn the psychological model of reading and criticism toward questions of critical ethics.

I believe that critics should be candid about what they are doing. If they are talking about their relationship to the poem, then their language should say so. It is, in that sense, vainglorious to claim that one's own concerns and values are those of a generalized "we." It is equally prideful to maintain that one is talking impersonally, "structurally," or "deconstructively" about the poem when it is not given to humankind to transcend self that way. All statements about literary works have an implicit "for me" modifying them.

I believe that it would be better to make that "for me" explicit. Critics therefore should not be afraid to use "I" to say what "I" believe or cherish or demand. I am impressed and amused by Robin Lakoff's arguments against "academese," the language of *we's* and passives. "The first and last resort of the coward who has fled the real world in the first place," she calls it.

> The passive says, "All errors aren't the author's—they belong to the unstated agent of sentences like, 'It has been shown above. . . .'" "We" means "blame him, whoever he is. Not me." The whole thing is reminiscent of a child's attempt to get out of difficulties by inventing imaginary companions who do the work."[7]

(As perhaps I have brought in Ms. Lakoff to do my polemics for me.) The very least a critic can do in this regard is acknowledge his own responsibility for what he says. In doing so he opens up the closures a "scientific," "objective" knowledge of literature threatens to all the myriads of different personal experiences possible for a given poem.

I would like to go even further. In the traditional, or at least New Critical, mode of reading a poem, the critic converges the surface texture of details around a thematic center so as to grasp the organic unity this particular work shares with all other works of art. Fine. I believe, however, that we can add another mode, an outward movement. That is, a critic can bring associations from outside the poem, as it were, to the poem; he can pass them through the poem and see how they interact with the poem. This is the way, for example, I used Dr. Johnson's critical opinion of the metaphysical poets. I remembered his phrase about yoking heterogeneous ideas together, and I brought it to the poem as a kind of free association. It seemed to me to parallel the first stanza's concern with the yoking together of mother and child in blissful fusion. That led me to another intriguing contrast: Donne does not want people yoked together, but ideas; and he does not want ideas united in bliss but by violence. I don't know how that suits you—my passing Johnson's phrase through the poem—but it feels rather fitting and satisfying to me. If so, why not adopt a procedure that leads to satisfying readings?

The earlier, New Critical method pressed the poem inward toward its center, as the outside of a crystal images its core. This associative method I am suggesting reaches outward from the poem as the petals of a daisy go out from the center of the flower and come back, go out and come back, go out and come back. . . .[8] One reaches out for associations and tests them against the poem to see whether they satisfy or not.

It is a special kind of activity with a poem that allows me, for example, to use Donne's to structure my experience of all kinds of things in my life beyond the one poem. Certainly the deepest thread in my reading of "The Good-Morrow" is my distrust of Donne's move away from physical, earthy, fleshly love to abstract thought. That is perhaps why I used my reading of the poem to voice my doubts about recent trends in our literary criticism imported from France: structuralism; post-structuralism; Lacanian psychoanalysis; and Derridean deconstructivism. They make up part of my association to the poem. They seem to me to move, as the poem does, from the earthy realities of human experience to airy abstraction. In effect, in the last lines, the word "love," the nominal subject of the poem, becomes deconstructed. The real issue becomes the relationship between two different and one the same, between perfect likeness and imperfect resemblance leading to decay. I find in Donne's last lines an expression of a French aspiration to complete and utter intellectual clarity at the expense of sucking, snorting, possessing, pleasures, and ultimately, "troth." I can read Donne's lyric as a parable of the present state of criticism in America.

If I turn from a parabolic "Good-Morrow" to my simple gut reaction, however, I have to confess that I enjoy the poem's intellectual game. I like explicating Donne's tangled metaphors and syntax, and I like finding an overall unity in this very sequential poem. But I don't enjoy the transition the poem makes, particularly in the last stanza. I feel the poem flees from a human, even animal, dependency to a precise intellectual balance. That runs exactly counter to my own intellectual and critical maturing—or at least the way I want to move.

The last half dozen years or so, I have been writing and teaching less of the abstract, highly intellectual analysis I prized earlier. Now, for many private and professional reasons, I am groping toward establishing, acknowledging, enjoying, and enlarging an untidy but more human relation to a text like Donne's. The new French games are fun, yes, but they are as unreal as a Court of Courtly Love.

By contrast, our theoretical discoveries at the Center for the Psychological Study of the Arts ground reading in our personal styles and identities. Transactive criticism and transactive teaching offer us a way to have literature, not as an abstract discipline removed from life, but as we have always believed literature to be: a way, perhaps our best way, of articulating ourselves to ourselves, finding out who we are (our identities) and discovering why we care about the things we care about, like "The Good-Morrow."

NOTES

[1] Text ed. from *The Poems of John Donne,* ed. Herbert J. C. Grierson, 2 vols. (London: Oxford Univ. Press, 1912), 1, 7-8.

[2] Bertram D. Lewin, "Sleep, the Mouth and the Dream Screen," *Psychoanalytic Quarterly,* 15 (1946), 419-34.

[3] *Civilization and its Discontents* (1930), Ch. i, *The Standard Edition of the Complete Psychological Worrks of Sigmund Freud,* trans. and ed. James Strachey (London: Hogarth Press, 1953-74), 21, 64-67.

[4] Heinz Lichtenstein, "Identity and Sexuality," *Journal of the American Psychoanalytic Association,* 9 (1961), 179-260; *The Dilemma of Human Identity* (New York: Jason Aronson, 1977), ch. ii.

[5] See my *Poems in Persons* (New York: Norton, 1973), ch. ii, and *5 Readers Reading* (New Haven: Yale Univ. Press, 1975).

[6] For DEFT, see "Unity Identity Text Self," *PMLA,* 90 (1975), 813-22 or "Transactive Criticism: Re-Creation Through Identity," *Criticism,* 18 (1976), 334-52.

[7] "Why You Can't Say What You Mean," *Centrum,* 4 (1976), 151-70, 165.

[8] See English 692, "Poem Opening: An Invitation to Transactive Criticism," *College English,* 40 (September 1978) 2-16. See also my "How Can Dr. Johnson's Remarks on Cordelia's Death Add to My Own Response?," in *Psychoanalysis and the Question of the Text,* ed. Geoffrey Hartman (Baltimore, Md.: Johns Hopkins Univ. Press, 1978), pp. 18-44.

NEGOTIATED KNOWLEDGE OF LANGUAGE AND LITERATURE

by
David Bleich

During the past few decades, many in the language and literature professions have tried to formulate sophisticated new systems for developing knowledge in this field. Generative grammarians and speech-act theorists have brought new perspectives on language; structuralists, phenomenologists, and deconstructionists have proposed new attitudes and new practices for literary interpretations. Most of these efforts have been animated by the need to give language-based knowledge authority comparable to that enjoyed by mathematically based knowledge for the past three or four centuries. These efforts have been complicated, however, by the widespread belief that binding authority and absolute truth shall never be a feature of linguistically articulated knowledge, or of knowledge about language itself. As a result, there exists a particularly rich and interesting collection of opinion, but with no clear consensus on which single epistemology shall govern this large common interest, or on whether the search for a common epistemology should be abandoned altogether.

Although previous crises in epistemology, such as that precipitated by Copernicus, have had revolutionary social and religious effects, today's ferment has an especially urgent character because the universal means of human discourse is the topic as well as the means of investigation. We are no longer dealing with an image of the earth in the universe or with an hypothesis regarding the origin of life. We are dealing, rather, with the fact that when any linguistically formulated proposal of knowledge is scrutinized long enough and thoroughly enough, even the most familiar and reliable knowledge can come to seem like a superstition. Furthermore, and perhaps more importantly, close attention to language has shown that each human being holds a significant share of responsibility for the use of a common language, and that each person's use of language changes it, whether that person speaks in clichés, writes the lyric poetry in the bathtub, or lectures in academic prose in public places.

There have been repercussions of this state of affairs in most universities in this country. Students entering the university meet language and literature teachers who don't know how much authority they should wield; they want to grant each student's interpretation its due, but they also want to say that there are objective ways of distinguishing good interpretations from bad ones. Students perceive this situation as a contradiction which devalues the whole subject of interpretation. This perception leads to the growing sense that one cannot "do" anything with knowledge of language and literature, and the consequent increase of enrollment in marketing, mathematics, operant conditioning, and sports. The fact that each of these fields is ultimately dependent on language and on the psychology of its use is simply not known by either teachers or students of language and literature. Put another way, the authority of language and interpretation is not known in such a way that it can be made available as a matter of course in pedagogical, critical, and scholarly activity.

Perhaps the main historical reason that this situation has developed now, rather than, say, five hundred years ago, is that only for the past several generations has literacy become universal. Literacy has shown that knowledge, like language, is accessible, in principle, to any person, and that, like wealth, it can no longer be hoarded and dispensed, but must be developed in common, shared, and negotiated contexts when each new demand for it arises. Yet the habits, customs, and institutions of authorizing knowledge are still based on those which prevailed when most people were illiterate, just as political institutions seem reluctant to react to the belief that if wealth is not shared, the human race won't survive. The negotiation of knowledge is considered the privilege of an elite group of leaders, whose resulting opinions are then passed down through the ranks of drones and functionaries called deadwood senior faculty, junior faculty, associate instructors, and textbook authors. I think that if these latter groups *took* the responsibility that is normally *accorded* or *conceded* to those who write theoretical books, there would be no chain of command in the matter of knowledge, fewer authoritarian practices in the classroom, and more knowledge developed by those who want it, need it, and seek it for themselves.

In looking to document my opinion on this issue, I am going to discuss a recent instance of an attempt to negotiate knowledge among a group of critics many have regarded as leaders in our profession. I will try to show that among the six participants there are six opinions, that none is obviously truer than any other, that no one opinion is shared by all, that immediate personal and professional motives play a major role in what knowledge is proposed, that the opinions issued depend greatly on when one enters the discussion and under what circumstances, and that nevertheless I and many other readers can say with certainty that we know much more after reading the negotiation than we did before. I will then try to explain what sort of authority this knowledge has and why this is more or less the same authority borne by knowledge developed by younger or less experienced people. Finally, I will say why I think deliberately and self-consciously pursued negotiated knowledge, derived by assuming a subjective epistemology, will help make knowledge seeking practices in language and literature more productive.

I am using the term "negotiation" the way it is used to apply to labor-management discussions and diplomatic conferences. At such meetings, areas of agreement are usually brought out only to clear the space for inquiry into the areas of dispute. When agreement is reached, the negotiation stops. In matters concerning knowledge this is not quite the case, however. Agreement could mean the dissolution of the community of discussants, but more often it means that the "school of thought" will aim to expand its influence. I am therefore viewing negotiation as the fundamental practice in the growth of intellectual and pedagogical communities. Such growth proceeds on Darwinian principles, where persuasion is the index of strength of any one person or subgroup. In trying to understand a given negotiation, I will use a motivational explanation, or teleological analysis, which I discussed and tried to justify in my book *Subjective Criticism.*[1] Although there are many risks in adducing the motives of others from insufficient acquaintance with them, I would like to stress that the motives I propose in the present discussion are meant more to show what can be done more responsibly when negotiators are face to face, than to tell some final truth about the negotiation I am studying now. Also, a printed series of opinions and responses is actually only an abbreviation of something that happens in live conversation. If I had a recording of a real oral negotiation of similar length and complexity, I would use it to make my argument. However, the material I am using has been very enlightening to me, regardless.

In the Spring 1976 issue of *Critical Inquiry,* Wayne Booth began an inquiry into interpretive pluralism, which drew one or more responses in five subsequent issues of the journal.[2] In the collection of materials I am treating, there are two essays by Booth, three by Meyer Abrams, one by J. Hillis Miller, two by James Kincaid, one by Morse Peckham, and one by Robert Denham. All of the essays address what I, and the editors of *Critical Inquiry* I assume, consider a common purpose, namely to say if they think there are limits to interpretive pluralism, and if so what are they, and if not, why not. Put another way, the basic question is: if there are two or more acceptable meanings for any literary text, what is the truth-status of each meaning, and to what extent can one distinguish right meanings from wrong ones? If the meanings contradict one another, does this imply that one or more are erroneous?

Booth's opening essay gives this general issue a specific locus. He is considering Meyer Abrams' treatise, *Natural Supernaturalism,* which is a historical and interpretive study of the phenomenon of Romanticism. Booth asks "just how pluralistic Abrams is willing to be. Has he given us *the* history of his subject as he defines it, or *a* history? If, as I am sure, he would answer the latter, how far will he go with that answer?" Booth then cites several instances from Abrams's previous work which bear on the question. In *The Mirror and the Lamp,* Booth quotes Abrams saying that criticism is neither a physical nor a psychological science and that its aim is not predictive; its purpose, rather is "to establish principles enabling us to justify, order, and clarify our interpretation and appraisal of the aesthetic facts themselves. And as we shall see, these facts turn out to have the curious and scientifically reprehensible property of being conspicuously altered by the nature of the very principles which appeal to them for support. . . . Any hope, therefore for the kind of basic agreement in criticism that we have learned to expect in the exact sciences is doomed to disappointment." Booth then cites Abrams' statement of what a critical theory does.

> A good critical theory . . . has its own kind of validity. The criterion is not the scientific verifiability of its single propositions, but the scope, precision, and coherence of the insights that it yields into the properties of single works of art and the adequacy with which it accounts for diverse kinds of art. Such a criterion will, of course, justify not one, but a number of valid theories, all in their several ways of self-consistent, applicable, and relatively adequate to the range of aesthetic phenomena.

These citations, as well as material subsequently given by Abrams, answer Booth's main questions. Abrams is willing to accept any theory that gives "coherent insight into single works of art and accounts for diverse kinds of art." Abrams cannot say in advance what is not acceptable as a theory because the number of acceptable possible theories is indefinite; one can only judge a theory to give insight after its presentation. In replying to Booth in the same issue, Abrams calls this attitude relativistic.

> A humanistic demonstration, unlike a scientific demonstration, is rarely such as to enforce the consent of all qualified observers. For it to carry the reader through its exposition to its conclusions requires some grounds for imaginative consent, some comparative ordering of values, some readiness of emotional response to the matters shown forth, which the reader must share with the author even before he begins to read; and these common grounds are no doubt in part temperamental, hence variable from reader to reader. If this assertion constitutes relativism, then we simply have to live with the relativism it asserts, for it is an aspect of the human predicament which the languages and complex strategies of proof in humanistic inquiries are designed to cope with, but can never entirely overcome.

Theories of a nonpredictive nature, Abrams argues, achieve truth-status by the imaginative consent of the reader in areas where proof is intrinsically unavailable. Abrams says that in retrospect you can tell if an explanation is true or not, but that you cannot specify in advance what kind of explanation is needed.

It is significant that Abrams sees humanistic inquiry as always trying to overcome relativism, though it "can never entirely" do so. Booth differs from Abrams on this key point. At the beginning of his next essay, Booth says that "I shall now behave like a *true* pluralist, quite probably the *only* true pluralist you will ever have the good fortune to meet." Where this statement could have a degree of irony, his concluding statement in the same essay probably does not: "If the first commandment issued by my commonwealth is 'Pursue some one chosen monism as well as you can,' the second is like unto it: 'Give your neighbor's monism a fair shake.'" Although many may consider that these statements really do not disagree with Abrams, I think the subtle difference in emphasis is extremely important, namely, Abrams believes he is pursuing the truth, but with less chance of success than the scientist has; Booth believes he is trying to persuade others of what *he thinks* is the truth, with the emphasis on "he thinks." I will try to document this claim by citing different kinds of statements from the essay exchange between Booth and Abrams.

At the end of Booth's first discussion of Abrams' work, he writes,

> . . . I found myself more deeply moved by his book [*Natural Supernaturalism*] and the re-reading it led me to than I have been by any Romantic literature since my late teens. Apparently, I rediscovered in it my own romanticism, while coming to understand better something of why I had for decades thought myself as somehow, absurdly, "against" Romanticism. My revaluation could occur only because Abrams moved me beyond a concern for literal causation into consideration of the permanent validity of some Romantic responses to evil and suffering.

Booth reports that reading Abrams' book effected a change in his self-image from "one against romanticism" to "one who has romanticism in him." His new understanding felt like both an enlightenment about himself, and about Romanticism. Booth's subjective language shows a further feature of his experience. First he said "I found myself . . . moved by his book," and finally he said, "Abrams moved me . . ." By "subjective language" I mean, "referring to the subject's own experience." Booth first describes the passive feeling of being moved, but then locates the cause of the movement in Abrams the person. I don't think that Booth's statements are mere rhetorical points, though, given Booth's longstanding interest in rhetoric, they may *also* be rhetorically motivated. I believe that mainly Booth is aiming to present a strong personal credential for engaging Abrams' work and for challenging it. Being an author himself, Booth must know that one of the most common wishes authors have is that their readers feel, in one way or another, moved by their work. Booth is telling what he thinks is the truth about himself in such a way as to win the credence of the person he is challenging. This way is to tell the person directly how Booth was able to make Abrams' point of view his own. Booth has created authorization for the knowledge he is proposing to Abrams, as well as to the readers of *Critical Inquiry.*

Booth must also be speaking as one of the editors of *Critical Inquiry*, as one who wishes the new journal success and influence, as one whose own professional esteem is now connected with the fate of this journal. In a sense, the journal has singled out Abrams work for "inquiry," and there must be the most urgent reasons for this inquiry to proceed in the most enlightened, respectful, and convincing way. Accordingly, much of Booth's essay is a documentation of the senses in which he was moved and convinced by Abrams; he takes pains to rearticulate each feature of Abrams' reasoning he was able to make his own. At the end of the essay, he even creates a dialogue between an imaginary challenger to Abrams view, with himself, Booth, as the respondent to each of the challenges. In the last reply to the last challenge Booth presents the response quoted above, and this response creates the most telling context for the methodological challenge which preceded it.

Throughout the essay, Booth orients his discussion toward Abrams the person, and not Abrams the agent of a certain theory or method. By implication which none can miss, Booth is raising a nonpersonal question about pluralism, but it first emerges as a personal question, "What kind of pluralist is he?" In so doing, Booth acknowledges that interpersonal, face-to-face ethics will apply to his discussion, and that he will not hide behind either language or print. Thus, Booth does not avoid seeing proposals of knowledge in terms of personal purpose or taste or even prejudice. Could it be, his challenge to Abrams is, that Abrams already had a "Platonic" idea of Romanticism in mind, and that the evidence for it was searched out and found? Put in more colloquial terms, Booth's challenge is, don't you really believe that although other people can say other things about Romanticism, you have told a most significant portion of the permanent truth about it?

In his reply to Booth, Abrams indicates that he very much appreciates the careful and respectful study of his work. He credits Booth's "just analysis" with making him (Abrams) discover "what a strange book *Natural Supernaturalism* is and how extraordinary the claims it presumes to make on its readers." He says that he accepts many of Booth's "Abramsian" answers to the possible challenges Booth devised; but most of the essay is spent denying the charge of platonism, showing that his work is empirically founded, and reaffirming his belief that other true histories may be written.

In the exchange of opinion, Abrams' position is different from Booth's in that Abrams and his work are the subject and occasion for discussion. Part of the agreed upon common purpose is that Abrams will speak on his own behalf. In so doing, however, he reacts to Booth only in terms of courtesy and gratitude for Booth's generous remarks. He does not engage Booth's more personal response to his work. For example, in trying to refute Booth's suggestion that Abrams may be committed to "some permanent human interest or eternal idea," he does not mention that Booth, in his own response, quoted earlier, considered possible "permanent validity of some Romantic responses to evil and suffering." Perhaps, in other words, Booth "saw" the commitment to the "permanent human interest" because that is how Booth *felt* after reading the book. To Abrams, Booth was just "wrong" because Abrams considers only the objective question of whether such a committment was or was not in his intention. he has no inclination to attribute any truth-value to Booth's response. Abrams's rejoinder shows no feeling of enlightenment about his own work that Booth felt about his own intellectual attitudes.

Two similar phrases used by Abrams make this contrast somewhat clearer. First Abrams says that "Even Wayne Booth . . . suggests that I may be committed to (Platonic) belief. . . ." A few pages later he says, "Even Booth . . . fails to specify one recurrent tactic in *Natural Supernaturalism.*" That phrase ("even Booth") suggests, I think, Abrams' feeling that "even the most generous of my critics does not quite understand my work." If such a feeling was present in Abrams' reply, then it would not quite accord with Abrams' announced expectation that "humanistic demonstration . . . is rarely such as to enforce the consent of all qualified observers." Abrams seems less willing to overlook what he considers Booth's false perception, than Booth is willing to overlook what he considers an inconsistency in Abrams' work.

A short exchange of letters between Booth and René Wellek shows a negotiative contrast similar to the one between Booth and Abrams. In Booth's second essay, "Preserving the Exemplar," Booth criticized a section of *Theory of Literature* for its curt dismissal of psychologism in literary theory. In the footnote citing this work by Wellek and Austin Warren, Booth mistakenly listed the second author as Robert Penn Warren. After defending his conception of New Criticism, Wellek says that Booth did not try to refute his position, and adds that he is "afraid that Mr. Booth simply does not know what phenomenology is. It does seem pointless to try to enlighten him on this matter in a letter to the Editor." He infers, further, that because Booth had been mistaken about the second author, "he cannot properly know *Theory of Literature.*"

In his response, Booth first allows that "there is no real excuse" for his error in attributing authorship. He then clarifies what he thought he had said in his essay, namely, that he objected to Wellek's and Warren's brief argument dismissing positions other than theirs, but that he did not oppose Wellek's argument for his own position. He then says, that "On reconsideration I do think it was unfair of me not to have mentioned that in other contexts you have addressed some of the other theories about what a poem is in much greater detail." Finally, he argues that refutations usually have the effect only of affirming the refuter's position rather than actually showing the faults of the criticized theory, and that phenomenology and psychology ought to inform, rather than oppose, one another. Answering these remarks, Wellek writes, "You wrote me such a friendly and generous letter that I felt like withdrawing my letter to *Critical Inquiry*. But on second thought I let it stand as I wrote it. Your paper has been heard and read by many." He then adds that "I can only plead that I do not reject psychology or the psychology of the reader," that "Actually I agree with almost everything you say about the 'deconstructionist,'" and finally, that "I trust that we are not really very far apart on fundamentals."

Booth's response to Wellek ended the debate and radically changed the tone of Wellek toward Booth. I attribute Wellek's change in tone to the fact that Booth recongnized and documented Wellek's personal authority as a critic. The fact that Wellek did not withdraw his first letter makes his negotiative attitude seem similar (in my mind) to that of Abrams, however. That is, in spite of the fact that the important interpersonal problem was solved, Wellek stuck to the principle of "the truth." Booth's use of objectivity begins with a self-objectification and his willingness to re-examine this objectification in the interest of productive negotiation. Abrams' and Wellek's use of objectivity is directed toward the task of deciding who is telling the truth about *the other person's views*. The more subjective sense of truth yields more negotiation; the more objective sense, more argumentation and more personal defensiveness.

The exchange of opinion between Abrams and J. Hillis Miller shows less negotiation than a mutual attempt at refutation. Though each is friendly and respectful toward the other, this cordiality is used only superficially by Abrams in engaging Miller's position, and it is not used at all by Miller, who concentrates on showing how the assumptions of deconstructionism yield richer critical possibilities than the assumption, which he attributes to both Abrams and Booth, that there is any literary text an "obvious and univocal meaning" on which deconstructionist readings are "plainly and simply parasitical."

Abrams claims that the deconstructionist method "goes beyond the limits of pluralism, by making impossible anything that we could account as literary and cultural history." Abrams then phrases this general objection in more personal terms: "His central contention is not simply that I am sometimes, or always, wrong in my interpretation, but instead that I—like other traditional historians—can never be right in my interpretation." In a sense, Abrams' distinguished career is predicated on the assumption that interpretations can be "right" in the scientific sense of "truthful." If a form of thought arises which seems to devalue such a hard won accomplishment because of its false assumptions, one can understand Abrams' rejection of deconstructionism. Yet if Abrams believed less strenuously in the absoluteness of truth and falsity, the deconstructionist claim would seem less dangerous to him. Abrams would take more seriously than he does Miller's judgment—cited by Abrams in his second essay—that Abrams' book is in the "grand tradition of modern humanistic scholarship, the tradition of Curtius, Auerbach, Lovejoy, C. S. Lewis." He would also take more seriously his own recognition of Miller's strength:

> There are, I want to emphasize, rich rewards in reading Miller, as in reading Derrida, which include a delight in his resourceful play of mind and language and the many and striking insights yielded by his wide reading and by his sharp eye for unsuspected congruities and differences in our heritage of literary and philosophical writings.

The traditional instinct for the scientific "true and false" of human experience is permanently part of Abrams' language system; it would be as difficult for him to redefine this vocabulary as it would for him to learn Yoruba. And there is every personal motive and justification for him to retain this traditional language and continue developing it as he has. Yet there is no need for him to think of Miller as a "double agent who plays the game of language by two very different sets of rules," meaning, the rules of discursive reasoning and the rules of deconstructive interpretation. Abrams had himself argued that to tell the truth about some things you use one form of evidence or justification, and to tell the truth about other things, different documentations apply. Why doesn't Abrams see Miller's two sets of rules as telling the truth in two different ways? The only possible answer shown in Abrams' essays is that he sees this form of thought as telling him that he can "never be right in my interpretation." And being objectively right is the belief that brought Abrams the great authority he already has.

Miller, in his presentation of deconstructionst criticism, did not see Abrams' second essay before writing his own; Miller is therefore responding to material that appeared in the first exchange between Booth and Abrams discussed above. Had he seen this second essay, his own effort would undoubtedly have been more directly responsive to the strong charges made by his friend Abrams. Nevertheless, Miller's remarks are enlightening with regard to his own point of view and his means of participating in the public negotiation.

In establishing his ground of dispute, Miller picked a formulation that combined statements made by Booth and Abrams; the phrase "plainly and simply parasitical" is Booth's; the phrase "obvious or univocal meanings" is Abrams'. In creating this combination, Miller defines an area of apparent agreement between the two critics. Whether it would remain an agreement in the context in which I compared the two is another matter. The main point is that relative to Miller's perspective, the two are in *sufficient* agreement for Miller's argument to proceed against them. Or, Miller *defined* his opposition in such a way as to facilitate his own argument. Miller implies, moreover, that Booth is not quite the pluralist he says he is because of his belief in the concept of parasitical readings; that is, Booth must believe that one sort of reading is prior to, or more basic than, all the others. In responding to Abrams' concern about the deconstructionist challenge to literary historians, Miller says that any *claim* that such histories cannot be written *does nothing to prevent* a critic from writing such a history. In this brief address to the separate concerns of his two co-negotiators, Miller argues that because their claims devalue or exclude his own work, their sense of pluralism is inadequate.

The bulk of Miller's argument to this effect is his discussion of the single word, "parasitical." With a series of etymological and literary citations, Miller reasons that it is indeterminate whether the critic is parasitical on the literature (with its univocal and obvious meaning) or whether the literature is parasitical on the "host" critic, whose store of culturally developed meanings for words and stories is the very thing that makes literature possible. His conclusion is that both of these views obtain:

> In fact, neither the "obvious" reading nor the "deconstructionist" reading is "univocal." Each contains, necessarily, its enemy within itself, is itself both host and parasite. The deconstructionist reading contains the obvious one and vice versa. Nihilism is an inalienable presence within Occidental metaphysics, both in poems and in the criticism of poems.

Although Abrams had charged Miller with Nietzschean nihilism, Miller goes on to affirm that nihilism is not only a part of his own critical attitude but that it is also "inalienable" from Occidental metaphysics. In this way, Miller accepts Booth's use of the term "parasitical" even in its critical opposition to Miller. What his critics used as a criticism, he considers a fact about his work. There is ground for claiming, therefore, that Miller's deconstructionism, relative to the foregoing discussion between Booth and Abrams, is more versatile, more flexible, more interesting, and more pluralist, than the earlier notions of pluralism. In the process of affirming that there is an absence of meaning at the center of a literary work, deconstruction reveals a whole collection of relevant meanings—and many irrelevant ones nevertheless admissible—that greatly enrich reading and criticism.

Miller's professional career followed a path somewhat different in intellectual allegiance than either Booth's or Abrams'. Miller's early work applied phenomenology to practical criticism; his later work applied deconstructionism. There is no comparably marked shift of affiliation for either Booth or Abrams. The attempt to apply independently developed systems of thought to literature—systems such as Marxism, Freudianism, Catholicism, or Structuralism—is viewed by many as a "parasitical" enterprise, where the critic is being parasitical on the system, deriving his sustenance from the preformed ideas, and then understanding the literature as an instance of these ideas. Critics like Northrop Frye have repeatedly argued that criticism ought to develop its own system of thought and its own unique vocabulary for explaining its subject, literature. Miller is admittedly not only investigating the single word, but is aiming to explore the concept and the critical practice that so-called "parasitism" involves. His point is, in part, that the destructive element in critical practice is inevitable, and that admitting it is there is more profitable than "to fool oneself or be fooled." His justification of parasitism is, then, an argument against Booth and Abrams, an affirmation of his own present perspective, a reconceptualization of his own career history, a claim of truth, and a claim of what he considers a critical attitude more valuable than traditional interpretation and historicism.

James R. Kincaid's first contribution to the larger inquiry

is his essay, "Coherent Readers, Incoherent Texts," which was originally written in response to an earlier debate in *Critical Inquiry* between Stanley Fish and Ralph Rader on a very similar issue. After the essay was accepted for publication, the editors asked him to change his essay so that it addressed the pluralism discussed as well as the Fish-Rader exchange. In so doing, Kincaid developed a wider perspective for his opinions and thereby broadened the scope of the negotiation in general.

Kincaid sees the debate—with Booth, Abrams, and Rader on one side, and Miller and Fish on the other—as presenting "positions so extreme and so starkly clear that no one needs a comparative listing of the assumptions at work." One position is that all texts have a determinate central core of meaning, and the other position is that such meanings are illusory—they simply don't exist. Kincaid aims to "mediate"—and hopefully solve—this dispute with a new idea namely, that "Booth and Abrams are right (or more right) about readers; Miller about texts and language generally." This means that determinate meanings are found in literary texts as a consequence of "our need for them." The reader's need for determinate meanings motivates him to see such in the texts; thus, at different times, a reader may use several different perspectives to establish meaning, even though both the perspectives and the meanings may contradict one another. Because texts may be shown to serve contradictory meanings, it follows that the texts are not intrinsically coherent. This position, he argues, does not lead to the "notion of genre or organizing pattern as a chimera of an out-dated positivism that falsely objectifies the text." Rather, "Signs, however various, come in patterns all the same," and these patterns "may and do cohabit very strangely indeed." In fact, critics ought not pretend, in conceiving what literature is, that "a busy whorehouse is a monastic cell." The primary "experience with literature" is created when the "text's impossible duplicity" clashes with attempts to deal with it using monistic notions of coherence. He had earlier claimed that the "basic principle governing reading is precisely the fear of logical contradiction, more narrowly and obedience to the law of identity. . . ." His essay gives several instances of texts that are duplicitous, but cites mainly Northrop Frye's scheme of generic classification as a monistic reading practice. Texts are duplicitous and promiscuous; readers are monastic and monistic.

It is probably a coincidence that Kincaid characterizes texts, casually, as helping to make reading a licentious activity, and that less interesting sorts of reading are practised by an ordained minister. Yet, Robert Denham's often sarcastic response to Kincaid's essay could be partially traceable to this fanciful—but serious—element in the essay. A more likely reason for Denham's strong reaction, however, is that he edited a Northrop Frye bibliography and a forthcoming collection of Frye's essay-reviews. Furthermore, he aligns himself with Rader and Hirsch as being committed to the discovery of determinate meanings in literary texts. He seems to feel that Kincaid is a rather sloppy or careless thinker who, typically, "slides rather easily from topic to topic, moving, for example, from 'intention' to 'structure' or from 'meaning' to 'form' with hardly a clue as to how we get from one to the other." Addressing the substantive issue in the essay, Denham says that Kincaid just did not do what he said he intended to do: "To mediate, at least, is his stated intention. But it is no less clear that his ultimate allegiance is to the deconstructionist camp." Because of this allegiance, he says that Kincaid believes that "there is, finally, very little knowledge to be shared, for our inquiries will always arrive at the same conclusion."

The dispute between Denham and Kincaid is mainly over the applicability of concepts of genre to explain individual texts, and less over which "camp" each is in. In both essays, however, this question of allegiance plays a very large role, in the sense that which camp one belongs to determines how generic explanation will be used. On this issue a difference between Denham and Kincaid becomes very clear. Kincaid, who believes that texts cannot be easily placed in camps, sees himself as a mediator between camps. Denham, who believes that texts can be so placed, sees himself and Kincaid as also easily placed. If the dispute is viewed as between two different tendencies of personality—one who prefers more categorical clarity and one who prefers less—we outsiders to the negotiation can discover the extent to which, in ourselves, each tendency plays a role. This knowledge then becomes a personally trustworthy guide for sorting out features in any series of differing opinions that will best help define our developing intellectual policies.

Just as Booth, relative to Abrams and Wellek, is the more

self-conscious negotiator, Kincaid is more self-conscious relative to Denham. Booth announces that he is a pluralist and then tries to show both personally and intellectually why he thinks so about himself. Kincaid announces that he is a mediator and likewise gives those two sorts of reasons for his claim. Kincaid gives his more personal reasons in his reply to Denham's essay. In responding to Denham's charge that he was confusing Frye's and Sheldon Sacks's generic system, Kincaid writes,

> I had thought that I was signalling clearly the switch from Frye to Sacks, that neither was using "genre" in an unfamiliar or restrictive sense, and that both presented useful systems that were comprehensive and thus adaptable—as time has surely shown—for the labeling and pigeonholing needs of those seeking coherence at all costs. Since Frye sees narrative patterns as "pre-generic," it would not be difficult to work out coordinations simply by saying that Sacks' three general categories of fiction could each exist in any of Frye's twenty-four phases. But things are not that simple, and more important, such devices would surely distract a reader I wanted to be in search of other game.

Very few critics present statements to the effect that "I want my reader to think in these terms or of these ideas." Perhaps because Kincaid is a Victorian scholar he more easily adopts usages of Victorian novelists. In its immediate context the thought comes as a reason for rejecting generic systems he generally respects but which he believes lend themselves to the abuse of the overly singleminded. Finally the thought announces that Kincaid aims to persuade his reader rather than tell him a truth he cannot but accept. This latter aim is also served by Kinciad's explicit indications of how parts of other systems are to be applied, and why certain uses of these systems do not answer to his own critical values. Although partial citation of other people's critical theories is widely practised, few critics allow that the selection is discriminatory, and even fewer allow that the discrimination is taking place in the service of their own point of view, which they already know to be different than that of the person whose work is cited as documentation. Abrams also argued for the selective use of documentation, but his justification is that the truth is better served as opposed to his own critical purpose.

In this connection, it should be noted that one of Abrams' ways of criticizing Miller is similar to one of Denham's ways of criticizing Kincaid. Abrams and Denham try to render Miller's and Kincaid's essays, respectively, as evidence against the principles the essays are advocating. Abrams sees Miller's discursive presentation to an audience as evidence of Miller's belief in determinate meaning. (This is why Abrams had called him a "double agent" in the game of language.) Denham tries to characterize Kincaid's own essay as an instance of textual incoherence. Kincaid's response, after getting over his exasperation at Denham's argumentative strategy, is to remind him that the topic of public discussion is the interpretation of literature, and not discursive negotiative practices; the same rejoinder could apply to Abrams' criticism of Miller. This is a typical instance of the problems that arise in the use of language to study language. There is no clear way to accept one use of language as more authoritative than another use. Kincaid's rejoinder to Denham implies that authorizing a specific use is a community decision, which, in this case, is the decision to discuss literary interpretation. However, since there was never any *explicit* definition of which sort of argument is inadmissible, two critics felt free enough to use other critics' text as analogous to literary texts, regardless of the key fact that the critic's text is an instrument of a living person facing his reader, and a literary text is a remaining artifact whose human source is extinct. Other distinctions between the two sorts of texts can be made, but unless negotiating communities *consciously* circumscribe their purpose, the justification of objective truth will permit any argumentative strategy to be acceptable. If each critic announces his purpose, a communal purpose is negotiated, and arbitrary shifts of context do not occur. In this instance the two critics advocating tighter limits on pluralism felt free enough to shift the context of discussion.

Morse Peckham entered the debate at the same time as Kincaid. His opinion, like Kincaid's, utilizes a retrospective advantage on the discussion. But where Kincaid sees himself "between" two camps, Peckham places his view above and beyond the others'. After summarizing what he considers the substance of the investigation, he reaches the following judgment about it:

It comes down to this. It is idle of Miller and Booth, and Abrams too, to talk about the methodology of interpreting complex literary texts before thay have determined what interpretational behavior is in ordinary, mundane, routine verbal interaction. The explanation for this statement lies in the logical and historical subsumption of written texts by spoken verbal behavior, in the subsumption of spoken verbal behavior by semiotic behavior, and in the subsumption of semiotic behavior by whatever it is we are responding to when we use the word "meaning."

Peckham argues that the principals in the "controversy" were not starting at the beginning, and that as a result, much of the foregoing debate is "idle." It is the case, however, that the "beginning" was *defined* as Abrams' methodology in *Natural Supernaturalism;* someone else's address to this defined beginning can be called "idle," only if the more fundamental matters that Peckham contributes are accepted as explanations of the issues at hand. I think it is the attitude of Peckham's that can call the whole debate "idle" that helped bring Abrams back to oppose him.

Booth's first essay cited Peckham's comment on Abrams' book: "Certainly the best book on Romanticism I have ever read." Booth then points out that after offering this praise, "Peckham summarizes the book in terms that he can easily repudiate." Why, then, would Peckham praise the book only to find a way to repudiate its main thesis? He does continue this repudiation in his present contribution. Peckham's essay suggests at least one possible reason for his negotiative strategy. He reports that

As long ago as 1900 George Herbert Mead said that the meaning of a sign is the response to it. More than a decade ago, without knowing of Mead's statement, I came to the same conclusion, backed into it by the failure of twentieth-century philosophy to deal successfully with the word "meaning."

On his own, frustrated by a monumental failure in a whole academic discipline, Peckham discovered the meaning of "meaning." Because of his belief in the fundamentality of his own discovery, Mead's earlier work notwithstanding, he feels able to judge his colleagues' discussion "idle." Peckham's sense of his own more inclusive perspective leads to his outline of interpretational genres, which permits the classification of Abrams' methodology, and provides the ground for disputing the thesis that emerges from the methodology. Abrams' work is the best of its kind, but its kind is not the best.

Peckham distinguishes two forms of interpretation, situational and emergent. Situational interpretation is historical and aims to see individual literary works as part of the culture upon which their authors drew. Emergent interpretation is the use of an independently developed ideology, whose practitioners believe in its supervening explanatory power to explain literary works as the manifestations of the forces described by the ideology. Examples of the latter are Marxism, Freudianism, Catholicism, Structuralism, Deconstructionsim, Existentialism, Phenomenology, and so on. Emergent interpreters believe that their ideology is in effect today, situational interpreters that the explanatory factors were all historically present at the work's time and place of origin.

Peckham claims to understand Abrams' work because of his own familiarity with and use of the same methods:

> He has identified his recurrent pattern as a Christian pattern which was continued in the post-Christian period by a semiotic transformation which he calls secularization of the pattern. His claim is that in this behavior he is repeating what his group of Romantic authors did, the perceptual disengagement of a pattern and its transformation. (I am reasonably sure that this is what he did because I did much the same thing long ago.)

Is Peckham saying that he has already done what Abrams has done? Perhaps so. Perhaps methodologically, perhaps substantively. Peckham is more clearly claiming that he has transcended the local sphere of situational interpretation, which he practiced "long ago." As a result of his own growth, he argues at the end of his essay, he has come to reject the redemption of the Romantics, secular or religious, because of its nefarious role in the creation of such twentieth-century villains as Hitler and Stalin. The twentieth century's "analytic tradition" in philosophy has fostered a pluralistic atmosphere in politics and art, with whose products Peckham feels more comfortable, and one of these is deconstructionism:

> It is worth considering how often in the past 190 years secular redemptionism has turned into brutal and bloody authoritarianism. I do not think Miller understands what he is doing, but I am glad that he is doing it, for he is maintaining the analytic tradition. Abrams assures us that the secular redemptionism of the early Romantics offers us reasonable grounds for hope.   We know better.

Peckham thinks Abrams understands what he is doing, but it is politically naive; Miller does not understand what he is doing, but Peckham thinks it represents a more humane politics. Wayne Booth's discussion is not engaged at all, and Booth appears in Peckham's essay as the imaginary man who orders coffee from a waiter in a restaurant as an instance of ordinary discourse the interpretation of which becomes a model for Peckham's theory of interpretation.

In responding to Peckham's essay, Abrams allows him a degree of rhetorical latitude but also does not fail to answer Peckham's debate-transcending posture.   About Peckham's argument Abrams says that his "behavioral theory of language neither clarifies nor helps to resolve the points at issue between traditional cultural history and Miller's deconstructionism." The reason for this failure is that "Morse Peckham belongs to the class of thinkers that A. O. Lovejoy called *esprits simplistes.*   That is, he is impatient with the clutter and tangle of our experience in using language and is convinced that a few simple principles underlie the seeming disorder and complexities." Abrams even implies a motive for this impatience, in citing a series of his formulations which view language and culture as instruments of controlling behavior.   Peckham's announced political interests, as well as the title of his forthcoming volume, *Explanation and Power: An Inquiry into the Control of Human Behavior,* support Abrams' implication, which is that Peckham's interest in control may be obscuring his perception of the uncontrollable, and thus devaluing the authority of his generalizations.

On the matter of political prudence, or historical prophecy, Abrams poses the following question to Peckham:

> Which of the following alternatives is more apt to open a cultural vacuum that will be filled by power-hungry authoritarians who have no doubts about what they want nor scruples about how to get it:—A systematic and sustained enterprise to deconstruct the grounds of all truths or values asserted by our culture-bearing texts, and to subvert even our confidence that we can communicate determinately with each other? Or a reformulated version of the central Romantic hope that, by a revolution of mind and heart, man may yet achieve unity with himself, community with his fellow men, and reconciliation with a nature in which, because it has been humanized, he can feel at home?

If Peckham tries to transcend Abrams, Abrams tries to transcend him right back, telling him, perhaps, to be more humble in the face of what will always resist scientific reduction. Yet the nature of this exchange between the two suggests that Peckham's belief in the impulse to control has been at least partially documented by this negotiation. Each has at least some interest in the intellectual control of the discussion, and then of the critical community which views the discussion. With his three essays, Abrams has already exercised considerable control—though obviously not command—of the issues before the group. It is either strange or even reprehensible that Peckham should try to take control by trying to place the issues in what he considers a more comprehensive and satisfying context? Is it not true that Kincaid's mediation or Booth's scrupulous pluralism also contribute concepts that, if believed, will control and order other contributions? Is it not also the case that the more doctrinaire arguments of Miller and Denham seek and exercise less control because of their concentration on developing their own points of view?

As much is told by the negotiating practices of the various critics as by the referential meaning of their claims. On the surface, practices and claims don't always correspond to one another; put another way, one cannot easily find the right language to articulate just how they correspond. It should be clear right from my own remarks, however, that one can define for each critic such a correspondence. This correspondence derives from how each of us integrates and unifies our perceptions of other people, what weight we assign to their thoughts, what weight to their manners, their vocabulary, their self-awareness, their consideration of our needs. Within the negotiation, these processes were taking place, and the nature of all the disputes may be understood in these terms.

Probably the most certain knowledge that I was able to derive from this negotiation is my clear concept of the six principles. I do not know any one of them personally. Furthermore, I don't think the path of my career will resemble the paths of any of these critics either in terms of subject matter or professional purpose. Yet the next time I see any of their names in print, I will look to see what they have to say, because, by virtue of today's public remarks, I have joined their community, and I am responsible to them because of the claims I made about their work.

This knowledge and this responsibility will be translated in some way into action, either in my classroom, other public forums, or in print. I will then be responsible to others, as I am to you, for persuading them of the integrity, validity, and reliability of what I say I know. In varying degrees, the six participants were likewise aware of their corresponding responsibility. Although I thought, for example, that Booth was more responsible than Denham, couldn't anyone say that because I agree more with Booth than with Denham, I justify this choice with moral encomiums? Yes, you could say just that, but then you and I will discuss a whole range of issues. You will identify yourself to me as much as I have to you, and in discussing pluralism and generic criticism, we will each try to define how important these issues are to us, what stake we have, professionally, pecuniarily, psychologically, traditionally, in the ideas we say we believe in. In other words, if we are to be responsible to one another, we shall not be able to avoid involving, through oral announcement, our subjective vocabulary of motives both as they appear to us in retrospect and as they appear to us in the present situation.

It should be obvious that this group of six discussants has not decided just what the limits of pluralism are. So much energy was spent in exploring the matter, yet nothing decisive was established in the sense that all readers will leave the debate with the same sense of pluralism and the same sense of how it ought to be limited. Yet it can't be denied that members of the negotiating community came out with knowledge similar in nature to the knowledge that I came out with, namely, they knew the other members of the negotiating community much better than before, both what their opinions are and how they handle these opinions as a function of their purposes and motives. As is well known, the latter component of this knowledge is considered an interference to the former. If, for example, Abrams is irritated with Peckham, Abrams will try to overlook this feeling and instead use an appropriately demeaning epithet, like "simplistic spirit" originated by yet another critic, but which aims to characterize the thought and not the individual. *Ad hominem* motives usually undergo elaborate disguises, with the result that ideas often are expressed with such sanctimony that one wonders, for example, how textual explication could ever become a cause. The reason for this is, though, that any studied articulation of ideas involves the thinker's full mobilization of personality, an adjustment of his personal life, an examination of his purposes and aims, an invocation of his ambitions and a suppression of abiding fears. To imagine that such forces are absent from the background and character of an intellectual document is superstition. There is no purpose but self-deception served by denying a person's own stake and involvement in what he urges others to know.

Leaders are more able, and less willing, than younger people and students to articulate their personal stake in what they consider knowledge. When these backgrounds are brought out, however, knowledge is shown to be age-specific: people think in certain ways *just because* they are older or younger. The fact that older people think they know more than younger people is based on the fact that as one gets older, one inevitably sees the actions of one's own youth as wasteful errors, that wisdom is what one has now. We too easily forget that younger people are now older than they were before, and their confidence in their own perspective is equivalent, though not identical, to our own. In proposing knowledge, a subjective epistemology aims to make use of that confidence and to explore its basis as fully as possible.

This epistemology is especially necessary when we wish to know about language and literature. The growth of our personal language system is the means we have of becoming aware of, and evaluating, our own growth. A proposal of knowledge about language requires knowledge of *whose* language we think we know about, and how our own language helped create our perception of that of others. In reading, we are perceiving someone else's language, and despite the understanding we get from apparently stable meanings and syntax, it is easy to be deceived about this understanding because we are just not aware of just how our less conscious or less palpable kinds of knowledge go to work. Knowledge such as this comes into play automatically, but it is always motivated—that is, it is always meant to serve an individual in one way or another. When we decide that we were "wrong" about something, we mean that our knowledge did not serve in our desired interests. Issues of right and wrong interpretation therefore depend on knowledge of our own interests.

Negotiated knowledge of language and literature is the only kind available under conditions of universal literacy. Received knowledge can come only from authoritarian sources; revealed knowledge comes from mystics, seers, and gods. Negotiated knowledge is created by us ordinary people when we decide to reduce our common ignorance.

NOTES

[1] Baltimore: Johns Hopkins Univ. Press, 1978. See especially, the beginning and end of Chapter Two. It should be noted that the present essay was undertaken in response to the important criticism by Michael Steig of the above treatise that it did not make sufficiently clear either the concept or practice of negotiation. The following discussion shows only one sort of negotiation that may be familiar. A motivational explanation is adaptable to many such common inquiries, but it remains to be shown just how the adaptation might be made.

[2] Here are the full bibliographical references to the essays under discussion. The text makes it relatively clear which parts of which essays

I am discussing at the moment, so I will not footnote the various citations individually. Also, all the essays appeared in *Critical Inquiry*, so I will not repeat this fact in the following list.

Wayne C. Booth, "M. H. Abrams: Historian as Critic, Critic as Pluralist," 2, No. 3 (Spring 1976), 411-446.

M. H. Abrams, "Rationality and Imagination in Cultural History: A Reply to Wayne Booth," same issue, 447-464.

Wayne C. Booth, "'Preserving the Exemplar': or, How Not to Dig Our Own Graves," 3, No. 3 (Spring 1977), 407-424.

M. H. Abrams, "The Deconstructive Angel," same issue, 425-438.

J. Hillis Miller, "The Critic as Host," same issue, 439-448.

James R. Kincaid, "Coherent Readers, Incoherent Texts," 3, No. 4 (Summer 1977), 781-802.

Morse Peckham, "The Infinitude of Pluralism," same issue, 803-816.

M. H. Abrams, "Behaviorism and Deconstruction: A Comment on Morse Peckham's 'The Infinitude of Pluralism,'" 4, No. 1 (Autumn 1977), 181-193.

Robert Denham, "The No-Man's Land of Competing Patterns," same issue, 194-202.

René Wellek and Wayne C. Booth, "Critical Response," same issue, 203-206.

James R. Kincaid, "Pluralistic Monism," 4, No 4 (Summer 1978), 839-845.

MOTIVES FOR INTERPRETATION: INTENTION, RESPONSE, AND PSYCHOANALYSIS IN LITERARY CRITICISM

by

Michael Steig

Having for some years considered myself a psychoanalytic critic, I cannot help but find it ironic that I now tell my students that I am not a "Freudian," that I don't believe in trying to psychoanalyze authors through their works, and that phallic and other body symbolism has no special status among meanings discoverable in the process of reading literature. The reason for such diffidence in the author of such monuments of purportedly objective interpretation as "Dickens' Excremental Vision" and "Anality in *The Mill on the Floss*" is that I have become too aware of the problematic nature of the critical enterprise—how, why, and indeed what we interpret—and too skeptical about the possibility of arriving at objective meaning through systematically applied psychoanalytic categories, to continue on my pathway of confident assertion about literary meanings.[1]

In an intellectual community where a Murray Krieger finds it necessary to write defenses of the "distinctness of the poetic response" and the usefulness of what he grants is the "myth of total interpretability,"[2] while varieties of reader-response and subjective criticism flourish, critical concepts which once seemed fairly stable are now up for grabs. Many of us are now not sure what literary meaning, intention, effect, and response are, and meanwhile post-structualist theorists preach the joys of endless interpretation, the continual production of discourse, once one is freed from the tyrannies of the author's intention, the intentionality of words, and of referentiality to anything but language itself.

The recent book by Gerald Graff, *Literature Against It-self*,[3] while revealing the self-contradictions and questioning the ethics of deconstructionism, does not fully grant the genuineness of the problem, and offers no alternative but a rival dogma of objective and referential interpretation. The ever-present difficulties stand out most clearly, I think, in the work of E. D. Hirsch, who was, in *Validity In Interpretation*, one of the staunchest defenders of the author's intention as equivalent to meaning.[4] In his later book, *The Aims of Interpretation*, Hirsch acknowledges, in reply to criticisms of his position, that "meaning" cannot be restricted to "conceptual meaning," but "embraces not only any content of mind represented by written speech but also the affects and values that are necessarily correlative to such a content."[5] The word "necessarily" is a giveaway, for who can tell us how to identify the necessary, as opposed to the idiosyncratic, "correlative affects and values"? As soon as we move out of the area of philological and historical explication of words in their immediate contexts we are in the dizzying realm of subjectivity, where nothing can really be proven. Yet in fact many literary critics today—psychoanalytic or otherwise—not only labor in that realm but do so without showing any signs of vertigo. Whatever doubts they may harbor in secret, their style usually exudes confidence in the truth of the interpretations they offer, though these will often be followed by others written with equal confidence, expressing different, even opposite, views. And this unwarranted confidence helps to fuel the "cognitive atheism" (to use E. D. Hirsch's term)[6] of post-structuralist theorists.

Why, apart from the need to publish or to have something to say to our students, do we bother with interpretation at all? It is my working hypothesis that the impulse to interpret, to create a new text about a previous one, follows upon some kind of affective reponse to the literary work. Like any emotional response that initial reaction is inchoate, and for some readers so private as to be threatened by detailed examination. All teachers of literature have had students who protest that it spoils a poem to analyze it. This *may* reflect intellectual laziness, but I think more often it is an expression of genuine anxiety, as though one might find out something one is afraid of knowing. But the professional interpreter, who does not suffer from this block, usually works out his unacknowledged impulse to understand the complex of his response in the form of an impersonal discussion of structure, style, plural symbolic meanings, and analogies to myth or Freudian, Jungian, or other system-derived categories. If the critic alludes to response at all, it is in a distancing, generalizing fashion: the "effect" of the work is mentioned as though there is a single correct way to respond. Even some current reader-response theory, notably that of Wolfgang Iser, tends to make such an assumption about the effect of a literary work.[7]

The need to come to terms with the affective impact of literature is evident in most varieties of interpretation, even in the *Anatomy of Criticism,* which, despite Northrop Frye's scientific pretensions, is perhaps the most elaborate structure ever created to both justify and distance one critic's responses. And while he insists that we read literature *as* literature and not as something else, Frye's discourse constantly moves towards the rationalizing of literature into "something else," namely myth, informed by a blend of anthropological and Freudian, Jungian, and Christian precepts. But few interpreters of literature are either as ambitious as Frye, or as pure as that fiction, the New Critic, remaining completely within the text. Most of us appropriate limited areas of literature, using whatever mixture of methodologies feels most congenial, and leads to the desired end: something like the "homeostasis" that Andrew Brink has recently described as the goal of creative activity.[8] We seek to still questions, reduce anxiety, to regularize the relationship between ourselves and the literary work. Yet because there is something fulfilling in the very activity of seeking and solving, we look for new areas to conquer and control, new puzzles to solve, new works to which we must define our relationship.

But what are the actual objects of such searches? Fredric Jameson has defined criticism as "not so much an interpretation of content as . . . a revealing of it, a laying bare, a restoration of the original method, the original experience, beneath the distortions of the censor."[9] This definition assumes that literature always elaborates and disguises an ideational, emotional, and situational content, which Jameson calls "the object forbidden" (p. 17). Although Jameson's perspective is Marxist, his hermeneutic model is derived from Freud. Indeed, it contains the basic Freudian assumption that manifest content is not equivalent to meaning. And, if the vexed question of conscious and unconscious meanings is laid aside, it looks very like a model of all interpretive acts. I shall come back later to Jameson's attempted distinction between "interpretation" and "revealing," but for the moment shall assume for the purpose of talking about the relation between reading, interpretation, and the author that meaning in literature is hidden, in a number of senses. First, there are all those modes of indirection and duplicity which characterize imaginative writing: if the author had nothing to disguise, one might say, he would have no need to write literature. Secondly, meaning is hidden from us by our own failures to conceptualize and objectify the aspects of the reading experience which are emotionally important for *us*. This idea, in turn, is based on an assumption that literary meaning in general is, functionally, hidden from us because it comes into existence only when it is constructed by a reader.

The difficulties of literary interpretation are compounded by the fact that literature is frequently, if not "normally," perceived as both the product of a purposive, historically located human activity, and a structure of what Roman Ingarden called "represented objects,"[10] which make vividly present to the reader purposive acts by fictive personae or characters. It has been common in modern critical practice to disregard one or the other of these qualities, to treat literature as either utterance *or* representation. We have yet to recover from the effects of Wimsatt and Beardsley's commandment, Thou shalt not consider the author (The Intentional Fallacy), and the deconstructionists have not only revived this commandment in more extreme and dogmatic form (no authors, only *écriture*), but have denied the referential or mimetic quality as well. The freedom such a denial is supposed to provide feels to me more like oppression, for it is a denial of what many serious readers commonly do: experience literary works as both vividly represented realities, and the productions, the utterances, of authors. (Michel Foucault identifies an "author-function" which he finds relevant only for certain eras in literature and criticism. His claim that we must now dispense with that function, as a hindrance to the free play of critical discourse, strikes me as an arbitrary proclamation, based on a narrow definition of how the "author" functions for readers.)[11]

It is because of what I sense as the prevalence in readers of this dual mode of literary apprehension that I consider it neither true to the act of reading to assert that literature does not make propositional statements (which is the position of Ingarden and the New Critical theorists),[12] nor to insist that literary meaning can be located satisfactorily *in* propositional statements (which Hirsch seemed to be close to saying in *Validity in Interpretation*). One's understanding of literary meaning lies somewhere on a continuum between the cognition of utterance and of representation. But when the reader is allowed into the model of interpretation we then have: the meaning elaborated and disguised by the author through representation and utterance, and the meaning in part apprehended and in part hidden from himself by the reader, and constructed for himself somewhere along that continuum. The goal of interpretation then becomes to discover one's own position in relation to the work and its author, and in relation to one's response insofar as that can be objectified and analyzed. The use of psychoanalytic schemata is not a privileged method in this process, and when taken beyond the basic model of hidden meaning presents the danger of getting between the reader and his experience of the text— though knowledge of such schemata can also be one kind of stimulus to the process.

Recently, in teaching a graduate course in children's literature, I re-read *Treasure Island* for the first time since childhood. At first, after years of doing what presumed to be objective, psychoanalytically based interpretations, I found myself laying out a neat pattern of "oedipal" meanings—oedipal, that is, with the element of incest fantasy repressed, and the son's fantasy of defeating or killing the father central. Thus, Jim Hawkins loses his father, encounters a series of substitute fathers (both good and evil), and ends in triumph over them all, defeating the pirates and exonerating himself in the eyes of the doubting "good" fathers. Yet at the center there remains Long John Silver, towards whom Jim's feelings fluctuate between affection, jealousy, and hatred, and who by the novel's end perfectly embodies the opposite qualities of paternal love and paternal threat. The pattern, as I say, seemed neat, but it also felt rather trivial, with little relation to my experience of the book.

The motivation for the kind of patterned psychoanalytic reading I constructed was likely the habitual need to come up with plausible interpretations for the purposes of teaching and publication. But at the same time I had a deeper motive for wanting to interpret *Treasure Island,* for quite unexpectedly the book moved, enthralled, and disturbed me in ways that the "oedipal" reading did not explain. Thus as a reader I could no longer limit my investigations to the text, but had to turn to myself. Using the method described by David Bleich in his book *Subjective Criticism,*[13] I sought for associations between the text, my feeling about it, and my own life; and, rather surprisingly since I was half-convinced that my Freudian abstractions had blocked any understanding of response, I found one dominant personal association. As Bill Bones, Doctor Livesey, Squire Trelawny, Long John Silver, and Captain Smollett provide Jim with important but often ambiguous substitute-father relationships, so I in childhood valued my five uncles as alternatives to my father. And, as Trelawny and Livesey appear to give up on Jim after he leaves the Block House, and as Silver is alternatively fatherly (or avuncular) and treacherous, so my relationships to my uncles alternated between close and distant, warm and antagonistic, and at times provoked jealousy and conflict in myself and my parents. This personal background, I realized, caused a good deal of the strength of my response to Jim's personal vindication at the end of the novel.

It may be felt that this reading is too idiosyncratic to be of any use other than clinical. Yet the associative interpretation of my response enabled me to understand what might be called the unconscious affective language system through which I experienced the reading of the text.[14] The distinction is that between a detached, "objective" interpretation of the work along roughly psychoanalytic lines, and the interpreter's definition of his own relation to the work. Even when the two kinds of interpretation produce results which—as in the present instance—look similar in general terms, the process gone through by the critic is qualitatively different, and provides a different kind of knowledge.

But because I normally experience literature as both representation and utterance, there remained for me the question of Stevenson's meaning: for of course he did not write *Treasure Island* with my relationship to my uncles in mind, nor did he consciously anticipate the theory of the oedipus complex. But it seems relevant for my reading that Stevenson wrote the novel in the company of, to some degree for, and possibly at the instigation of, his stepson Lloyd Osbourne, who was about fourteen at the time.[15]   For a story involving the death of a father, a series of substitutes, and ultimate triumph for the boy-protagonist might be an appropriate fantasy for a step-father to write for his stepson's enjoyment. In particular, Jim's feelings of love and jealousy towards Long John Silver suggest ambivalences related to the difficult situation in which Stevenson and Lloyd had found themselves for the previous six years in regard to the boy's vivacious but hysterical mother, and his handsome but philandering father.[16]

The unsettled family context in which the book was written suggests to me that both my Freudian and personal readings have a bearing on the meaning of the text for its author and first reader.   It seems significant that Stevenson reported that "It was to be a story for boys, no need of psychology or fine writing; and I had a boy at hand to be a touchstone.   Women were excluded."[17]   This disclaimer sounds rather like a denial which reveals the truth of what it seems to negate—that the novel is indeed full of "psychology," in the sense of emotional content, and that women (who are not, in fact, totally excluded, since Jim's mother is there in the early chapters, and Silver's wife is referred to several times) were somehow at the bottom of it all, as Mrs. Osbourne featured so importantly in the re-lationship between Stevenson and his stepson. But I must stress that these meanings, nowhere stated or implied propositionally in the text, are, like my oedipal allegory and my associative response, interpretive constructs, and that my Robert Louis Stevenson as author of *Treasure Island* is also such a construct. My own general motivation for creating such biographical con-structs is a desire to define and stabilize my response to the text by finding a link between the author's subjectivity and my own; but I doubt that any critical interpretation which takes the author into account can do anything *but* create a fantasy figure of some kind.   To take a familiar example, what is probably the most famous critical biography of our time, Leon Edel's life of Henry James, seems to me a full-length demonstration of the process. However accurate the presented facts, Edel's portrait of the novelist is a portrait of *his* James—and no less important or interesting thereby.

A student of mine put the matter rather neatly in saying that critical interpretation is motivated by a need to "make the book feel right." I want to turn now to a novel which some critics have tried to make feel right, and which others have rejected because they could not do so. Lionel Trilling begins his essay on *Mansfield Park* with the observation that there are many reasons why we should expect to dislike the book. "No other great novel," he writes, "has so anxiously asserted the need to find security, to establish, in fixity and enclosure, a refuge from the dangers of openness and chance. There is scarcely one of our modern pieties that it does not offend."[18] Moreover, it "seems to controvert everything that its predecessor *[Pride and Prejudice]* tells us about life" (Trilling, p. 211). Yet Trilling is determined to demonstrate *Mansfield Park*'s greatness, and to this end he employs the strategy of for the most part dismissing the heroine, Fanny Price, as one with whom it is difficult to be sympathetic, and reading the novel less as a representation of character than as dramatized utterance, as society depicted in such a way as to imply certain propositional points.

In doing this, he constructs a Jane Austen who is an agent of what he calls the "Terror of secularized spirituality" (Trilling, p. 230), under which every individual is to be judged not on the basis of actions, but rather according to his or her internal spiritual condition in a secularized world. Thus Mary Crawford is scored off by Trilling's Austen for the pure "style" of her behavior, her lack of any principle of "sincerity," just as the Price family of Portsmouth is condemned as vulgar for their lack of interest in Fanny. Yet it seems that for the novel ultimately to satisfy Trilling it must ironically undercut itself, and the irony Trilling finds is that the final, ideal state of existence in the reconstituted household at Mansfield Park includes Lady Bertram, a vegetable-like figure whose self is "safe from the Terror of secularized spirituality." So the irony is directed by Trilling's constructed Jane Austen against her own criteria of personal adequacy, by admitting indirectly her own fatigued dream of a blissful existence, a dream that, Trilling says, "speaks to our secret inexpressible hopes" of shutting "out the world and the judgment of the work" (Trilling, p. 230).

I cannot, of course, divine Trilling's motives for reading Jane Austen this way, but it seems an inescapable conclusion that the meanings he finds are constructed according to his own needs and preoccupations. It is one among many evidences that critics tend to construct authors in fantasy and endow them with certain privileged qualities. For some critics these are qualities from which the real author deviates at her peril: and thus for Marvin Mundrick, *Mansfield Park* is a disappointing failure for Austen's ironic vision.[19]

My own way of accommodating *Mansfield Park* to my general sense of Austen as the champion of a limited liberation of spirit within a society especially oppressive to women has been to distinguish it from the other novels as the one in which the super-ego dominates, and in which are revealed fantasies of brother-sister incest and ruthless dreams of omnipotence, in which the insipid Fanny gets all the prizes and shows the falsity of Mrs. Norris's confident prediction that bringing up cousins in the same household is a guarantee against "unnatural" sexual involvement.[20] My 1973 reading was no less than Trilling's a set of constructions based on a selection from among the novel's represented objects and aspects of the author's utterance, constructions which fulfill certain of my subjective needs, including a feeling of discomfort with the novel based on the difficulty of identifying with its protagonist. Although I did not fully realize it at the time, my essay was another attempt to make the novel "feel right," to make it accord with both my own constructed Jane Austen and my biases and values.

But I should stress that my interpretation involved no reading beyond the literal events of the text—no symbol-hunting or elaborate psychoanalytic superstructure. Mrs. Norris does make a prediction which is based on assumptions about the incest taboo; and Fanny does carry all before her, as in an omnipotence fantasy. A less timid reading might have included the observation that Fanny Price's name has contextual meaning: that her fanny is available only at a price, and that when one looks at the number of exiled and miserable characters at the novel's close, the price has been high. Even Sir Thomas must acknowledge his moral inferiority, and Edmund must go through a humiliating period of contrition for his understandable attraction to Mary Crawford. I do not claim that Austen had any such meaning consciously in mind (though surely she did see Fanny as a pearl of great *price*); but at least, anyone aware of the existence of an earlier novel's heroine punningly named Fanny Hill will have the possibility of that interpretation somewhere near the surface of consciousness.

Are there any rules of prescribed method possible for interpretation which tries to take the author and reader simultaneously into account? A colleague of mine, Stephen Black, believes that we can get close to the author's subjectivity by adopting an attitude, which he calls "neutral empathy," rather like that of the classic psychoanalyst: listening, as it were, with heightened sensitivity to what the author is saying and doing and, at the same time, to our own response. But even if one works out this procedure with great care, it can produce no more than a conviction that one is right, rather than an objective knoweldge of an author's subjectivity; for our own subjectivity, through which we apprehend the author's, is never neutral, if only because our self-knowledge is never clearly complete. There are, I believe, always motives for the act of interpretation and for particular interpretations. My reading of Fanny Price's name as a sexual pun is at least in part motivated by my frustration with *Mansfield Park* and my need to undermine its excessively virtuous heroine; and yet, rather like Lionel Trilling in his attribution of a dream of safety from the world's judgment to Jane Austen, I want to find authority for that process of undermining in the author's intention, conscious or unconscious.

Frederick Jameson's interpretive model, which I cited earlier, implies a commitment to the scientific possibilities of criticism, to the idea of an objectively discoverable meaning. And Jameson, in criticizing certain systematic methodologies (structuralism in particular), remarks that true criticism requires "standing back" in order to apprehend "the very categories of our understanding as reflections of a particular and determinate moment of history" (Jameson, p. 15). It would seem that no systematic methodology can "lay bare" the meaning of a literary work because that methodology will help to determine the outcome of the process; it is necessary to take into account the "perceptual instruments" (to use Jameson's term) of the method itself. Even this implies the possibility of arriving at objective truth, but one might ask whether Jameson's distinction between "interpretation" and "laying bare" of content can really be sustained. For surely we can attempt to "reveal" content only by writing a new text to clarify the original one; and if we repeatedly examine our "perceptual instruments," there is the danger of an infinite regress.

The fear of such a regress, one might speculate, could be a source of the wish to ground one's interpretations in a received or invented system of ideas—whether myth, psychoanalysis, Marxism, or even "deconstruction." I do not consider myself free of such anxiety, but I suggest that recognizing motivation as the interpreter's ground provides a more flexible, open approach to interpretation. For we are what we ask: the kinds of problems we choose to tackle in literary interpretation reflect who and what we are. I am fairly confident that J. Hillis Miller's search for joyous free play in the deconstruction of literary works into their etymological atoms, until he reaches the "uncanny" condition where interpretation must cease,[21] is as much a reflection of his emotional needs, and of an anxiety about infinite regress, as my search for links between the author's subjectivity and my own is a reflection of my emotional needs and of the same interpretive anxiety. Lionel Trilling's account of the "Terror of secularized spirituality" may be great critical wisdom, but surely it carries the force of conviction because of Trilling's personal involvement in the question. If interpretation is always motivated, one problem with any critical system is that it too easily becomes a means of concealing motivation.

This said, I feel an obligation to "stand back" a bit further than I have so far done. My teacher at the University of Washington, Wayne Burns, wrote in 1956 that "we must give up what has come to be known as psychoanalytic criticism in favor of a theory of criticism that includes but is not dominated by Freudian awareness . . .; a theory that places Freudian awareness under the aesthetic controls provided by the individual

work of art."[22]   To this, I would now add, under the controls
provided by an awareness of one's own motivations as critic,
one's response to the text, and one's relation to the author whom
one constructs in the process of interpretation.   My motives
for taking this position are of several kinds.   I have a need to
assert my importance as reader, and yet to retain the idea of an
author to help provide authority for my readings.   And on a
more personal level, I have a need to move beyond my teacher
of twenty years ago, without rejecting his influence completely.

Yet I should like to think that on another level my motivation is less personal.   In the present state of confusion and anxiety in literary theory, which affects not only the practice of
criticism but the teaching of literature, there are those of us who
feel a need to re-unite reader, text, and author (including historical and social milieu).   While conclusive, objective knowledge
of any of these elements may be unattainable, it does not follow that all sense of the "real" must be abandoned, that we
must all become "cognitive atheists."   Those who believe that
we are trapped in a prison-house of language seem overly
attached to their jailor, and by a leap of logic transform their
imprisonment into what is supposedly freedom.   Acknowledgment and analysis of the critic's own motivation and response,
together with a regard for authors—incomplete and unverifiable
as our portraits of them must be—is in some ways analogous
to Freud's original interpretive method, as in *The Interpretation
of Dreams.*   And it is an alternative, on the one hand to the
systematic application of methodologies, including psychoanalysis, which claim to yield objective knowledge, and on the
other hand to the new logorrhea of self-perpetuating discourse.[23]

NOTES

[1] Michael Steig, "Dickens' Excremental Vision," *Victorian Studies,*
13 (1970), 339-354; "Anality in *The Mill on the Floss,*" *Novel,* 5 (1971),
42-53.

[2]Murray Krieger, *Theory of Criticism* (Baltimore: Johns Hopkins University Press, 1976), pp. 10, 194.

[3]Gerald Graff, *Literature Against Itself* (Chicago: University of Chicago Press, 1979).

[4]E. D. Hirsch, Jr., *Validity in Interpretation* (New Haven: Yale University Press, 1967).

[5]E. D. Hirsch, *The Aims of Interpretation* (Chicago: University of Chicago Press, 1976), p. 8.

[6]Hirsch, *The Aims of Interpretation,* p. 49.

[7]This tendency is more apparent in Iser's book *The Implied Reader* (Baltimore: Johns Hopkins University Press, 1974) than in *The Act of Reading* (Baltimore: Johns Hopkins University Press, 1978), in which Iser acknowledges diversity of response, though he does not make such diversity a crucial factor in his model of the act of reading literature.

[8]Andrew Brink, *Loss and Symbolic Repair: A Psychological Study of Some English Poets* (Hamilton, Ontario: The Cromlech Press, 1977), p. 5.

[9]Frederic Jameson, "Metacommentary," *PMLA,* 86 (1971), 16.

[10]Roman Ingarden, *The Literary Work of Art,* transl. George G. Grabowicz (Evanston: Northwestern University Press, 1973), pp. 217-254.

[11]Michel Foucault, "What Is an Author?" in Josué V. Harari, ed., *Textual Strategies: Perspectives in Post-Structuralist Criticism* (Ithaca: Cornell University Press, 1979), pp. 141-160.

[12]Roman Ingarden, *The Cognition of the Literary Work of Art,* transl. Ruth Ann Crowley and Kenneth R. Olson (Evanston: Northwestern University Press, 1973), pp. 146-167; René Wellek and Austin Warren, *Theory of Literature,* 2nd ed. (New York: Harcourt, Brace, 1956), pp. 13-26.

[13]David Bleich, *Subjective Criticism* (Baltimore: Johns Hopkins University Press, 1978).

[14]The concept of individual language systems is developed by David Bleich in *Subjective Criticism,* pp. 84-85, 136-137.

[15] James Pope Hennessy, *Robert Louis Stevenson* (London: Jonathan Cape, 1974), p. 155.

[16] A sense of this ambivalence and conflict is given in Lloyd Osbourne's own account of his relationship to Stevenson, *An Intimate Portrait of R. L. S.* (New York: Scribner's, 1924), especially pp. 19-21.

[17] Pope Hennessy, *Robert Louis Stevenson,* p. 156.

[18] Lionel Trilling, "Mansfield Park," in *The Opposing Self* (New York: Viking Press, 1955), p. 210.

[19] Marvin Mudrick, *Jane Austen: Irony as Defense and Discovery* (Princeton: Princeton University Press, 1952), p. 180.

[20] Michael Steig, "Psychological Realism and Fantasy in Jane Austen: *Emma* and *Mansfield Park*," *Hartford Studies in Literature,* 5 (1973), pp. 126-134.

[21] J. Hillis Miller, "The Critic as Host," *Critical Inquiry,* 3 (1977), 439-447.

[22] Wayne Burns, "The Critical Relevance of Freudianism," *Western Review,* 20 (1956), 305.

[23] For an extended example of an attempt to apply this approach to a particular work, see my article, "At the Back of *The Wind in the Willows*: An Experiment in Biographical and Autobiographical Interpretation," *Victorian Studies,* 24:3 (Spring 1981), 303-323.

CRITICISM AS THE SITUATING OF PERFORMANCES: OR WHAT WALLACE STEVENS HAS TO TELL US ABOUT OTHELLO

by
Charles Altieri

Literary theorists have become so serious about their work, or so pretentious, that they spend a good deal more effort justifying themselves philosophically than proving their utility for practical criticism. On other occasions I would defend this tendency in my own work,[1] but now I want to take advantage of being invited to contribute to this collection by focusing on the question of what consequences my theoretical work has for reading and enjoying literary texts. This means I shall not try to ground or defend my ideas in conceptual terms. Instead I shall concentrate on three practical concepts—performance, situating, and identification. Moreover I shall derive them here from a literary work, Stevens' "Of Modern Poetry," so that the terms I use shall be closely tied to an actual performance. I hope this will both deepen the theory and illustrate some of the basic existential stakes involved in getting such ideas straight. By staying close to texts, I will necessarily be submitting my claims to one obvious form of testing. But it is very difficult to formulate tests for how representative or universal theoretical concepts are. Representativeness is not merely a matter of extension across cases; it involves questions of significance which, in turn, involve complex, circular arguments. Criticism then must seek representativeness much as literary works do, that is by the power of examples to create types and to suggest possible uses. As an attempt to meet such a test I shall try to extend Stevens to *Othello* in order to show the general heuristic value of specific formulations spawned by modernism. And rather than simply apply my critical ideas to a second text, I shall assume that the application is obvious in order to show how Shakespeare's play is a richer meditation on Stevens' subject than is any work of Stevens. My ultimate aim is to show how our obsession with modern theoretical questions can serve the dialectical function of deepening our grasp of classical texts.

Steven's poem is so strong a source of theory because its movement as a poem fulfills and concretizes the notions of performance and act of mind it sets out abstractly:

> The poem of the mind in the act of finding
> What will suffice. It has not always had
> To find: the scene was set; it repeated what
> Was in the script.
>   Then
> The theatre was changed
> To something else. Its past was a souvenir.
> It has to be living, to learn the speech of the place.
> It has to face the men of the time and to meet
> The women of the time. It has to think about war
> And it has to find what will suffice. It has
> To construct a new stage. It has to be on that stage
> And, like an insatiable actor, slowly and
> With meditation, speak words that in the ear,
> In the delicatest ear of the mind, repeat,
> Exactly, that which it wants to hear, at the sound
> Of which, an invisible audience listens,
> Not to the play, but to itself, expressed
> In an emotion as of two people, as of two
> Emotions becoming one. The actor is
> A metaphysician in the dark, twanging
> An instrument, twanging a wiry string that gives
> Sounds passing through sudden rightnesses, wholly
> Containing the mind, below which it cannot descend,
> Beyond which it has no will to rise.
>   It must
> Be the finding of a satisfaction, and may
> Be of a man skating, a woman dancing, a woman
> Combing. The poem of the act of the mind.[2]

The discussion of act is sustained primarily by the poem's careful, self-reflexive movement. The initial abstraction creates a sense of negation contrasting past and present. The need to define and come to terms with this difference then establishes a pressure which takes imaginative form as a litany of necessities. The intensity of this litany focuses the mind's attention on its own needs, processes, and powers, so that reflection on bondage generates a new attitude towards the imagination. The meditation makes it possible in the poem's closing lines to resolve the issues by celebrating the mind's power to compose and inhabit what I can best describe as spaces or sites where the mind can both stage and appreciate its ways of giving value to particulars.

Stevens treats all poems as acts of mind: the modernist difference is simply the nature of the stage. A fixed symbolic theatre, presumably where the minds' energies can transform content into the imaginative "meanings" sustained by acknowledged cultural or religious scripts, gives way to a form of activity whose value cannot be externally justified. The remainder of the poem charts the conditions of internal or gestural self-justification in performance, while at the same time enacting what it describes. Now it is not the script that is repeated but a litany of necessities that define what historical conditions have to be met, as if the mind could learn its own powers only by first acknowledging the external, historical pressures upon it. Then the mind can change attitudes from simply observing its condition to the self-conscious creation of theatrical (not conceptual) structures. Now the mind can take form as author of its own performances and thus an emblem of autonomy. In other words the poem as an act projects an increasing intensity of thinking which creates a movement from the mind's sense of the content it must produce (11.7-10), to a recognition of how the content must be projected (on a new stage), to a celebration of the specific qualities of the unfolding performance that might suffice on and as that stage. In this movement, the developing intensity produces an increasingly lyrical and inward sense of both act and stage (11.11-19). Here inwardness becomes also the principle of community because of the identifications made possible once the mind can put on stage the delicate desires that express its demands. The self-conscious lyrical exuberance makes it appear as if the sounds could literally reproduce the wiry string's music and capture self-consciously "the sudden rightnesses" it speaks of. This physical texture embodying the statement (as its stage) then itself becomes the focus of reflection at the end of the third stanza, where the idea of containing the mind must be taken quite literally. A mind displaced from a symbolic theatre now finds a physical form in its own articulate expression, so that it conceives all alternatives as either a return to the violent rebellion and satiric energy characterizing the alienated wanderer or an evasive escape to a mythic trans-lunar paradise. By composing a space for a thinking that engages and expresses desire, the poem establishes a sense of self-sufficing presence; there is no displacement because there are no energies of thought that cannot be expressed and accepted.

The nature of this composed space is the subject of the final stanza. Stevens makes the break by shifting from the anaphoric "it has" to "it must." This is not simply elegant variation. Where the "it has" introduced external compulsions, the "must" offers an inward psychological correlate of those conditions. "It must be/the finding of a satisfaction" transforms external necessity and states it as an internal demand so that the image of a space wholly containing the mind rests on a profound correlation of lucid observation and educated will. This is how the mind can literally construct its own stage while still addressing a real historical situation. And this is how Stevens can justify his next and most daring move: once the "must" is acknowledged, the modality of necessity gives way to one characterized by a range of permissions. The new stage replaces the fixed script by a set of conditions of attention open to any content. What matters is the attitude towards content: the poet recognizes that his need is not opposed to his imaginative acts but it opens for him a form of attention capable of erotic satisfaction in the most casual of appearances.

Rich as it is, the thematic aspect of the dramatic performance does not suffice for Stevens. He reinforces the idea of the act of mind creating a space in which to dwell and adapts to modernist ontology the Keatsian idea of stationing, by calling attention to the spatial features of the poem as a construct within which dynamic movement takes place. As the poem steps free into the permission to revel in particulars it also steps back to repeat the sense and syntax of the opening line. To go forward is also to circle back. In this circling Stevens makes a concrete figure of the abstract idea that the performance reveals the ground on which a liberated act of mind can take place. This ground or place is characterized by the syntactic feature of the poem's framing sentences lacking a main verb. This grounding structural repetition echoes and partially interprets the many other syntactic repetitions which compose the delicate sonorities of the third stanza. (All the repetitions also suggest the literal construction of a stage, since the echoes give an illusion of substance because particulars seem to build on others.) The frame for erotically attaching to particulars, then, is a grasp of "the poem of the act of the mind" as a continual state of desire, where an external "must" and internal quest for a sense of sufficiency are balanced. By syntactically projecting a dimension of the act of mind which exists outside of time, the denial of transitivity and the repetition suggest the timeless quality of a meditative theatre composed by and hushed for the sounds that can wholly contain the mind and unite author with audience. Yet to view these static qualities as pure aesthetic form would be to impose contraries where Stevens sees complements operating on different levels. His point is not how space contrasts to flux; rather he insists on our seeing how the act of mind is at once a force and a space reciprocally creating and valuing each other as performance and staging conditions. (Burke's scene and act become fused.) Thus the act of mind is without verbs because its framing power and its awareness of the pressure of self-reflective need imposing the frame are the preconditions of all verbs. We move from "must" to "may be" to a series of participles which serve as emblems for the continual generating of imagined subjects—all poised between the substance of nominalized states and the activities which elicit and satisfy desire. The details of combing, etc., are absolutely casual, and the casualness is never transformed into symbol. The transformation that does take place is on a different level, casualness itself becomes resonant and reverberates without ever tempting us to confuse the energies of composition with putative meanings *in* the world. As a treatment of objects, the poem inhabits a totally modern poetic universe, deprived of symbols and dependent on the energies of perception. Then in this world it seems that even with the poetic act of mind, "nothing has been changed at all"; the world goes on. But, as Wittgenstein suggested in his early works, there can be total transfigurations

of the world that alter none of its factual qualitites. Simply
by understanding that one must construct an attitude towards
a range of objective processes, Stevens sees that one can educate
one's desires to the world until desires themselves appear as
permissions (perhaps a secular, subjective analogue of God's
creative fiat): it *may be* any particular that becomes "Part of
major reality, part of/an appreciation of a reality/And thus
an elevation, as if I left/With something I could touch, touch
every way." *As* the poet imagines, he performs modes of thinking which are not merely regulative forms or the confirmation
of ideas about maturity, if not the thing itself. Rather the poet
constitutes the multiple frames which allow us to treasure
the varied world we have, and he reminds us that in the vital
perception of differences we find ourselves more truly and
more strange as the possessors of a power we all share.

II

While many of Stevens' concerns are distinctly modernist,
I think they are grafted on a view of literature and of the mind's
needs which can sustain a general literary theory. This can be
shown fairly briefly by abstracting three ideas from the poem
and then showing how the poem deepens their theoretical significance. What Stevens treats as act I shall explore as a general notion that literary texts invite us to approach the work
as performance displaying qualitites of the various agents involved; what he establishes structurally I shall take as acknowledging the need for readers to "situate" the performance in a
context or site that brings out the nature and significance of
the qualities; and what he takes as the identification between
authorial and audience emotions I shall treat abstractly as the
terms by which literary texts are representative and hence
serve cognitive functions.

The essential attribute of a performance is the equation
Stevens makes between act and actor, for performance is the
projection of action so that instrumental assessments are sub-
ordinated to conditions of qualitative review. By concentrating on the various kinds of reviews we might bring to actions
we can then indicate the aspects of performance relevant to
literary theory. First, a performance obviously involves assess-

ing something in terms of what an agent does. This means that statements or propositions per se, that is utterances judged for descriptive truth conditions, are not performances. As Russell indicated, a truth functional logic depends on separating the properties of a statement from any self-reflexive or self-qualifying conditions (such as we find in the Cretan Liar paradox). But it is precisely these conditions which are the basis of performance—the how of a what or the construction of the stage as part of the activity. We arrive then by a somewhat circuitous route at Austin's distinction between constatives and performatives—the former a category for propositions carried in an utterance and the latter a term for aspects of meaning achieved *in the act* of saying something.[3] This circuitous route, however, makes possible our going well past Austin's limiting performatives to rule-governed activities, as if he created the stage for performances and then could find no fully human actors. Austin wanted to preserve space for expression and judgment, but only within the constraints of formal procedures. Austin ignores any constitutive power in the expression which requires attention to the agent's purpose and the qualities revealed when those purposes are carried out in actions.

Stevens, on the other hand, recovers an important principle of idealist thought about actions. His concern for building and embodying the stage of one's act allows us to make a distinction between external and internal relations established by the act. External relations are lines of projections between an agent and world in which the terms of the relations can be taken from categories not affected by the purpose or beliefs of the agent. These range from obvious biological attributes of actions to symptomatic features of an act which indicate class bias, social preconditioning or neurotic behavior which the agent does not control. Internal relations, by contrast, are those Hegel imagined as expressing the subject fully in the predicate.[4] In other words an action self-consciously projects internal relations—and thus become a performance—to the extent that it embodies in its articulate properties qualities the subject wants to be represented by. The performance can fail, but primarily only by not capturing qualities one is led to expect, either because one knows the script and recognizes mistakes or because the agent offers an implicit script he fails to follow (for example, when a speaker uses a passionate rhetoric to make a banal point). Conversely, performances succeed to the extent that they elicit qualitative review of the predicates as reflections of the powers, attributes and desires of an expressive agent. This allows us to take as the unit of performance any segment of a text that elicits qualitative review in terms of an agent's expressive purposes. Ultimately we shall have to posit a single performative act by an author if we are to see the work as coherent or satisfy a standard way of scrutinizing works of art. But within this overall interpretive performance, several smaller acts of both character and implicit author can be isolated for reflection. These range from local features displaying stylistic mastery of a medium to patterns among stylistic choices which become integrated into our sense of the overall act. In narrative or dramatic works, we extend our sense of authorial presence to the actions of individual characters. These agents need not be self-conscious performers, but we cannot read critically without imposing conditions of review or transferring to them the stage we see the author constructing. And once we project a stage, we see the variety of acts—combing, dancing, etc.— as intimately connected with a more general need to find satisfaction in and through the overall performance they participate in and take meaning from.

The easiest way to grasp the importance of Stevens' sense of the poem as performance is to contrast it with other models for describing the internal unity of a text and for correlating that aesthetic dimension with the existential and thematic issues a text raises. Organicist views of coherence base internal relations on an analogy with natural objects, and these logically require an autonomous impersonal author. This makes it difficult to conceive anything but an aesthetic unity for the text and gives no terms for describing an overall synthetic stance and the judgments we might make of it. Similarly, when we lack a model of what occupies the stage a text constructs, we are easily tempted to replace dramatistic by thematic categories, with a corresponding reduction in what can be qualitatively reviewed.[5] In Stevens' poem, for example, a purely thematic view would leave no way to integrate style and idea and produce no way to understand the poems' movement or the significance of the spatial organization which grounds the performance. Mimetic views do somewhat better, since they attend to the work's actions. But they normally concentrate only on represented acts and lack categories for the authorial presence which alone can make dramatic sense of style and structure. (Otherwise they are only controls of affect—not constituents of complex meaning.) Finally, views of performance like Paul de Man's and recent post-structuralist views of the text as a continual process of producing possible structures can handle all the complexity of Stevens' poem, but I have serious doubts about the cognitive uses to which they can put that complexity. If texts produce infinite levels of signification and subversion, the only performer is the text: we are left with no synthesis, not much of a stage, and no principle for identifying with the performer.

I have used "review" as a central defining term and criticized other positions for not establishing significant terms for review. Now I must explain the kind of review required by Stevens' poem. I call this a process of situating and see it as the single most important feature of a performative approach to criticism. If one takes a performative act on a stage as what Keats called a process of stationing the mind, situating is the corresponding critical process which establishes the contexts required for recognizing and appreciating the qualities exhibited. Situating makes explicit the terms of staging so that an appropriate review is possible and the specific permissions a poem wins can be seen against a backdrop of the apposite necessities.[6]

Situating takes place on two basic levels—as a means for establishing concrete contexts which clarify the nature and internal relations of the performance and as a means for establishing the significance of a performance by showing what contexts it is representative of and what possible forms of acting or assessing actions might follow from our identifying with the site a critic sees constructed by the work. Thus one situates the specific performances in Stevens' poem by showing how the poem asks us to take up a process of thinking about its own processes as they stage a way to acknowledge and satisfy basic desires informing modern poetry. Once we see where Stevens locates the mind—at a threshold between necessity and permission constructed by an increasingly intense process of self-conscious reflection—we can indicate the relevant qualities of the act which make the site constructed a significant and representative one. This is what I hope I did in my reading of the poem. Then, were this a specific treatment of Stevens, we could go on to situate the situating by showing how Stevens' poem resolves problems basic to Stevens' career or modern poetics or modern culture or by arguing pragmatically about what might follow were we to grant the identification Stevens seeks and take up in our experience the stance his act composes.

There is a sense in which I am now performing the second of these roles in a highly abstract way. For I am trying to situate the value of Stevens' act in the limited realm of literary theory. And, again, the more one brings problem contexts to bear (primarily created by the failure of other critical perspectives), the more clearly, deeply, and positively, we can assess Stevens' achievement. The third basic theoretical claim I want to make provides one of those problem contexts. This concerns the possibility of indicating how Stevens' view of identification enables us to explain the cognitive role of literary texts. I have discussed the cognitive dimensions of performances in other essays, so I shall be very brief here. Cognition is a question of how one can use in non-textual experience constructs one derives from carefully reading a specific literary text. When we situate a text as a performance, it exemplifies a possible stance toward experience which we can at once identify with and reflect upon as a possible element in our lives, as if what were two emotions could become one. Extensive literary experience, then, creates a complex grammar or repetoire of attitudes we can employ as possible projections of our behavior and ways of engaging ourselves in the actions of others. Grammars are permissions. And as containers of the mind, this repetoire can become the object of reflection so that our finding satisfaction in its various aspects becomes a principle for acknowledging the mind's powers and the value of the cultural frameworks the mind depends upon. Grammar builds a "major man."

The relationship between situating and the cognitive functions of examples is to me the most appealing feature of a dramatistic theory. Unlike other approaches, it enables us to attend to both the productive and mimetic energies in a work, to acknowledge the uniqueness of the actions, and still to make the distinctive and whole action (not simply some mimetic feature of it) the constituent which becomes a feature of our cultural grammar. It is Stevens poem as a process and attitude—

not one of its themes or what it imitates or its textual dance—
which exemplifies the nature of poems as performances and the
poet's vision of situating his own act of mind. Similarly there
is no gulf between rhetoric and mimesis, or what Edward Said
calls the production and achievement of meaning, because
the object of knowledge is not an idea (displaced by desire)
but a stance displaying both desire and the process of locating
predicates adequate for its expression and interpretation. Acts
of mind as Stevens presents them capture both the production
and articulation of staging.   And finally because this approach
makes attitudes objects of knowledge it offers a rich solution
to a need I consider basic to any literary theory—developing
text-psyche correlations so that what we treat as significant
principle of aesthetic integration in a work can also be seen
as significant aspects of the knowledge, or at least states of
mind, a text can produce.   Here the poetic syntax for structural relationships (or what Coleridge called poetic logic) derives from the poem's power of giving intensity and internal coherence to acts of mind and thus is directly equivalent to attitudes we can possibly use or reflect upon in ordinary experience.

III

Lyric poetry is the best medium with which to illustrate
the process of situating because poems come, as it were, so
naked into the critical stream that they require us to create
elaborate contexts for them. And this very need makes it hard
to contain them within the type of ordinary descriptive contexts usually appropriate for the popular novel. This means
that if my critical terms are to be representative they must
apply to other genres. As indeed they do. I could, for example,
show the enormous differences that follow if we situate a Lawrence novel as a traditional mimetic fiction and as the expressive
exploratory act he calls *Women in Love* in his preface to that
work.[7]   In the former case we have no way to explain our
fascination with sloppy ideas or to judge the shifting distances
between author and character. But an expressive view sees the
style and identification with Birkin as deliberate efforts on
Lawrence's part to explore imaginative alternatives to the discursive thought and forms of emotion characterizing a dying
culture. I prefer, however, to concentrate on a drama. First,

the idea of situating has obvious analogies to the critical process of staging. But at the same time, the idea of situating acts of mind can remind us of the narrowness frequent in our modern theatrical practice. Situating is a form of staging intended to capture literally the performance of states of mind which often cannot be confined to the temporal and spatial models of coherence required by the stage. Second, the particular drama I have chosen, Othello, affords both a clear instance of classical literature and a very complex meditation on the ideas of performance and situating. At one pole *Othello* makes central the internal psychological pressures impinging on basic aspects of performance, and at the other it captures dramatically and metadramatically the problems of mediation which derive from the ways performances depend on frameworks they cannot completely control. Precisely because Shakespeare so fully renders the philosophical and psychological ramifications of Othello's performative needs, his play forces us to ask how one can situate a staging of the play so that the theatrical production does not become a disfiguring or highly reductive medium. Shakespeare's plays can only be experienced fully if one can take as literally present a range of forces from philosophical abstractions to absolutely immediate psychological states usually sublimated in practical behavior. This is the underlying reason for Romantic arguments that the plays cannot be staged. As Stevens might put it: in appealing to the delicatest ear of the mind the plays demand that we seek alternatives to the realistic theatre which is now our set scene where directors only repeat an outworn script. I do not here want to argue the strong claim that Shakespeare's imagination is too fine and complex to be situated on any but imagined, readerly stages, but the recent BBC productions and a lot of academic "psychological" criticism make clear how much our usual critical mirrors contaminate what they should display in its full performative intensity.[8] So while I cannot here deal with specific questions of staging, I shall try to bring out in my reading metaphorical dimensions of the actions which are most compelling when imagined as literally present on a stage that is not easily realized in a theatre.

In this respect it is important to remember that the allegorical dimensions of *Othello* are not simply traces of an earlier mode not yet outgrown entirely. Shakespeare had shown in the history plays and in most of *Hamlet* that he could make the stage mirror quotidian reality. So the allegory is chosen, primarily to extend the action and make the audience aware of what unearthly stuff rounds a scene. Allegory is a mode of making literal what is not empirical. It makes demons enter men like Iago and an angel appear in Desdemona. Shakespeare, however, uses the space of allegorical thinking without letting his plays resolve into a single allegory dominated by one master code giving coherence to the symbolic elements. We must then distinguish the allegorical as a form of imagining forces at play from allegory as a form of semantic coherence. In the allegorical mode, the central feature is simply setting symbolic elements in internal patterns so that they reverberate against one another. As in abstract painting, the reach beyond empirical, descriptive concerns becomes a means for intensifying and deepening one's sense of forces and relations that can take concrete form. Dramatically this means staging the characters so that we must respond to the abstract forces they embody and, in their interrelationships, develop as significant. For example, Iago is not simply a devil but a figure for the complex idea of the monstrous, and how the monstrous is understood depends on the variety of ideal forces in Othello's actions which Iago can demonically reverse. In fact, the more fully we understand the needs of Othello as a performer, the richer becomes our sense of how deeply embedded in these needs are the vulnerabilities and potentially perverse energies which make us all capable of monstrous acts. If we do not take the monstrous literally, Othello and Willy Loman could inhabit the same stage, one where needs and causes are evident, disaster is never dignified by ritual, and the psyche can pity its needs so fully that it need never confront its own demons. Conversely, once one acknowledges an allegorical mode for situating the actions, Rhymer's insistence on a highly empirical form of dramatic coherence fades away as simply a reductive attitude.

The best way to disclose the central energies engaged by *Othello* may be to work out the dialectical pressures that give the monstrous force Iago represents its power, and its terror. My way of doing this will be to concentrate on what it is in Othello he can corrupt—namely Othello's power to perform his identity in a way that fully satisfies his imagination of nobility. One could deal with this in terms of Renaissance ideas of the ideal human image and its defacement or contamination. Yet this seems to me too abstract to capture fully the play's vision of the dynamics of performance. So I shall instead borrow from and freely modify some ideas on performance and "the imaginary" from a contemporary thinker, Jacques Lacan. Because he is so indebted to Hegel, Lacan speaks largely from within a neo-platonic tradition that preserves Renaissance concerns, but he also tries to capture dynamic, affective features of those concerns which are not explicit themes in Renaissance philosophy.[9] Even with this historical justification, I need to insist on a difference between situating and explaining. I intend here no psychoanalytic explanation of Shakespeare or even of the play; instead I use Lacan as a kind of conceptual dye which, when added to the play, will clearly bring out structural patterns and qualitative features of some of the actions. From this perspective Lacan helps us see the basic desires motivating most performances and the ways in which performance involves dependencies and paradoxes that give a conceptual place and depth to Iago's monstrous presence. Moreover, with this philo-sophical and psychological background we can see some of what Shakespeare's imagination makes literally present in a space perhaps no merely physical actor can inhabit.

Lacan takes as a central theme the ironies inherent in the need of expressive performances to be mediated (or proven) for an audience whose affirmation they require. Performance is the expressive vehicle of self-identification. It is how the self becomes an identity for another, and hence for itself—ideally by projecting qualities which compel from the other the idea and the response the agent desires. Lacan proposes as the psycho-analytic base (or perhaps metaphor) for this process the child's desire to repeat the state of satisfaction achieved in moments of maternal care in which the child's name is uttered as a sign of his pure individuality in the mother's eyes. The name, then, seems at once to depend on and be supported by the mother's establishing virtually a magical mirror which reflects back to the child the child's specialness. In subsequent experience, the child's private, fantasized or "imaginary" sense of individuality seeks substitutes for this reflective glass. But the mirror is not an innocent one. The child develops its sense of an inward iden-tity by depending on someone else's reflection, which is also a projection of the reflector's needs and desires. So individuality is inextricably caught up in dependency—on both the media of names and mirrors and the reactions of other people—and within and without become enormously complicated phenomenological experiences because the sense of inward identity depends on external reflection. The actual structure of dependencies constitutes the radical opposite of the maternal order. Lacan conceives it as "the symbolic" or the order of the father. Here the father assumes a castrating presence because he negates the mother's love and invites an understanding of the child in terms of an impersonal, social system based on names as signs of properties, roles, and duties. The child can only survive this threat to its identity by restructuring its sense of self. The child must sublimate imaginary demands and define itself through identification with the father and the roles he exemplifies and mediates. Yet the imaginary can never be entirely suppressed because it is the source of an individual's desires and attachments.

Shakespeare's theatre, in fact, is one medium where the interplay between the symbolic and the imaginary manifests itself clearly—if we can free ourselves from the habits of realistic theatre and novel reading. Consider the theatrical presence of the King (and by obvious metonymy the hero as the man of noble imagination). Here we have on stage at once the active man on whom social orders depend, the authoritative man through whom religious and political symbols are focused, and the psychological man with the possibility of enjoying full performative powers to compel the attention of others in the exact terms he desires. I call the last of these "the King's demand" and I see it as a central force in the tragedies and a central vehicle for leading us to identify with the actions as literal states. I suspect that we all at our least sublimated project ourselves as Kings and Queens with respect to our fantasized selves. Any example, of course, becomes a breech of sublimated discourses and leaves one vulnerable to judgment, so as a modern man I will stay with sexual analogies. The King can, simply by being King, expect persons he desires to reflect back the sovereign's ideal image of his own potency, or his power to exist for others as one can imagine existing for one's mother. Yet the King's power is really not personal at all. He depends on a symbolic order in the same way that the child depends on a reflection he really does not create. The King's demand, in short, is also the King's vulnerability because what most exalts "the imaginary I" and often actually produces "noble" actions is what it least controls.

This logic of desire and ironic dependency is beautifully rendered by the tension between the King's dream of himself and the mirrors that he depends on in *Richard II, King Lear,* and *Julius Caeasr.* More complex explorations of the imaginary and its dependencies inform *Macbeth* and *Antony,* but it is *Othello* which most powerfully connects the ideas of performance and vulnerability to the demands of the imaginary. This very conjunction of ideas, in fact, may go a long way toward explaining why *Othello* is the basis for our greatest tragic opera. Opera is the form most insistent on opposing the emotional and intellectual limitations of popular realism, and it thus achieves its richest intensities when the action presents abstract emotions which seem to take place as literal states of feeling free of standard contextual qualifications.

IV

The opening scenes of *Othello* set a stage dominated by questions about who or where someone is. We move from Roderigo's efforts to understand who Iago is, to Iago's paradoxical "I am not what I am" (1, 1, 65) to Brabantio's questions and painful discoveries about Roderigo and Othello, to two parties searching for Othello. All this is prelude to a comic revelation scene in which Othello's identity is proclaimed and secured by the confirmation of his beloved. But the terms of Othello's imaginary self-identifications are already in the process of being rendered problematic. For one possible reflection of his identity is the one Brabantio possesses but refuses to surrender in order to establish comic harmony. The fragility of identity is more strikingly rendered in the gulf between Othello's confidence and what each of the two groups searching for him wants in a world where blind passions or political expediency dominate. What each group demands cannot be reconciled with the Othello he or the others perceive, so as we begin to hear Othello believe in proof we also see the possibility of definitive proof, the presence of an agreed upon method of inquiry, collapsing into dividing and divisive questions. Yet the dominant mood of the scene is quite different. There we are made to feel the power of someone's imaginary demands to motivate noble actions. Othello's confidence allows him to appear as a successful Brutus or Richard II who can, momentarily at least, combine private worth and public sustenance of identity because his powers seem so obviously expressed on the surface in his manner and deeds.

We need here, however, to begin looking forward and examining the particular nature of Othello's imaginary demand and the difficulties of continuing to satisfy it. At this point in the play Othello appears Iago's absolute opposite. For Othello there is absolutely no gulf between appearances and reality because he takes all the world as his mirror. Both men share the personal power to control how others regard them, but Othello does so as a matter of unselfconscious essence rather than competitive will. Othello's opening words all reflect a sense of pure plenitude, an imagination gratified by appearances, which even Panurge might accept.

"This better as it is"

Let him do his spite; (1, 2, 6)

My services which I have done the signiory

Shall out-tongue his complaints . . . (1, 2, 17-19)

My parts my title, and my perfect soul

Shall manifest me rightly. (1, 2, 30-32)

This is Othello's first, and not least problematic reliance on ocular proof, and it explains his differences from Iago, his particular reliance on Desdemona and, ultimately the reason he succumbs so totally to jealousy. Where Iago's basic form of language is a manipulative rhetoric positing and playing identities rather than expressing personal traits, Othello's characteristic mode of self performance, before his jealousy, is the naive heroic narrative. For him stories suffice to indicate character, and there is no gulf between records from the past and the projection of qualities essential to the present self. Because he is no de Manian modernist about allegory, all time is no time for

Othello, whereas Iago's willful control of ironies requires that
he project any imaginative ends for himself into the future
(a future he perhaps knows is a fiction, but also which is his to
create because he masters the suspiciousness central to a modern
sense of history.) Yet even if stories unite past and present, they
still involve other dependencies. They require an appropriate
audience although audiences can change quickly, thus altering
the terms for being reflected in a satisfying way. To the extent
that Othello is a simple military man, like Coriolanus, he hopes
that the character expressed in his stories can be appreciated
and reflected by any audience: We have seen how he expects
the duke to know him, and the speech in which he tells of cap-
tivating Desdemona modulates to her from an initial account of
how Brabantio loved his stories (1, 3, 127-70).

Desdmona, however, serves as a very complex figure for the
status of an audience. On the one hand, as I have suggested,
Othello consciously sees her largely both as an extension of
the men who love his stories and his reward for them, as if her
approval were a metonymic symbol putting in essential female
form the effect he has on all people. Yet Shakespeare insists
on differentiating Desdemona from other audience figures.
She loves because "I saw Othello's visage in his mind" and she
"consecrates" herself to that (1, 3, 252-54). She, then, loves
the essence or ideal behind the stories. She reads in a noble
but, as we shall see, problematic way not available to Othello.
But the effects of her reading do affect him: although she sees
in a special way, in effect situating the true performer whom
others see only in an empirical theatre, he takes her way of responding as an emblem of how all people should see him. He
feels the effects of specialness, but emotionally tries to make
the special qualities symbolic of general conditions. These
symbolic extensions are clearest in the speech grounding his
later metaphysical sense of what her fidelity symbolizes. I
refer to the virtually transcendental form of satisfaction or
contentment he feels in returning to her:

> It gives me wonder great as my content
>
> To see you here before me. O my soul's joy!
>
> If after every tempest came such calm,

May the winds blow till they have wakened death.

If it were now to die,

'Twere now to be most happy; for I fear

My soul hath her content so absolute

That not another comfort like to this

Succeeds in unknown fate. (2, 1, 183-92)

Such wonder is terribly close to woe. These are not the rewards of the soldier or public man. This is what Antony feels, what brings the imaginary close to bursting because it literally transports one to a place where life takes on a different cast and metaphors are truer than descriptions, where, for example, Egypt is more the home for one spirit than Rome can be. For even the exalted language is a demand for something to make it true and reflect it as having a place to dwell. Once we see this stage Othello can live on because he responds to, if he does not understand, a love that recognizes and lives in terms of his visage in his mind, the metaphysical aura he surrounds Desdemona with is in no way surprising. He often identifies her love as a literal place establishing his identity "There, where I have garnered up my heart,/Where either I must live or bear no life;/The fountain from which my current runs" (4, 2, 57-59). And given the nature of the contentment he gains from her reflection, the stakes are ultimately metaphysical: any fall from Eden or any contamination of this mirror will bring chaos again (3, 1, 92) or show "nature erring from itself" (3, 3, 226). The statement of content, then initiates an important allegorical dimension of the staging. It raises Othello into a world far beyond the one dominated by political concerns in the first act, while measuring in literal dramatic terms what a fall from this state will demand. In order to present these forces and prepare the need for a fall not into simply jealousy but into monstrosity, the actors' tasks here are remarkably like the lovers'—to preserve an alternate world free of the contamination in which fountains become cisterns and Desdemona appears "like" other women for whom common sense requires the divided loyalties Othello most fears:

I had rather be a toad

And live upon the vapor of a dungeon

Than keep a corner of the thing I love

For other men . . . (3, 3, 270-72)

It is worth repeating that Othello's fear is not silly. One cannot live in an alternate world if that world can at any moment collapse into momentary fiction or space shared by others. Conversely the burden of preserving that world demands a radical investment of one's identity which is inherently unstable because Othello gives Desdemona such power he will be tempted to overdetermine her slightest gesture. Shakespeare, however, is not content with this psychological basis for motivating his tragedy. He employs his allegorical framework and structural patterns to spin out a complex enactment of what is at stake in imaginary identification, especially in terms of the roles Desdemona must and cannot play. Consider first how Shakespeare surrounds the scene of Othello's most exalted feelings in order to show how his other main actors treat identity. On one side we find Iago's first victim Cassio suffering a fate that parallels Othello's. Cassio's basic lament is for his reputation, a form of imaginary self-regard that requires largely the public mirror of a symbolic order which seems fatally easy to restore. Cassio sees his tarnished image as the result of error, not of fatal contamination, so he dreams of a cure which makes only limited demands on Desdemona's capacity to reflect identities. From her point of view a corner of her attention will suffice, but this form of reflection is unimaginable to Othello. Equally foreign, but of a quite different order of being, is the control of images in the scene of social banter between Desdemona and Iago which precedes Othello's return. Here we notice several features of Desdemona's power to establish ideal worlds. She begins the banter, I think, in order to rescue Emilia from Iago's nasty and vulgar cracks. Iago's identity comes not from someone else reflecting his image but from his observing in others signs that their actions reflect his power to control. Confronted with this Desdemona, we must assume, sympathizes with Emilia, and more important, simply cannot bear the tawdry domestic melodrama that is now the stuff of our empirical stage.   If Cassio has a beauty that repels Iago, Iago's actions have a daily ugliness that is virtually metaphysical to her and requires her projecting a light theatrical alternative.   But the theatrical space she creates brings an odd tension into ordinary life.   First it embarrasses Iago by forcing him to a mode of being, a playful delicacy, which he can only handle by the force of a sharp critical intelligance that can negate the terms Desdemona wants to make him live up to, "thou praisest the worst best."   Her capacities cannot transform Iago but only bring out in compensation what is perhaps *his* visage in his mind, the dream of ultimate critical lucidity.   Much of the play is here in embryo: best and worst will depend on perspectives so that "proof" is relative to identity and the worlds one inhabits, and Desdemona's insistence on a world she can reflect as noble provokes only a social version of the violence Othello will wake in Iago.   Desdemona sees Iago's cynicism as a most lame and impotent conclusion, but she cannot see that this stance is his only form of potency.   Under the pressure of her elegance and Cassio's gentlemanly skills, Iago has no glass that can return a satisfying imaginary version of himself except one created out of his own will and intelligence and authorized by its power to invert the self-congratulatory forms of civility oppressing him.   Thus, it is only after this scene that Iago begins to revel in an imaginary future where his oppressors will get what to him is "justice."

    This apparently incidental scene is even more crucial to the play than the contrast between Cassio's victimage and Othello's. For Iago and Desdemona serve at once to outline the moral poles of Othello's world and to indicate by what they share the essential doubleness of all idealizations.   Typologically this interaction displays the historical forces competing to control and interpret heroic narrative and all it stands for.   Iago's versions of motivation and proof threaten to reduce heroism to an illusion or mask for crass power which manipulates illusions.   At the other pole, Desdemona's clarity before her father suggests that she sees Othello's true visage (even within his role as wooer) because she embodies an attitude that can read out the essential truths of narrative, although such a vision depends on forms of proof increasingly difficult to trust or to make others trust. Dramatically the very possibility of proof supporting Desdemona's view may depend on a destructive single-mindedness not unlike the willful blindness of Iago. This leaves Othello, and perhaps everyone seeking a performative identity that satisfies the imaginary, between two impossible options. There is the way of the critic and manipulator who bases his own ideal being in a distrust of all reflections from others so that he has only his own demonic compulsion to disprove ideals, at least all ideals but that of pure will—itself ironically absolutely dependent on there being others to victimize. Or there is the way of the philosopher who can see beneath appearances to capture essences, but whose identification with a world of ideals creates an equally narrow and isolating distance from the vagaries of the desires to which she must give meaning and value.

If I am correct about these allegorical forces, there is a good deal of truth in contemporary criticisms concentrating on Desdemona's goodness as a central fibre in the net that enmeshes them all (3, 3, 361-62). But I would reverse the cause—Desdemona helps bring about the final tragedy not because of her sexuality but because of limits inherent in her form of mirroring and giving meaning to identities. Her distance from Othello, who by this distance becomes a more representative figure, is most evident in the fact that like Iago she has no need for any "other" to reflect an identity back to her—Iago because his identity depends on a self-reflective sense of the power inherent in actualizing one's will, and Desdemona because she clearsightedly makes no excessive demands and needs no substitutions. Her existence is virtually identical to her essence. Consequently neither agent has much sympathy for those who seek an imaginary identity through another person. And this produces what is probably the most frightening dilemma in the play—that for Othello to pursue a King's demand on these ultimate terms of essential images held in the mind he must come to depend on principles which cannot fully enter or comprehend life in time and the vacillations of vulnerable psyches. While Desdemona never lapses from nobility, that very righteousness makes it impossible for her to comprehend what cannot be staged as nobility. Just as she must try to transform the signs of Iago's tawdry domestic arrangements, she refuses to accept any interpretation of Othello which would deny the ideal she holds and the level of motive she can accept as noble. She simply will not live in a world where vulgar names abound and men bely their nobility in degrading jealousies and tortured efforts to prove what to her is apodictic. What she cannot know on her terms she will not admit into existence: "My lord is not my lord; nor should I know him/Were he in favor as in humor altered" (3, 4, 124-25). And what her mind can reflect needs no caution or qualification. Unaware of the jealousy about identity built into the conditions of the imaginary, she can easily offer to reflect without contradiction the virtues of both Cassio and Othello. Her mirror is always whole, even if its allows corners for other uses, so there remains a sad truth to Othello's laments. Othello discovers in embryo what will become a basic problem for Western intellectual life: when a form of ideality in which we invest our ideas of nobility can no longer reflect empirical conditions, there is little alternative but the endless suspiciousness of Iago, with its need for absolute will as the only supplement for all the forms of proof suspiciousness destroys.

There is a sense then, in which Othello's feelings about adultery are plausible if not justified. For to the extent that Desdemona cannot bring herself to imagine the real plight of Othello, she presents him with neither an imaginary nor a real identity. She only reminds him of all she is not, and hence all that he can no longer be because his original image is now fractured within and without. A contentment beyond the natural becomes a self-division in which natural and ideal are as dislocated, as easy to confuse, as the forms of integrity Iago and Desdemona come to represent for Othello. There is no longer a mirror which coherently reflects things as they are and identity as one imagines one can take satisfaction in it.

These abstract analogies establish a remarkable conjunction between doubt, a philosophical form of aporia, and the psychological sense of self that emerges as one's vulnerable needs seem no longer sustained by imaginary identifications. So by the third act Shakespeare has constructed a set of forces so encompassing that they allow the monstrous to emerge as something considerably more than a moral idea or trope in a Christian allegory. As we come to fully recognize the forces Iago embodies and opposes, we begin to see how the allegorical properties of his characterization cease to depend on Christian terms but instead point to cosmic dimensions of what the play itself literally demonstrates. The devil becomes a figure for monstrosity, and monstrosity deepens because its full source is not Iago but a human condition susceptible to Iago. Monstrosity appears inseparable from the self-division of noble wills and the frustrations that entails. Then monstrosity becomes increasingly frightening as we are asked to contemplate the necessity for and difficulty of restoring something much deeper and more encompassing than a tarnished reputation. (That Othello's acts ruin his reputation with the Venetians appears as almost a trivial byproduct of a tragedy taking place on another, metaphysical stage.) The easiest way for me to demonstrate this briefly is to trace the process of mirrors becoming contaminated and identities doubled until the stakes involved in desiring proof seem more monstrous than the deeds one can "prove." Othello can no longer trust Desdemona to reflect a self and give him an image (proof) capable of resisting Iago, and he cannot find in Iago's pure demonism a lyrical or imaginative enough role to dignify fully the pain and rage he feels at being vioated. The stage itself must locate new sites for proving the consequences of such dilemmas.

Once its terms are set up, Othello's plight can be captured in a single, profoundly resonant gesture. Its context is again a scene where Cassio's identity is the subject. Cassio's appeal to Desdemona to restore his "place" creates intead Iago's opportunity to occupy that place. The imaginary does not correlate with social functions. This lack of coincidence then takes more profound form in the ironies attendant upon the agent's place when Othello requests Desdemona, "Leave me but a little to myself" (3, 3, 85). We notice first that this request is not a fully sincere utterance but a mask: because of his shame at his doubts and fears Othello is unwilling to express himself and risk his "true" image. That truth would to Desdemona be "untrue" with respect to the Othello she "knows." So there is, in a sense, no longer one self to be left to. There is instead only a need. And the need in turn becomes an opening for a rush of increasingly complex feelings for which no image is adequate and no idealization possible. The need, moreover, involves a paralyzing double bind as the monstrous now takes the form of forces which disfigure any possibility of reflecting with pride or pleasure on one's self-image. The inhuman becomes inseparable from the human. For Othello seeks not

Iago's truth but his love. Othello has learned from his experience of Desdemona to base criteria for truth on a form of passionate attachment—the only truth that can matter is one that commands affective assent and ennobles the thinker. But that makes him susceptible not simply to error but to enslavement by the demonic. Othello needs love to rescue standards of proof, but he needs standards of proof in order to know whom to love:

> I think my wife be honest, and think she is not;
>
> I think that thou [Iago] art just, and think thou art not.
>
> I'll have some proof. (3, 3, 384-86)

This is what remains when the hero fostered on imaginary demands is left to himself. Othello literally becomes the Othello who is not Othello, a condition that utterly puzzles the direct, "monological" Desdemona.[10]

The final irony of this withdrawal into self occurs at the conclusion of the seduction scene where Othello virtually marries Iago. Needing an identity, he identifies with a demonism which is most unlike the imaginary nobility he is trying to preserve. And as he develops this identification, the play begins to insist on contrasts from more realistic, sublimated drama. The play as performance raises questions about how it can be mediated, not primarily for metadramatic purposes but in order to deepen our sense of Othello's encounter with dimensions of the monstrous. While the other characters in the fourth act still seek an empirical understanding of events, Iago and Othello increasingly enter a world of pure metaphysical principles. Yet the more Othello evokes the demonic, the more he becomes degraded, and knows it—"a horned man's a monster and a beast" (4, 1, 61). All these forces are clear in the play's perverse use of the standard comic scene of mistaken identities. The reversal of genre in relation to the scene's content is the first aspect of degradation. Within this reversal we see a man descending to spy on his wife and so obsessed he himself serves as the unwitting tool of another. The need for the man who has commanded by appearances now to spy is painful enough; that he is so easily duped brings him very close to losing all his claim on humanity.

All his claim, that is, except the pathos and intensity of his pain. Shakespeare carefully brings in the Venetian envoy in order to preserve Othello's humanity, or at least his condition as something not reducible to empirical explanations. For the envoy makes the obvious judgment that he is acting badly, but the envoy's socially based evaluation simply misses both the nobility and the degradation.

It is important not to explain away the theatre of cruelty in the fourth act. It creates two contradictory pressures on the rest of the actions. First of all it puts extreme demands on the ways Othello's plight can be resolved. Having sunk so low, and having involved himself in demonic ritual, his purging act must take the form of a compensatory ritual. Shakespeare uses this need for a purgation equal to the degradation in order to project a striking sense of tragic heroism. If Othello is to redeem such debasement even partially, he must create for himself a new performative stage and project on it qualities of action neither Desdemona nor Iago could understand or reflect. Thus he partially breaks from all dependencies. Shakespeare's means is again structural contrast between Othello's desires and the comparatively banal monstrosity of Iago's negative will. For while Iago dictates the deed of murdering Desdemona, he is content with the literal fact. It is Othello who writes the script for the deed. His profound sense of the need for purgation, with its power to recognize the value of all he has lost, enables him to exalt a strangely right, yet perverse moment of religious submission to an utterly monstrous justice. But now "monstrous" ceases to be an adequate moral term. It can describe the deed but not truly evaluate the sense of justice carried by the blend of self-assertion and desperate self-punishment of the great speeches in his murder scene. Further implicating and partially justifying these passions is an equally intense allegorical contrast between the tawdry, practical murder presided over by Iago's light and the pathos of Othello's light, as he pursues a nobility inseparable from self-evasion and self-contempt, yet persuades us of the emotional rightness of his doomed and foolish violence. Where Iago saves himself by his cleverness, but does nothing to redeem "the savage spectacle" he presides over, Othello produces a sacrifice which by its intensity virtually creates the need for gods who can appreciate its desperate justice. This is a performance matched only by Lear's last speech to Cordelia: it almost creates its own truth and audiences to make it true. Desdemona is not wrong to cry "That death's unnatural that kills for loving" (5, 2, 42) but her philosophical clarity now stands out as incapable ultimately of reflecting what Othello has become. We see on stage something which is proof of quite another order of being. Othello acts because he has seen loving as unnatural, as a submission to conditions which allow one to become a monster whose continued love only further contaminates all it should exalt, until only some impersonal "it is the cause" can possibly point to a divinity capacious enough to take in such utterly human inhumanity. Othello's only truly monstrous deed is in some ways his most human act, but only for an audience capable of making identifications allowing it to see how Desdemona's final sympathy for Cassio (5, 2, 73-81) so mistakes the scene as an ordinary drama among rational human agents that for a moment one is tempted to think she deserves to be sacrificed.

This new level of performance, however, cannot entirely dominate the stage. Balancing it is a constant pressure in the fifth act towards the parodic pole of realism where one cannot separate the demonic, the noble, and the farcical. We are reminded in effect that there is no simple way, dramatically or metadramatically, to use an idea of tragic dignity as a means for restoring Desdemona's power to ground an idealized imaginary sense of noble identity. There is, in fact, on stage the reminder of Desdemona's dead body, a final ironic instance of a proof that the world will not yield entirely to metaphoric self-creation, however lyrical and repentant. Moreover, as Othello's power to dominate the present collapses, the play reminds us that the hero unfortunately lives beyond his most exalted moments. Time fractures every glass. So Shakespeare makes Othello his one hero whose climactic act is based on an absolute mistaking of obvious proof (similar to a Hamlet whose great moment was killing Polonius). So the empirical truth then cuts very deeply at the play's conclusions, leaving the play itself totally unresolved, or resolved as inescapably divided between passion and pathos, dignity and something close to degeneracy. He finds in her dying self-condemnation absolute proof of Desdemona's love, but it is an absolute which only confirms her difference from Othello and, as we shall see more fully in a moment, renders inescapable the division in himself between the one who acts and the one who imagines the meaning and value of the act as an expression of identity. Farce enters the situation, at least as potential, with the somewhat ludicrous effort of Desdemona to assert a calm truth within a scene at once cloyingly sentimental (the songs and marriage bed business) and passionately monstrous. And farce emerges as an inescapable element of the scene when her truth ultimately renders Othello virtually impotent. He bungles his thrust at Iago, is degraded before the Venetians, and above all, fails to elicit even from Emilia the slightest awareness of a visage in his mind which can redeem his bestial roaring. Critics have complained about these scenes as diminishing the tragic impact. But I consider it appropriate to end a tragedy about doubleness and monstrosity by refusing any humanistic self-congratulations about tragic dignity. When Desdemona can only prove the value of her glass by her death, there is nothing left by which to project and comprehend a purely heroic Othello.

Those actions Othello can now perform only recapitulate his self-division. His final statement of identity mirrors all the plays's contamination and dependencies. Once again we find groups searching for Othello. But now there is no confident sense of deeds as supporting a claim to worth. When asked where Othello is, Othello points to Iago and he cries "That's he that was Othello; here I am." (5, 2, 284). What is here is something very close to a pure absence, whose humanity remains in a Dantesque pain roaring as its only outlet. The source of identity he desired is silent on her bed, vindicated as truth but speechless for desire.

The best Othello can do is reflect upon his own contaminated state. Yet his version of justice cries out for a form of justice that is more ennobling than his vengeance on himself. And even here the moment of self-recognition—Othello's grasp of truth—cannot quite dispel the impotence and pathos of self-division. Tragic recognition becomes largely the awareness of unbearably unreconciled aspects of demand and need. Neither priest nor monster, he performs his final act in the guise of a simple heroic soldier, an earlier identity now set against the uncircumcised dog who had dared to make an exalted lover's form of the King's demand. Othello finds himself at the beginning of a modern history in which there often seems no way to destroy apparent monstrosity without turning oneself and all one believes into at least an equivalent monstrosity that mars all that is spoken (5, 2, 3, 57). The permissions that remain for his heirs take place on a much narrower stage built by performers who have no glass but that of the solipsist's interior paramour.

NOTES

[1] I develop the philosophical basis for my claims most fully in *Act and Quality: A Theory of Literary Meaning*, Amherst, University of Massachusetts Press, 1981.

[2] Wallace Stevens, *Collected Poems* (New York: Alfred Knopf, 1954), pp. 239-40. At the end of my reading I also quote from Stevens' "As You Leave the Room," in *Opus Posthumous* (New York: Alfred Knopf, 1957), p. 116.

[3] See J. L. Austin, "Performative Utterances," in his *Philosophical Papers* (New York: Oxford University Press, 1970). For my use of Austin in relation to expression see "The Concept of Expressive Implicature," *Centrum*, 6 (Fall, 1978), 90-103.

[4] See Hegel's *Phenomenology of Spirit*, trans. Karl Miller (Oxford: Clarendon Press, 1977) pp. 174-75, 187-207. And see Wallace's footnotes to his translation of Hegel's *Logic* (London: Oxford University Press, 1975), pp. 306-07.

[5] The best theoretical framework I have for clarifying ideas of situating is David Lodge's discussion in *The Modes of Modern Writing* (London: Edward Arnold, 1977) of differences between logics of historical inquiry and those required by metaphoric structures. For practical criticism, Richard Poirier's reading of the qualities in Frost's acts in *Robert Frost: The Work of Knowing* (New York: Oxford University Press, 1977) serves as an excellent example, although my theory would support more attention to the imaginative site of the discourse characterized by such qualities.

[6]Were I allowing myself theoretical arguments I would claim that situating the "meaning" involves capturing the intended performance; other forms of situating are inquiries into significance.

[7]I quote the relevant passages from his "Forword";

> The novel pretends only to be a record of the writer's own desires, aspirations, struggles; in a word a record of the profoundest experiences in the self. Nothing that comes from the deep passional soul is bad or can be bad. . . .
> Any man of real individuality tries to know and to understand what is happening, even in himself, as he goes along. This struggle for verbal consciousness should not be left out in art. It is a very great part of life. It is not superimposition of a theory. It is the passionate struggle into conscious being.
> We are now in a period of crisis. Every man who is acutely alive is acutely wrestling with his own soul. The people that can bring forth the new passion, the new idea, this people will endure. Those others that fix themselves in the old idea, will perish with the new life strangled unborn within them.

See Lawrence, *Women in Love* (New York: Random House, 1948), p. x.

[8]It would be an endless task to be specific about all of one's critical debts and disagreements with respect to Shakespeare. I hope it will suffice here to indicate the general lines of criticism I think partially mistaken. Howard Felperin, in fact, does a good job of describing both forms of thinking—one conservative and attentive to allegorical and "historical" frameworks, the other treating the plays as dramatic and relevant today. See Felperin, *Shakespearean Representation* (Princeton: Princeton University Press, 1977), pp. 79, 84-87. Felperin is very close to my concerns about the place of allegory and the concern in the plays for "the impulse to self-dramatization" (p. 85), but we take almost completely opposite approaches. He sees allegory as continually being demystified and reconstructed, while I argue there is an allegorical space beyond character in which the abstract forces are coherent and virtually literal. And he sets up as a dialectic of self-representation the playing and casting off of roles, as if there were substances beyond the roles, where I concentrate on the need to find a stable glass outside the self for men's performative energies. Felperin's ultimate commitment is to a sense of real beyond or at odds with language, mine to spaces of reflection opened by taking metaphoric constructs in terms of the relations they make literal. For

brief evidence of problems with Felperin's perspective, consider the following statement: "It is precisely their (Othello's and Iago's) ultimate inde-
terminancy in relation to their earlier models that sets them apart from
those models and makes them unconventional and life-like" (p. 85). This
means that they only become real as the play progresses. I suspect, however, that their reality is established by a few brief strokes—the rest of the
play gives complex ideal dimension to that reality. Felperin, in short,
is overly realistic, differing from Bradley only in his more epistemological
and to me more impoverished sense of realism. I have similar quarrels with
two of the most intelligent recent commentaries on the play—by Stephen
Greenblatt, "Improvisation and Power" in Edward Said, ed. *Literature and
Society* (Baltimore: Johns Hopkins University Press, 1980), pp. 57-99
and Stanley Cavell, *The Claim to Reason* (Oxford: Clarendon Press, 1979),
pp. 481-96. Both stress the implicit sexuality of Desdemona as a crucial
factor in the play. I will argue the opposite, only partially because I am
acutely aware of the danger of reducing questions of performance to a
melodrama about potency. More significant is the fact that their readings
reduce both Othello's condition and the typological ironies of Desdemona's
characterization in the service of features of her life that must be inferred
from off-stage behavior, as if drama were the bourgeois novel. Such attention to boudoir dimensions in plays like *Othello* only confirm John Barths'
allegory of Telemachus who is frustrated in his desire to hear epic adventures of his father because Menelaus insists on telling the tale of how he
humped Helen in the eighth year after the war. For Barth this is what
the modern spirit tempts us to make of the epic imagination.

[9] For Lacan's view of "the imaginary," see his *Ecrits* (Paris: Editions
de Seuil, 1966), pp. 93-124, 588-645. The less courageous or masochistic
may be content with the summary in Anika Lemaire, *Jacques Lacan*, trans.
David Macey (London: Routledge and Kegan, Paul, 1977), pp. 67-107. And
for Lacan's thought as a modern restatement of Renaissance Platonist concerns, see Eric La Guardia, "Lacan's Full and Empty Words, and Literary
Language," in *Proceedings of the VIth Congress of the International Comparative Literature Association* (Stuttgart: Eric Beiber OHG, 1973), 757-60.

[10] J. Hillis Miller defines a similar state of doubleness in *Troilus and
Cressida* as the dialogical set against the monological. See "Ariachne's
Broken Woof" *Georgia Review*, 31 (Spring, 1977). In my reading, I am
speaking of the idea of the dialogical as part of how we situate a performance, so for me the dialogical is a dramatic and not primarily a textual
condition and thus not the play's ultimate ontological stance.

LEARNING TO READ: INTERPRETATION AND READER-RESPONSE CRITICISM

by

Steven Mailloux

Interest in reader-response criticism has grown considerably in the last few years, though at times the basic premises of this approach seem only poorly understood. My purpose in this essay, therefore, is twofold: to clear up some misconceptions about this criticism by providing a detailed description of assumptions and strategies; and also to maintain a metacritical perspective that uses reader-response criticism as an example of how approaches to literature generally function. This dual purpose requires that I alternate between presenting reader-response criticism on its own terms and viewing its claims from outside its premises. First, I seek to outline my metacritical position; then in sections I and II, I represent the basic interpretive assumptions and critical practice of much reader-response criticism. Section III begins and ends with a further development of my metacritical perspective, while between these theoretical explanations is a more detailed survey of specific descriptive moves made by reader-response critics.

Every critical approach embodies a set of interpretive conventions used to make sense of literary texts. Such interpretive conventions are shared procedures for creating meaning, and they consist of interpretive assumptions manifested in specific critical moves.[1] A critic adopts (and is adopted by) these conventions in his attempt to describe, explicate, and explain any discourse, whether one line of poetry, a complete novel, or an entire literary tradition. The history of literary criticism is a chronicle of the changes in these shared interpretive strategies. For instance, conventions of Anglo-American New Criticism dominated in the United States during the nineteen-forties and fifties; the kind of text constituted by that criticism is known for its levels of unity, patterns of imagery, ironic tensions, and objective meanings. In the sixties and seventies, reader-response criticism joined many imported and domestic challengers to the New Critical hegemony, and like them it visualized other texts with different formal properties and changed literary effects.[2]

In this essay I focus on the most widely-reviewed version of reader-response criticism, that practiced by Wolfgang Iser, Stephen Booth, and Stanley Fish.[3] Like the New Criticism before it, reader-response criticism is not just one set of interpretive conventions; rather it consists of various sets gathered under one critical term because of a common focus on the reader. Partly due to the present moment in the history of criticism (with its reactions against the Intentional and Affective Fallacies), the focus on readers has become foregrounded, disguising the many interpretive assumptions not held in common by various reader-response critics. Among these differing assumptions is one that defines the relation between reader and text: for example, Gerald Prince and his followers focus on the reader *in the text;* David Bleich and Norman Holland on the actual reader's complete dominance *over the text;* and Iser, Booth, and Fish on the ideal reader's interaction *with the text.* Or again: for Prince the inscribed reader (the narratee) is part of the meaning in the narrative; for Bleich and Holland meaning is a creation by and in the individual reader; for Iser, Booth, and Fish meaning is a product of the interaction of reader and text.[4] It is the critical moves made in describing this interaction that I will portray in section II and analyze in section III of this essay. First, however, I will examine more closely the interpretive assumptions underlying this version of reader-response criticism as practiced by Iser, Booth, Fish, and their followers. By describing these assumptions and the critical moves arising from them, I hope to clarify one influential version of reader-response criticism and simultaneously allow it to stand as an example of how all critical approaches function as sets of interpretive conventions.

I. Assuming Readers Read

All of the critical strategies I discuss in section III assume a reader who is an active participant rather than a passive observer during the reading process. In his practical criticism, Wolfgang Iser focuses on "gaps" in the text that stimulate the "reader's creative participation" (*IR*, p. 275); while Stephen Booth's analyses of sonnets emphasize the "reading experiences that result from the multiplicity of organizations [formal, logical, ideological, etc.] in which, over the course of fourteen lines, the reader's mind participates" (*ESS*, p. ix). Therefore a typical (and, for my purposes here, central) act of reader participation is his contribution to the lessons he learns from a text: for example, Iser describes many reading experiences in which the reader works things out for himself instead of being told (e.g., *IR*, pp. 41-45, 154), and Stanley Fish often examines a text that "does not preach the truth, but asks that its readers discover the truth for themselves" (*SA*, p. 1).

In such practical criticism, the stage for action moves from the literary work to the reader's mind. What Fish says of *Paradise Lost* is true for most texts discussed by reader-response criticism: the mind of the reader becomes the "poem's scene" (*SS*, p. 1). In its strongest form, such criticism sees meaning itself as "an *event*, something that happens, not on the page, where we are accustomed to look for it, but in the interaction between the flow of print (or sound) and the actively mediating consciousness of a reader-hearer" (*SS*, p. x). Reader-response critics offer descriptions of this interaction, descriptions that often take the form of talk, not about "what a work *says* or *shows*," but about "what it *does*" (Booth, VH, p. 138).

A crucial issue for these critics is the identity of the reader whose experiences they portray; that is, whose reading responses are being described? Iser refers to the "implied reader" of his book's title as a term incorporating "both the prestructuring of the potential meaning by the text, and the reader's actualization of this potential through the reading process" (*IR*, p. xii). Iser also refers to the "educated reader" (p. 58), a close relative of the "ideal" or "informed reader," whom Fish describes as a person "sufficiently experienced as a reader to have internalized the properties of literary discourses, including everything from the most local of devices (figures of speech, etc.) to whole genres" (*SA*, p. 406). In actual critical practice, all of these theoretical constructs become identical to the "intended reader," the person "whose education, opinions, concerns, linguistic competences, and so on make him capable of having the experience the author wished to provide."[5] In this version of reader-response criticism, the author becomes a *manipulator* of readers, his techniques guiding the reader to the intended response.

To describe these reactions, reader-response critics adopt a temporal model of the reading process. Fish has made the following helpful distinction between formalist and reader-response enterprises:

> The lines of plot and argument, the beginnings, middles, and ends, the clusters of imagery, all the formal features that are observable when we step back from the reading experience, are, during that experience, components of a response; and the structure in which they are implicated is a structure of response. In other words, there is no necessary relationship between the visible form of a work and the form of the reader's experience—one is a complex of spatial, the other of temporal, patterns—and since it is in the context of the latter that meaning occurs, a criticism which restricts itself to the poem as 'object' will be inadequate to its pretentions. (*SS*, pp. ix-x)

Iser and Booth share Fish's preference for a temporal over a spatial model of the reading experience. Booth describes a "succession of actions upon the understanding of an audience" (VH, p. 139), while Iser focuses on the "potential time-sequence which the reader must inevitably realize" (*IR*, p. 280).

The interpretive assumptions of every critical approach form the enabling beliefs upon which its enterprise is founded. So it is with reader-response criticism: interpretive assumptions about the reader and the temporal reading process provide a basis for the strategies of its practical criticism. In the following section, I will adopt the interpretive conventions of reader-response criticism so that I can provide an extended example using in combination some of the critical moves that I discuss separately in section III.

II. A Sample Analysis: Using Up a Narrator

The question of the vanishing narrator in *Moby-Dick* has perplexed critics since the earliest reviews of the novel. The reviewer for the London *Spectator* expressed his concern in these words: "It is a canon with some critics that nothing should be introduced into a novel which it is physically impossible for the writer to have known: thus, he must not describe the conversation of miners in a pit if they *all* perish. Mr. Melville hardly steers clear of this rule, and he continually violates another, by beginning in the autobiographical form and changing ad libitum into the narrative."[6]   Though the first criticism results from the epilogue missing in *The Whale* (the British edition of *Moby-Dick*), the complaint about the change from autobiography to narrative is a precursor to later questions about what happens to Ishmael as narrator in the last quarter of the novel. Critics most often arrive at one of two conclusions: one side in the debate claims (with the *Spectator* reviewer) that Melville creates an artistic problem by changing narrators in mid-story; the other side denies that Ishmael actually disappears. Another interpretation is also possible: Ishmael does vanish as narrator, but his disappearance serves an aesthetic purpose.[7] My own view follows from this last interpretation. I see the vanishing narrator as a consequence of Melville's careful rhetorical plan: teaching the reader to read.

Outside the pages of his fiction, Melville spoke disparagingly of the "tribe of 'general readers,'" who were most responsible for the fact that "it is the least part of genius that attracts admiration." In his novels Melville took forms popular with this audience—whaling adventures, sensational Gothic romances, picaresque travel tales—and used them for his own kind of truth-telling. He wrote with a disguised dual purpose: to entertain and deceive the popular audience, to write books that sold because they could not be known for what they were by "the superficial skimmer of pages." These same books would reveal to the "eagle-eyed reader" the truth "covertly, and by snatches."[8]   Thus, Melville began *Pierre* with the intention of writing a lady's magazine romance for the popular audience, while he simultaneously composed a profound psychological exploration for his more perceptive reader.[9]

It was upon this "eagle-eyed reader" that Melville focused his rhetorical attention in *Moby-Dick*. Early chapters of the novel prepare the way for later ones, not simply by revealing new information but by arming the reader with interpretive habits, specific ways of reading. In the early chapters, Ishmael (a schoolmaster on land) teaches his readers to see the rich significances of the later chapters. Indeed, reading *Moby-Dick* is a process of learning to read it.

From the first, in "Loomings," Ishmael encourages the reader to "dive," to search for the deeper meanings. "He exhorts us to confront, and, if we can, to explain the meaning of a series of analogical situations, stated in various images."[10] The mysteries of the first chapter are followed by others, as Ishmael makes out of everything a puzzle, a problem: the true identity of the "Black Parliament" (Ch. 2); the "boggy, soggy squitchy picture" in the Spouter-Inn[11]; the "mystifying and exasperating stories" told by the landlord; the use of a mysterious "door mat"; "what to make of this head-peddling purple rascal," Queequeg (Ch. 3); the meaning of Queequeg's tatoos, which were like "an interminable Cretan labyrinth"; the memory of a childhood "mystery" (Ch. 4); Father Mapple's dragging up of his pulpit ladder, an act which "must symbolize something unseen"; the pulpit itself, so "full of meaning" (Ch. 8); and the map to the Nantucket Try Pots (Ch. 15). At one point Ishmael makes his lesson explicit: "All these things are not without their meanings" (Ch. 7). In fact, all of these early puzzles prepare the reader for the more complicated puzzles of Ahab and the Whale. Later in "Moby Dick" and "The Whiteness of the Whale," the reader's instruction continues, as Ishmael struggles to explain to him the "symbol" of the White Whale, first in its unitary significance to Ahab and then in its multiplicity of meaning to himself.

By the last quarter of the novel, the reader's training is complete. If he has learned his lesson well, he no longer requires an explicit guide to encourage him to make puzzles out of everything. He now sees the signifying nature of all things on his own. Thus, Ishmael disappears as narrator in the later chapters because he is no longer needed as a teacher. The reader uses him up by learning his lesson—the lesson of how to read the novel.

However, the structure of the reader's response can be further particularzied.   The specific habit of mind that Ishmael encourages in the reader is best illustrated (as Harrison Hayford has shown) by the first chapter: the crowds (including the reader) are confronted by the mystery of the sea, and what these inlanders discover is not an easy solution to the mystery, not an obvious signification for the symbol, but rather the "ungraspable phantom of life" (Ch. 1).   The reader is taught to follow the example of Ishmael (and later Ahab) in turning "every object, situation, and person they confront into a problem, one which cannot be solved, a mystery whose lurking meaning cannot be followed to its ultimate elucidation" (Hayford, pp. 121-122).   The pattern Hayford describes for Ishmael's puzzling is also an accurate depiction of the reader's experience: "confrontation-exploration-nonsolution of a problem."   This pattern is repeated in later chapters for both Ishmael and the reader.   "Moby-Dick," for example, is a chapter that begins with the problem of what the White Whale means to Ahab.   This question is explored and a theory set forth, but the chapter ends with Ishmael admitting that he cannot understand why the crew follows Ahab: "all this to explain, would be to dive deeper than Ishmael can go" (Ch. 41).   Again and again, Ishmael and the educated reader recognize that, though "some certain significance lurks in all things" (Ch. 99), that significance cannot always be captured.   The guiding lesson is clear: "Read it if you can" (Ch. 79).

The reader's education and the pattern of his response indicate the temporal structuring of *Moby-Dick,* the care in Ishmael's "careful disorderliness" (Ch. 82).   Not only does this interpretation dissolve the problem of the vanishing narrator, it also suggests a perspective on another critical controversy: it is not Ishmael who changes in the telling but the *reader* who changes in his reading.

III. The Critical Moves

The success or failure of the preceding critical performance depends on the persuasiveness, not of its evidence, but of the interpretive conventions that employ (and constitute) that evidence.[12]   These conventions (those of reader-response criti-

cism) consist of the interpretive assumptions I discussed in section I and the critical moves that I will now classify and describe.
Several of these moves are closely related because they arise
from the same interpretive assumptions; for example, the description of successive reading activities and the analysis of response
patterns both derive from the adoption of a temporal reading
model. Some strategies have an added relationship, being refinements of more basic moves; the variations on the reader-character axis will serve as an example. All critical approaches manifest a similar network of strategies, strategies arising out of an
inner core of premises and interrelated either as derivations
from a common assumption or as variations and refinements of
other critical strategies.

The *description of successive reading activities* is the most
common move made by the reader-response critics I am discussing. These critics focus on "the mind in the act of making
sense, rather than on the sense it finally (and often reductively)
makes" (Fish, *SA,* p. xii). Their descriptions of the temporal
reading experience often proceed section by section, line by
line, even word by word. The following compact example
of the strategy is from Fish's analysis of a passage by Augustine:
"The first part of the sentence—'He came to a place'—establishes a world of fixed and discrete objects, and then the second
half—'where he was already'—takes it away" (*SA,* p. 41). Here
the reader is first given something and then he loses it. By contrast, Fish would argue, a holistic interpretation of Augustine's
sentence ignores this temporal experience and provides only
an impoverished meaning extracted after that experience. Booth,
Iser, and others use this same strategy on longer passages, just
as I do in my analysis of the successive puzzles in *Moby-Dick.*
What such a move demonstrates is that "form also has a *temporal* dimension, manifest in the reader's sequential experience
of a work."[13]

A related strategy is also based on this assumption of a
temporal reading model: any patterns found are placed not in the
text but in *the structure of the reader's response.* For instance,
Booth writes that "the audience's sensation of being unexpectedly and very slightly out of step is repeated regularly in
Hamlet." This pattern plays a central role in Booth's thesis
that the play "is insistently incoherent and just as insistently

coherent" (VH, pp. 140, 139). Patterns of a similar temporal nature are posited throughout Fish's applied criticism. In a recent book, he demonstrates how the poems in Herbert's *The Temple* work "by inviting the reader to a premature interpretive conclusion, which is first challenged, and then reinstated, but in such a way as to make it the vehicle of a deeper understanding" (*The Living Temple*, p. 35). This pattern is a more complex version of that described in his previous book: in the "self-consuming artifact," the reader "is first encouraged to entertain assumptions he probably already holds and then is later forced to reexamine and discredit those same assumptions" (*SA*, p. 10). Still earlier, Fish found a simpler pattern in *Paradise Lost*: "mistake, correction, instruction" (*SS*, p. 42). Similarly, my analysis of *Moby-Dick* uses the "pattern of confrontation-exploration-nonsolution" that Hayford sees for Ishmael as a description of the reading experience the novel provides.

The attempt to describe these sequential activites and temporal patterns is an attempt to close the gap between criticism and reading: "it may be truer to the reader's experience of the text to speak of a succession of moments that yield varying effects."[14] Reader-response critics make the description of reading identical to the act of criticism and claim that they accurately represent the temporal reading process in their analyses. To convince others that this descriptive claim is valid, the reader-response critic often resorts to the device of *citing other readers' reactions*. Booth's "Preface" best illustrates this device of using evidence external to one's own reading experience:

> The responses I attribute to my hypothetical reader of the sonnets cannot ultimately be more universal or other than my own. I have attempted to demonstrate that the responses I describe are probable in a reader accustomed to Elizabethan idiom. I have also quoted at length from the responses of the critics and editors who have preceded me in the study of the sonnets; their comments, glosses, and emendations provide the best available evidence that the responses I describe are not idiosyncratic. (*ESS*, p. x)

In his discussion of *Hamlet*, Booth also uses other critics' responses in demonstrating the confusion he claims to see in the reader's experience of the play; thus, he argues that it is intended incoherencies in the text that cause critics to propose stage directions to "make sense of Hamlet's improbable raging at Ophelia in III.i" (VH, p. 137).

I use a similar strategy in my analysis of *Moby-Dick*, when I cite the perception by Melville critics that Ishmael disappears as narrator; I use their interpretation as support for the final act I posit in the reader's education—the reader' learning of his lesson and the resultant loss of his teacher. Fish also uses such evidence but pushes it in different directions. For example, he takes a critical controversy over the meaning of a passage and uses the controversy to show that two contradictory meanings are equally available, his usual conclusion being that the recognized ambiguity is to be experienced, not resolved, by the reader. In fact, recognizing ambiguity becomes the meaning *(Is There a Text in This Class?* pp. 150-151.) Another strategic use of other critics' readings is to show how successful an author is in trapping his reader; that is, a critic's interpretation is taken not as the "right" response but as evidence that the author encouraged the "wrong" response so that he could later correct his reader (e.g., *SA*, pp. 219-21).

This first group of critical moves is derived from the basic assumption that criticism should analyze the temporal reading experience: the reader-response critic tries to describe successive reading activities and patterns of response and validates his descriptions with evidence from other critics' reactions. Another strategy is used to support not individual analyses but the whole enterprise of concentrating on the reader: the accumulation of external evidence to demonstrate authorial concern with readers. This strategy is less a part of the reader-oriented analysis than an argument for its critical respectability. Thus, we find Iser referring to letters in which Richardson states that "the story must leave something for the reader to do" and other letters in which Thackeray shows he "did not want to edify his readers, but to leave them miserable" (*IR*, pp. 31, 116). Roger Easson makes a similar move in his reader-response analysis of *Jerusalem*, which begins: "Repeatedly, in his correspondence, in his marginalia, and in his poetry, William Blake expresses an abiding concern with his audience."[15] My use of a Melville letter and his essay on Hawthorne has the same rhetorical purpose as these other critical moves: to prove that my emphasis on the reader was shared by the author of the text I am analyzing.

An even more basic strategy is to cite direct references to the reader in the text being discussed (see Iser, *IR*, pp. 29, 38). Such a procedure not only justifies the reader-centered focus but also becomes a part of the description of the reading experience. The next series of moves are really only refinements of this basic strategy. All of these moves either place the reader in the text in some way *or* demonstrate correspondences between elements in the text and the reader's experience.

The first move in this group shows how *the reader's response is a topic of the story.* For example, Booth demonstrates that the "illogical coherence—coherent madness" experienced by the audience of *Hamlet* is "a regular topic of various characters" in the play (VH, p. 172). And for Shakespeare's sonnets, he argues that the author "evokes in his reader something very like the condition he talks about" (*ESS*, p. 59). In fact, this strategy of demonstrating response as topic sometimes expands into a claim that *the subject of the text is the reader.* For Booth, *Hamlet* becomes "the tragedy of an audience that cannot make up its mind" (VH, p. 152). For Fish, *Paradise Lost* has as its center of reference "its reader who is also its subject" (*SS*, p. 1). The potential self-reflexiveness of this strategy is apparent in Easson's essay: Blake's *Jerusalem* "is a poem about itself, about the relationship between the author and his reader. . . . *Jerusalem* may be read as a poem about the experience of reading *Jerusalem*" (Easson, p. 309).

Instead of putting the reader in the text, a related critical move demonstrates how settings and events already in the text correspond to the reader's experience of that text. "*Jerusalem* mirrors the state of the reader," claims Easson (p. 314). More specifically, Fish shows how in *Paradise Lost* Michael's teaching of Adam in Book XI resembles Milton's teaching of the reader throughout the poem (*SS*, p. 22); and in his discussion of Herbert's poetry, Fish argues that "what is happening in the poem"—the "actions" of the speaker—corresponds to "what is happening in (and to) the reader" (*SA*, p. 165). Booth also exemplifies this recurrent strategy when he writes, "As the king is threatened *in* scene one, so is the audience's understanding threatened *by* scene one" (VH, p. 147).

A refinement of this last move is to point out a specific model in the text for the entire reading experience. Here a section of the reader's response is taken as a type of the whole. In discussing *Vanity Fair*, Iser finds "an allegory of the reader's task at one point in the novel"—a brief scene which "contains a change of standpoints typical of the way in which the reader's observations are conditioned throughout this novel" (*IR*, pp. 110-111). In Hamlet's "little poem on perception and truth," Booth also discovers "a model of the experience of the whole play" (VH, p. 173). And in my analysis of Melville's novel I cite the strategy of one reader-response critic who calls Ishmael's attempt to interpret the Spouter-Inn painting "a useful model . . . for the would-be interpreter of *Moby-Dick*" (see note 11).

The next group of critical moves I will describe focuses on the reader's relationship to the narrator and characters. The simplest of this group is the strategy (traditional in discussions of satire) which points out implicit references to the reader's life outside his present reading experience. Robert Uphaus's chapter on *Gulliver's Travels* illustrates this move when it emphasizes that the "transference from manifest fiction to the reader's [life] experience . . . is, perhaps dismayingly, insisted upon" (Uphaus, p. 18). Another move for the reader-response critic is to note how the narrator explicitly comments on the reading activities that the critic has posited. Iser, for instance, points out where Fielding, in *Joseph Andrews*, "makes various observations about the reader's role as producer"; for Iser, this is a reference to the reader's filling of gaps, his imaginative participation (*IR*, p. 39). A refinement of this critical strategy is to apply a character's comment to reading responses; for example, Booth writes that Horatio's comment "describes the mental condition evoked in an audience by this particular dramatic presentation of events as well as it does that evoked in the character by the events of the fiction" (VH, p. 142).

A commonplace of much traditional criticism is the identification of reader with characters, and, not surprisingly, reader-response critics use this device. (See Booth, VH, p. 150, and Iser, *IP*, p. 117.) More interesting, however, are the variations performed on this reader-character axis. Distinctions must be made, for example, among critics' (1) having the reader identify his life experiences with a character's, (2) having the reader become self-consciously aware of resemblances between his *reading* experience and characters' actions, and (3) simply declaring that a character's act mirrors the reader's activities during the reading process with no reader awareness of that resemblance. For example, Fish uses the second strategy when he argues that "a large part of the poem's meaning is communicated" to the reader through his awareness that Adam's experience in the poem "parallels" the reader's experience reading the poem (*SS*, p. 29). Here the resemblance between character actions and reader activities is made a part of the reading experience. The third move mentioned above makes no such claim for reader awareness; the critic simply demonstrates a correspondence between a character's acts and the reader's response, as in Carole Berger's description of *Pride and Prejudice*: "Instead of guiding us to accurate judgments of Darcy and Wickham, Austen creates an experience analogous to Elizabeth's in its bewildering complexity and susceptibility to distortion" (Berger, p. 539). This is the same move that Fish makes in his discussion of Herbert's poetry where the speaker and reader are associated in similar disorienting and educational experiences: "Like 'The Holdfast,' 'A True Hymne' proceeds in stages, and again like 'The Holdfast,' its stages represent levels in the reader's understanding as well as plateaus in the spiritual history of the speaker" (*SA*, p. 200).

A final move using the reader-character relation detaches the two "actors" from each other: "in the *Phaedrus,* there are two plots; Socrates and Phaedrus are busily building a picture of the ideal orator while the reader is extracting, from the same words and phrases, a radical criticism of the ideal" (*SA*, p. 13). In this move Fish does not identify reader with character but rather contrasts the two. In another variation on this strategy, Iser shows that *Vanity Fair* "denies the reader a basic focal point of orientation. He is prevented from sympathizing with the hero" (*IR*, p. 107). Such detachment from characters is a prerequisite for judging them, even when that judgment is a result of prior identification or resemblance; for example, Fish describes a version of the Herbertian "double motion" in which "the speaker and the reader part company and the latter becomes a critic and corrector of the former's words and thoughts" (*SA*, p. 178).

Having the reader judge the characters is often, even in traditional criticism, only a step on the way to having the reader judge himself.   But in reader-response criticism, describing such self-evaluation becomes a central concern, and this concern manifests itself in a variety of critical moves.   In one move the critic shows how the reader is pressured to judge his own actions and attitudes performed outside his reading of the text: Uphaus, for instance, argues that in *Gulliver's Travels* the reader's attention is called not simply to some of "the arbitrary niceties that are the domain of royalty" but to some of "the dubious distinctions . . . that the reader may unconsciously accept or consciously sustain" (Uphaus, p. 17).   Here the reader judges the characters in the text *and* himself in his everyday life.

A related move is to describe the reader correcting himself but not the characters; this move abandons the reader-character axis and its depiction here initiates the final series of critical strategies I will discuss.   In this move, *the reader becomes a judge of his own reading responses.*   As Fish puts it for *Paradise Lost*, the reader is "simultaneously a participant in the action and a critic of his own performance" (*SS*, p. xiii).   The object of judgment here is not the reader's everyday life but his actions performed during the reading of the text causing those actions. Thus, Iser shows how the author of *Joseph Andrews* encourages a feeling of superiority in such a way that the reader eventually becomes embarrassed ("trapped") by that feeling (*IR*, p. 44). Iser does not pinpoint the moment of entrapment; rather he suggests that at some *unspecified* time following the initial feeling of superiority, the reader becomes embarrassed by it. In contrast, Fish and Booth repeatedly describe precise moments when a reader turns on himself because of a specific textual event or statement.

Before describing these more precise specifications of reversal, I need to explain the critical move upon which they depend: the description of reader expectations and their disappointment.   Howard Anderson provides one of many examples that I could cite: "Sterne repeatedly manipulates us by deliberately disappointing expectations of narrative form which we have developed through our prior reading."[16]   Shattered expectations result in disappointment, disorientation, confusion; these effects recur again and again throughout applied reader-response criticism. Such disappointed expectations especially proliferate in the reading experiences Fish describes in *Surprised by Sin*. His description of the Guilty Reader is typical: beginning with assumptions about epic tradition and Christian myth, the reader is startled to discover what seems to be an admirable Satan. The speciousness of the devil's argument becomes apparent to the reader only after Milton's epic voice intervenes. Then the reader admonishes himself for "the weakness all men evince in the face of eloquence" (pp. 4-9). This example not only illustrates how Fish uses unfulfilled expectations in his analyses; it also shows how he pinpoints the moment when a reader becomes his own critic.

In reader-response criticism a reader's disappointed expectations are never viewed as ends in themselves; rather, such disorientation always becomes an authorial means for a more significant end, such as the moral trial of the reader. In reader-response analyses, we find many statements describing this authorial purpose: *Mansfield Park* includes "a test of the reader's moral perceptiveness" (Berger, p. 535); in *Vanity Fair* the reader "is constantly invited to test and weigh the [moral] insights he has arrived at as a result of the profusion of situations offered him" (Iser, *IR*, p. 119); in *Paradise Lost* Milton puts the reader on trial by "fitting temptations to our inclinations and then confronting us immediately with the evidence of our fallibility" (Fish, *SS*, p. 41). The last statement in this sampling indicates the specific use to which reader-response critics put the reader's disorientation: the text contradicts the reader's expectations as it corrects his actions. Trial thus becomes entrapment. For example, after being encouraged to judge every word and act of the devils in Hell, the reader of *Paradise Lost* continues this associational and judgmental practice in a totally different and inappropraite situation—unfallen man in Edenic Paradise; the reader is thus "forced to admit again and again that the evil he sees under everyone's bed is his own" (Fish, *SS*, p. 102). Self-criticism is the result, then, of misplaced assumptions, shattered expectations, trial by error, and correction from the text.

According to reader-response critics, however, even self-evaluation is not the final resting place intended for the reader. The last move I want to discuss is the critic's demonstration that self-judgment is simply an authorial means for *educating the reader*. This brings me to a final pair of strategies used in reader-response criticism—the descriptions of two different but related processes: learning by reading and learning to read. Both assume that the reader learns as an active participant rather than as a passive observer. The reader's education is therefore "not so much a teaching as an intangling."[17] That is, the reader is involved "in his own edification " (Fish, *SS*, p. 49). In the experiences Iser portrays, the disappointment of expectations pushes the reader toward discovery, and the entanglement of the reader in moral conflicts forces him to formulate solutions of his own (*IR*, pp. 35-45). What Iser describes here are the lessons of the text—learning by reading—rather than a lesson on reading that text.

Describing this latter process—learning to read the text— is the paradigmatic move of reader-response criticism. It is one I make use of in my analysis of *Moby-Dick* in order to resolve an interpretive crux: Ishmael "disappears" because he has served his purpose of teaching the reader to read his book. This critical move is ingeniously duplicated throughout reader-response criticism. Iser describes essays in *Tom Jones* as "guide-lines" for showing the reader "how he is to view the proceedings" (*IR*, p. 47). Discussing *Hamlet*, Booth notes that "after the fact, the play often tells us how we should have reacted" (VH, p. 160). Anderson argues that "Sterne uses the example of false judgments of minor characters to guide the reader's judgment of his major character in the future" (Anderson, p. 970). And again Iser: "the potential experiences of the first two monologues [in *The Sound and the Fury*] serve to sharpen the reader's critical eye, creating a new background against which he will judge Jason's clear-cut actions" (*IR*, p. 149). In all these examples, critics describe how earlier passages in a text prepare the reader to judge, to interpret, to read later passages.

Descriptions of this cumulative training are made possible by all the groups of critical moves I have discussed: accounts of temporal reading responses, refinements of seeing the reader in the text, variations on reader-character analyses, and versions of having the reader judge himself. Fish uses all these critical strategies in his analysis of reading *Paradise Lost.* In one place he demonstrates that the result of corrections by the epic voice "is the adoption of a new way of reading." Taken in by Satanic rhetoric, the reader "proceeds determined not to be caught out again; but invariably he is" (*SS*, p. 14). Here the reader learns to read so that he can be shown how difficult it is to read the text (and the world) correctly. In this case, learning to read ultimately becomes learning by reading.

The critical moves I have discussed are the most common strategies used in applied reader-response criticism. However (to return one final time to my metacritical position), these strategies are not simply techniques employed by critics to describe a text and a response. Rather, they are manifestations of interpretive conventions that constitute that text and its effects (see notes 1 and 2). It is true that reader-response criticism claims to approximate closely the content of reading experiences that are always assumed to pre-exist the critical performance. But what in fact takes place is quite different: the critical performance fills the category of "reading experiences" with the content of its own interpretive moves. Like all critical approaches, reader-response criticism is a set of interpretive conventions that constitutes what it claims to describe.

Moreover, the interpretations (presented as neutral descriptions) not only function as warrants for specific readings; they also serve as an argument for the whole reader-response enterprise. To return to just one illustration from the previous discussion: reader-response critics often interpret the subject of a text to be the reader. This strategy works by describing the reader's relation to the text (he is the subject of it), and this description simultaneously provides the evidence that legitimizes the reader-centered focus of which it is a part. That is, the description of the reader as subject of the text is at the same time a justification for focusing on the reader. Here an interpretation generates evidence that is taken as validation of the attempt at making that interpretation in the first place. It would be a mistake, however, to judge this argument as a vicious circle that could be avoided. Actually it is merely a special case of the way all criticism works: facts do not cause interpretations; interpretations constitute facts. (Of course, this is as true of my own metacritical description as it is of the critical analyses I describe.) Every act of criticism would persuade us to adopt its conventions and to "write" the text it "describes."[18]   If we are convinced by an interpretation, it is finally the critic who teaches us to read.

NOTES

[1] For more on this critical theory, see Steven Mailloux, *Interpretive Conventions: The Reader in the Study of American Fiction* (Ithaca: Cornell Univ. Press, 1982).

[2] See the theory of interpretation elaborated in Stanley Fish, *Is There a Text in This Class? The Authority of Interpretive Communities* (Cambridge, Mass.: Harvard Univ. Press, 1980), especially pp. 163-73. Fish's book develops a metacritical position that calls into question the descriptive claims of his applied reader-response criticism.

[3] Subsequent references to works by these critics will be made in the text using the following key: Wolfgang Iser, *The Implied Reader: Patterns of Communication in Prose Fiction from Bunyan to Beckett* (Baltimore: Johns Hopkins Univ. Press, 1974) [*IR*]; Stephen Booth, "On the Value of *Hamlet*," in *Reinterpretations of Elizabethan Drama: Selected Papers from the English Institute*, ed. Norman Rabkin (New York: Columbia Univ. Press, 1969), pp. 137-76 [*VH*]; Stephen Booth, *An Essay on Shakespeare's Sonnets* (New Haven: Yale Univ. Press, 1969) [*ESS*]; Stanley E. Fish, *Surprised by Sin: The Reader in Paradise Lost*, 2nd ed. (Berkeley: Univ. of California Press, 1971) [*SS*]; Stanley E. Fish, *Self-Consuming Artifacts: The Experience of Seventeenth-Century Literature* (Berkeley: Univ. of California Press, 1972) [*SA*].

[4] For detailed comparisons of various reader-response approaches, see Mailloux *Interpretive Conventions*, pp.19-65, and Susan R. Suleiman, "Introduction: Varieties of Audience-Oriented Criticism," in *The Reader in the Text: Essays on Audience and Interpretation*, ed. Suleiman and Inge Crosman (Princeton: Princeton Univ. Press, 1980), pp. 3-45. Also see *Reader-Response Criticism: From Formalism to Post-Structuralism*, ed. Jane P. Tompkins (Baltimore: Johns Hopkins Univ. Press, 1980).

[5] Fish, *Is There a Text in This Class?*, pp. 160-61. Cf. Jonathan Culler,

Structuralist Poetics (Ithaca: Cornell Univ. Press, 1975), especially pp. 113-30 on "literary competence," and Mailloux, *Interpretive Conventions,* pp. 94-113 on·"inferred intention."

[6]Review of *The Whale,* London *Spectator,* 25 October 1851, rep. in *Moby-Dick as Doubloon,* ed. Hershel Parker and Harrison Hayford (New York: Norton, 1970), p. 12.

[7]For examples of these interpretations, see Leon Howard, *Herman Melville* (Berkeley: Univ. of California Press, 1951), p. 179; Walter E. Bezanson, *"Moby-Dick:* Work of Art," in *Moby-Dick Centennial Essays,* ed. Tyrus Hillway and Luther S. Mansfield (Dallas: Southern Methodist Univ. Press, 1953), pp. 30-58; Glauco Cambon, "Ishmael and the Problem of Formal Discontinuities in *Moby-Dick,*" *MLN,* 76 (1961), 516-23; Paul Brodtkorb, Jr., *Ishmael's White World* (New Haven: Yale Univ. Press, 1965), pp. 1-10; amd William B. Dillingham, "The Narrator of *Moby-Dick,*" *English Studies,* 49 (1968), 20-29.

[8]The first quotation in this paragraph is from Melville's letter to Nathaniel Hawthorne, June 1 (?) 1851. All the other quotations are from Herman Melville, "Hawthorne and His Mosses," *Literary World,* 17 and 24 August 1850. Both of these documents are reprinted in the Norton Critical Edition of *Moby-Dick,* ed. Harrison Hayford and Hershel Parker (New York: Norton, 1967), pp. 535-60. All quotations from *Moby-Dick* in this section are taken from this edition.

[9]Brian Higgins and Hershel Parker, "The Flawed Grandeur of Melville's *Pierre,*" in *New Perspectives on Melville,* ed. Faith Pullin (Edinburgh: Edinburgh Univ. Press, 1978), p. 162.

[10]Harison Hayford, "'Loomings': Yarns and Figures in the Fabric," in *Artful Thunder,* ed. Robert J. DeMott and Sanford E. Marovitz (Kent, Ohio: Kent State Univ. Press, 1975), p. 123. My interpretation of *Moby-Dick* is derived from the essays and lectures of Harrison Hayford; his readings have been developed further and passed on to me by Hershel Parker. Though neither Melvillian should be held accountable for what I do with their insights, I owe a great debt to both for they have taught me how to read Melville's masterpiece. I should also note here that in his recent article, "Unnecessary Duplicates: a Key to the Writing of *Moby-Dick,*" in Pullin, pp. 128-161, Hayford provides in passing a very different explanation than the one I suggest for the disappearance of Ishmael as narrator.

[11]In a recent reader-response analysis of *Moby-Dick,* Carey H. Kirk

notes that this picture "provides a useful model as well as a disconcerting initiation for the would-be interpreter of *Moby-Dick*," ("*Moby-Dick:* The Challenge of Response," *Papers on Language and Literature*, 13 [1977], 384). Cf. Morton L. Ross, "*Moby-Dick* as an Education," *Studies in the Novel*, 6 (1974), 71-73.

[12] See Stanley Fish, *The Living Temple: George Herbert and Catechizing* (Berkeley: Univ. of California Press, 1978), pp. 170-73, and *Is There a Text in This Class?*, pp. 365-69.

[13] Carole Berger, "The Rake and the Reader in Jane Austen's Novels," *Studies in English Literature, 1500-1900*, 15 (1975), 544.

[14] Robert W. Uphaus, *The Impossible Observer: Reason and the Reader in 18th-Century Prose* (Lexington: Univ. Press of Kentucky, 1979), pp. 17-18.

[15] Roger R. Easson, "William Blake and His Reader in *Jerusalem*," in *Blake's Sublime Allegory*, ed. Stuart Curran and Joseph A. Wittreich, Jr. (Madison: Univ. of Wisconsin Press, 1973), p. 309.

[16] Howard Anderson, "*Tristram Shandy* and the Reader's Imagination," *PMLA*, 86 (1971), 967.

[17] Fish quoting Milton, *Complete Prose Works of John Milton*, II, ed. Ernest Sirluck (New Haven: Yale Univ. Press, 1959), p. 642 (*SS*, p. 21).

[18] The hermeneutics advocated here is ultimately neither realist nor idealist; it is *rhetorical*. See Steven Mailloux, "Convention and Context," *New Literary History*, 14 (1983), 399-407, and "Truth or Consequences: On Being Against Theory," *Critical Inquiry*, 9 (1983), 760-766; both essays correct the epistemological idealism found in Mailloux, *Interpretive Conventions*, pp. 192-207.

CHEAP THRILLS: LOST 'AUTHORITY'
AND ADVENTITIOUS AESTHETIC *FRISSONS*

by
Hershel Parker

Now that formalists have gone underground, few will come forth to testify to their belief in the certain authority of an uncertain literary text, that mystical source of power we used to call "the text itself." Academic journals where New Critics used to celebrate "imagery in" and "unity of" are now crowded with critics who exult in the authority of a subjective reader or the authority of an interpretive community over the poor remnants of the once omnipotent text; and jostling the subjectivists and the interpretive communards aside are the deconstructionists who propose to undermine all authority through essays they have humbly submitted to the whim of editorial boards. A handful of hermeneutists such as E. D. Hirsch (and his recent follower P. D. Juhl) and a dozen or two textualists still quaintly believe that literary authority comes, if at all, from the author, despite the widespread suspicion that he has perished somewhere during his prolonged banishment from literary discussion. As a textual scholar I belong to this small crew, content to wait out the fads until everyone comes back to the study of literature as the product of men and women living in particular times and subject to particular experiences and influences, literary and otherwise.

Yet intentionalist though I am, I hesitate to follow Hirsch in claiming without qualification that the meaning of a literary work cannot change, or to assert like Juhl that the meanings of textual details are always intended by the author.[1] In many of the standard American novels I am familiar with, authorial words evoke from the reader responses unintended by the author. The meanings which the authors built into their texts have been changed, and most of the changes are not only unintended but unimagined by the author or anyone else besides the reader. The attentive reader who progresses through such a novel will experience not only genuine authorial rewards but also some perfectly real aesthetic *frissons* which, although coming from words the author wrote, are haphazard and spurious. I am not talking about the chance results of outlandish literary experiments but about the everyday inadvertent consequences of a writer's imperfectly altering a text, usually after it had been complete in an earlier form. These adventitious thrills, passing for authentic authorially-created goosebumps, are more abundant than anyone has suggested, and are of a significance which shames that notorious example of a fatuous literary response to a textual error, the cheap thrill F. O. Matthiessen felt when he was brushed by a "soiled fish," a single-word compositor's error in a modern reprint of a nineteenth-century novel.[2]

I will draw my illustrations from four novels with diverse textual histories: *Pudd'nhead Wilson,* salvaged by a process of drastic excision plus tiny bridging of gaps; *The Red Badge of Courage,* fitted for genteel readership by the excision of an entire chapter, three chapter endings, and other small cuts; *Tender is the Night,* rendered partially incoherent by a reordering of sections; and *An American Dream,* greatly damaged by tiny excisions.[3] While we can produce documents showing how the authors of these works reacted to the prospect of being asked to make changes in some of their other works, we have no specific authorial comments on the creation of adventitious meanings in these four novels. Whether a jackleg novelist (as Mark Twain bragged he was) or highly self-conscious students of novelistic techniques like F. Scott Fitzgerald and Norman Mailer, these writers do not seem to have had any notion that they were creating inadvertent aesthetic effects by their alterations. The sloppiest among them, Mark Twain, at least actively hoped that what he ended up with would *work*, somehow, without his having to revise to *make* it work; he contented himself with a bit of retro-fitting and a great cloud of vague retro-wishing. Stephen Crane seems to have operated under duress, making the cuts he had to make and forgetting all about it as soon as he could. Fitzgerald focused on one wishful goal: if he reordered the book, readers would know for sure at the outset that it was about Dick Diver, and then perhaps it would belatedly gain the success it deserved. I suspect Mailer felt the need, at some stage or stages of his prolonged, intense revision, to protect himself from having readers take the hero as even more autobiographical than he was and from having readers distort the portrayal of male sexuality. Whatever their motives and whatever their skills, these writers seem to have assumed wrongly that the unchanged words would continue to mean what they had meant when they were written, or mean all they had meant except for whatever aspects were to be removed or disguised. Later they apparently did not realize they had done their works any harm, never behaved as if they had left a legacy of inadvertent aesthetic effects.

I will lay out my case histories tersely, with a glance, each time, at the kinds of adventitious effects we can expect to occur from the particular textual situation. If you want to experience some adventitious aesthetic effects by yourself first, in the privacy of your study, go ahead. No one will know what you're doing. Just read *Pudd'nhead Wilson, The Red Badge of Courage* (except in the new Norton text edited by Henry Binder), *Tender is the Night* (in the Cowley edition), and *An American Dream* (in book form). You'll have cheap thrills aplenty. If you can resist this temptation, read on, and I'll show you other readers, dressed in their little brief authority as literary critics, reveling in cheap thrills the authors had no notion anyone would find in their altered texts and, almost incidentally, taking some cheap shots at the authors or loading them with cheap praise. Afterwards I will discuss some of the biases critics reveal as they celebrate these maimed texts—and as they celebrate the authors for their adventitious effects and castigate them for not being able to do what they really did.

Mark Twain saved the incriminating evidence about *Pudd'n-head Wilson,* so we know that he started writing a farcical story about Italian brothers, conjoined twins with two heads, four arms, one body, and two legs, who come to Dawson's Landing, a village downriver from St. Louis, where they meet a lawyer without a practice, Pudd'nhead Wilson, and a local young sneak thief, Tom Driscoll. After many elaborate one-joke scenes dealing with the sensation the twins occasion among the townspeople, the bickering over their incompatible habits and beliefs, and the difficulty of ascribing the results of their actions to the proper causes (Luigi drinks and Angelo gets the hangover, but how can you know which twin kicks Tom?), Mark Twain had a new brainstorm: Tom would be a changeling, part black and a slave. He continued writing some farcical pages about the twins even in between writing pages in which Tom treacherously sells his (newly-created) mother down the river and murders the man who is now only his supposed uncle. Mark Twain wound up with a spectacular trial in which Pudd'nhead saves the falsely-accused twins and exposes Tom as a slave and a murderer. After writing this ending, he went back and wrote a new beginning in which Roxy exchanges her son for her master's, the boys grow up, Roxy is freed and goes away steamboating, and Roxy's return then soon reveals to Tom that *he* is the slave Chambers and she is his mother. Into this new material Mark Twain stuck many early-written pages about the arrival of the twins and their misadventures, then he slapped the last of the new passages, what we know as Chapter 10, up against a passage written fairly early, where Tom has nothing on his little lily-white mind except the pleasant chance to sew dissension and the momentary fear of having Pudd'nhead read his thievery in his palm. (In the published book, the reader will have the adventitious thrill of thinking that Tom draws back his hand out of fear that Pudd'nhead will read his blackness there.) Early in 1893 Mark Twain had a typescript made of this big thing in Florence, where he had written most of it, and sent it to his publisher in New York, who gave it back to him the next time he crossed the Atlantic. Months later, back in Europe with the typescript, Mark Twain salvaged what we know as *Pudd'nhead Wilson* by discarding about half of the pages, mainly escapades of the twins but also some other material, including some passages about Roxy. Then he glanced over some of what was left and separated the twins whenever he noticed that they were referred to as conjoined, wrote a few short bridge passages, and called the result a success. It may have taken him several hours.

You can see where adventitious effects will occur. What can we expect of characterization in a novel where chapters survive (unrevised) from stages in which two characters were conjoined twins, other characters were not invented, and one was invented but not yet declared part black and a slave? Can we expect passages written as extravagant farce to gain profound social significance merely because the author later placed in front of them later-written passages imbued with such significance? Can we expect passages to be meaningful when they survive without their original reason for being? (The twins playing duets on the piano, for instance, is remarkable only if they have one torso and four hands.) If you know anything at all about recent criticism you will ask other questions. Can, for instance, the slavery theme or the heredity *vs.* training theme (each a product of the decision to make Tom a changeling) inform brief passages or longer units of the book which were written before Mark Twain introduced those themes into the manuscript?

Sometime around the beginning of 1894, while *Pudd'nhead Wilson* was being serialized triumphantly in the *Century,* Stephen Crane completed *The Red Badge of Courage,* my second example. S. S. McClure accepted it for his newspaper syndicate but sat on it for six months, all the while assuring the young and literally hungry author that he would publish it soon. In desperation Crane finally sold rights for a condensation to the Bacheller syndicate, and on the measure of fame which resulted he took first the clippings then the whole manuscript to Ripley Hitchcock, the editor of Appleton's. Hitchcock wanted to publish the work which had created such a genuine small sensation, but when he saw the entire manuscript he scented danger: while the newspaper portions had dealt with ordinary soldiers in battle in a remarkably fresh way, concluding with a moment in which Henry Fleming and his friend Wilson feel like young heroes, the full version contained a portrait of Fleming which was not suitable for the Appleton imprint: he was shallow, egotistical, vainglorious, blasphemous in his recurrent debates with the forces of the universe, and not, by any definition, a hero. Tantalizingly close to having the novel printed by a reputable house, Crane agreed to cut out one entire chapter and three chapter endings where Henry justified his cowardice by haranguing the universe, as well as a number of smaller passages, many of them in the last chapter. Not required to rewrite, except to put in a couple of sentences, Crane let the book be printed without even making good bridges for the omitted passages.

Once again you can see where problematic areas will be.

Any analysis of authorial irony will be undercut since the attitude toward young Fleming is so fragmentary. Any discussion of Crane's ideas about the nature of heroism and about man's relationship to the universe and to other human beings will be vitiated since the manuscript was purged of the strongest bits of the main character's pseudo-philosophizing. Characterization will be damaged, particularly in the case of Fleming, whose state of mind throughout the middle and latter parts of the book was reduced and sanitized by cuts, though left with confusing pieces of the original meaning. Any image study, also, will be weakened in two ways: the count of images (and critics have painstakingly counted images in the truncated text) will be off by whatever number was in the deleted portions, and the significance of the images which remained in the Appleton edition may well be blurred by the lack of related images in the deleted portions, especially since the parts cut out were the very parts where imagery, like meaning, was presumably most strikingly unconventional.

My third example reached print as the author wanted it, the best he could write at the time. All during his work on the various drafts of *Tender is the Night*, Fitzgerald used the flashback structure which appears in the 1934 serial and book. A few years later, worried over the collapse of his reputation and the failure of this novel in particular, he took apart a copy and put the sections into chronological order, so that the first pages dealt with Dick Diver's student days in Zurich rather than what is now known as the "Rosemary section," set some years later on the Riviera. For all we know, Fitzgerald may have decided against trying to have the book reprinted this way, but in 1951, a decade after his death, Malcolm Cowley printed a new edition containing almost all of the words of the 1934 text (he made a few editorial alterations) but arranged in chronological order. Apparently the closest Fitzgerald came to perceiving any problem with the reordering was when he realized that if he put the four Zurich student-days pages first he could no longer retain the words describing the effect he had designed those pages to have when the reader encountered them after reading the Rosemary section: "it is confusing to come across a youthful photograph of some one known in a rounded maturity and gaze with a shock upon a fiery, wiry, eagle-eyed stranger." Although he marked these words for deletion, he did not cancel the words

which followed them: "Best to be reassuring—Dick Diver's moment now began." This reassurance in the Cowley edition seems
to prepare the reader to expect that Dick may soon be "called
to an intricate destiny," an adventitious meaning which takes
the place of the original poignant emphasis on the word "moment." Sometimes, as here, the reordering made only a sense
which is partly or wholly adventitious, and sometimes it made
no sense at all. Fitzgerald was simply wrong in assuming that
the parts in the new order, aside from the spot he noticed and
doctored, would still make sense without being rewritten, or
make an even clearer sense by focusing more sharply on Dick
at the beginning.

Again, you can anticipate some of the kinds of inadvertent
effects that resulted, but you may want to look at the detailed
analysis Brian Higgins and I made some years ago. Very obviously, the mystery of what happened in the bathroom in the Villa
Diana, a mystery which informs much of the Rosemary section,
in the Cowley edition becomes absurd mystification, since every
reader already knows just what sort of mad scene Nicole must
have enacted there. Less obviously, and on a much smaller scale,
the screening of Rosemary's movie, *Daddy's Girl*, seems to
gain an appalling luridness in its new placement, since the reader
knows already in the Cowley edition that Nicole, who is in the
audience, was driven mad by incest with her father. The function of characters is altered, also, as when in the Cowley edition
Abe North, from the time he enters the book, must be perceived
as a man like Dick, wasting his talents, when he was designed
to be perceived at first as a contrasting figure to the Dick who
is so idolized by Rosemary and to a great extent by the reader.
Fitzgerald's favored device of paired scenes is largely sabotaged
in the Cowley edition, where there is no full circle, beach scene
to beach scene structure, and where in the reordering a later
scene may occur before the scene it was meant to recall, while
even if the scenes remain in the same order they may function
differently because the second scene is a lesser or a greater number of pages away from the scene it is meant to recall and comment upon: what counts in the reading experience is not the
factual chronology, that one scene deals with Dick at 25, another
at 30, but how many pages have intervened between the paired
scenes. Most important, perhaps, Dick's decline in the Cowley
edition seems miserably gradual rather than precipitous, so the

poignant sense of what Dick almost was is sacrificed along with the reader's most sympathetic feelings toward him. You might want to test your responses to a scene Higgins and I did not analyze—Nicole's stream-of-consciousness passage, the four pages which bridge the years between the pre-nuptial negotiations and the first arrival of Rosemary on the Divers's beach at the Riviera. You'll find some curiously muddled effects in the Cowley order: some wholly authorial still, some distortedly authorial, and some wholly adventitious.

My last example is a descendant of *Tender is the Night*, Norman Mailer's *An American Dream*, which in the *Esquire* version (January-August 1964) even more plainly than in the 1965 Dial book version employs the Dick Diver theme—talented young hero sells out to riches and leaves his most ambitious work unwritten. For the book version Mailer revised many passages, making many fine small excisions, rewordings, local reorderings, and additions. During the revision he also retrenched in ways that damaged the characterization of the hero, Stephen Richards Rojack, and altered the structure of the book. Some three dozen deletions or revisions, (one word or a few words long) remove some of Rojack's fears—fear of women, fear of failing in sex, fear of being raped homosexually, fear of (if imprisoned) longing to rape young men. Three of his memories of Harvard (enough to have filled a page or so in the book) make up, in number of words, roughly half of these deletions. Two very short deletions, the most damaging of all, remove Rojack's response first to Detective Roberts then to Shago Martin as men of psychological complexity and power to equal his own—a response in which Mailer had bravely violated the venerable American taboo against portraying men as being sensitive to each other in ways which cannot exclude awareness of each other's sexuality.

From the little I've said here you may not be able to anticipate the extent to which the book was damaged, so I'll look now at how some critics have gone wrong, relying as they have on the Dial edition. The critic who says that "Rojack, in accord with Mailer's own biases, is caught up in the savage world of *machismo*," is unfair to Mailer himself and to his achievement in the *Esquire* version, where the burden of *machismo*, the difficulty of growing up to be a man in a macho society, is a major theme; however, the reduced scrutiny in the book version of what it means to be masculine is not such as to plainly exclude the critic's accusation.   And when the same critic says that the three actions which "demand the utmost courage from Rojack" are "killing Deborah, loving Cherry, and going to see Kelly," he is relying on the confusing evidence in the Dial version, so that he ignores one major character, Roberts, and quite mistakes Mailer's purpose in introducing another major character, Shago Martin.[4]   In this case it's hard to blame the critic: Mailer brought upon himself the situation where everyone who has written on the structure and characterization in *An American Dream* has been more or less wrong, and where everyone who has railed against Mailer's portrayal of masculinity in *An American Dream* has been using the imperfect evidence of the book version.

Authors take warning: critics are not apt to recognize adventitious effects for what they are.   And even when we do see that some of the effects in a novel are not authorial but inadvertent, there's little we can do about it.   There's no hope at all for *Pudd'nhead Wilson,* since what Mark Twain cut it down from already had a good share of the unintended anomalies which throng the novel as we know it.   California may publish the full text as Mark Twain completed it, but as a resource for scholars and critics, not as anyone's notion of a lost masterpiece.   We can restore, and have restored, almost all of the original *Red Badge.*   Thanks largely to good instincts of Scottie Fitzgerald, *Tender* has been restored to its original form.   I have hopes of persuading Norman Mailer to repair the damage he did to *An American Dream.*   That would be something, indeed, but even gaining general recognition for the category of adventitious aesthetic effects would be a minor breakthrough in literary criticism.

Now to look at more of the critics reveling in adventitious effects as they play with the vocabulary of biographical criticism, discussing authorial preparations and purposes.   Wayne C. Booth, whom you would expect to be especially sensitive in his reponse, experiences an astonishing number of adventitious *frissons* as he praises authorial preparation in the Cowley edition of *Tender is the Night:*

Consider, for example, the scene in which Rosemary has learned that Nicole and Dick are to meet for love-making at four. If we read Rosemary's jealous reactions ("It was more difficult than she thought and her whole self protested as Nicole drove away") without ever having seen Dick's and Nicole's love in the early years, and without knowing anything of all the qualities besides sex that enter into that love, we can hardly avoid feeling all on the side of Rosemary: too bad about that poor man trapped by the mysterious and obviously dangerous Nicole. But in the revised version our sympathies are properly divided: we see two women fighting over the drowning man, himself a victim of both, though each is in her own way sympathetic. A fairly trivial affair has been transformed, through proper preparation, into a significant step in a moral collapse that none of the principals sees as clearly as we do.[5]

This analysis is notable for the argument that authorial preparation is found not in the text into which Fitzgerald worked his developing intentions page by page; instead, "preparation" is discovered and celebrated in the edition where hunks were reordered without being rethought or rewritten. Critics pay tribute to the construction of *Pudd'nhead Wilson* in similar terms, commenting upon what happens "as the novel develops," on what the author did "from start to finish," on a phrase that "echoes threateningly and ambiguously throughout the novel," on "the novel's chief concern, from the first to the last chapter," on an "inexorable process" in the book, on how the "opening chapter, with considerable adroitness and economy, prepares us for the major ironies of the narrative to follow," on the "long, carefully plotted preparation," on the author's coming "to grips with the animating issue of slavery in a sustained effort which, challenging him more deeply as he wrote, called upon the deepest resources of his imagination."[6] Malcolm Bradbury finds purposeful ambiguity in *Pudd'nhead Wilson,* scoffing at critics who have tried to pretend that the plot is simpler than it is or have blamed the author for "evading the significance of his 'slavery' theme," while in reality the "very variety of their interpretations suggests the ambiguous quality of the book," and therefore, of course, its high literary merit.[7] Donald Pizer, likewise blinded by the New Critical valorization of ambiguity, finds that "Crane's mature narrative voice was one which "made for complexity and fuzziness." Like Bradbury, Pizer speaks in praise—praise of what he earlier called "a moral ambiguity in Crane's conception of man's relationship with his fellows, an ambiguity which permeates his entire vision of man," an ambiguity which really resulted from Crane's hasty excisions for Hitchcock, not from anything Crane wrote.[8]

Such critics have the author at least vaguely in mind as they talk about preparation and purposeful ambiguity, but most of the time the critics treat the text as if it were a New Critical aesthetic object, in discussions of which an author is to be named only incidentally, a peg to hang an analysis on. Mark D. Coburn ignores Mark Twain's own confessions about the way he salvaged *Pudd'nhead Wilson* from the larger typescript in which the twins were very prominent characters and were conjoined, all the way through; looking only at "the text itself," he is much moved:

> Twain devotes most of chapter 6 to an account of Aunt Patsy's reception, where Dawson's Landing swarms to meet the handsome young noblemen it has acquired. Twain's unusually heavy irony belittles the celebrants, compelling the reader to find their desperate need for public approval both amusing and pitiful. The contrast between the surface gaiety of the scene and the underlying blackness of Twain's satiric vision makes the chapter almost painful to read.[9]

The pangs which make the chapter almost painful to read are, one hesitates to say, pure cheap thrills. Equally pure are the cheap thrills John Freimarck has when he says that Luigi's kicking Tom is "a direct reversal of Tom's kick which lifts Chambers over the doorsill,"—this although Luigi's kick was written before Chambers was invented and before Tom had any black blood. Equally pure are the cheap thrills James B. Haines has in saying that "Luigi, by kicking Tom—as one might kick a dog—, is literally launching him into an orbit of subsequent actions and reactions, all of which have as their animating and sustaining force, the thrust of Luigi's foot, the impelling power of blackness"— this despite the fact that the foot belonged equally to Angelo and to Luigi when the passage was written, the fact that Tom was not black when it was written (nor, in case Haines makes you wonder, was Luigi), and the fact that many of Tom's later actions and reactions date from the time when he was white. Donald Pizer says that much of *The Red Badge of*

Courage "is devoted to Fleming's loss and recovery of his feeling of oneness with his fellows,"[10] when, quite the contrary, the direction of the novel as Crane wrote it was toward Henry's climactic conviction that death—like lesser discomfitures such as public exposure for misdeeds—was for others, not for him. Robert J. Begiebing names the four main characters Rojack has to confront in *An American Dream:* "Deborah, Ruta, Cherry, and Kelly"—a list possible only because the deletions muffled Roberts's and Shago Martin's roles as two of the worthy opponents Rojack confronts. Without the controlling force of Roberts's psychological quality with the hero, a force which governs the reader's response to subsequent contests, the hierarchy of characters seems to break down, and Begiebing magnifies the wrong encounters: "Rojack tests his courage and new psychic powers against the ex-prize fighter Romeo and the mafioso Tony to win Cherry from them."[11] As Mailer wrote it, the psychic warfare was something like a parody of the greater confrontations engaged in by Rojack in drunkenness and near-hysteria after the more dangerous opponent, Roberts, has released him from questioning. Such critical comments go wrong by assuming that the novels are not only in the author's words but also carry the author's meanings, when in fact many of the aesthetic effects are adventitious, not authorial.

Underlying many of the essays which celebrate cheap thrills the writers have discovered in *Pudd'nhead Wilson, The Red Badge of Courage, Tender is the Night,* and *An American Dream* is a common failure in American literary study—the failure to take seriously the existence of the creative process, a process that begins, continues with varying admixtures of excitement, boredom, anxiety, and discomfort, and ends, ends so completely that writers may forget the intentions which they built into the text during the act of composing it and treat it as a piece of merchandise, something which they may change at will, with more concern for present convenience than possible damage to what they had created in the past. Textual editors, of all people, do not really believe in the creative process, or else they could not have accepted that part of W. W. Greg's rationale of copy-text which advises adopting any later authorial reading into the early copy-text—advice which is based on the notion that a writer retains, as long as he lives, a constant control over all of his literary productions, no matter how much time has elapsed since he composed them. Literary critics do not believe there is such a thing as the creative process, either, or they would not cheerfully put the burden of establishing the text they read upon the author (as in arguing that we should read the expurgated Appleton text of *Red Badge* because there is no evidence that "Crane ever expressed later in life a desire to publish the *Red Badge* in its original manuscript form")[13] or upon the editor (as in assuming that a modern edition is "an authoritative text" because the title-page declares it is). Rejecting any responsibility for thinking about how a text came to be the thing they hold in their hands, critics take full responsibility only for demonstrating its formal perfections, just as if New Criticism were not dead. And most American literary theorists, with the exception of Murray Krieger, are also unwilling to acknowledge there is a creative process.[14] Michael Hancher's influential definitions of three kinds of authorial intention, for example, deal with the time before the process of composition starts, with the moment that process ends, and with some indefinite time after it ends, not at all (except in one sentence in a footnote) with the time the process is going on.[15] Almost no one, editor, critic, or theorist, stops to consider the circumstances under which an author can lose control over his own literary work, so that the text he "authorizes" is not the text he "authored." The most we have had is a series of *ad hoc* arguments in CEAA editions designed to explain away the editor's failure to follow Greg in particular cases.

Not believing in the reality of the creative process, critics look with an olympian aloofness upon the labor of making a novel, the real struggles and achievements of the writer. They routinely overpraise Mark Twain for his slapped-together *Pudd'nhead Wilson*—that "tragic masterpiece" which surpasses *Huckleberry Finn* "in unity of theme and general organization," which has "artistic and philosophic" unity, and a "unity of vision" as well. Working backwards from a text maimed at a publisher's insistence, critics condemn Stephen Crane as incompetent, as when James B. Colvert exposes "the insecurity of the author's control over his point of view" in *The Red Badge of Courage.*[16] Or critics patronize the author, as Wayne C. Booth does: "The achievement of the revision is, in short, to correct a fault of over-distancing, a fault that springs from a method appropriate to other works at other times but not to the tragedy Fitzgerald wanted to write." Presumably at the moment Fitzgerald re-ordered a copy of *Tender is the Night* he miraculously wrote the tragedy he had "wanted to write" all during his years of labor on the novel: immaculate reconception. Robert Maxwell counts on his fingers the months during which Mailer wrote *An American Dream* and dismisses any possibility that the result could be very good: "The circumstances alone call it all into question: there could not have been time for a grand design; he began publishing long before the novel had been worked out in his mind." Another poor ambitious fool of an author! Over-praising or underpraising, these critics are posturing at the expense of the author, blind to his actual achievements and mistakes.

Perhaps the most curious aspect of lurking New Criticism in this writing on novels which contain adventitious aesthetic effects is the tendency to treat the original product of the creative process as merely hypothetical, an imaginary construct, while the real work is the familiar "text itself." In his ecstatic praise of *Pudd'nhead Wilson* Leslie Fielder comments on how the duel between one of the twins and Tom Driscoll "was to have been in the book as originally planned" and "what mad complications would have ensued," when in fact the duel did take place and such complications did ensue, as can be seen in the manuscript at the Pierpont Morgan Library.[17] Edwin H. Cady comments that since "discursive patches mar *The Red Badge*, it is not surprising that Crane suppressed his intend-ed Chapter XII. He was right to do so"; Cady knows better, of course, but his wording seems to minimize the actual chapter, the one Crane wrote and tried for a year and a half to get into print, as one only "intended," not actualized. Joseph Katz goes so far as to say that the manuscript version of *Red Badge* is "a work that was never meant to exist," as if it had not in fact existed. Wayne C. Booth talks coolly about the "restor-ation of chronological order" in *Tender,* when the surviving drafts show that there never had been a chronological order to restore, only the flashback structure, according to which the whole novel was built. Robert Solotaroff, who read the *Esquire* version of *An American Dream* with distaste as it appeared, forgets the function Roberts had in that version and comments frivolously on the detective's presence in the Dial version: "I am left with the feeling that Mailer did not worry about the jarring contrast between the level of reality on which Roberts exists and the one, with all of its allegorical reverberations, of the other characters. Roberts was a type for whom Mailer has expressed much admiration, Mailer wants to play him, and so he's included in the novel." So much for the actuality of authorial achievement. In this curious phenomenon, critics let their acute sensitivity to the text they are reading make them defensive of it, and therefore rather brutally insensitive to the real text the author wrote and to the author who completed it.

Aesthetic experiences such as I have described are cheap thrills indeed—cheap because they do not cost the author much, if anything at all, since he does not have to set them up painstakingly, does not have to calculate just what effect will be achieved when he puts one word after another, one scene after another. These thrills are cheap for editors too, since they are retained in print when the editors take the easy way and edit without doing the elementary, preliminary chore of reading what the author actually wrote when he was in the process of composing the book and the elementary, preliminary chore of studying the original functions of the parts in relation to the whole as it then stood. Instead, editors edit, most often, by the simple expedient of reprinting whatever form of the work first reached print, and they congratulate themselves upon permitting the author to have "the last word," even if they have denied him hundreds of his words, and perhaps the most meaningful words he had put into the text. The thrills are also cheap to the critic and the theorist who pay very little for their adventitious aesthetic experiences when they content themselves with any edition which comes to hand rather than seeking out and understanding what the author actually wrote.

Until the day we all share a theory of criticism which acknowledges the prevalence of adventitious aesthetic effects in works imperfectly altered by their authors (and acknowledges as well the more elusive category of adventitious aesthetic effects which were caused by some smaller or larger lapse of the writer during the period of composition),[18] I offer a measure of encouragement. A reader who pays the rare coin of alertest attention seldom buys a cheap thrill. Anyone attuned to the mind and style of the writer and the remnants of structure in even a maimed text may be capable of saying something like

John Berryman said when he encountered a nonsensical passage in the last chapter of *Red Badge*: "But then comes a sentence in which I simply do not believe."[19] Berryman did not know why the sentence was not to be believed, did not know that for meaning it depends upon something which was deleted, but he knew it violated the pattern Crane had set up earlier in the novel. In other cases readers sympathetically alert may experience at least some subliminal uneasiness with a flawed text, may find themselves stopping and turning back to discover some lost clue, some link they think they must have dropped, may even find themselves looking for some textual explanation for an intrusive anomaly. We need to be armed with sympathetic, skeptical alertness when we read, for if cheap thrills abound in the texts of the novels I have discussed, and abound in many more I could list (*Moby-Dick, Pierre, Billy Budd, Sailor, Huckleberry Finn, The Ambassadors, The "Genius", The Great Gatsby, Satoris,* to name some obvious American examples), what about the novels for which no textual history has been established, or those for which almost no textual history *can* be established? What reason do we have to think that there are no such comparably adventitious aesthetic effects in other books we all pride ourselves on reading well, and criticizing brilliantly?

NOTES

[1] E. D. Hirsch, Jr., *Validity in Interpretation* (New Haven: Yale Univ. Press, 1967), pp. 6-10; P. D. Juhl, *Interpretation: An Essay in the Philosophy of Literary Criticism* (Princeton: Princeton Univ. Press, 1980), pp. 129-35.

[2] John W. Nichol, "Melville's 'Soiled Fish of the Sea,'" *American Literature,* 21 (November 1949), pp. 338-39.

[3] See, for an overview, Hershel Parker, "The 'New Scholarship': Textual Evidence and Its Implications for Criticism, Literary Theory, and Aesthetics," *Studies in American Fiction,* 9 (Autumn 1981), pp. 181-

97. I have forthcoming in *Resources for American Literary Study* a long essay on *Pudd'nhead Wilson* relevant to the present essay. See also the special number on Stephen Crane, *Studies in the Novel,* 10 (Spring 1978), ed. Hershel Parker, especially Henry Binder's "The *Red Badge of Courage* Nobody Knows," pp. 9-47, and Steven Mailloux's *"The Red Badge of Courage* and Interpretive Conventions: Critical Response to a Maimed Text," pp. 48-63, two of the better seminar papers I received in 1976. Binder's text of *Red Badge* is available in the *Norton Anthology of American Literature,* Vol. 2 (New York: W. W. Norton, 1979), pp. 802-906, and in a 1982 Norton separate publication. See Brian Higgins and Hershel Parker, "Sober Second Thoughts: Fitzgerald's 'Final Version' of *Tender is the Night,"* *Proof* 4 (1975), pp. 129-152. Finally see my "Norman Mailer's Revision of the *Esquire* Version of *An American Dream* and the Aesthetic Problem of 'Built-in Intentionality,'" *Bulletin of Research in the Humanities,* 84 (Winter, 1981), pp. 405-430 (published in January 1983).

[4]Stanley T. Gutman, *Mankind in Barbary* (Hanover, N. H.: Univ. Press of New England, 1975), p. 110 and p. 116.

[5]Wayne C. Booth, *The Rhetoric of Fiction* (Chicago: Univ. of Chicago Press, 1961), p. 195.

[6]All these quotations are genuine, but I identify only the author of the last one, because my point is better made by using someone of his prestige: James M. Cox, *Mark Twain: The Fate of Humor* (Princeton: Princeton Univ. Press, 1966), p. 226.

[7]Introduction to *Pudd'nhead Wilson* (New York:Penguin Books, 1969), p. 29.

[8]"'The *Red Badge of Courage* Nobody Knows': A Brief Rejoinder," *Studies in the Novel,* 11 (Spring 1979), p. 80; Pizer's Norton Critical Edition of *The Red Badge of Courage* (New York: W. W. Norton, 1976), p. 300.

[9]Mark D. Coburn, "'Training is everything': Communal Opinion and the Individual in *Pudd'nhead Wilson,"* *Modern Language Quarterly,* 31 (June 1970), p. 213. The following quotations are from John Freimarck, *"Pudd'nhead Wilson:* A Tale of Blood and Brotherhood," *University Review,* 34 (June 1968), p. 306; and James B. Haines, "Of Dogs and Men: A Symbolic Variation on the Twin Motif in *Pudd'nhead Wilson,"* *Mark Twain Journal,* 18 (Winter 1976-1977), p. 17.

[10] Norton Critical Edition, p. 299.

[11] Robert J. Begiebing, *Acts of Regeneration* (Columbia: Univ. of Missouri Press, 1980), p. 62, p. 71.

[12] "The Rationale of Copy-Text," *Studies in Bibliography*, 3 (1950-1951), p. 32.

[13] Pizer, "A Brief Rejoinder," *Studies in the Novel*, 11 (Spring 1979), p. 78.

[14] *Theory of Criticism* (Baltimore: Johns Hopkins Univ. Press, 1976), Chapter 2 in particular.

[15] Michael Hancher, "Three Kinds of Intention," *Modern Language Notes*, 87 (December 1972), pp. 827-51; the sentence is in footnote 10, p. 831.

[16] Norton Critical Edition of *Red Badge*, p. 302; Booth, p. 195; Maxwell, "Personal Reactions to a Presidential Candidate," *Minnesota Review*, 5 (August-October 1965), p. 250.

[17] Norton Critical Edition of *Pudd'nhead Wilson,* ed. Sidney E. Berger (New York: W. W. Norton, 1980), p. 225. See also Cady in the Norton *Red Badge*, p. 250; Katz in his Editor's Note to the *Portable Stephen Crane* (New York: Viking Press, 1969), p. xxii; Booth, p. 192; and Solotaroff, *Down Mailer's Way* (Urbana: Univ. of Illinois Press, 1974), pp. 176-77.

[18] Krieger has a characteristically lucid passage in *Theory of Criticism*, pp. 41-42, on this category.

[19] "Stephen Crane: *The Red Badge of Courage*," in *The American Novel: From James Fenimore Cooper to William Faulkner*, ed. Wallace Stegner (New York: Basic Books, 1965), p. 91.

PART THREE

Speculations and Interconnections

REINVENTING HISTORICISM: AN INTRODUCTION TO THE WORK OF FREDRIC JAMESON

by

Michael Sprinker

"In every era the attempt must be made anew to wrest tradition away from a conformism that is about to overpower it."
                    —Walter Benjamin, "Theses on the Philosophy of History"

Somewhere in the middle of Woody Allen's *Annie Hall*, Allen says mockingly to his New York intellectual, social-climbing wife, "I thought *Commentary* and *Dissent* had merged to form *Dysentery*." Like many of Allen's memorable one-liners, this touches on something profoundly true about American politics, here that corner of it which is so savagely pilloried in all of Allen's recent films: the ideology of the liberal intelligentsia. In *Manhattan*, Allen retorts to the not quite rhetorical question about how best to deal with a neo-Nazi group in New Jersey "Don't you think satire is more effective than violence?" with: "No, with Nazis baseball bats are much more effective. Gets right to the point." We laugh knowingly, confident that of course he doesn't really mean it. But if he does? And what if our liberal intellectual traditions, which we don't so much cherish as take for granted, are precisely the object of bitter criticism here, though, as is Allen's way, in a form and style that allow most of us to walk away unaware that we've just been knifed in the back?

Let me take another example, more direct, less open to mis-understanding and equivocation. In his most recent book, E. P. Thompson writes of the bankruptcy of liberalism with especial fervor and insight:

> The truth is that our liberal intellectual often does not notice
> the real forces which determine our political life, because he does

not feel *himself* to be unfree.   In his island of mild dissent he is
able to speak, to argue, and to communicate with others like himself to his heart's content.   Where he has a grievance, there is generally a remedy to hand which does not entail any major appeal
to public opinion.   He may say what he wants because he wants
to say so little; and the more intemperate radical can often be
'nobbled' before he becomes an irritant within the system.   If
the intellectual thinks of the forces of conditioning, he thinks
of them as something done *to* other people—the masses—*by* other
people—the advertisers or the press—not as something which is
also being done to him, and in the doing of which he has active
complicity.[1]

Upon this essential innocence of liberal intellectuals, it is difficult to make an impression, particularly at an historical moment,
like the present, of relative calm and outward (though by no
means real and underlying) stability.   After the awkward dis-
comforts of the 1960's, academic intellectuals are especially
eager to be left to cultivate their gardens, having glimpsed something of the real world at Kent State, Berkeley, Columbia, and
Cornell and found it a bit too real and too immediately conse-
quential.   For what the liberal consensus signifies most of all is
the comfort of the liberals themselves, who have given up genuine dissent for the active complicity about which Thompson
speaks.   In return, they get a relatively untroubled life—for
the moment.

Marx's judgment in the *18th Brumaire* concerning the
tendency of history to repeat itself in the form of farce takes on
a local habitation and color in the current atmosphere of literary
studies in the academy.   Surely it was fitting that only a few
years ago the Lionel Trilling Seminar given at Columbia by M. H.
Abrams celebrated "tact" as the preeminently necessary critical
virtue of the moment.[2]   A more Arnoldian judgment cannot
be imagined, and the author of *The Liberal Imagination,* were
he alive, would have nodded in agreement.   Certainly Trilling
himself must have made a similar plea when confronted with
the quite palpable threats to academic freedom in the late forties and early fifties.   And then it made some sense to appeal
to the liberal virtues, even though they were no more effective
in stopping the McCarthyite juggernaut (it took the army to
do that) than Abrams' cautionary statements have been in

curbing the supposed excesses of Bloom, Derrida, and Fish. This is what I mean about the farce of it all. Whom do these people threaten but Abrams and his generation of scholars, and what threat do they really pose save to the peace of mind of a few people in literature departments who wish to be left alone to intone piously lines from Yeats and Wordsworth, while lamenting the decline in their students' ability to comprehend what the lines mean literally, let alone symbolically?

For if, as Derrida and others claim, there is a scandal spreading in the groves of academe, it concerns less the spelling of difference with an "a" than with the continuing and increasingly foolhardy innocence and impotence of academic intellectuals themselves. The price paid for this insulation is becoming increasingly difficult to bear. What is needed, perhaps, is a Nietzschean gesture of defiance. No body of criticism within the academy at present lays more rightful claim to such a label than the work of Fredric Jameson, our most defiantly anti-liberal critic, and also the most paradoxical figure in contemporary criticism. The paradox of his work is that of the historical situation itself, indeed of the very mode of thought that can be called historical. If there is a currently viable alternative to the liberal consensus in the academy, it lies here, in the attempt to redeem historicism from its current state of poverty. For to be authentically situated within history is perhaps the only redemption from its essential innocence for which contemporary criticism may with reason strive. Criticism, like men, must make its own history, though it cannot do so just as it pleases.

* * * * *

Confronted by much the same situation in Germany over a century ago, Friedrich Nietzsche packed his bags and left his position as Professor of Philology in Basel. The immediate issue of this flight was the *Unzeitgemässe Betrachtungen,* which, then as now, and despite the obvious irony of their title, were timely thoughts indeed. For one of these reflections, *Vom Nutzen und Nachteil der Historie für das Leben,* remains, *pace* Karl Popper, the classic critique of historicism in the Western tradition. Its power as a critique derives most from its situation

within and acceptance of the problematic of history and historical writing, from which it cannot finally escape. Nietzsche announces in the Preface: "We do need history, but quite differently from the jaded idlers in the garden of knowledge, however grandly they may look down on our rude and unpictures-
que requirements. In other words, we need it for life and action, not as a convenient way to avoid life and action, or to
excuse a selfish life and a cowardly or base action. We would
serve history only so far as it serves life; but to value its study
beyond a certain point mutilates and degrades life: and this
is a fact that certain marked symptoms of our time make it as
necessary as it may be painful to bring to the test of experience."[3] Paraphrasing Marx, we may sum up Nietzsche's project thus: hitherto, historians have only interpreted the past in
various ways; the point is to change it.

That such a project flies in the face of that most sacred
of historical cows, the objectivity of the historian, his faithfulness to the truth of his data and to the inviolability of the
past, indicates once again why Nietzsche still has the power to
make us squirm. In making history useful for life, Nietzsche
strikes an Orwellian note, placing the needs of the present
above any respect for the reality of the past and condemning
the historian to the creation of useful fictions. Suddenly what
appeared at the outset as an epistemological problem—the
relationship of the knower in the present to the object of his
knowledge in the past—becomes a moral one involving the
integrity of the historian and his faithfulness to the facts of
history. But this is to move too quickly and down a false trail,
as Walter Benjamin reminds us: "To articulate the past historically does not mean to recognize it 'the way it really was' (Ranke). It means to seize hold of a memory as it flashes up at a
moment of danger. Historical materialism wishes to retain that
image of the past which unexpectedly appears to man singled
out by history at a moment of danger. The danger affects both
the content of the tradition and its receivers. The same threat
hangs over both: that of becoming a tool of the ruling classes.
. . . Only that historian will have the gift of fanning the spark
of hope in the past who is firmly convinced that *even the dead*
will not be safe from the enemy if he wins. And this enemy
has not ceased to be victorious."[4] Benjamin's point is, in a way,
a simple one: the appropriation of the past is not something one

chooses to do or not do; the only question is who will appropriate it and for what purposes. The circumstances of the present, the "moment of danger," always determine the shape of our vision of history. This is not to say that the past itself, "the way it really was," is ontologically altered by historical writing, rather that certain historical moments present themselves as significant and portentous, moments of danger in which the present is suddenly illuminated by the events of the past, as, to cite one of Benjamin's examples, the French Revolution recognized in itself the reincarnation of ancient Rome. The past remains volatile, subject to reinterpretation and reappropriation at every moment; history itself is the struggle among competing interpretations whose validity and significance can only be judged historically, that is, *post festum* in a future they will have helped to create but cannot have entirely foreseen or willed. The writing of history is thus less an epistemological or moral problem than a political one; it enables actions and legitimates the exercise of power by one group (or class or party) over another.

This would seem also to be Nietzsche's point, the use or utility or perhaps advantage *(Nutzen)* of history for life. Nietzsche's principal antagonists are those antiquarian and monumental historians for whom the past shines forth either in its own right and for the intrinsic value of itself (the antiquarian), or as an admonishing and impregnable superior form of life that stands in judgment over the present and urges us on to imitate its stirring example (the monumental). Nietzsche also postulates a third kind of history, which he calls critical history, and it is from this mode that he particularly wished to deliver his contemporaries, so intoxicated had they become with the instruments of historical criticism. But to escape from this impasse is no simple feat, and, as Paul de Man has shown, Nietzsche's critique of historicism discovers its own most radical historicity:

> From the start, the intoxication with the history-transcending life-process is counterbalanced by a deeply pessimistic wisdom that remains rooted in a sense of historical causality, although it reverses the movement of history from one of development to one of regression. . . . [Nietzsche's] description of life as a constant regression has nothing to do with cultural errors, such

as the excess of historical disciplines in contemporary education against which the essay polemicizes, but lies much deeper in the nature of things, beyond the reach of culture. It is a temporal experience of human mutability, historical in the deepest sense of the term in that it implies the necessary experience of any present as a *passing* experience that makes the past irrevocable and unforgettable, because it is inseparable from any present or future.[5]

Moreover, the critique itself is implicated in the very crimes it indicts: "Only through history is history conquered; modernity now appears as the horizon of a historical process that has to remain a gamble. Nietzsche sees no assurance that his own reflective and historical attempt achieves any genuine change; he realizes that his text itself can be nothing but another historical document, and finally he has to delegate the power of renewal and modernity to a mythical entity called 'youth' to which he can only recommend the effort of self-knowledge that has brought him to his own abdication."[6]

De Man's subject in the essay from which these quotations are cited is "Literary History and Literary Modernity," and he concludes by drawing out the implications of the Nietzschean deconstruction of historical knowledge, first for the comparatively narrow concerns of literary history, but finally for the limits of historical knowledge itself: "To become good literary historians, we must remember that what we usually call literary history has little or nothing to do with literature and that what we call literary interpretation—provided only it is good interpretation—is in fact literary history. If we extend this notion beyond literature, it merely confirms that the bases for historical knowedge are not empirical facts but written texts, even if these texts masquerade in the guise of wars or revolutions."[7] Leaving aside for the moment the problem of what precisely would constitute "good interpretation" (a question whose full significance I believe de Man has never adequately confronted), we may focus on the implications of de Man's final sentence: that history is textual, that historical knowledge (upon which, presumably, one bases a course of action) is not knowledge at all, strictly speaking, but interpretation, and that even the brute material circumstances of wars and revolutions (and purges, physical repression, famines, pestilence, and all the other material events of history) are accessible to understanding only in a purely textual mode. I can only indicate briefly here the consequences of this position as de Man has subsequently worked them out, notably in his latest book, *Allegories of Reading*. De Man patiently undoes the authority of historical knowledge by showing its epistemological fallability, which is always made evident in the rhetorical mode of its articulation. Thus de Man, in explicating the "text" of Rousseau's *Social Contract,* discovers at one and the same time the perfect model for the structure and functioning of any text and the constraints that structure history in textual ways: "In the description of the structure of political society [in the *Social Contract*], the 'definition' of a text as the contradictory interference of the grammatical with the figural field emerges in its most systematic form. . . . We call *text* any entity that can be considered from such a double perspective: as a generative, open-ended, non-referential grammatical system and as a figural system closed off by a transcendental signification that subverts the grammatical code to which the text owes its existence. The 'definition' of the text also states the impossibility of its existence and prefigures the allegorical narratives of this impossibility."[8] By de Man's own judgment, what can such "allegorical narratives of this impossibility" be but history itself? De Man himself says as much some pages later: "to the extent that [it] is necessarily misleading, language just as necessarily conveys the promise of its own truth. This is also why textual allegories on this level of rhetorical complexity generate history."[9] De Man effectively reverses Marx's famous dictum in the *18th Brumaire,* asserting that men do not make their own history, but rather that history, in the form of allegorical narratives, produces the actors necessary for its own performance. The logic of historical process conceptualized as textuality appears quite as rigid as any of the iron-law economic schemes in the successors to Engels.[10] But it may be that the de Manian textual machine is really modelled on the quite different Althusserian concept of history as a "process without a subject."[11] At this conjuncture of Marxist philosophy and formalism stands the embattled figure of Fredric Jameson, locked in unequal struggle with both.

* * * * *

Jameson's situation is a difficult one. Teaching and writing within the humanist establishment of the American academy where both theoretical speculation and open political engagement are at best highly suspect, at worst completely ignored or suppressed, Jameson invokes the wrath and also the misunderstanding of two otherwise opposed factions among literary intellectuals: traditional humanists who reject out of hand Jameson's theoretical emphases; and theorists who wish to defuse the critical power of Jameson's Marxism by denying the validity of his principal theoretical category, history. Thus Jonathan Culler, in an otherwise sympathetic review of *Marxism and Form*—judged the most important theoretical work in English since Frye's *Anatomy of Criticism*—criticizes Jameson's hypostatization of history as something more than a theoretical model.[12] By history Culler seems to mean simply the passage of time ("just one damned thing after another"). But for Jameson history is no mere diachronic sequence (though it can be said that any genuinely materialist history must take as its starting point the raw data of events in linear succession in time); it is a structure of complexly related events, forces, and conditions whose functioning, though not precisely determined by rigid scientific laws, is nonetheless subject to rational comprehension and explanation and thus to reasoned calculation and control. If Culler's reading risks turning Jameson into a naive empiricist and thus making him vulnerable to Popperian attacks, conversely, my ascription to him of a putatively structuralist view of history suggests what is at once true of Jameson's work, namely, its serious engagement with an Althusserian theory of history and ideology (about which more later), but equally problematic, if for the opposite reason. E. P. Thompson has claimed (incorrectly in my view) that structural Marxism is an idealism of the classical sort.[13] And this is perhaps the more pressing danger for Jameson's project—indeed, for much contemporary Marxism.

Walking this particular tightrope, unfamiliar a feat as it may be in Anglo-American literary criticism, is an old problem in European philosophy, particularly in aesthetics. This is not the place to discuss the rich heritage of classical German aesthetics and its impact upon the Marxist tradition from Marx and Engels down to Lukács and Adorno. Suffice to say here that any genuinely historical cirticism—I am tempted to say any criticism whatever—must confront the claims of, on the one hand, a trans-historical logical model of history (which for purposes of notation we may identify with Hegel), and, on the other, the existential historicism familiar in Dilthey and Ranke and elaborated perhaps most fully for an academic discipline in the work of art historians in the first half of this century. For the sake of getting down to a specific instance in Jameson's own writings, I would denote this latter alternative by the name Michelet. For it is in commenting on a famous passage in the *Historie de la révolution française* that Jameson most explicitly characterizes the historicist project of Marxism. Jameson movingly evokes Michelet's personal and epochal relationship to the historical events of 4 August 1789 and argues that, similarly, Marxism is historically situated such that Marx's own discoveries, though they may be "scientific" and objectively verifiable, are nonetheless themselves the products of a historical development over centuries of human struggle:

> What needs to be stressed here is that we no longer have to do with the contemplative relationship of an individual subject to the past, but rather with the quite different relationship of an objective *situation* in the present with an objective *situation* in the past. Indeed, in so far as Marxism is itself a historicism—not to be sure a geneticism or a teleology in Althusser's sense of this word, but rather, as I have termed it elsewhere, an "absolute historicism" —its historical grounding is analogous, and Marx takes pains at various places in *Captial* to underscore the objective and historical preconditions of his discovery of the labor theory of value in a social situation in which for the first time labor and land are fully commodified. . . . Marx's "personal" discovery of this "scientific truth" is therefore itself grounded within his system, and is a function of the originality of a historical situation in which for the first time the development of capital itself permits the production of a concept—the labor theory of value—which can retroactively "recover" the truth of even millenia of precapitalist human history.[14]

Jameson's task here is to answer the critique of historicism emanating in different forms from a variety of contemporary thinkers for whom the claim of Marxism to be scientific presents insuperable logical and epistemological problems. Althusser's solution is well-known: retain the axial distinction between science and ideology, but renounce the Kantian claims of philosophy to guar-

antee the objectivity of knowledge, leaving the sciences and philosophy distinct, though not unrelated, activities. Hindess and
Hirst's post-Althusserian position is less well known, in America
at least, but perhaps more congenial in the long run to a certain
ruthlessly pragmatic sense of what the relationship between theory and practice entails. Their solution to the historicist dilemma,
as Jameson remarks, strikes a familiar Nietzschean note: all history is determined by the political needs of the present moment.
Finally, there is the explicitly Nietzschean critique of the subject,
and thereby of the basis of existential historicism, in Deleuze's
and Guattari's *Anti-Oedipus* and in the recent work of Jean Fran-
çois Lyotard. In these works, the impossibility of thinking or
conceptualizing a condition of human society different from the
present transforms the entire historicist project into a colossal
myth, and one that serves to reproduce the hegemony of the
bourgeoisie to boot. Moreover, as Jameson readily admits, the
obvious initial response to this position, that Marxism is an absolute historicism which "grounds the possibility of a comprehensive theory of past societies and cultures in the structure of the
present, or of capitalism itself," is subject to an opposite but no
less powerful objection. For "this would seem at best to reinvent
some 'place of truth,' some ethnocentric privilege of our present
as inheritors of world culture and as practitioners of rationalism
and science, which is not visibly different from the imperializing
hubris of conventional bourgeois science, and which would tend
at the same time to confirm the current line of the *nouveaux
philosophes* on the innate or intrinsic 'Stalinism' of the Marxian
world view."[15] Marxist historicism seems trapped between a relativist rock and a totalitarian hard place.

In response, Jameson suggests three necessary ways of
rethinking the problem. First, there is the reorientation of the
category of the subject itself, hence of the epistemological short-
comings of individual understanding: "we must try to rid ourselves of the habit of thinking about our (aesthetic) relationship to culturally or temporally distant artifacts as being a
relationship between individual subjects. . . . It is not a question of dismissing the role of individual subjects in the reading
process, but rather of grasping this obvious and concrete individual relationship as being itself a mediation for a nonin-
dividual and more collective process: the confrontation of two
distinct social forms or modes of production. We must try to
accustom ourselves to a perspective in which every act of read-

ing, every local interpretive practice, is grasped as the privileged vehicle through which two distinct modes of production confront and interrogate one another. Our individual reading thus becomes an allegorical figure for this essentially collective confrontation of two social forms."[16] Second, and consequent upon the first, is a reformulation of the implications of studying the social formations of previous epochs such that "the past . . . will begin to come before us as a radically different life form which rises up to call our own form of life into question and to pass judgment on us, and through us, on the social formation in which we exist."[17] Finally, and most importantly, Jameson, drawing upon Ernst Bloch, reorients Marxian historicism from a mere meditation upon and appropriation of the past toward a projection of a possible but as yet imperfectly visible future. Here the central dilemma of historicism is, if not solved, restructured so that the opposite pitfalls of historical relativism and idealist totalization are both avoided:

> [Marxism] is, however, also the anticipatory expression of a future society, or, in the terms of our discussion above, the partisan commitment to that future or Utopian mode of production which seeks to emerge from the hegemonic mode of production of our own present. This is the final resason why Marxism is not, in the current sense, a "place of truth," why its subjects are not centered in some possession of dogma, but are rather very precisely historically decentered: only the Utopian future is a place of truth in this sense, and the privilege of contemporary life and of the present lies not in its possession, but at best in the rigorous judgment it may be felt to pass on us.[18]

As in a great deal of Jameson's work, the task of restructing the categories and the actual practice of historical criticism is not realized here but is projected as a vector for contemporary criticism to follow. As I shall show further on, this future-directed moment in Jameson's criticism produces certain difficulties of its own, for it leaves Jameson in what Benjamin denominated "no-man's land," writing to abolish the very historical conditions which have produced his own work, at the same time aware that the conditions impelling his writing must be taken as a sign that his project has thusfar been a failed one. But for the moment it is sufficient to remark on the importance of the "Utopian impulse" to a genuinely Marxist historicism. The distinctive feature of this vision of history is its projection of the future out of the material conditions (mode of production) of the present.

Jameson's restoration of the properly Utopian task of Marxist criticism is apparent at a number of points in his work, perhaps most poignantly, and also most powerfully, in the final chapter of *Marxism and Form*, "Towards Dialectical Criticism." In the Preface to *Marxism and Form*, he acknowledges the enormous difficulty of moving literary criticism off the dead center of its present impasse, a difficulty exacerbated by the almost total absense of any speculative tradition in philosophy or the social sciences in this country. At the same time, the speculative impotence of the theoretical disciplines has produced a uniquely privileged position for literary criticism as an arena wherein the struggle toward dialectical thinking is still possible:

> [Literary criticism] appeals to other disciplines in vain: Anglo-American philosophy has long since been shorn of its dangerous speculative capacities, and as for political science, it suffices only to think of its distance from the great political and Utopian theories of the past to realize to what degree thought asphyxiates in our culture, with its absolute inability to imagine anything other than what is. It therefore falls to literary criticism to continue to compare the inside and the outside, existence and history, to continue to pass judgment on the abstract quality of life in the present, and to keep alive the idea of a concrete future. May it prove equal to the task![19]

Now this sounds more than a little Utopian, in the bad sense of that term, and one could scarcely maintain that in the decade since these sentences were written literary criticism has proven anything like equal to the task Jameson set for it. And yet to charge Jameson with misplaced optimism and historical naivete misses the point of this passage, indeed of the whole of his work. Such a reading imposes the static, ahistorical categories, taken over unexamined from post—Kantian analytic philosophy, which Jameson exposes as ideological projections throughout *Marxism and Form* and elsewhere in his work.[20] A more productive reading would follow Jameson's own description of the relationship between the philosophical "systems" of Marx and

Hegel: "The only concrete correction of Hegel's system is therefore the passage of time, the development of the socio-economic
situation beyond those limits, which is to say that the only adequate critique of Hegel is the philosophy of Marx. Thus philosophical thinking, if pursued far enough, turns into historical
thinking . . . ."[21] Thus, to judge the incipient optimism in Jameson's work to be impossibly Utopian and incommensurate with
the contemporary conditions of literary criticism as an institution is, first of all, irrelevant, since the point of Jameson's writing
is to project a future that, per definition, conflicts with the
content of the present. Secondly, it is a symptom of the ideological conditioning Jameson himself exposes in his critique of
the ahistorical categories of bourgeois philosophy. The content of Jameson's writing cannot be completely evaluated within
the present historical situation, since the constitutive fact of the
present is that, while it contains the material for the structuring
of the future, it must itself be abolished for this future to appear.
Jameson's explication of a Marxist theory of historical determination as itself a "historical trope," along with his characterization of the *post festum* situation of Marxism as a mode of
thinking, provides the most useful commentary on the content
of his own work: "For the attempt to predict is but one of the
symptoms of a failure to think in a situational way; and as a
mode of philosophical thought, we may say that Marxism itself
operates primarily after the fact with respect to other philosophical positions. It is in this sense also, then, that Marxism may
be seen as the 'end' of philosophy, in that in its very structure
it refuses system, or what amounts to the same thing, metaphysical content."[22]

Though the work of Ernst Bloch offers an explicit projection of a Utopian Marxism,[23] the difference between Jameson's
Utopian historicism and the more conventional historicism
familiar in the scholarship of "late bourgeois humanism" (Erich
Auerbach's phrase) is best articulated in Jameson's essay, "The
Case for Georg Lukács." Lukács's writings are close in spirit
to, just as Lukács himself grew to maturity in, the cultural am-
bience of post-Hegelian historicism in Germanic scholarship, with
its powerful nostalgia for an imagined social and cultural environment prior to the characteristic alienation in modern society.[24] Lukács's early writings on the German Romantics culmi-
nate in that continually puzzling masterpiece of modern specula-

tive criticism, *Theory of the Novel,* with its famous opening chapter on "Integrated Civilizations" evoking the world of Greek epic as the vanished Eden of a civilization now irredeemably estranged from reality. The text is founded, as Jameson says, on "a kind of literary nostalgia, on the notion of a golden age or lost Utopia of narration in Greek epic."[25] This early work of Lukács's (which could be fruitfully compared to some of the familiar monuments of humanist scholarship written in succeeding decades, Curtius's *European Literature and the Latin Middle Ages,* Auerbach's *Mimesis,* Kahler's *The Inward Turn of Narrative,* and lesser but no less influential studies like Booth's *The Rhetoric of Fiction* and Abrams's *Natural Supernaturalism*) presents the inverse of Marxist Utopianism, an image of history as regression, of human consciousness suffering under the burden of an ancient disaster from which it strives in vain to recover. Except that in the very working through of this scheme of the history of Western narrative, Lukács projects a transcendence of its present contradictions in a Utopian future whose lineaments can be glimpsed in the novels of Dostoyevsky:

> For it is clear to Lukács, at the end of his work, that the transformation of novel into epic has as its precondition not the novelist's will but the transformation of his society and his world. The renewed epic cannot come into being until the world itself has been transfigured, regenerated; and his final comment, that the novels of Dostoyevsky offer a glimpse into such an ultimate, totally humanized Utopia, must be taken more in the way of prediction than of formal analysis.[26]

The "logic of content" (Jameson's phrase) forced upon Lukács in the writing of *Theory of the Novel* led him to the threshold of Marxism; thinking through the contradictions presented by the modern form of the novel compelled him to recognize in modern alienation, not a metaphysical condition but a historical one, hence not an eternal or natural necessity but a situation subject to change. And indeed Lukács's next major work, *History and Class Consciousness,* overcomes the historicist contradictions of *Theory of the Novel* by projecting a transcendence of modern alienation in an as yet to be realized aesthetic experience:

> Thus with its humiliation of middle-class philosophy, *History*

and Class Consciousness lays the groundwork for that differentiation of the aesthetic experience which Lukács will later exhaustively work out in the *Aesthetik,* where indeed narration is valorized in that it presupposes neither the transcendence of the object (as in science) nor that of the subject (as in ethics), but rather a neutralization of the two, their mutual reconciliation, which thus anticipates the life experience of a Utopian world in its very structure.[27]

Lukács's writing between *History and Class Consciousness* and the *Aesthetik* did scant justice to this Utopian impulse in his work. The attack on modernism in literature, the defense of socialist realism, and the championing of the critical realism of Balzac, Tolstoy, and Thomas Mann were in effect regressions to the historical typology of *Theory of the Novel,* and thus Lukács's literary criticism of the thirties and forties is marred by the same theoretical deficiencies of a nostalgic historicism as was the early work, whose contradictions one thought *History and Class Consciousness* had laid bare and to a large extent overcome. At the same time, however, these deeply flawed analyses of the European narrative tradition evolve the categories by means of which a properly dialectical criticism can be realized. Lukács's key terms are "typicality," "realism," "reification" (the latter definitively formulated in *History and Class Consciousness,* a decade before the surfacing of Marx's *1844 Manuscripts* which present the now classic arguments concerning this concept), and "totality." On the typical, Jameson remarks: "the form of the work is dependent on some deeper logic of the raw material itself; the word *typical* merely serves as a name for the articulation into individual characters of this basic reality which is the substance or content of the work of art."[28] "Typicality" is an aesthetic category denoting the representation in art of material reality; Rastignac and Goriot are typical characters insofar as they present the social reality of petty bourgeois ambition, its temporary successes and ultimate failure, in France during the period of the July Monarchy.

The concepts of reification, totality, and realism are elsewhere taken up by Jameson to formulate a more properly dialectical theory of modernism than that presented in the middle works of Lukács himself, and in delineating the contours of the realism/modernism debate, Jameson establishes the boundaries of his own critical project. He first reorients the Lukácsian formula of the "decadence" of modern works away from the explicit moral critique it entails toward "an interrogation of their buried social and political content."[29] He then situates these works within the social formation of late capitalism and outlines the critical project which offers the best hope of overcoming the reification of life and art within this historical situation:

> The reification of late capitalism—the transformation of human relations into an appearance of relationships between things— renders society opaque: it is the lived source of the mystifications on which ideology is based and by which domination and exploitation are legitimized. . . . reification necessarily obscures the class character of that structure [of the social totality], and is accompanied, not only by anomie, but also by that increasing confusion as to the nature and even the existence of social classes which can be abundantly observed in all the "advanced" capitalist countries today. . . .

> Under these circumstances, the function of a new realism would be clear; to resist the power of reification in consumer society and to reinvent that category of totality which, systematically undermined by existential fragmentation on all levels of life and social organization today, can alone project structural relations between classes as well as class struggles in other countries, in what has increasingly become a world system. Such a conception of realism would incorporate what was always most concrete in the dialectical counter-concept of modernism—its emphasis on violent renewal of perception in a world in which experience has solidified into a mass of habits and automatisms.[30]

With this passage we reach the very center of Jameson's critical enterprise: the situation and function of modern art, its formal and substantial properties, its ideological force, and its potential as an instrument to transform the dominant mode of production from capitalism to socialism. For it is Jameson's explicit reversal of the Lukácsian judgment on modernism that animates virtually all of his literary criticism, but is most fully worked out in his study of Wyndham Lewis, to which we now turn.

* * * * *

Near the end of *Marxism and Form,* Jameson sketches an analysis of the novels of Hemingway that establishes a model for the later, more detailed, study of the works of Lewis. Jameson's strategy is to reverse the familiar direction of criticism which moves from the personality or the experiences of a writer to his style, the latter understood as the embodiment of the writer's personality or perhaps his *Weltanschauung.* In opposition to this familiar practice of stylistics (whose exemplary representative for American criticism would be Leo Spitzer), Jameson asserts that for Hemingway the sentence itself precedes all experience whatsoever, and in itself effectively produces the experiences we typically associate with Hemingway's works. But this is not to limit the significance of Hemingway's writing to the concept of an individual style. Rather, "Hemingway" comes to signify a certain practice of writing that functions in a certain way because of the pressures of the social and economic reality under which the writer is compelled to labor:

> the experience of sentence-production is the form taken in Hemingway's world by nonalienated work. Writing, now conceived as a *skill,* is then assimilated to the other skills of hunting and bullfighting, of fishing and warfare, which project a total image of man's active and all-absorbing technical participation in the outside world. Such an ideology of technique clearly reflects the more general American work situation, where, in the context of the open frontier and the blurring of class structure, the American male is conventionally evaluated according to the number of different jobs he has had, and skills he possesses. The Hemingway cult of *machismo* is just this attempt to come to terms with the great industrial transformation of America after World War I: it satisfies the Protestant work ethic at the same time that it glorifies leisure; it reconciles the deepest and most life-giving impulses toward wholeness with a status quo in which only sports allow you to feel alive and undamaged.[31]

Comparable analyses of the ideology of technique are featured in Jameson's essays on Raymond Chandler and Norman Mailer.[32] Mailer's extraordinarily intimate and aggressive style, for example, is seen to be a response to the situation of the writer under late capitalism. His "muscular" prose (too often glibly attributed to his career as an amateur boxer) provides "a way of working up close to the American reader, body against body, naming with relish precisely those things which have been repressed by the deodorized culture, using a revulsion as much social as personal to revive the reader's numbed perception of the state of the organism among the computers. So what looked like private obsession and arbitrary sensory symbolism turns out to be an implied political commentary on the American way of life itself, as well as a new and more direct and exasperating way of relating to readers formed in that way of life."[33] Suddenly any writer, almost, can be enlisted in the fight against capitalism, for every writer, insofar as he presents the contradictions and the painful isolation of just being a writer in the *société de consommation*, forges the instruments for a frontal assault on capitalism itself. Nor do the writer's explicit political views matter ultimately, for shattering the smooth surface of postindustrial culture is as much a characteristic of writers on the right as of those on the left. Enter Wyndham Lewis, prophet, iconoclast, least read and most misunderstood of the major figures of Anglo-American modernism.

Fables of Aggression, Jameson's first book-length study of a single writer since his early work on Sartre, presents even a sympathetic reader of Jameson's work with a number of problems. To some extent, Jameson seems to have assumed the tone and at least some of the indignation and outrage of his subject. The writing in this book is at times as openly terroristic as that of Lewis himself. Passionate, satiric, often brutally direct, even crude—these familiar features of Lewis's prose can be seen to have affected Jameson, as he writes with much the same fury that animated Lewis's assaults on the proprieties and decorum of the fading world of pre-1914 European culture into which he was born. Drawing on the work of Deleuze and Guattari, Jameson identifies the tension in Lewis between the "molecular" and the "molar" aspects of the latter's writing: "Yet considered on its own terms, Lewis's molar forms, the macrologic of his narratives, prove to have a very different dynamic from the momentum of the sentences themselves: what was in the latter sheer production and energy now veers about into the negative element, into an intolerable closure, an atmosphere of violence and destruction which the narratives articulate into a self-perpetuating sequence of rape, physical assault, aggressivity, guilt and immolation."[34]   And something like this very process of veering about from the production and sheer energy of this sentence to an inverse of destruction and immolation can be seen in the conclusion to *Fables of Aggression* itself, in the culminating passage (to which I shall return) in which Lewis's excoriation of European intellectuals of the twenties and thirties is transferred to Jameson's own vitriolic attack on the American intellegentsia of the fifties and sixties. Jameson's pent-up rage pores out on the page in such barely controlled fury that the entire project of his criticism is put into question.   For if the character of the contemporary intellectual is such as Jameson portrays it, what point can there be in writing to or about him at all? Certainly Jameson knows very well how he has implicated us all in the crimes he denounces, but at the same time there seems no way out of the passage down which we all tumble. Jameson comes quite near in this book to closing off that Utopian space which his previous work had consistently defended as the foundation of a viable Marxist historical criticism.[35]

Then, too, we have in *Fables of Aggression* tendencies toward an almost pure formalsim that make Jameson's reading of Lewis all but indistinguishable from contemporary critical methods of a more programmatically ahistorical kind:

> Thus at length a veritable self-generating image- and sentence-producing machine comes into view behind the dextrous and imperceptible substitutions of literal and figural levels for one another. . . . Indeed, the entire text of [*Cantleman's Spring Mate*], which collapses sex and war or aggressivity—the organic and the machine—together into a single "ruse of Nature," can in this repsect be read as a projection of the process of representation itself, or in other words, of the unnatural or artificial redoubling of "nature" by its expression, or by Language.[36]

Though Jameson will consistently link this aspect of Lewis's writing to the historical situation of the writer in the period of the demise of European culture and the rise of mass social movements, one wonders about the possible complicity between Jameson's own version of a formalist valorization of technique over content and that most powerful contemporary theorization of the text as machine, deconstruction.[37]

Nevertheless, the project of *Fables of Aggression* remains an aggressively historical one: the discrimination of modernism as a specific movement in literature, and the liberation of the term from the twin ideological determinations, one negative the other celebratory, now shackling it. Jameson's book is an attempt to see beyond these two apparently irreconcilable theories of modernism, the one conveniently represented by Lukács's condemnation of modern art as decadent and his consequent valorization of nineteenth-century realism, the other articulated in a variety of movements from Anglo-American ideologues of modernism, to the Russian Formalists and their current heirs among the *Tel Quel* group, and finally to Adorno, for all of whom high modernism is the embodiment of the revolutionary spirit itself. Both groups, Jameson argues, attack the modern fact of reification, though from opposite positions. It is important to realize here that reification produces a fragmentation of the psyche, a "division of labor" among mental faculties in which thought (in the form of instrumental reason) is cut off from the feelings or any form of inner life, and thus the private and the psychological is made completely distinct from the public and the social. Jameson concludes:

> But if this is the case, then it becomes clear that modernism not only reflects and reinforces such fragmentation and commodification of the psyche as its basic precondition [Lukács's point], but that the various modernisms all seek to overcome that reification as well, by the exploration of a new Utopian and libidinal experience of the various sealed realms or psychic compartments to which they are condemned, but which they also reinvent.[38]

The Utopian impulse at work in Lewis is most fully developed in what Jameson labels his "theological science fiction," the three volumes of *The Human Age*, about which Jameson writes with stunning clarity and with an acute sense of the place of this curious work in the long tradition of Utopian writing in the West. As, in its own way, the culmination of the Utopian impulse in modern literature, *The Human Age* recapitulates the entire tradition, at the same time highlighting the inherent contradiction that gives life to and simultaneously renders futile the modernist projection:

From the hindsight of the modern Utopian tradition, from Fourier to Marcuse and Ernst Bloch, we may suggest that such thinking is an attempt to expand the hegemonic religious code to accommodate what is essentially a vision of the Utopian body, of the libidinal transfiguration of human life in some nonalienated state.

Lewis's angels thus retain their instinctual content but dramatize the formal dilemma of the Utopian imagination itself, which must open a space for itself beyond this fallen world of contingency, to which however its categories remain corporeally shackled. The truth of the Utopian imagination indeed may be said to lie not in the representation it achieves, but rather ultimately in its failure to imagine its object; the greatest Utopias are thus those which, dramatizing the limits and the impoverishment of our visions of Utopia, denounce the imprisonment of the reading mind in the asphyxiating immanence of its here-and-now.[39]

Once more, and here in a writer whose work is impelled by the most virulent anti-Marxism, the paradoxical prognosis of Marxian historicism emerges. The task of the present is the abolition of itself, the creation of the necessary conditions for a future that will overcome all the conditions that made its coming into being possible. Thus the ideology of modernism is self-contradictory, and this may account for its current accommodation to the socioeconomic system of late capitalism, which has adopted all the strategies and many of the artifacts of the *avant-garde* as instruments of the market system in which the production and consumption of commodities is enhanced by endless swift changes in fashion which the mechanisms of advertising and the media disseminate through the various strata of consumption. Such is the depth and extent of penetration of this ideology into all the corners of our lives that there remains scarcely any "safe" position from which to denounce it cleanly and without a sense of guilt over one's own implication in the vast functioning of the global capitalist order. And so Jameson ends his book on Wyndham Lewis with an analysis of Lewis's castigation of intellectuals, which turns into a self-flagellation (in *The Revenge for Love*) by Lewis of his own crimes as a political intellectual who produced "paper weapons that cut down real bodies . . . ." Finally, in a passage alluded to earlier, Jameson draws out the conclusion of this line of argument for his own work, and also for us, insofar as we fancy ourselves to be and in reality do function as political intellectuals whose intentions for realizing a more humane, perhaps even more just, world inevitably come up against the realities of political power and its all too real consequences for those who, unlike the intellectuals themselves, are not insulated from its naked manifestations:

> Not the crimes themselves, indeed, are what is here condemned: not the mindless executions, the sheer blood-guilt alone, which any garden-variety gangster or torturer could provide, and which it would not require Lewis' genius to arraign. No, it is rather the essential "innocence" of intellectuals which is here in question: this private inner game of theoretical "convictions" and polemics against imaginary conceptual antagonists and mythic counterpositions, of the monad's projection of its own shadow sign systems upon the historical struggles of living people, of passionate private languages and private religions, which entering the field of force of the real social world, take on a murderous and wholly unsuspected power. So the facist theoreticians of the twenties and thirties, many of them quite genuinely shocked to discover the things for which the words really stood; so the post-war generation of American liberal theoreticians, elaborating enthusiastic apologies for the "free world" and exulting in the ingenuity of their own paper strategy and contingency planning, which were at length to realize themselves in the smoking and bleeding genocide of South-East Asia. Not that they meant that, exactly, for it is precisely this reality isolation of the intelligentsia of power, it is precisely its blind imprisonment in its own world of words, which is at issue. That was not our fault; that was not what we had in mind at all![40]

The passage reopens the central question posed by Jameson's entire *oeuvre*, certainly the nagging question for any contemporary Marxist criticism: for whom does the Marxist critic write? How is it possible given the anomie, the uniformity of surface, and the reification of modern culture, given its tenacious resistance to basic (as opposed to superficial) changes in the distribution of power and even to changes in the categories by means of which reality is conceptualized, given, in short, the extraordinary capacity of late capitalism to absorb and defuse all challenges to itself—given all this, how is it possible to produce a critique that both adequately represents the contemporary reality of our socioeconomic experience and offers the instruments by which it may be overcome?

There is, of course, no simple solution to this dilemma, no immediate or obvious means, to take one of Jameson's own frequently invoked figures, to square this circle. It is, in a way, a resurfacing of the original problem of historicism, though now with the epistemological difficulty of the relation of the present to the past recast in the form of a political and rhetorical difficulty, that of the present in relation to itself; for the present is precisely that which must be surpassed in order to see it for what it is, at the same time that the present is that which appears incapable of ever being other than what it already has become. To paraphrase Derrida, the future is what we already know we have not yet begun. The work of Fredric Jameson dramatizes in its energy, its commitment, and perhaps, from our present perspective, its inability to make a dent in liberal intellectuals' armor, the paradoxical situation of the Marxist critic in our culture. Jameson is what Lukács hypostatized in the figure of the essayist, "the pure type of the precursor," one who, like John the Baptist, "goes out to preach in the wilderness about another who is still to come, whose shoelace he is not worthy to untie."[41] Jameson's work can only be justified in a future that he has both helped to bring about and that will finally of necessity abolish him. But the relationship of the essayist to the course of history and to the great transformation he envisions is more complicated still, particularly in the present, when the "system" predicted by contemporary Marxist criticism is already in existence. For is it not Marxism itself, fully articulated if not always and everywhere politically effective, that Jameson's work envisions? And is it not, then, in some sense a superfluous role in which Jameson, and every contemporary Marxist critic, has been cast? To answer this question in the affirmative is to succumb to either of two powerfully tempting—but, I hasten to add, unsatisfactory—ways of understanding the present historical situation. The one, which might for the sake of convenience be denominated post-structuralist, is to interpret the present as the actualization of an absolute closure which has been present *in potentia* throughout history. One then beholds in history what Paul de Man once called "the sad time of patience," or what he would now identify as the ineluctable irony of the historical project itself, which simultaneously proposes its fulfillment and, with rigorous and merciless technical skill, exposes the necessary aberration of its own aims and actions.[42]   The other, more easily recognizable and certainly more accessible, temptation is the familiar Utopian projection of the end of history. Its most powerful spectre has been the iron-law determinism of the Second International associated (rightly or wrongly) with the later work of Engels. From this perspective, the production of the Marxist corpus, and in particular Marx's "scientific" writings on the structural formation of capitalism and the materialist theory of history, are signs of the "end of ideology" and the imminence of the millenial social revolution that will usher in the realm of freedom and the "Sunday of life" of a post-capitalist collectivity. Thompson's charge that Althusserianism leads inexorably to political quietism has been echoed by numerous commentators on and critics of Althusser from Rancière in France to Hindess and Hirst in England, and all are linked to this hypostatization of the imminence of the revolutionalry millenium which they (wrongly, in my view) believe Althusser's work projects. Their charge fails to account for that scandalous Althusserian insistence that even in a communist society ideaology will continue as a necessary means of social cohesion. But the argument does serve to highlight the problem which a project like Jameson's presents to Marxist political practice, and which his recent detailed engagement forgrounds.[43] The site of this engagement is the theory of ideology and the relation of this concept to political praxis.

* * * * *

The Political Unconscious, Jameson's most recent book, presents a sustained engagement with Althusser, and indeed with the theory of ideology itself. It is not possible to do full justice here to Jameson's reading of Althusser (much less to the remainder of the book, which offers an analysis and critique of a variety of Marxist and non-Marxist theories of cultural production, along with the projection and enactment of a more mature and more properly historical theory and practice), but the essential issue for Jameson's own position can be telescoped by laying out the revision of the science/ideology antinomy in Althusser which *The Political Unconscious* accomplishes. To anticipate, Jameson manages or contains the Althusserian attack on historicism by appropriating the Althusserian theory of ideology and reorienting it in relation, not to science, but to history itself, or rather, to that feature of history which he has consistently labelled Utopian. The problem is worked out most thoroughly in the final chapter, "The Dialectic of Ideology and Utopia," though it depends to some extent on the prior discussion of Althusser in which the Althusserian category of structure as the "absent cause" within a mode of production is transcoded through Jameson's absolute historicizing project to become History:

> history is *not* a text, not a narrative, master or otherwise, but . . .
> as an absent cause, it is inaccessible to us except in textual form,
> and . . . our approach to it and to the Real itself necessarily passes
> through its prior textualization, its narrativization in the political
> unconscious.[44]

This is to say that any narrative or any form of cultural production (including theory itself) is necessarily ideological in the more or less conventionally negative sense of the term that stigmatizes ideology as "false consciousness." The attempt to comprehend History produces forms that are, in Carlyle's phrase, "Hyperbolic-Asymptotic,"[45] more or less *adequate* (a word Jameson has recourse to on several occasions) representations of a, never entirely graspable, but nevertheless real, plenitude. Marxism's claim to priority among competing narrativizations of History is its greater "semantic richness,"[46] that is, its superior theoretical power. Marxism remains within ideology, though, somewhat miraculously, it theorizes ideology itself and proclaims its privileged access to a realm beyond ideology, namely History. Marxism thus proposes both a negative hermeneutic (with respect to other theories) and a positive hermeneutic (with respect to History). The latter claim, Jameson recognizes, is the more problematic.

We must return to the title of the chapter under discussion: "The Dialectic of Ideology and Utopia." For the resolution (if not the solution) of this dilemma within the Marxian theory of history lies in the relationship between ideology and Utopia, a relationship that can only be adequately conceived through dialectic, that mode of thinking which remains imperfectly realized in the present historical formation but which at the same time constitutes the horizon of thinking itself. For the dialectic fully realized is "the thought mode of a social formation of the future"; it must remain for now "the *anticipation* of the logic of a collectivity which has not yet come into being."[47] Jameson's projection of "a whole new logic of collective dynamics, with categories that escape the taint of some mere application of terms drawn from individual experience" (he cites most pertinently for the beginnings of such a logic the "machinery of Sartre's *Critique of Dialectical Reason*") is as yet, he knows, a Utopian desire. Such a logic is not merely the theorization of an object—the authentic collectivity—but the decisive product of a real historical development—the emergence of classless society. In this sense, Marxism, like other narrativizations of History, is necessarily ideological, the expression of class interest and the (for now) imaginary resolution of a real contradiction. Thus one can see what Jameson means when he says that "the effectively ideological is also, at the same time, necessarily Utopian."[48] This formulation explains how one can understand even the ideology of the ruling class as Utopian, and in the following way:

> The achieved collectivity or organic group of whatever kind—oppressors fully as much oppressed—is Utopian not in itself, but only in so far as all such collectivities are themselves *figures* for the ultimate concrete collective life of an achieved Utopian or classless society. Now we are in a better position to understand how even hegemonic or ruling-class culture and ideology are Utopian, not in spite of their instrumental function to secure and perpetuate class privilege and power, but rather precisely because that function is also in and of itself the affirmation of collective solidarity.[49]

Sympathy for the devil? Perhaps, but the advantage of Jameson's reformulation of the Marxist theory of ideology from merely a negative hermeneutic to both a negative (ideology) and a positive (Utopia) hermeneutic lies in its liberation of thought from the sterile ethical oppositions that have plagued so much Marxist ideological critique and also in its refusal of the ultimately debilitating determinism of a theory of history in which Marxism (or any other theory) occupies the "place of truth." For, as E. P. Thompson has said:

> there is no error more disabling and actively dangerous to the
> practice of any human freedom than the notion that there is
> some "socialist" mode of production . . . which will afford a
> categorical guarantee that some immanent socialist society (values,
> ideas, institutions, etc.) will *unfold itself:* not, perhaps, instantan-
> eously . . . but in good time, out of the womb of the mode of pro-
> duction itself. This is wholly untrue: every choice and every insti-
> tution is still to be made . . . .[50]

This is the very point that Jameson makes at the end of *The Political Unconscious* by reminding us (and himself) of Walter Benjamin's grim assessment of the price at which any mode of cultural production must be purchased: "There has never been a document of culture which was not at one and the same time a document of barbarism." No doctrine or theory, no program or project, no narrative or representation, however "progressive" or Utopian is ever free from the taint of ideological distortion which suppresses, manages, and contains the objective contradictions of Reality and History, which is to say that every ideology, however Utopian, is purchased at the cost of the domination of competing ideologies. Only at the end of History, with the disappearance of social fragmentation in the dissolution of classes, can the full human collectivity be realized. Within the present, it is worth keeping open this possibility, without giving in to the temptation of thinking its arrival imminent or inevitable.

NOTES

[1] E. P. Thompson, "The Segregation of Dissent," in *Writing by Candlelight* (London: Merlin Press, 1980), p. 8. The most notable Marxist theoretician of such "traditional intellectuals" is of course Antonio Gramsci; see *Selections from the Prison Notebooks,* ed. and trans. Quintin Hoare and Geoffrey Nowell Smith (New York: International Publishers, 1971), pp. 5-23.

[2]M. H. Abrams, lecture delivered at the Lionel Trilling Seminar, Columbia University, February 23, 1978; an expanded version of this paper was published as "How to Do Things with Texts," *Partisan Review,* 46 (1979), 566-88.

[3]Friedrich Nietzsche, *The Use and Abuse of History,* trans. Adrian Collins (Indianapolis: Bobbs-Merrill, 1957), p. 3.

[4]Walter Benjamin, *Illuminations,* ed. Hannah Arendt, trans. Harry Zohn (New York: Schocken Books, 1969), p. 255.

[5]Paul de Man, *Blindness and Insight: Essays in the Rhetoric of Contemporary Criticism* (New York: Oxford University Press, 1971), p. 148.

[6]*Ibid.,* pp. 150-51.

[7]*Ibid.,* p. 165.

[8]Paul de Man, *Allegories of Reading: Figural Language in Rousseau, Nietzsche, Rilke, and Proust* (New Haven: Yale University Press, 1979), p. 270.

[9]*Ibid.,* p. 277.

[10]On rigidity in de Man's method, revealed in his troping of the logical category of rigor, see Jonathan Arac, "To Regress from the Rigor of Shelley: Figures of History in American Deconstructive Criticism," *boundary 2,* 9 (Fall 1980).

[11]Louis Althusser, "Marx's Relation to Hegel," in *Politics and History,* trans. Ben Brewster (London: New Left Books, 1972), p. 182.

[12]Culler's review of *Marxism and Form* appeared in the *Modern Language Review,* 69 (July 1974), 599-601.

[13]See E. P. Thompson, "The Poverty Of Theory," in *The Poverty of Theory and Other Essays* (New York: Monthly Review Press, 1979), pp. 1-210. I see no justification whatever, incidentally, for the charge by the anonymous *TLS* reviewer of *Marxism and Form* (see *TLS,* 3712 [27 April 1975], 462) that Jameson is guilty of "popular frontism." Jameson's work is capacious, even at times eclectic, but it is always written

from a carefully conceived, if not always explicitly articulated, theoretical position. Even a cursory reading of the final chapter of *Marxism and Form* demonstrates that much.

[14] Fredric Jameson, "Marxism and Historicism," *New Literary History*, 11 (Autumn 1979): 57-58.

[15] *Ibid.*, p. 69.

[16] *Ibid.*, pp. 69-70.

[17] *Ibid.*, p. 70.

[18] *Ibid.*, p. 71. Earlier in the essay (p. 58), Jameson cites a similar bursting forth of the Utopian impulse in Benjamin's *Theses on the Philosophy of History*, which I have cited above. It is worth remarking here that the contemporary attempt to "theologize" Benjamin's *Theses*, to read in them a deconstruction of historical materialism as a "disguised theology" (see, for example, Geoffrey H. Hartman, *Criticism in the Wilderness: The Study of Literature Today* [New Haven: Yale University Press, 1980], pp. 72-85), while it derives a certain plausibility from Thesis I, nonetheless sublimates the powerful rethinking of historicism that the *Theses* accomplish at the same time it discounts entirely the incipient Utopianism that Benjamin's critique of diachronic succession makes possible. The final sentences of the *Theses* can stand as the explicit rejoinder to this reading: "We know that the Jews were prohibited from investigating the future. The Torah and the prayers instruct them in remembrance, however. This stripped the future of its magic, to which all those succumb who turn to the soothsayers for enlightenment. This does not imply, however, that for the Jews the future turned into homogeneous, empty time. For every second of time was the strait gate through which the Messiah might enter." (Benjamin, *Illuminations*, p. 264)

[19] Fredric Jameson, *Marxism and Form: Twentieth-Century Dialectical Theories of Literature* (Princeton: Princeton University Press, 1971), p. 416.

[20] See especially in *Marxism and Form* the pages on Lukács's *History and Class Consciousness*, Sartre's *Critique of Dialectical Reason,* and the whole of the final chapter; elsewhere, the essays "Imaginary and Symbolic in Lacan: Marxism, Psychoanalytic Criticism, and the Problem of the Subject," in *Literature and Psychoanalysis—The Question of Reading: Other-*

wise, ed. Shoshana Felman, *Yale French Studies,* 55-56 (1977), and "The Ideology of the Text," *Salmagundi,* 31-32 (1975); and finally, the first chapter of *The Prison-House of Language: A Critical Account of Structuralism and Russian Formalism* (Princeton: Princeton University Press, 1972), entitled "The Linguistic Model."

[21] Jameson, *Marxism and Form,* p. 346.

[22] *Ibid.,* p. 361.

[23] Jameson's most succinct formulation of the importance of Bloch's work is as follows: "For Bloch's work suggests that even a cultural product whose social function is that of *distracting* us can only realize that aim by fastening and harnessing our attention and our imaginative energies in some positive way and by some type of genuine, albeit disguised and distorted, content. Such content is for him what he calls 'Hope,' or in other words the permanent tension of human reality towards a radical transformation of itself and everything about it, towards a Utopian transfiguration of its own existence as well as of its social context. To maintain that everything is a 'figure of Hope' is to offer an analytical tool for detecting the presence of some Utopian content even within the most degraded and degrading type of commerical product" (Fredric Jameson, "Introduction/Prospectus: To Reconsider the Relationship of Marxism to Utopian Thought," *Minnesota Review,* 6 (1976), 57-58). Among the astonishing feats of *Marxism and Form* was to have discovered "the presence of some Utopian content" in virtually every major figure in the twentieth-century Marxist tradition, even in so intransigently pessimistic a writer as Adorno and so melancholy a personality as Benjamin.

[24] I have discussed this relationship elsewhere in an essay on the work of Erich Heller, "The Tragic Vision: Erich Heller and the Critique of Modernism," *Salmagundi,* 52 (Spring 1981).

[25] Jameson, *Marxism and Form,* p. 179.

[26] *Ibid.,* p. 178.

[27] *Ibid.,* p. 190. Though Jameson makes no mention of it here, surely the most important precedent for such a theory of aesthetic transcendence of modern alienation is Schiller's *Letters on the Aesthetic Education of Man.* But cf. Jameson's criticism of Schiller's implicit substitution (much imitated in subsequent theories of "aesthetic education" like

those of Frye and the American New Critics) of cultural revolution for social revolution (*Marxism and Form*, p. 91), and also Lukács's essay on "Schiller's Theory of Modern Literature," in Georg Lukács, *Goethe and His Age*, trans. Robert Anchor (London: Merlin Press, 1968), pp. 101-35.

[28] Jameson, *Marxism and Form*, p. 193.

[29] Fredric Jameson, "Reflections in Conclusion," in *Aesthetics and Politics*, ed. Ronald Taylor (London: New Left Books 1977), p. 202.

[30] *Ibid.*, pp. 212-13.

[31] Jameson, *Marxism and Form*, p. 412.

[32] See Fredric Jameson, "On Raymond Chandler," *Southern Review*, 6 (1970); and "The Great American Hunter, or, Ideological Content in the Novel," *College English*, 34 (1972).

[33] Jameson, "The Great American Hunter," p. 189.

[34] Fredric Jameson, *Fables of Aggression: Wyndham Lewis, The Modernist as Fascist* (Berkeley and Los Angeles: University of California Press, 1979), p. 8.

[35] I hasten to add that this apparent imbalance is perhaps merely a matter of emphasis, a featuring of the ideological rather than the Utopian character of modernist writing. I shall return to this problem of "the dialectic between ideology and Utopia" in the final section of this essay. Given the recalcitrance and just plain blindness of most literary intellectuals to the ideological function of their work, it may be that Jameson's tone and temper in the Lewis book are not all that extreme, perhaps not even extreme enough. Thus, a recent review of the book by Charles Molesworth can tolerate the fierceness of Jameson's (not to mention Lewis's!) indictment of liberal intellectuals quite well by completely misconstruing Jameson's understanding of ideology and declaring that "his critical strategy is, finally, essentially moral" (Charles Molesworth, "Frightful Fashions and Compulsive Occasions," *Salmagundi*, 50-51 [Fall 1980-Winter 1981], 333). Liberal intellectuals will swallow most anything, provided they can transform the adversary into an image of their own bland moralism, a metamorphic power they seem to possess in abundance.

[36] *Ibid.,* pp. 28-29.

[37]Cf. Paul de Man on Rousseau: "In the general economy of the Revêrie, the machine displaces all other significations and becomes the raison d'etre of the text. Its power of suggestion reaches far beyond its illustrative purpose, especially if one bears in mind the previous characterization of unmotivated, fictional languages as 'machinal.' The underlying structural patterns of addition and suppression as well as the figural system of the text all converge towards it. Barely concealed by its peripheral function, the text here stages the textual machine of its own constitution *and* performance, its own textual allegory. The threatening element in these incidents then becomes more apparent. The text as body, with all its implications of substitutive tropes ultimately always retraceable to metaphor, is displaced by the text as machine and, in the process, it suffers the loss of the illusion of meaning. The *deconstruction of the figural dimension is a process that takes place independently of any desire; as such it is not unconscious but mechanical, systematic in its performance but arbitrary in its principle, like a grammar"* (de Man, *Allegories of Reading,* p. 298; emphasis added).

[38]Jameson, *Fables of Aggression,* p. 14.

[39]*Ibid.,* pp. 152-53.

[40]*Ibid.,* pp. 176-77.

[41]Georg Lukács, *Soul and Form,* trans. Anna Bostock (Cambridge: MIT Press, 1974), p. 16.

[42]See Paul de Man, "Impasse de la critique formaliste," *Critique* 12 (1956), 500; idem, *Allegories of Reading,* pp. 277, 298-301; and idem, *Blindness and Insight,* pp. 142-65.

[43]See especially the essays "Marxism and Historicism" and "Imaginary and Symbolic in Lacan" cited above.

[44]Fredric Jameson, *The Political Unconscious: Narrative as a Socially Symbolic Act* (Ithaca: Cornell University Press, 1981), p. 35.

[45]Thomas Carlyle, "On History Again," in *Essays,* 2 vols. (London: J. M. Dent, 1915), II:99.

[46] Jameson, *The Political Unconscious*, p. 10.

[47] *Ibid.*, pp. 117, 294.

[48] *Ibid.*, p. 286.

[49] *Ibid.*, p. 291.

[50] Thompson, "The Poverty of Theory," pp. 161-62.

IMAGINATION AND MEANING: AESTHETIC ATTITUDES IN MIRCEA ELIADE'S THOUGHT[1]

by

Matei Calinescu

> Every exile is a Ulysses traveling toward Ithaca. Every real exis-
> tence reproduces the *Odyssey*. . . . I had known that for a long
> time. What I have just discovered is that the chance of becoming
> a Ulysses is given to *any* exile *whatsoever* (precisely because he
> has been condemned by the gods, that is, by the 'powers' which
> decide historical, earthly destinies). But to realize this, the exile
> must be capable of penetrating the hidden meaning of his wander-
> ings, and of understanding them as a long series of initiation
> trials (willed by the gods) and so many obstacles on the path
> which brings back to the hearth (toward the center). That means:
> seeing signs, hidden meanings, symbols, in the sufferings, the de-
> pressions, the dry periods in everyday life. Seeing them and read-
> ing them even *if they aren't there;* if one sees them, one can build
> a structure and read a message in the formless flow of things
> and the monotonous flux of historical facts.
>
> M. Eliade, *No Souvenirs* (January 1, 1960)

The term "aesthetic" is used here in a broad "existential"
sense. It certainly refers to, but is not limited to, the experience
provided by the arts. There is, in fact, an aesthetic way of appre-
hending the world and of structuring experience which sometimes has little or nothing to do with what we conventionally
relate to the domain of the arts. It is known that Benedetto
Croce considers Vico the true founder of modern aesthetics,
although the author of *La scienza nuova* never specifically tried
to define art and was preoccupied mainly, if not exclusively,
with the problem of comprehending a *forma mentis* that he
called "poetic" and that we now would call "mythic." Even
if Croce's viewpoint seems somewhat exaggerated, there is no

doubt that the founder of the modern study of myth has, directly or indirectly, played a major role in the history of aesthetic consciousness. Finally, Vico's use of "poetic" instead of "mythic" is more than a simple case of synonymity. It involves a complex conception of poetic imagination. Opposed to the already very strong Cartesian tradition of rationalism of the early eighteenth century, Vico displayed a fruitful cult of fantasy, originality (in the etymological sense), and ingenuousness and revealed the inexhaustible metaphoric powers of mythical thought. Even more, metaphor and myth were for Vico a *means to knowledge:* the sphere of the poetic was not only extended, but also given a philosophical dignity in perfect contrast to its status in rationalist aesthetics as a mere "plaything of the mind" or a form of "ornate" discourse.

From this point of view, Vico is perhaps the first great modern thinker to have suggested an existential approach to the problems of both mythology and poetry. His anthropology definitely contains an aesthetic, and this aesthetic is based on a system of values which defines a mode of being. I think it is not at all fortuitous that Vico was led to his revolutionary discoveries by his contact with the manifestations of "primitive" religious creativeness. It seems to me that Vico's emphasis on richness, implied in his conception of mythical thought, suggests an important aspect of the aesthetic attitude, even when we do not accept the Italian philosopher's emotional-expressive view of myth and his particular historicism of *corsi* and *ricorsi.*

More generally, I would say that the "aesthetic Weltanschauung" is characterized by the presence, in a variety of ways, of certain elements: a deep sense of multiplicity and diversity; a consciousness of the secret network of relationships connecting the various phenomena of life, coupled with the realization that any kind of reduction eventually kills a vital richness which is in and by itself one of the highest values; and a special interest in "ambiguity" or polysemy, also regarded as a bearer of value (a value, I would add, not challenged by the dramatic polarizations brought about by ethical thought).

These are only some of the ideas I have in mind when speaking of aesthetic attitudes in Mircea Eliade's work conceived as a whole. Eliade is known in the West mostly, if not exclusively, as a scholar and thinker. He is "by nearly unanimous consent the most influential student of religion in the world today," as Harvey Cox put it a few years ago in the *New York Times Book Review*.[2]   As for his abundant literary *oeuvre*— whose themes and structures might illuminate some of his major choices in the study of religion—there are few readers in the West who are even aware of its existence. This may be due, among other things, to Eliade's own curious disinterest in the promotion of his fiction, a disinterest that is in perfect contrast to his passion for fiction writing, to which his *Fragments d'un journal* (covering the period 1945-69) bear ample witness. It is indeed strange to think that Eliade, parallel to his brilliant scholarly career in postwar France, and then in the United States, has created an impressive body of fiction and seems satisfied with its publication in occasional translations (mostly French and German, and only very recently English[3]) and with the appearance of the Rumanian originals in little émigré magazines or in small editions sponsored by friends. It is as if the experience of success during his youth in Rumania—where he was known and acclaimed primarily as a novelist—had been sufficient to him and, moreover, had armed him with a certain wariness with regard to literary success.

I am certain that one day Eliade's literary work will enjoy the wider readership it deserves. Until then, the simple awareness of his passion for fiction and for art in general can be of help in an attempt to define his personality as a thinker and his particular directions of interest in the study of religion. The appeal of myth, the special use he makes of hermeneutics, his deep-rooted belief in the existential value of images and symbols, the quality of attention he devotes to narrative structures—all these draw to a large extent on his aesthetic, and specifically creative, experience. One should not therefore be surprised to discover that for Eliade *artistic imagination* and religious creativeness present many analogies, which justify basically similar approaches. This is so because both art and religion are concerned with the problem of meaning—a problem which is central to his whole work as a thinker, novelist, and scholar.

Speaking recently of his stories of the supernatural and the occult, Eliade made a significant theoretical statement when pointing out that the elements by which these stories belong to what is called *littérature fantastique* "disclose, or more precisely create, a series of 'parallel worlds' which do not pretend to be 'symbols' of something else. . . . Each tale creates its proper universe, and the creation of such imaginary universes through literary means can be compared with mythical processes. . . . One can speak of a certain continuity between myth and literary fiction, since the one as well as the other recounts the creation (or the 'revelation') of a universe parallel to the everyday world." And, in the same "Introduction"—written especially for the English translation of two earlier stories, "Nights at Serampore" and "The Secret of Dr. Honigberger"—Eliade compares the problems that confront the historian of religions and the writer of fiction, adding that both have to deal "with different structures of (sacred and mythological) space, different qualities of time, and more specifically with a considerable number of strange, unfamiliar, and enigmatic worlds of meaning."[4]

Eliade's belief in the "creative" (and "revelatory") nature of both mythical and literary imagination seems to be a consequence of one of his early philosophical illuminations or intuitions, an intuition which determined his lifelong preoccupation with what he calls "the unrecognizability of miracle." I found the first mention of the idea of unrecognizability in one of the feverishly youthful aphorisms collected in 1932 in the volume *Soliloquies.* "The question," Eliade writes, "is not that God is invisible, but that he is unrecognizable. God has made himself impossible to be recognized anywhere."[5] Two years later in *Oceanography* (1934), another collection of short essays and aphorisms, he goes further in that direction, speculating about a possible phenomenology of miracle. While in the world of Greek antiquity a miracle was defined in terms of *contrast* (in regard to human expectation), in Christianity it is described rather in terms of *contact*. In the latter case, Eliade thinks, miracle tends to become an element of daily reality; there is nothing spectacular about it, no dramatic opposition between it and the most humble events of which our lives are made. If there still is any contrast, we should look for it in the difference between the *exceptional* way we would expect a miracle to occur and the unrecognizable way it actually occurs. "A miracle," Eliade affirms, "is distinguished from an ordinary event (that is, an event that can be explained as resulting from natural causes—cosmic, biological, or historical) by the impossibility of isolating it. The unrecognizable is the perfection of divine revelation: the sacred no longer *manifests* or makes itself present by contrast; it acts directly on mankind by contact or union.''[6]

Twenty years later, in 1953, trying to answer the question of how he was able to reconcile his scholarly activity with the apparently divergent set of goals implied by creative writing, Eliade pointed out that both his religious studies and his fiction were essentially concerned with the same problem—again the "unrecognizability of miracle." Scholarship and literary creation, he wrote, "eventually lead to the same problem: the unrecognizability of the Transcendent that camouflages itself in History."[7]   Eliade's diary contains a large number of similar statements, some of which will be discussed later.

One of the central oppositions underlying Eliade's thought is clearly implied in such passages as those I have just referred to, namely, the opposition between unknowable and unrecognizable. The agnostic thesis that ultimate reality is unknowable is replaced here by the hypothesis of unrecognizability—a variant of the Platonic doctrine of *anamnesis*. At first sight, the difference between the two approaches may seem slight, indeed irrelevant. Let me stress therefore that in the case of agnosticism the main concern is that of epistemological validity (implying a relativistic theory of knowledge) while in the second case true knowledge is in principle accessible to everyone who can recognize it (or who can remember it, according to Plato). The latter way of thinking is structurally symbolic, and its main concern is to discover the actual *meaning* of the innumerable signs which constitute our consciousness. The idea that the "transcendent" has made itself "unrecognizable"—which should be taken as a philosophical metaphor, no less legitimate than Freud's psychological metaphor of the "censorship" of consciousness— leads to a theory of interpretation or hermeneutics, interested in the disguises, variations, and analogical ramifications of meaning. As a method, hermeneutics can certainly be made use of for an indefinite number of theoretical and practical purposes. Eliade's particular use of hermeneutics—which in his *Journal* he has called "imaginative hermeneutics"—is determined by his conception of the sacred and the profane, and more broadly by his theory of "camouflage." To anticipate what will be discussed later in more detail, I would say that for Eliade meaning (whose plenitude is realized in the sacred) undergoes a process of occulation in history, whose linear and irreversible character is directly opposed to the circular and timeless pattern of mythical thought. Meaning shrinks, as it were, disappears behind meaningless appearances. Its signs, which no one can read any longer, are hidden *among* and not beneath the trivia of day-to-day life. From this standpoint, hermeneutics, whose task is to recover lost worlds of meaning, may be defined simply as the *science of recognition.* The concept of "camouflage" also occurs in Eliade's essays of history of religions: it is basic, for instance, in the last chapter of *Myth and Reality* [Aspects du mythe (1963)], which is significantly entitled "Survivals and Camouflages of Myth." The focus here is on the "unrecognizability of myth" in modern desacralized societies. But the problem comes up more directly, and more strikingly, whenever Eliade is speaking of his literary works. Another example from his journal is the entry of December 28, 1963, in which the author discloses the "intention" of a short story ("The Bridge") he was working on at the time: "In the story I'm writing," the diarist notes, "I am obsessed with getting across its secret meaning: the camouflage of mysteries in the events of immediate reality. Consequently, I want to bring out the ambivalence of every event, in the sense that an apparently banal happening can reveal a whole universe of transcendent meanings, and that an apparently extraordinary, fantastic event can be accepted by those who live it as something that goes without saying and at which they wouldn't even dream of being surprised."[8]

Eliade's insistence on "ambivalence"—in the quoted passage and in so many other places—is another key to the understanding of what I would call his metaphysics or even "theology" of meaning. For both writer and thinker, the question is not so much to go beyond the camouflage in order to grasp the one "hidden" truth or "principle" as to become *aware* of a richness which participates in the nature of the miraculous and whose existence would be impossible without the plurality of meaning brought about by the very action of camouflage. Eliade seems to believe that the process through which the mystery, the transcendent, or the miracle become unrecognizable creates a *richness* of parallel worlds of meaning that the interpreter is supposed to discover, assess, and fully disclose to the conscious mind. Paradoxically, the sacred hides itself in the very process of revealing itself, and vice versa.[9] Interpretation, Eliade suggests, should preserve and even amplify the richness which results from the dialectic of unrecognizability. The value of hermeneutics derives, among other things, from the fact that it enlarges the circumference of what might be termed man's "semantic imagination."

To be aware of richness and to create more richness of meaning is, in Eliade's eyes, the essential task of both the student of religion and the poet—taking the word "poet" in its original sense of "maker." His personal interest in archaic religiosity and myth is a direct consequence of his passion for, and obsession with, creation, for *myth* "tells how . . . a reality came into existence, be it the whole reality, the Cosmos, or only a fragment of reality—an island, a species of plant, a particular kind of human behavior, an institution. Myth, then, is always an account of a 'creation'; it relates how something was produced, began to *be.*"[10]   But myth is not only an account of a creation; it is itself a creation, an "existence." All myths are true, though it may seem paradoxical, both symbolically and literally. Eliade's vision of religion might be superficially characterized as somewhat neo-Platonic, in the sense that all past and living religions are, despite boundless diversity, *one.* They are emanations of the same creative Oneness. His vision of religion is based on what I have already called a *"theology" of meaning.* More specifically, it is as if the sacred or God (absolute creativeness) manifested itself through the innumerable parallel "worlds of meaning" of which man, as a historical being, tends to be unconscious. So it would be perhaps correct to say that for Eliade the sacred is simply the meaningful or real, whereas the profane is the meaningless or *false,* illusory, misleading.

In this respect, literature (fiction), as a modern substitute for myth, has the function of tearing up the illusory veil of meaninglessness. As I indicated earlier, there is no substantial difference between the mythical and literary imagination. The novel, for which Eliade has a marked and explicable preference, is one of the main cultural activities that perform a secretly mythological role in our world. Essentially, the analogy between novel and myth rests on their common narrative structure. In spite of many differences, they both are articulated successions of images and symbols (even if the latter are not recognized as symbols). To imagine and tell *stories*— that is what mythmakers and novelists are supposed to do. The almost metaphysical value attached to the fact of storytelling explains why Eliade has been a consistent enemy of the contemporary "antinovel," of the novel that, for whatever reasons, fails to fulfill its narrative mission. Realistic or fantastic, psychological or antipsychological, traditional or technically innovative, the novel simply loses its *raison d'être* when it turns against storytelling. To narrate acquires in Eliade's eyes an ontological significance: the imaginary events which compose a story can actually enrich the world and make it more meaningful. This conviction, expressed several times in the *Journal,* is seen in the following passage: "The novel must tell something, because narrative (that is, literary invention) enriches the world no more and no less than history, although on another level. We have more creative possibilities in imaginary universes than we do on the level of history. The fact *that something is happening, that all kinds of things are happening,* is just as significant for the fate of man as the fact of living in history or of hoping to modify it."[11]

II

At this point, it might be useful to examine more closely the novel that Eliade himself considers his most accomplished literary work, namely, *The Forbidden Forest.* "Great novels are above all great fairy tales," Vladimir Nabokov used to say. This was certainly meant as a paradox, since the fairy-tale nature of the works Nabokov had in mind (Flaubert's *Madame Bovary,* Tolstoy's *Anna Karenina,* or Proust's *A la recherche du temps perdu,* among others) is by no means easy to grasp; indeed, to become aware of it, one must first realize that, according to another typically Nabokovian dictum, "Life is the least realistic of fictions." Most serious novelists would be surprised and a little annoyed to hear someone state, no matter how admiringly, that all they do is recount fairy tales. Not so Mircea Eliade. Actually, his most carefully constructed and most ambitious novel, *The Forbidden Forest,* achieves some of its most powerful effects by showing how many unobserved elements of the marvelous enter into what we call reality, and conversely, how real certain aspects of the marvelous are.

The Forbidden Forest has an entirely *self-conscious* fairy-tale dimension. And this goes beyond the significant fact that three of the central motifs of the novel are explicitly linked to some of the best-known Rumanian *basme* (folk-tales): the motif of the unrecognizability of miracle or the sacred to "Făt-Frumos și merele de aur" ("Prince Charming and the Golden Apples"), in which the prince will be put to death if he is unable to choose the one apple of real gold out of a hundred gilded ones; the motif of the search of eternal life to "Tinerețe fără-batrînețe și viața fără de moarte" ("Youth Without Old Age and Life Without Death"); and the motif of unattainable love to the various tales about Ileana Cosânziana, the inaccessible fairy princess of Rumanian folklore. Essentially, for Eliade fairy tales perform, on the level of imagination, an *initiatory* function which is analogous to those performed, on different levels, by other kinds of narrative. This function is rooted in the "human condition" itself, man's life having the character of a "story," and specifically of an initiation story—"Every existence," Eliade writes, "is made up of an unbroken series of 'ordeals,' 'deaths,' and 'resurrections' . . ." (*Myth and Reality*, New York, 1968, p. 202). In substance, then, if not in form, a novel, insofar as it attempts to make sense of the fate of human individuals, functions as a "doublet" for initiatory rites and myths, very much like a fairy tale. Among contemporary writers, Eliade is one of the few who could fully subscribe to Nabokov's para-doxical formula, but we must not forget that *Non idem est si duo dicunt idem.* Eliade, unlike Nabokov, attaches religious, not only aesthetic, meaning to the manifestations of Imagi-nation: thus myths, fairy tales, novels, can all be said to "exist within an epiphanic structure: they *are* because they have ap-peared. . . ." (*No Souvenirs: Journal 1957-1969*, New York, 1977, p. 14).

The title of Eliade's novel in English, *The Forbidden For-est*, a direct translation of the French *La Forêt interdite*, pre-serves little if anything of the sense of the marvelous that the Ru-manian *Noaptea de Sânziene* so unmistakably conveys. *Noaptea de Sânziene* (The Night of the Sânziene) is the midsummer night, the night preceding the feast of the nativity of St. John the Baptist on June 24. It is a night of proverbial importance to love and lovers, and also the one time of the year when, accord-ing to various folk traditions, supernatural beings moved freely about (Shakespeare's famous comedy draws on such beliefs, and I think that certain passages in Eliade's novel, particularly those at the beginning, dealing with the strange, entrancing magic of the forest where Stefan and Ileana first meet, have something to do with *A Midsummer Night's Dream;* the whole atmosphere evoked in these passages presents a sharp contrast with the final pages of the novel, which justify the French and the English title, since the forest of Royaumont is indeed *forbidden,* charged with the infernal symbolism of Dante's "selva oscura"). While the word "Sânziene" in Rumanian may derive, as philologists point out, from "sanctus dies Johannis," its meaning in folklore is nevertheless totally non-Christian: the "Sânziene" are fairies, often also called "Drăgaice" (from "dragoste"=love), and they perform a wide variety of roles in the mythology of Eros. Both in sound and in meaning, "Sânziene" is close to the generic word for fairy, "Zână." The latter also has a Latin origin, for it comes from Diana, the Italic goddess, conceived as a patroness of birth, both human and animal, that is, a deity of fertility. The Night of St. John is about the time of the *summer solstice,* and that is why it has been associated since long before Christianity with diverse fertility (and erotic) cults. The names of Eliade's main characters are also highly significant in this context: Ioana, Stefan's wife, is the feminine of Ioan (=John); Ileana is obviously related to Ileana Cosânziana, the fairy-princess, whose *pagan* feast coincides with the Christian celebration of John the Baptist; as for the hero of the novel, Stefan (=Stephen, derived from the Greek Stephanos = "crown"), he bears the name of St. Stephen, the first Christian martyr, whose feast, according to the Eastern Orthodox calendar, falls on December 27, only a few days after the *winter solstice.* This detail is very important. The key scenes in the novel are, in terms of the solar cycle, directly related to the solstices (the night of St. John, Christmas, the Day of St. Stephen, the New Year). The very etymology of *solstice* may be relevant here: when it reaches the solstice, the sun seems to "stand still" for several days. The solstice represents therefore a *different quality of time,* a privileged time, a pause in the ineluctable on-going flow of Chronos. The major theme of Eliade's novel—the conflict between primordial (sacred) time and historical (profane) time—makes the use of solstitial mythology quite natural.

A novel and a fairy tale, *The Forbidden Forest* recounts, through the stages of Stefan's quest, an attempt to rediscover "lost time," not so much the personal time of which Proust speaks as the larger time of myth: a time in which stories, all sorts of stories, are told and happen, and in which happenings themselves are made of the stuff that tales are made of—epiphanies. The book is important for any student of Eliade's philosophy of myth, but it should also interest any serious student of the post-World War development of the novel. From the latter point of view, *The Forbidden Forest* (written roughly between 1949 and 1954, and published in French translation in 1955, and in the original Rumanian in 1971, by the émigré publisher Ioan Cusa), is one of the first novels in which one can identify the signs of what has been called "magic realism," a phenomenon that has been widely discussed in connection with recent Latin American literature, but whose independent variant, as it emerged in Rumania, the only neo-Latin country in Eastern Europe, has received only little attention. Eliade's project, namely, writing a vast narrative on the theme of Time, including the numerous and dangerous paradoxes brought about by the specific time consciousness imposed upon us by our modernity, has led him to the discovery of certain techniques that are very close to those used by the representatives of magic realism: the point of departure is "realistic" (recognizable events in chronological succession, everyday atmosphere, verisimilitude, characters with more or less predictable psychological reactions), but soon certain strange discontinuities or gaps appear in the "normal," true-to-life texture of the narrative. The author sets out to explore these gaps. There are countless *images* floating there, some of them archetypal, some purely idiosyncratic, which combine and separate according to the laws of the logic of myth (or dream), a logic that somehow compels the writer to take it at least as seriously as he takes the ordinary one. The traditional unity of character is consequently disrupted; there are sudden passages from one plane of vision to another; shifts of identity; and bizarre multiplications or dispersions of the self. Basically, one can say that sequential phenomena tend toward the simultaneity of a mythical present. The main difference between Eliade and the magic realists is the latter's experimentalist bent, often combined with a polemicism which is both aesthetic and social (usually leftist radical), as opposed to Eliade's more serenely meditative outlook. Both the magic realists and Eliade share a deep interest in mythical thought and in "primitive" religious experience, but Eliade's "modernism"—his literary work being undoubtedly an offshoot of the large movement of artistic modernism—does not imply a blunt rejection of the narrow "tradition" that most modernists construe as the enemy but, on the contrary, an effort to *understand* it, even though this understanding means relativizing it, and assigning it the rather modest place that belongs to it within a greater and fundamentally *plural* Tradition.

For Eliade there are always several traditions that must be taken into account *at the same time*, because only by using them all, in spite of their often heterogeneous or even mutually contradictory aspects, can a writer hope to attain some kind of "totality." This totality, whose possibility, in Eliade's eyes, is granted by the immanent symbolic power with which everything in the world is endowed, has an *epiphanic* quality, which can be seized only when reality is observed with what I would call an inspired attention—an attention so great that it becomes visionary. *The Forbidden Forest* is a perfect example of how Eliade's dialectic of the sacred and the profane functions within the context of a work of fiction. The starting point is the hero's intuition that the sacred hides itself in the world, that it takes on the appearances of the profane and makes itself unrecognizable. The problem is how to uncover and recognize it.

Hence we come to the first of three central motifs of the book referred to earlier: the unrecognizability of miracle. Stefan *knows* (as he tells Ileana on the night of St. John in 1936) that "all kinds of miracles could happen. . . . But someone has to teach you how to look at them so you'll know they are miracles. Otherwise you don't even see them. You pass right by them and you don't know they *are* miracles. You don't see them" (p. 7). How to look at things, the most common things of everyday life, in order to *see*—that is what Stefan sets out to learn. His is an initiatory quest. But from the point of view of the reader, even this quest is hidden, its major stages being almost indistinguishable from among the more or less "extraordinary" events of the life of a Rumanian intellectual in a period of shattering historical crises (the rise of fascism; the rebellion of the Iron Guards in 1940; the military dictatorship

of General Antonescu who, about the time of the summer solstice, in 1941, joined Hitler in the attack on the Soviet Union;
the Russian occupation and, after the war, the imposition on
the country of brutal Stalinist rule), and of natural catastrophes,
such as the 1940 earthquake that hit Bucharest, or the 1946
drought in Moldavis, as a result of which thousands died from
starvation.   Such upheavals naturally affect Stefan's life.   He
suffers cruel losses—his wife and son die in the bombing of
Bucharest in the spring of 1944, his best friend, Biris, a teacher
of philosophy, passes away under torture by the Communist
secret police in 1947, while Stefan has become a refugee in the
West.   But the hero's quest takes place on *another plane.*   What
he does and says while pursuing his initiatory quest, himself
not altogether conscious of it, *seems* to the other characters,
and at times to the reader as well, slightly ridiculous, and even
plainly *irresponsible.*   What Eliade suggests is that the search
for the sacred, in our desacralized modern world, masquerades
as absent-minded dreaminess, as comic inadequacy, as childish
behavior in an adult—a behavior which is not without a certain
charm, but whose real significance is never understood.   Stefan
himself, insofar as he is a modern man, and he cannot help but
be one, fails to understand it.

The search for eternal life—that is the second constitutive
motif of *The Forbidden Forest.*   In the opening chapter of the
novel, Stefan tells Ileana, in answering her question, "What
must I search for?"   "To escape from Time, to go out of Time.
Signs come to you from all sides.   Trust these signs.   Follow
them" (p. 25).   This emphasis on the hero's urge to escape
from historical time strikes a note that will be repeated, in different contexts and with different effects, throughout the
book.   Going beyond the "terror of history" is the same thing
as achieving a paradisiacal condition.   But Stefan does not
believe that to do this one must simply turn one's back on
history.   In fact, if history were not what it is, a nightmare,
if the tragic did not exist, paradise would lose its significance.
Modernity, with its acute awareness of history and historicity,
must be assumed before being transcended.   If in the past there
were other ways to paradise, today this is the only one: passing
through history is unavoidable.   In an important discussion with
Anisie, a "saint" of sorts, who fascinates Stefan because of his
ability to harmonize his existence with the great rhythms of

cosmic time (but at the price of completely ignoring history by leading the life of a recluse on his farm at the foot of the Carpathian Alps), Stefan clearly realizes that the hermit's solution is not the right one: "Human existence," he tells Anisie, "would seem vain to me if it were solely reduced to mythical categories. Even that ahistoric paradise would be hard for me to endure if it didn't have the hell of history accompanying it. I believe—I even hope—that an exit from time is possible even in our historical world. The Kingdom of God is realizable at any time on earth, *hic et nunc*. . ." (p. 314). This *hic et nunc*—the "here and now" of historical consciousness—is essential: the sacred *is* in the midst of the profane and nowhere else. It is this absolute *immanence* of the sacred (and hence its ambiguity if not downright indeterminacy) that one must first understand. Stefan is right—this seems to be the author's view—when he discovers that the end or *telos* of his quest is so close, so breathtakingly close to its point of departure: paradise *hic et nunc*. But paradise, one must keep in mind, is only a possibility. The hero, in his passionate initiatory pursuit, gets lost, perhaps precisely because what he was seeking was so close that he could not *see* it. It is hard to say what causes his failure.

Is it his love for Ileana—his fascination with the unattainable? Does he stray from the right way due to his cult of the impossible, embodied in Ileana, a cult that is indistinguishable from the idea of romantic love (in the sense defined in *L'amour et l'Occident,* the famous essay by Denis de Rougemont)? As the narrative unfolds, the two women in Stefan's life, Ioana and Ileana, both of whom he strives to love with a love that is more than love (another facet of his cult of impossibility), acquire a symbolic significance. Simplifying and disregarding numerous nuances that make the two women entirely *credible* as literary characters, Ioana, the wife, represents Stefan's "life instinct," while Ileana his secret penchant toward self-destruction, the temptation of Thanatos, his "death instinct." Interestingly, while working on the novel, Eliade himself was largely unaware of the symbolism of his two major female characters, Ileana in particular. Only when he came to the very last scene, which describes the meeting between Stefan and Ileana in the wood of Royaumont and the accident in which the two of them perish on the night of St. John 1948, exactly twelve years, or a Cosmic Year, after their first meeting—did the author realize that Ileana was, and had been all along, "an angel of Death."[1 2]

And so Eliade's "great fairy tale" ends unusually as far as normal fairy tales go, with the death of the hero and his beloved. In the diary entry for July 7, 1954 (the day when he finished writing the book), he notes that he had been unable to avoid this ending. "All these days I have written struggling against sadness and also against an almost physical sense of oppression. I was unable to oppose *destiny* [italics mine], which had decided long ago, and without my knowledge, the ruin of Stefan and Ileana. . . ."[1 3] Actually, the novel ends, quite befittingly, I think, for a work so rich in literary, mythological, and philosophical suggestions, by raising a series of questions. Stefan, we are told in the closing sentence, "had known that this last moment, this moment without end, would suffice." Is this the paradisiacal instant of infinite bliss he had longed for all through his initiatory quest? Or is it, on the contrary, a final and truly irreparable act of self-deception? And if so, what went wrong, and when, and why? Such questions, when they arise in the mind of the reader, are nothing but a thinly disguised temptation to reread. They suggest the "circular" structure of both the novel and the kind of time its hero is dreaming of; they suggest the very "circularity" of literary time itself.

III

It is therefore the role of the novel to tell us that all sorts of things *occur* (believable and unbelievable, expected and unexpected, important and unimportant, tragic and humorous, etc). Not only Eliade's conception of fiction, but that of imagination in general, could well be characterized by the formula of "symbolic realism." We live in a world of images—yet are not images just surfaces of symbols? Reality is deeply symbolic, but, accustomed to looking only at its surfaces, we fail even to realize that there is something lying deeper. From this point of view, "realism" in the common sense would be nothing but an instance of false consciousness.

"The most commonplace existence," Eliade writes in the introductory part of *Images and Symbols*, "swarms with images, the most 'realistic' man lives by them. . . . Symbols never disappear from the *reality* of psyche."[14] These images with multiple, indeed inexhaustible, symbolic functions cannot and should not be evoked in purely "analytical" terms. In his view, interpretation is, if properly used, entirely opposed to any kind of directly or indirectly *reductive thinking*. To interpret an image, therefore, is not to "discover" its *one* true and generalizable meaning (which is sometimes construed as a cause) but, on the contrary to explore and reveal its multiple levels of meaning, to comprehend and communicate its depth in all its symbolic wealth. Through interpretation, the latent richness of the image is brought to the surface and made accessible to consciousness. Thus, we may say, instead of diminishing the perceivable "ambiguity" of almost any image considered with some degree of (aesthetic) *attention*, the interpreter does the right thing when he succeeds in increasing that "ambiguity."

In this final part of my essay I will discuss at more length the large theoretical implications of Eliade's commitment to imagination in his consistent efforts to defend hermeneutics against its major reductionist deformation (psychoanalysis) as well as against its direct negation in structuralism, and particularly in the version of structuralism represented by Claude Lévi-Strauss.[15]

To begin with, I think that Eliade as a student of religious symbolism has always been conscious of the dangers of reducing the infinite complexity of meaning of any particular image to an analytically simple and univocal signified. If for purely linguistic purposes the hypothesis of the arbitrariness of the (verbal) sign is acceptable, the study of more complex symbols becomes almost impossible without the admission of a large— if obscure—degree of "semantic motivation" in the relationship between signifier and signified. This motivation itself, involving both conscious and unconscious elements, and being the result of a great many nonhomogeneous cultural processes, is practically impossible to unravel completely. Nevertheless, the more closely we consider the symbol in one or another of its concrete instances, the more compelling the feeling that a profound motivation is there, no matter how invisible or "unrecognizable." Interpretation should not go against this intuition but, rather, justify it and make it even more intense, for both in religion and literature, the signified per se—however complex—is always infinitely less important than the manner in which it is related to the signifier. If we agree that meaning has nothing to do with either signifier or signified taken independently, but only with the relationship between the two, we can understand the apparently paradoxical assertion that interpretation reveals and even *increases* the hidden richness of its object (let me stress that to interpret is much more than, and sometimes just the opposite of, to decipher or to "decode"). Broadly speaking, what matters in the interpretation of both religious and poetic symbols is the consciousness that meaning is not to be identified with any one of its possible projections on the "screen" of the signified. These projections (or constructions), which may complement each other, but may also be mutually exclusive (in logical terms), modify, each in its own way, our perception of the signifier. The awareness of the progressively and mutually enriching relationship between signifier and signified, the sense of *coincidentia oppositorum* (a notion frequently referred to by Eliade), the experience of what might be called "semantic energy" are some of the rewards of the interpretive effort.

Eliade's constant and consistent criticism of Freudian psychoanalysis is interesting to discuss in this context. This criticism in no way obscures the importance, indeed the essentiality, in the history of modern hermeneutics of psychoanalysis as a theory and practice of interpretation. But Freud—Eliade maintains—has not succeeded in freeing himself from some of the basic prejudices of positivism. Thus, the founder of psychoanalysis, in his effort to demonstrate that sexuality is the all-determining cause in the life of the psyche, makes the methodological error or taking sexuality as an *isolated* entity. Freud operates, as it were, with the "utopian" concept of "pure" sexuality. But sexuality is never "pure," Eliade argues. It is sufficient to think of its definitely *cosmological* function, through which the sexual act acquires the meaning of an "integral action" and becomes "also a means to knowledge." And this is only one of the many functions of sexuality.

To get at the gist of Eliade's argument against orthodox psychoanalysis (parenthetically, he is an admirer of the dissenting C. G. Jung), let us examine more closely the way he discusses the fundamental Freudian theory of the Oedipus complex.

In this discussion, as we shall see, he makes some of his clearest statements concerning the problems of interpretation and meaning.

According to Eliade, the attraction that the infant feels toward its mother should not be analyzed as such but presented as "so much imagery." "Because," he writes, "it is the image of the Mother that is really in question, and not this or that mother *hic et nunc.*" To translate such images into concrete terms, Eliade believes, is a fallacy; the same applies to the efforts of psychoanalysis to elucidate the problem of the "origins" of images. Let us consider the following passage from *Images and Symbols:*

> Philosphically, these problems of the "origin" and of the "true interpretation" of the Images are pointless. We need only remember that the attraction to the mother, if we interpret it on the plane of the immediate and "concrete"—like the desire to possess one's own mother—*can never tell us anything more than what it says;* whereas, if we take account of the fact that what is in question is the Image of the Mother, this desire means many things at once, for it is the desire to re-enter into the bliss of living matter that is still "unformed," with all its possible lines of development, cosmological, anthropological, etc. For . . . Images by their very structure are *multivalent.* If the mind makes use of images to grasp the ultimate reality of things, it is just because reality manifests itself in contradictory ways and therefore cannot be expressed in concepts. (We know what desperate efforts have been made by various theologies and metaphysics, oriental as well as occidental, to give expression to the *coincidentia oppositorum*—a mode of being that is readily, and also abundantly, conveyed by images and symbols.) It is therefore the image as such, as a whole bundle of meanings, that is *true,* and not any *one* of its meanings, nor one alone of its many frames of reference. To translate an image into a concrete terminology by restricting it to any one of its frames of reference is to do worse than mutilate it—it is to annihilate, to annul it as an instrument of cognition.[16]

This lengthy quotation leaves little doubt that Eliade is opposed to the artificial separation of image from its many frames of reference. Images are untranslatable, and precisely because their meaning is multiple they are valuable as "instruments of cognition." In orthodox psychoanalysis, images and symbols are never important in themselves: what actually matters is to pierce the deceptive appearances and discover the actual content hidden beneath.

Freud's crucial contribution has been that of extending, psychologically, the realm of the meaningful. A great many apparently meaningless phenomena, traditionally ignored by psychologists as irrelevant, were proven to have unexpected and sometimes urgent significance in *The Interpretation of Dreams, The Psychopathology of Everyday Life,* and elsewhere. I am certain that to this point Eliade would completely agree with the major assumptions and course taken by psychoanalysis. As I have indicated, what he objects to is the eventually positivistic character of the Freudian doctrine. To clarify Eliade's point, let me reiterate that for him interpretation is justified only insofar as it opposes any tendency toward reduction and is conceived as a totalizing *activity,* as an attempt to grasp the organic whole which this or that particular image or symbol is part of. The task of interpretation is, then, through its emphasis on multiplicity and complexity, to restore that sense of imaginary and imaginative totality which is lost not only in daily common experience, but also—and with spiritually more dangerous consequences—in the fragmentary world of science in which unity is usually attained through reduction. Whereas analysis divides, decomposes, separates, and isolates, interpretation links in a *religious* sense, closes the gaps, integrates. It offers the mind the possibility of contemplating infinitely complex and inexhaustibly rich worlds of meaning.

The conception of interpretation as a totalizing activity is clearly expressed in the important essay which closes *The Two and the One* [Méphistophélès et l'Androgyne]. The study of "apparently heterogeneous but structurally related" symbolisms—Eliade argues—"does not imply the reduction of all these significances to a common denominator. One cannot sufficiently insist on this point: that the examination of symbolic structures is a work not of *reduction* but of *integration.* One compares and contrasts two expressions of a symbol not in order to reduce them to a single, pre-existent expression, but in order to discover the *process by which a structure is capable of en-*

riching its meaning" (italics mine).[17]

Centered around the problem of imagination, Eliade's philosophy of symbolism is opposed not only to various reductionist doctrines (as exemplified in his critique of psychoanalysis) but also to conceptions and procedures characteristic of the structuralist approach to mythology and, more generally, to religious anthropology. Eliade is certainly aware of both the newness and the importance of some of the positions of contemporary structuralism, namely, its *theoretical courage* (so refreshing when compared with the narrow empiricism of the traditional Anglo-American school of anthropology) and its consistent criticism of European anthropological historicism. What he deems difficult to accept in structuralism, as represented by Claude Lévi-Strauss, is its neopositivistic aspect, its assumption that "la science est déjà faite dans les choses" and that "logic is already prefigured in nautre." "That is to say," Eliade writes in his essay "Cultural Fashions and History of Religions" (1966), "man can be understood without taking consciousness into consideration. *La Pensée sauvage* presents to us a thinking without thinkers and a logic without logicians. This is both a neo-positivism and a neo-nominalism, but at the same time something more. It is a reabsorption of man into nature—not, evidently, dionysiac or romantic nature, nor even the blind, passionate, erotic drive of Freud—but the nature which is grasped by nuclear physics and cybernetics, a nature reduced to its fundamental structures . . . ."[18] The main reason why Eliade disagrees with the structuralist approach seems, however, to lie elsewhere. It is useful here to recall Lévi-Strauss's conception of mythical thought as "bricolage" and his almost exclusive interest not in meaning as such (and in its existential value) but in the instruments and relations involved in the *production* of meaning. Lévi-Strauss, whose conception can be summarized in the notion of *Homo significans,* considers that the system of myths works essentially as language does—its specific function being that of "signifying the significance."[19] I think it is this extension of linguistic formalsim to the study of myth (and its inevitable consequences) that is in direct contradiction to Eliade's "theology" of meaning. Finally, I may say, structuralism operates on the basis of another kind of reduction, less easy to recognize because it is not "substantial" but, rather, "relational." Structuralism reconstitutes the mechanism of the production of meaning (using the linguistic model), but it avoids the question of *what* various myths, images, and symbols signify (beyond the mere fact that they "signify the significance") and also the related question of what *value* they may have in different cultures, times, and societies. Such questions, structuralism assumes, are scientifically irrelevant, or even antiscientific.

Another characteristic feature of structuralism is that it establishes a perfect "homology" between mythical thought and scientific thought. Given its material limitations, mythical thought is governed by exactly the same laws and processes as scientific thought (this is illustrated by Lévi-Strauss's famous comparison between "bricolage" and engineering). Here is the conclusion of his "Structural Study of Myth": "If our interpretation is correct," Lévi-Strauss writes, "we are led toward a completely different view—namely, that the kind of logic in mythical thought is as rigorous as that of the modern science, and that the difference lies, not in the quality of the intellectual process, but in the nature of things to which it is applied."[20] Such an approach not only abolishes traditional distinctions such as Lévy-Bruhls' (between the magical or "prelogical" mentality of the primitive and the "logical" one of the civilized man), but simply leaves no room for any kind of hermeneutics. Specifically, Lévi-Strauss rejects the idea that any one of the constitutive elements of a myth has a meaning by itself. Extending the Saussurean principle of the arbitrary character of linguistic signs to the domain of mythology, Lévi-Strauss states that it is the *combination* of mythical "constituent units" (mythemes), not the units themselves, which provide significance. To try to deal with images, symbols, or mythological patterns and discover their meaning is to be the victim of a serious misconception. Jung's theory of archetype is an example of that erroneous approach. "Let us consider, for instance, Jung's idea that a given mythological pattern—the so-called archetype—possesses a certain meaning. This is comparable to the long-supported error that a sound may possess a certain affinity with meaning. . . ."[21] Obviously, "sacred" and "profane" are concepts completely out of place in such a system.

If we were to look at the personalities of Eliade and Lévi-Strauss from a certian distance, it would be tempting to distinguish two opposing types of world views. Eliade strikes me as a thinker for whom diversity is so precious in itself that any attempt to reduce it—for either theoretical or practical purposes, or both—becomes illegitimate. His conception of integration implies an aesthetic consciousness of multiplicity. Eliade's interest in, and treatment of, primitive religion is characteristic in this respect. Unlike most modern religious anthropologists, he does not use myth to demonstrate one thesis or another; what he tries to do is to get at the lost or "unrecognizable" meaning of myth as a manifestation of the sacred. The thinker engages in an arduous quest whose ultimate purpose is imaginative *recognition* and *restitution.* This implies, wittingly or not, a trust in a variety of ways (both rational and intuitive) through which enriching knowledge is accessible. It is indeed remarkable how frequently Eliade employs phrases like "instrument of cognition" or "means to knowledge." I do not think that Eliade is, as some have said, a kind of neoromantic irrationalist. He has never denied the validity of scientific cognition, a cognition which depends on imagination as much as any other, although he is definitely an adversary of the "scientific myth," of the perfectly irrational belief that "science" can solve every problem and that the "scientific" mind has a legitimate monopoly in all matters of knowledge.[22] Eliade seems to suggest that the modern scientific "myth" is responsible precisely for the fact that a variety of other "means of knowledge" have become "unrecognizable" to man. Here Eliade is consistent with his deep-rooted conviction that reality is irreducibly manysided. His intolerance starts to manifest itself only when he is faced with the intolerance of one-sided intellectual dogmas.

Eliade's thought is pervaded with admiration for the diversity of processes in nature and the mind, and more—with a sense of emulation of all forms of creativeness in the world, a sense which can account for a particular kind of intellectual expansiveness. This latter quality is sufficient to single him out from among his colleagues in the highly specialized field of religious anthropology. Eliade's cult of vitality and energy, his unabated belief in what E. M. Cioran calls, in a remarkably penetrating portrait of Eliade,[23] "fertility for its own sake," is a disconcerting quality in the world of scholarship, in today's largely pessimistic, if not apocalyptic, cultural atmosphere.

Lévi-Strauss's philosophy is not without a certain element of metaphysical bitterness. Paradoxically, the inventor of *Homo significans* discovers at the same time what I would call the "misery" of meaning. In an unexpected acceptance of Buddha's pessimistic message, Lévi-Strauss realizes the "destructive" character of all knowledge and the fact that the knowing mind is faced eventually, and inescapably, with meaninglessness. This movement is parallel to that of the world itself as it approaches its final state of inertia, or entropy. Toward the end of *Tristes tropiques,* Lévi-Strauss writes:

> For what, after all, have I learnt from the masters I have listened to, the philosophers I have read, the societies I have investigated, and that very Science in which the West takes such a pride? Simply a fragmentary lesson or two which, if laid end to end, would reconstitute the mediations of the Sage at the foot of his tree. When we make an effort to understand, we destroy the object of our attachment, substituting another whose nature is quite different. That other object requires of us another effort, which in its turn destroys the second object and substitutes a third—and so on until we reach the only enduring Presence, which is that in which all distinction between meaning and the absence of meaning disappears: and it is from that Presence that we started in the first place.[24]

The readiness to accept the conclusions of the stern philosophy of Buddhism (as opposed to the philosophy implicit in traditional Hinduism, to which Eliade is so close) can explain Lévi-Strauss's very acute consciousness of contradiction, not only at the intellectual but at the social level as well—whence his inclination toward radicalism. "Between Marxist criticism which sets Man free from his first chains, and Buddhist criticism, which completes that liberation, there is neither opposition nor contradiction. (The Marxist teaches that the apparent significance of Man's condition will vanish the moment he agrees to enlarge the object that he has under consideration.) Marxism and Buddhism are doing the same thing, but at different levels."[25] In light of such considerations, it is not surprising that structuralism has been one of the sources of recent philosophies of the "death of Man" (and the theoretical antihumanism of Marx himself, as put into relief by Louis Althusser—a thinker not unaffected by structuralism—may be another illustration). Such tendencies are not unrelated to the "dehumanization" of thought, achieved through Lévi-Strauss's conviction that "la science est déjà faite dans les choses." In regard to orientations of this type, Eliade may appear as a substantially more traditional thinker, which is a matter of remarkable intellectual courage in today's world tyrannized by fashion. Anyway, there is a clear-cut opposition between structuralism's basic antivitalism and antihumanism (and subsequent technologism) and the unambiguous vitalism under-lying Eliade's philosophy—which may explain, among other things, his passion for continuity, growth, process, and, finally, his conception of "sacred time," viewed as "eternal return."

It has been repeatedly observed that structuralism, which appeared as a reaction against positivist historicism, is essen-tially an ahistorical method: structures are obviously synchronic constructs, and, theoretically, structuralism is incapable of accounting for change. (Practically, the structuralist is incessant-ly confronted with problems of change, transition, evolution, or involution, with which he deals, when he cannot avoid them, according to his particular philosophy of history; but this philo-sophy of history is ultimately a matter of personal choice. There is nothing in the structural method to indicate a preferential direction or to limit this freedom of choice.) In this context, both Lévi-Strauss and Eliade are quite explicably opposed to nineteenth-century historicism. That is perhaps why Eliade has been sometimes regarded as a kind of structuralist *sui generis;* Cox, for instance, uses the strange and confusing label "neo-Hin-du-structuralist" to characterize his thought.[26] It is true that Eliade conceives the history of religions as a science of religious "patterns," but these result from a dialectic of the sacred and the profane (the basic contradiction being that between sacred, reversible, and substantially *continuous time* and historical, linear, irreversible, and *discontinuous time*). But the problem of time consciousness—central to Eliade's philosophy—does not play any significant role in Lévi-Strauss's thought, which is dominated by *spatial* (static) categories.

This essay does not attempt to be even a fragmentary ac-count of Eliade's achievement as a thinker, student of religion, or writer. As I indicate at the outset, my purpose is to bring to light his multifaceted personality in regard to his aesthetic-imaginative experience and activity, which I consider of essential importance throughout his work. The description of his major theoretical options, the analysis of his views on symbolism and meaning (what I have called his "theology" of meaning), the examination of his attitudes toward some crucial issues and intellectual trends of our time (his constant rejection of reductionist methods, his defense of creativeness and diversity against the encroachment of pseudomythical scientism), contain sufficient elements to justify the assertion that Eliade's Weltanschauung is largely an aesthetic one. His understanding of religion is especially significant in this respect. I am not referring now to his contribution to scholarship (which is amazingly vast and solid), or to the originality of his philosophy of religion as compared with that of other contemporaries. What I wish to do is to discuss Eliade's own "existential" response to religion. Some of those who have written about his religious studies have noticed his open-mindedness, his deep tolerance, his disinterest in problems of religious conflict and in the *dark side of religion* (fantacism, destructiveness, mythical forms of self-violence, obsession with sin and damnation). This line of thought is suggested, for instance, by E. M. Cioran in "Beginnings of a Friendship": "Everything *negative*, everything that promotes self-destruction on the physical as well as spiritual plane, was then, and still is foreign to him—whence his inaptitude for resignation, for remorse, for despair, for all feelings that imply the bogged-down, the rut, the nonfuture. Again, I may be going out on a limb, but I believe that if he has perfect understanding of sin, he lacks a sense of it; he is too feverish for that, too dynamic, too hurried, too full of projects, too intoxicated with the possible."[27] If this is so, we can say that Eliade offers us a broadly aesthetic, possibilistic and imaginative, vision of religion. Is it necessary to guard against the rather widespread misconception of using the epithet "aesthetic" to denote—or connote—gratuitous, disinvolved contemplation? I hope this essay leaves little room for such a possibility. A genuinely aesthetic attitude has an *existential* dimension, which is evident in all of Eliade's major themes of reflection. To conclude, I am tempted to characterize Eliade's implicit metaphysics as an *aesthetic ontology* based on the idea of creativeness, in which *imagination* appears both as a means to knowledge and as a mode of being. It is only through imagination that one can reach that consciousness of universal creativeness which constitutes the dynamic and inexhaustible *meaning of life.*

NOTES

[1]This essay is a revised version of the article with the same title, published in *The Journal of Religion,* 57, 1 (January 1977), 1-15, and of the review article of Eliade's *The Forbidden Forest,* "Between History and Paradise: Initiation Trials," published in *The Journal of Religion,* 59, 2 (April 1979), 218-223. I have dealt more specifically with the *literary* aspects of Eliade's work in "Mircea Eliade's Journals," *The Denver Quarterly,* 12 (Spring 1977), 313-316; "The Disguises of Miracle: Notes on Mircea Eliade's Fiction," *World Literature Today,* Autumn 1978, 558-564; and "The 'Function of the Unreal': Reflections on Mircea Eliade's Short Fiction," in Norman J. Girardot and Mac Linscott Ricketts, eds., *Imagination & Meaning: The Scholarly and Literary Worlds of Mircea Eliade* (New York: The Seabury Press, 1982), 138-161.

[2]Harvey Cox, review of Mircea Eliade, *Gods, Goddesses and Myths of Creation. . . .: A Thematic Source Book of the History of Religions* (New York: Harper & Row, 1974), in the *New York Times Book Review,* August 11, 1974.

[3]The fact is that even now, after the publication in English translation of Eliade's major novel, *The Forbidden Forest* tr. by Mac Linscott Ricketts and Mary Park Stevenson (the University of Notre Dame Press, 1978), only a fraction of this prolific author's fiction is available to the English reader. Of his older short stories and novellas only two, "Nights at Serampore" and "The Secret of Dr. Honigsberger," originally published in Rumanian in the 1940's, have appeared in book form as *Two Tales of the Occult,* tr. by William Ames Coates (Herder & Herder, 1970). A more recent novella, *The Old Man and the Bureaucrats,* tr. by Mary Park Stevenson (original title: *Pe strada Mântuleasa,* 1968), certainly one of Eliade's most brilliant achievments in short fiction, was translated in 1979 (the University of Notre Dame Press). As for Eliade's journal, which contains a great many enlightening reflections on the recurring themes of both his research and imaginative work, his American publisher decided rather arbitrarily to leave out the first half of the French edition of *Fragments*

d'un journal (1973), which covers the period 1945-1957, retaining only the second part that deals with the author's experiences after his moving from Europe to this country in 1957. Cf. *Fragments d'un journal*, traduit du roumain par Luc Badesco (Paris: Gallimard, 1973) and *No Souvenirs: Journal 1957-1969*, tr. by Fred H. Johnson, Jr. (New York: Harper & Row, 1977).

[4] *Two Tales of the Occult*, "Introduction," pp. xii,xiii.

[5] *Soliloquii* (Bucharest: Colectia "Cartea cu semne," 1932), p. 61.

[6] *Oceanografie* (Bucharest: Editura "Cartea Poporului," 1934), p. 97.

[7] "Fragment autobiografic," published in the Rumanian émigré magazine *Caete de Dor*, No. 7 (July 1953).

[8] *No Souvenirs*, p. 205.

[9] *Ibid.*, p. 268 (entry of October 1, 1965). Eliade writes: "When something sacred manifests itself (hierophany), at the same time something 'occults' itself, becomes cryptic. Therein is the true dialectic of the sacred: by the mere fact of *showing* itself, the sacred *hides itself*"

[10] *Myth and Reality*, tr. by Willard R. Trask (New York: Harper & Row, 1963), pp. 5-6.

[11] *No Souvenirs*, p. 205.

[12] *Fragments d'un journal*, pp. 219-220.

[13] *Ibid.*, p. 221.

[14] *Images and Symbols*, tr. by Philip Mairet (London: Harvill Press, 1961), p. 16.

[15] For a more specific discussion of the conflict between hermeneutics and structuralism in literary criticism and aesthetics, see my article "Hermeneutics or Poetics," *The Journal of Religion*, 59, 1 (January 1979), 1-17.

[16] *Images and Symbols*, p. 15.

[17] *The Two and the One*, tr. by J. M. Cohen (New York: Harper &

Row, 1965), p. 201.

[18]"Cultural Fashions and the History of Religions," *Monday Evening Papers*, No. 8 (Middleton, Conn.: Center for Advanced Studies, Wesleyan Univ., 1967), p. 17.

[19]Claude Lévi-Strauss, *Le Cru et le cuit* (Paris: Plon, 1964), p. 346.

[20]Claude Lévi-Strauss, *Structural Anthropology*, tr. by C. Jacobson and B. G. Schoepf (New York: Basic Books, 1963), p. 230.

[21]*Ibid.*, p. 208.

[22]That is why Eliade endorses with enthusiasm the view of numerous modern scientists summarized in the following general statement by Jacob Bronowski, quoted in the Preface to *No Souvenirs:* "The step by which a new axiom is adduced cannot itself be mechanized. It is a free play of the mind, an invention outside the logical processes. This is the cultural act of imagination in science and it is in all respects like any similar act in literature." Commenting on this passage, Eliade speaks specifically of the "structural analogy between the scientific and the literary imagination" (pp. IX-X).

[23]E. M. Cioran, "Beginnings of a Friendship," in *Myths and Symbols: Studies in Honor of Mircea Eliade*, ed. by Joseph M. Kitagawa and Charles H. Long (Chicago: University of Chicago Press, 1969), p. 408.

[24]Claude Lévi-Strauss, *A World on the Wane* [Tristes Tropiques], tr. by John Russell (London: Hutchinson, 1961), p. 394.

[25]*Ibid.*, p. 395.

[26]See Note no. 2.

[27]Cioran, *loc. cit.*, p. 413.

THE SEMIOTICS OF CULTURE AND THE INTERPRETATION OF LITERATURE: CLIFFORD GEERTZ AND THE MORAL IMAGINATION

by
Giles Gunn

In an essay in progress at the time of his death, Lionel Trilling initiated an unusually fruitful dialogue with the social and cultural anthropologist Clifford Geertz.[1] The ostensible reason for Trilling's interest in Geertz's work was the way it confirmed certain suspicions Trilling had come to entertain about the traditional assumptions of humanistic scholarship as a result of a course he had recently taught on Jane Austen. However, the substance of his own unfinished meditation, together with Geertz's subsequent response,[2] possess a critical importance that far transcends the particular circumstances of their origin. By setting the discussion of literary as well as anthropological interpretation in the wider context of intra- and cross-cultural understanding, their dialogue sheds significant light on what a semiotic theory of culture like Geertz's has to do with a moral theory of criticism like Trilling's, and also suggests along the way what cultural semiotics, if I may use so modern a term to describe Geertz's method, has to learn from literary hermeneutics, to employ a description awkwardly recherché for Trilling's. More than this, their dialogue provides a welcome relief from the mystifications of so much recent critical theory, mystifications that have almost succeeded in removing critical discussion from the plane of cultural discourse altogether.

I

In his typically canny way, Trilling had been both disturbed as well as challenged by the experience of teaching the major novels of Jane Austen to an audience so culturally distant from her own because it raised certain troubling questions about the conventional assumptions of humanistic pedagogy and research. Central among those assumptions, as Trilling pointed out, is the notion that the products of other minds, the expressions of other selves, possess a crucial relevance to the nature of our own moral existence, and that they can be placed in the service of our own moral lives precisely because, no matter how distant in time or how different in temperament, they are more or less fully accessible to us. This purported accessibility is possible, so the conventional argument goes, because the humanist has traditionally been convinced that beneath all the surface differences and apparent variations between one mind and another, one mode of being and its neighbor, there exists both within cultures and across them an unbroken continuity. And from this derives the humanist's whole theory of the past "as a source of remedial wisdom, a prosthetic corrective for a damaged spiritual life" ("FIT," p. 799). As Trilling put it,

> Humanism does not in the least question the good effect of reading about the conduct of other people of one's own time, but it does put a special value upon ranging backward in time to find in a past culture the paradigms by which our own moral lives are put to the test. In its predilection for the moral instructiveness of past cultures, humanism is resolute in the belief that there is very little in this transaction that is problematic; it is confident that the paradigms will be properly derived and that the judgments made on the basis they offer will be valid. Humanism takes for granted that any culture of the past out of which has come a work of art that commands our interest must be the product, and also, of course, the shaping condition, of minds which are essentially the same as our own.[3]

Yet is was just this comforting reassurance about the essential continuities between minds other than our own that had been put in question by Trilling's recent experiences in the classroom. If any such continuities exist—and no study of other selves, much less other cultures, could proceed without assuming that they do—Trilling's problems in placing Jane Austen's world before a group of students so culturally ill-equipped to grasp its general outlines, much less its deeper nuances, still convinced him that there are real discontinuities as well. And it was in the interest of understanding the nature of, and the reasons for, these discontinuities and disjunctions that he was initially drawn to the work of Clifford Geertz.

The essay he focused on is one in which Geertz disputes the view widely shared by humanists and social scientists alike that our knowledge of other peoples depends in large part on our capacity to empathize, to imagine our way into the subjective life of someone else. On the contrary, Geertz argues, our ability to empathize has very little to do with it, because the anthropologist is not engaged in learning how to think and feel as others do but how to define and assess what, so to speak, they are up to. The task is not to put oneself in their place but to learn how to comprehend the symbolic forms in which they represent themselves to each other. And this is accomplished, Geertz goes on, in the same way one undertakes any other act of understanding: by submitting oneself to what has been acknowledged since the time of St. Augustine and referred to since the time of Wilhelm Dilthey as "the hermeneutic circle."

The "hermeneutic circle" is but a complicated way of referring to a comparatively simple process. We cannot understand the parts of anything without some sense of the whole to which they belong, just as we cannot comprehend the whole to which they belong until we have grasped the parts which make it up. Thus we are constantly obliged to move back and forth in our effort to understand something "between the whole conceived through the parts which actualize it and the parts conceived through the whole which motivates them" in an effort "to turn them, by a sort of intellectual perpetual motion, into explications of one another."[4] Hence the understanding of other peoples, as of other minds, normally proceeds by way of a kind of dialectic in which knowledge increases as we alternatively press two kinds of questions, the first having to do with the nature of the general form of their life, the second having to do with the specific vehicles in which that form is embodied. From this perspective, the goal of the anthropologist, Geertz reasons, cannot be to achieve communion or identity with those lives but only to enter into a kind of conversation with them. While we cannot assume their mode of being or take on their form of existence, we can at least establish a relationship with them by attempting, from our own vantage point, to comprehend what they are about.

It was just here, however, that Trilling began to express reservations concering Geertz's formulations. While he could respect Geertz's realism about the staggering problems involved in any act of cultural interpretation and found this realism a salutary antidote to humanism's customarily facile indifferences to such problems, he was still perplexed and alarmed by Geertz's apparent refusal to concede that the imagination plays any determinative role in this hermeneutical transaction. Since Trilling's reflections break off when he became too ill to proceed, it is difficult to be certain of all Trilling intended to say in response to Geertz's view of the way we gain knowledge of other minds, of different sensibilities, but the gist of his argument seems to be as follows: Even if we can never succeed in imagining ourselves so completely into the innerness of lives other than our own so that we can take on their modes of thought and feeling, put ourselves in their place, nevertheless we can learn how to think more and more like them, to think more intelligently and concretely and sympathetically about them, as we learn, to borrow an expression from Archibald MacLeish, how to put our thought in the place where our imagination goes. And the proof that we can do this is provided by our own experience of being able to think *against* ourselves, of being able to overcome, or at least to resist, the movement of our own sensibilities by responding imaginatively to alternative modes of being which threaten to disrupt or destroy them.

The example that offered itself to Trilling was the one Geertz himself had employed in his essay on "From the Native's Point of View," namely, Keats's "Ode on a Grecian Urn." But where Geertz has read the poem as constituting an assertion of the priority of the aesthetic over the historical, Trilling read it instead as an effort to assimilate, without subordinating, the historical to the aesthetic by seeing pastness as an essential attribute of beauty. In such terms as these, Trilling in fact believed that Keats's poem spoke directly to the question currently in dispute between Geertz and himself. For if the aesthetic incorporates the historical within it and thus refers to something which is finished, completed, and, to that degree, static and even death-like, then by effecting a transmutation of what is living and changing into a state of fixity and inertness, the poem actually invites us to repudiate the essence of the Western ideal of personality, of self-realization, by conceiving the goal of life as something dependent not upon the exercise of the will but on the negation of it. Such a reading did not mean to Trilling that Keats had succeeded in undermining certain of the most cherished spiritual aspirations of Western culture; it signaled only that he had been responsive to, and in turn been able to make his readers aware of, the paradoxical character of that ideal itself. And, by the use of this example, Trilling therefore seemed to be winding his way back to his initial reservations about Geertz's skepticism concerning the role of the imagination and to be preparing to ask if the very dialectic of our own imaginative life in culture isn't itself the surest, if not the only, guarantee that we can obtain a knowledge of what we ourselves are not, namely, of other minds, even of alien cultures.

II

In his otherwise sensitive and probing response to Trilling's essay, Geertz never quite succeeds in facing the issue Trilling seems to have been raising. Yet he does manage, and that very effectively, to clarify the nature of their common enterprise. Referring to that common enterprise in his subtitle as "the social history of the moral imagination," Geertz defines it most succinctly as the question of how other peoples' imaginations enter into and color our own. Like Trilling before him, Geertz finds this an immensely difficult question to answer for at least two reasons: first, because of the suspicions aroused by historical relativists that there may be no connections at all between the lives of others and the way we live now; and, second, because of the awareness urged upon us by cultural historicists of the interfering glosses between. But if Geertz rejects the relativist argument on the grounds that we can certainly know as much about the minds of others as we can know about anything else not our own, he finds equally reasonable grounds for dismissing the historicist argument on the assumption that if we can never go around those glosses or see behind them, we can still look through them.

For Geertz this means that there is a deep and undeniable "equivocality" about the things studied by the literary critic and the anthropologist. Each is continually confronted with objects that "speak with equal power to the consoling piety that we are all like one another and to the worrying suspicion that we are not" ("FIT," p. 796). This is a paradox that cannot be evaded or dismissed but only confronted and accepted. However, to confront this paradox is to realize that everything that comes to us from the past, everything that crosses to us from other minds, reaches us in the form of translation, as something that has been filtered through, perhaps, countless intervening readings. And to accept this paradox is to resist the temptation to remove these filters and instead try to learn how to see by them, to discover what modes of insight they afford as well as deny, enhance as well as obscure. If we are all "lost in translation," as James Merrill suggests in the poem that Geertz takes as the point of departure for his remarks, then the way out is not through some form of intellectual escapism where, as for the deconstructionists, for example, all translations are deprived of any validity but that which attests to their own willful subjectivism, but through submission to what Conrad's Stein would have called "the destructive element," that hermeneutical tangle of interpretations that constitutes the filtered character of virtually everything we encounter in culture, where, to continue the Conradian analogy, you learn how to "make the deep, deep sea keep you up" by "getting straight," as Geertz puts it, "how the massive fact of cultural and historical particularlity comports with the equally massive fact of cross-cultural and cross-historical accessibility—how the deeply different can be deeply known without becoming any less different; the enormously distant enormously close without becoming any less far away" ("FIT," pp. 803-804).

Without blinking the extent of the problem, Geertz holds that the only possibility of coming to grips with it, much less of resolving it in individual instances, lies in the exercise of what he refers to as "the moral imagination," and in the broadest sense his whole theory of culture is an attempt to define the scope of this imagination and explain its task. Geertz's theory of the symbolic forms which constitute culture is in effect an attempt to lay the basis for a moral analysis of culture itself; and what unites the cultural analysis of symbolic forms—in our case predominantly aesthetic forms—with the moral analysis of culture is the interpretive character of both. But to understand how interpretation operates culturally, it is necessary to see how culture for Geertz is an interpretive system, or a series of such systems; and this leads one back from the question of what other peoples' imaginations have to do with our own to the question of what characteristic forms the imagination uses to express itself, and of how those forms relate to the others that comprise culture and to the particular function all cultural forms serve in human experience.

III

As Geertz would be the first to concede, neither his ideas about art and its relation to culture, nor his views of the semiotic nature of culture itself, are in any way particularly novel. Their theoretical importance lies elsewhere: in the way he has combined them into a coherent system that attempts to "cross the border" and "close the gap," as Leslie Fiedler once put it, not only between high culture and low but also between individual expressions of mind, collective forms of experience, and the immense thicket of social and historical fact that surrounds them. By doing so, Geertz has mounted what may well become one of the more significant modern alternatives to all theories of art and culture that attempt to isolate them from the practical contexts that give them life—either as the old New Critics did, through their definition of the self-interpreting text, or, to employ Geoffrey Hartman's phrase, as the "new New Critics" do, through their notion of the self-deconstructing text. On Geertz's reading, such "pure" theories are almost inevitably misleading because they typically obscure the very problem they were designed to overcome—for the old New Critics, the problem of how the totally distinctive can be known at all if it is so unique; for the "new New Critics," the problem of how the essentially indeterminate can be deconstructed when it is unstable and self-cancelling to begin with.

Geertz's theory of culture, and of the imaginative forms in which it has its being, so to speak, is therefore partially conceived as a response to certain widespread misconceptions. Against those, for example, who, like many modern formalists, tend to view culture as a more or less self-contained and historically transcendent reality with purposes and procedures intrinsic to itself; or, again, in reaction to those who, like certain historical positivists as well as behavioral psychologists, typically associate culture only with those most explicit patterns of behavior that are observable in any identifiable community; or yet, again, in response to those who, like many contemporary Marxists as well as ethno-scientists, come close to reducing the notion of culture to the ideas and assumptions one must share in order to operate in a manner deemed acceptable by the dominant social group or class—over against all these various misconceptions, Geertz conceives of culture as an imaginative world (or worlds) in which acts are constantly being translated into signs so that human beings can attach a meaning to things which the things themselves do not intrinsically possess. The purpose of such translation, especially as individual signs become absorbed into the interrelated system of significant signs or symbols we call culture, is to provide a context in which the raw materials of experience—events, objects, acts, persons, other signs—can be interpreted. Thus the concept of culture Geertz wishes to advance is a semiotic one. "Believing, with Max Weber, that man is an animal suspended in webs of significance he himself has spun, I take culture to be those webs, and the analysis of it to be therefore not an experimental science in search of law but an interpretive one in search of meaning."[5]

But the interlinked system of significant signs and symbols Geertz calls culture—sign and symbol being roughly interchangable words to refer to "any object, act, event, quality, or relation which serves as a vehicle for a conception" (*IC*, p. 91)—does more than help make sense out of what would otherwise remain opaque and threatening. Taken as a whole, it also furnishes a set of patterns, blueprints, programs (Geertz also calls them "templates") by which many social and psychological processes can be organized in advance. Thus cultural symbol systems do a kind of double duty both to interpret the "already" and to anticipate the "not yet."

The necessity for such strange behavior, Geertz maintains, derives from the fact that human beings are unequipped genetically to deal with the environment in any other fashion. Unlike other animals who possess sufficient internal sources of information to make their actions and reactions effective in response to the outer world, our own internal sources of information, our own genetic endowment, is in some ways deficient and must therefore be supplemented by what we can receive or acquire externally. And this is precisely what cultural symbol systems provide us, in the form of models or templates that help familiarize the strange and regulate behavior in relation to it. Often overlooked, however, is the fact that the information these templates provide is not only mental or conceptual but also affective and emotional. As human beings, we not only need to acquire various kinds of information; we also need to determine how the information feels to us and how we feel about it before we can successfully negotiate our relations with the environment. And this is the service rendered by those particular cultural symbol systems we typically think of as aesthetic—myth, ritual, art. By providing us with public images of sentiment and sensibility, they help us to know what we feel and to feel what we know.

Geertz is here drawing upon what he terms the "control mechanism view of culture," since it associates culture with the set of mechanisms that govern behavior rather than with the concrete patterns of behavior that result from such governance. And there are several important corollaries to this. The first is that thinking is essentially a public rather than a private affair and therefore one that has less to do with events that occur inside the head than with events that result from man's interaction with what George Herbert Mead once called "significant symbols," referring to "anything, in fact, that is disengaged from its mere actuality and used to impose meaning upon experience" (*IC*, p. 45). Such symbols are for the most part inherited rather than created and thus constitute the commercial tender by which individuals as well as groups transact their business with the world. The second is that, without the intervention of such symbols and symbol systems, human beings would be completely at the mercy of events and their behavior therefore utterly chaotic. Cultural symbol systems give their actions specificity and purposefulness and thus are one of the essential components of human existence rather than a mere adornment. The third is that, according to this view, man is to be defined exclusively neither in terms of his capacities alone, nor in terms of his actions, "but by the link between them, by the way the first is transformed into the second, his generic potentialities focused into his specific performances" (*IC*, p. 52). As Geertz puts it elsewhere, in addition to being "the tool-making, laughing, or lying animal, man is also the incomplete—or, more accurately, self-completing animal" who must create "out of his general capacity for the construction of symbolic models the specific capabilities that define him" (*IC*, p. 218). Hence the clue to man's nature is not to be found in the commonalities of human behavior as they are exhibited throughout history and across cultures but in the processes and procedures whereby the scope of his inherent capacities are transformed into the concrete form of his actual accomplishments. Man's nature is to be inferred from his career "in its characteristic course" and not visa versa, Geertz likes to assert, "and though culture is but one element in determining that course, it is hardly the least important" (*IC*, p. 52).

The most dramatic support for this control mechanism view of culture comes from recent advances in the field of physical anthropology, and particularly from new discoveries which have been made about the nature of human origins. Three of the most significant advances have to do, first, with the abandonment of a sequential view of the relations between physical evolution and the emergence of culture in favor of an interactive or overlap view; second, with the discovery that the most important biological changes associated with man's evolution from his most immediate progenitors seem to have occurred in the central nervous system, and particularly in the brain; and, third, with the growing realization that what differentiates man from the other animals is not so much the sheer scope of his capacity to learn as the scope and character of what he *must learn* in order to get on in life at all.

What all these advances suggest is the close correlation both between the evolution of man and the emergence of culture and between the emergence of culture and the development of the human mind. Indeed, Geertz sees the growth of human mentality as not only instrumental to the creation of human culture but in significant part the result of it. The relationship between culture and mind is therefore more than complementary; it is integral. Thinking is but the ability to translate experiences into symbols in order to make sense of them. Culture is but the accumulated system of significant symbols by which this process of sense-making is accomplished and furthered.

This distinctively functional but anti-behaviorist view of

mind and culture can be traced back through Talcott Parsons and Max Weber all the way to Giovanni Battista Vico, but it is also compatible with the phenomenological perspective of such thinkers as Maurice Merleau-Ponty and Michael Polanyi and owes an even larger debt to the later philosophy of John Dewey. Geertz is drawn particularly to Dewey's redefinition of mind as neither an object nor a thing but an organized set of dispositions, capacities, propensities, abilities. But Geertz is equally attracted to Dewey's emphasis upon the essentially directed or pragmatic character of thinking. Mental activity begins in puzzlement and terminates in its resolution. Thought results from what sociologists sometimes refer to as information deficit; it ceases when the deficit is, so to speak, overcome. Or, to use another paradigm which Geertz borrows from Galanter and Gerstenhaber and which converges more directly with a theory of culture that places so much emphasis upon images and symbols, thinking can be conceived as "neither more nor less than constructing an image of the environment, running the model faster than the environment, and [then] predicting that the environment will behave as the model does. . . ." (quoted, *IC*, p. 77). In both cases, thought is related to the solution of a problem, and the discovery of the solution depends upon the mind's ability to exploit certain resources with which it is not genetically endowed to provide the information that is lacking.

For this reason Geertz is inclined to define all the forms of mental acitvity that can be differentiated culturally, from the scientific to the ideological and from the common-sensical to the religious, as "symbolic strategies for encompassing situations." This phrase is, of course, Kenneth Burke's who uses it in his dramatistic theory of art and criticism to describe all forms of symbolic expressive activity, discursive as well as imaginative, physical as well as mental. What differentiates the various kinds of symbolic expression from one another is, according to Burke, the distinctive way they "size up" the specific situations they are designed to encompass: by naming their structure and essential components, and by naming them so as to convey a particular attitude toward them. The advantage this definition of symbolic expression possesses over a good many others is that, in addition to stressing the puposeful intentions and implications of such actions, it leads away from personal and historical subjectivism toward what might be considered a kind of cultural empiricism. And it does so, Burke insists, because "the situations are real; the strategies for handling them have public content; [and] in so far as situations overlap from one individual to another, or from one historical period to another, the strategies possess universal significance" (quoted, *IC*, p. 230).

Thus Geertz can define ideology, for example, as a response to the loss of social and political orientation. The resultant confusion about what to make of the civic world of rights and responsibilities in the absence of suitable models for comprehending it sets off the frantic search for alternative models which will provide fresh images through which the opportunities and conditions of the civic realm can be sensibly grasped. As cultural systems designed to provide new maps to a world become strange and new sets of directions by which to find one's way, ideologies should be thought of as highly figurative solutions to very concrete problems. But in this they are no different from other cultural symbol systems like science or religion. What separates the one from the other is the particular procedure they individually employ to define the structure of situations, and the specific manner in which this process of defining or "naming," as Burke calls it, determines the range of attitudes that can be taken in response to those situations. Thus science defines the structure of situations in such a way as to promote an attitude of disinterestedness toward them, whereas ideology, on the other hand, defines them in a manner which elicits an attitude of commitment.

By virture of the oft-repeated claims made in behalf of their cultural uniqueness, aesthetic forms might seem to represent the one exception to this rule. Ever since the appearance of texts like I. A. Richards' *Practical Criticism* and T. S. Eliot's *The Sacred Wood,* it has been modish to suppose that if aesthetic forms are not uniformly self-referential and, as Paul Valéry believed, autotelic, they are in any case far more responsive to the complications of their own nature than they are to forces associated with the social and historical world surrounding them. As we shall see, however, Geertz is prepared to dispute this; indeed, it is aesthetic forms in general, and art forms in particular, that represent for him the essential paradigms of a theory that conceives of culture as an interwoven system of functional, which is to say meaningful, symbolic forms.

IV

Geertz's aesthetics rests on the premise that art forms typically deal with dimensions of experience that are normally well hidden from view. These forms organize those dimensions into an encompassing structure that throws into relief some specific understanding of their essential nature. The purpose, or at least the effect, of such strategies of representation is not so much to depict the way things literally *are* in experience as to portray how, from certain perspective, they *might* be. Thus the range of attitudes that can be indicated or provoked through such procedures is delimited by the nature of the imaginative situations they define. Dealing with what *could be* or, under certain circumstances, just *may* be the case, rather than with what necessarily and under all circumstances almost certainly *is* the case, they are intended to give expression to certain suppressed, or at least partially obscured, facets of human subjectivity and not to provide evidence for a specific argument or to validate a general view of life. As Northrop Frye suggests, we go to *Macbeth* not "to learn about the history of Scotland" but "to learn what a man feels like after he's gained a kingdom and lost his soul" (quoted *IC,* p. 450). By bringing selected experiences or dimensions of experience to a focus, art forms give us what Aristotle designated as the typical or recurrent or universal human event, or what Geertz prefers to describe as the "paradigmatic human event—that is, one that tells us less what happens than the kind of thing that would happen if, as is not the case, life were art and could be as freely shaped by styles of feeling [and states of mind] as *Macbeth* and *David Copperfield* are" (*IC,* p. 450).

It is no coincidence that these comments about art are to be found in Geertz's widely quoted essay on the Balinese cockfight, an essay which, until the publication of "Art as Cultural System," remained his most sustained discussion of aesthetics. Geertz's notion of art in fact extends to cultural forms built out of any materials, including social ones. The key to their peculiar nature lies in the effects of the imagination which produces them, for it is the imagination, Geertz believes, which permits artists to render the ordinary experiences of everyday life in terms of acts and objects dissociated from their practical consequences so that we can perceive their potential as opposed to their actual meaning. As Geertz puts it elsewhere, "if there is any commonality among all the arts in all the places one finds them . . . that justifies including them under a single, Western-made rubric, it is not that they appeal to some universal sense of beauty" but that "certain activities everywhere seem specifically designed to demonstrate that ideas are visible, audible, and —one needs to make up a word here—tactible, that they can be cast in forms where the senses, and through the senses the emotions, can reflectively address them"[6] Thus Geertz views the Balinese cockfight as he would any other aesthetic form: as an effort to place a construction on certain themes drawn from everyday life, to "make them, to those historically positioned to appreciate the construction, meaningful—visible, tangible, graspable—'real,' in an ideational sense" (*IC,* pp. 443-44). What thereby sets the cockfight apart from any other events with which it might be compared is not that it performs certain social functions, such as the reinforcement of status discriminations, but that it serves a hermeneutic function, by disclosing certain partially concealed dimensions of Balinese experience. "An image, fiction, model, metaphor, the cockfight is a means of expression; its function is neither to assuage social passions or to heighten them . . ., but, in a medium of feathers, blood, crowds, and money, to display them" (*IC,* p. 444).

Inherent in this way of putting the relations of art to experience is the danger, as Geertz realizes, of placing too much emphasis on the mimetic and expressive character of art and too little on the generative and creative. For if art forms refract and express certain meanings, they also help shape and sustain them. Art not only imitates life but equally influences it, and it does so by providing, often for the first time, a significant form for those very aspects of subjective human experience it purports only to reflect.[7] Here one confronts what Geertz takes to be one of the great paradoxes of aesthetic theory, what Eliseo Vivas meant by the dialectic of "creation and discovery." Art objects seem to do no more than reorganize aspects of experience in terms of styles of feeling and states of mind that were presumed to exist before. Yet the most highly valued among them, as one of the reasons why they are so highly valued, succeed simultaneously in convincing us that those same styles of feeling and states of mind never fully or "truely" existed until they were cast in an aesthetic form that shed significant new light on their essential nature.   Hence Geertz can conclude that "quartets, still lifes, and [Balinese] cockfights are not merely reflections of a pre-existing sensibility analogically represented; they are positive agents in the creation and maintenance of such a sensibility" (*IC*, p. 451).

This realization that art forms are simultaneously generative as well as refractory, creative as well as mimetic, clearly leads away from the notion, popularized by the New Critics, that art objects cannot be talked about but only enjoyed, that their function is not to mean but simply to be. Even if most art forms leave us with the impression that they can say in their own behalf far more than we can say about them, no one—and least of all artists themselves—can resist the temptation to talk about them, and that incessantly. And except when this talk is purely technical, its purpose is somehow to situate the discussion of works of art within those larger contexts of meaning which endow the rest of our experience with sense and significance. The corollary to this is that there is no such thing as a purely aesthetic definition of art. To the degree that all talk about art demands to be assimilated into the patterns of meaning by which we lend import to everything else we experience, any theory of art is implicitly a theory of culture as well.

But this broadly cultural view of art and the nature of our talk about it is also to be contrasted with the notion most often opposed to "pure" theories of the sort espoused by the New Critics. I refer in this case to the more functionalist view, associated with many anthropologists and sociologists, which has now been taken up in a variety of refined but not always consistent forms by the literary structuralists—the view that works of art are highly complex verbal mechanisms which define semantic worlds, or sustain linguistic codes, or strengthen the grammar of values sedimented into the syntactical components of speech itself.   In setting his own theory of art over against this functionalist-structuralist view, Geertz is not intending to propose that art lacks a social function but only to redefine it. Where many structural anthropologists and their literary compatriots tacitly assume that aesthetic forms help to support social systems that would begin to collapse without them, Geertz wants to argue that aesthetic forms simply permit certain things which are felt partially as a result of those systems to be said within their confines. And when those things can no longer be said, then they may in time no longer be felt, whereupon life suffers diminishment, impoverishment. Hence the office of aesthetic forms is not, at least primarily, to sustain social structures, much less to reify them, but to "materialize a way of experiencing" within them, to "bring a particular cast of mind out into the world of objects, where men can look at it ("ACS," p. 1478). Their relation to society is thus ideational rather than mechanical, semiotic rather than instrumental. They are what Geertz would call, borrowing a term from Robert Goldwater, "primary documents; not illustrations of conceptions already in force, but conceptions that themselves seek—or for which people seek—a meaningful place in a repertoire of other documents, equally primary" ("ACS," p. 1478).

The typical objection to this line of argument is that it may very well apply to the art of so-called primitives, or people who are unreflective generally, but that it has little bearing upon most of the more complex forms of Western art which are sufficiently sophisticated to operate according to laws internal to their own nature. Geertz finds this to be a wholly specious distinction and one which can be readily discredited by examining some of the more complex forms of Western art itself. Taking as his example quattrocento painting in the Renaissance, Geertz notes that such painting existed not only to depict spiritual concerns but also to deepen them. The artist was interested in doing more than presenting religious material on his canvas; he was also anxious to invite the beholder to reflect on it in a religious manner. The artist's aim, in other words, was not merely illustrative or even exegetical but evocative; his object extended beyond the transcription of certain concerns to include the creation of an artistic situation in which others would be obliged to respond to those concerns. What the painter was attempting to do, Geertz observes with the help of Michael Baxandall's *Painting and Experience in Fifteenth Century Italy,* "was to construct an image to which a distinctive spirituality could forcibly react." His public did not need what it already possessed; what it needed, Geertz continues, "was an object rich enough to see it in, rich enough, even, to, in seeing it, deepen it" ("ACS," p. 1483).

The relation between the painter and his audience in this

most complex of art forms, then, and, more precisely, the relation between his painting and the wider culture to which it
was addressed, was complementary rather than expository, interactive rather than merely expressive. The beholder was in
effect to complete the image presented to him in the painting
by reflecting on it in the light of the whole of his religious
experience and then by adjusting that experience accordingly.
"'For it is one thing to adore a painting,' as a Dominican preach-
er defending the virtuousness of art put it, 'but it is quite another
to learn from a painted narrative what to adore'" (quoted,
"ACS," p. 1483). Yet this capacity "to learn from a painted
narrative what to adore" was not in the fifteenth century, and
is not in the twentieth, the result of individual gifts or subjective intuitions only, but a wider collective form of experience of
which this capacity is one component. Put another way, the distinctive sensibility to which the quattrocento painter addressed
his art was not the creature of his own invention but one that
the whole of the life of his time has participated in forming.

Such observations lead inescapably to a conclusion as ger-
mane to secular art as to religious, to what we like to think
of as wholly imaginative forms as well as to didactic: the artist
does not so much produce a reflection or imitation of the thing
he would have his audience know and feel, and know through
feeling, as create an object capable of eliciting in response those
feelings that will enable his audience to learn what he wants
them to know. In this sense, then, the meanings of his art
might fairly be described as being determined by that art without, as many structuralists contend, being imprisoned within
it. As something his art as fully draws out of his audience as
renders for them, its meanings clearly belong to a larger field of
experience than any that either the art form itself or its audience
may be said to define, refract, or epitomize. And this wider
realm of meaning that supervenes our experience of art is every
bit as real a datum of consciousness as our sense of the poverty
of mind that compels us to intervene by interpreting it. But
this is only a roundabout way of asserting that artist, audience,
and aesthetic form alike are part of a collective experience that
considerably transcends them, and that it is out of their mutual
participation in this larger collective experience of meaning
we call culture that, as Geertz says, their participation in the
particular form of it we call art, "which is in fact but a sector

of it, is possible" ("ACS," p. 1488).

V

With this as background, Geertz's critical theory, or theory of criticism, makes a good deal more sense. What we require, Geertz believes, is a semiotics of art, a science of aesthetics, concerned with how signs signify. What differentiates his own semiotics from almost all contemporary variants is that it would not be a formal science, like mathematics and logic (the models for structuralism), but a social science, like history and anthropology (the models for hermeneutics). This distinction is crucial to Geertz, for he believes that it is one thing to describe the structure of a work of art but quite another to account for the sources of its spell. The former activity can content itself with the definition of relationships; the latter must undertake the investigation of meanings and the assessment of their significance. In pressing this distinction, Geertz has no intention to discount the importance of the formal analysis of works of art; he only wishes, like Trilling before him, to delimit the scope of that analysis on the grounds that "one can no more understand aesthetic objects as concatenations of pure form than one can understand speech as a parade of syntactic variations, or myth as a set of structural transformations" ("ACS," p. 1477).

By a semiotics of art Geertz therefore refers to "a kind of natural history of signs and symbols, an ethnography of the vehicles of meaning" ("ACS," p. 1498). Such a semiotics or ethnography must move beyond the study of signs dissociated from the uses to which they have been put in society and toward a study of signs defined in relation to those uses. Instead of regarding signs as assertions to be deconstructed, codes to be deciphered, or messages to be demystified, Geertz wants to conceive of them as idioms to be interpreted, texts to be read. The first leads only to "a new cryptography" in which one kind of sign is replaced by another more opaque. The second issues in what Geertz wants to call "a new diagnostics" where signs are investigated in terms of the circumstances of their significance ("ACS," p. 1499). The clinical overtones of this last phrase should not be allowed to discredit its utility. In calling for "a new diagnostics," Geertz intends to point to a procedure which will be concerned with heuristics, not pathology, with signification, not symptoms. Insofar as it can be called a science, this "new diagnostics" will not be concerned with determining the nature and causes of disease but with determining "the meaning of things for the life that surrounds them" ("ACS," p. 1499).

Geertz's proposal for "a new diagnostics" provides the link between the cultural analysis of artistic forms and the moral analysis of culture. By shifting the analysis of cultural forms from the analogy of dissecting an organism, decoding a message, or dismantling a system to interpreting a text, and by viewing all cultural texts, whether they be constructed of social materials or imaginative, as symbolic strategies for encompassing situations, Geertz intends to argue that such strategies can never be adequately understood without sufficient comprehension of the situations they were designed to encompass. The moral analysis of culture is therefore an ingredient within the cultural analysis of art, because the study of culture in all its forms involves a study of the social uses these symbolic strategies serve, or the social uses to which they can be put, in man's continuous effort to make sense of, and find significance in, the great variety of things that happen to him. The study of such uses is what Geertz means by "the social history of the moral imagination" and what, like Trilling before him, he assumes to be the one subject common to all students of culture.

As I observed earlier, Geertz has a highly sophisticated sense of the complexity of that history and thus of the devious ways our imaginations are influenced by those of others. The process by which the imaginations of others insinuate themselves into our own involves a subtle but continuous series of interpretive translations that we can never comprehend by reversing, as it were, in the hopes of reaching some ultimate goal of deinterpreted immediacies, but only by penetrating, so to speak, in an effort to discover how the immediacies of one form of experience are translated into the metaphors of another. The key to unlocking this metamorphic process for Geertz and rendering it intelligible is to set its successive phases in their social frames, to place its stages of evolution in the practical contexts in which they occur and from which they derive their meaning.

Yet it is just here that Geertz's semiotics becomes vulnerable to criticism. For what are those social frames, as he calls them, in which we are urged to set the translated object in the various phases of its existence so as to make it intelligible to us but another translation of our own, and one which is just as susceptible to manipulation and distortion as any other? Fredric R. Jameson has recently argued that if the Burkean model of the text is to be applied with critical consistency, then it must be realized that the attempt to establish social frames within which to place the existential phases of the interpreted object represents in its turn a strategy of our own for encompassing situations—the situation in this case being the necessity of making sense out of the text before us.[8] We do so, it would seem, only by supplying a secondary text to interpret the primary one, the secondary text being a fabrication of our own constructed out of that collective fund of wisdom which happens, for whatever reasons, to serve us best in making sense out of the past.

To assume, then, that we can always successfully differentiate between the interpreted transformations of the translated object and the social contexts of its various forms of existence is as treacherous as supposing that we can work our way back through the phases of translation and recover the immediacy of experience from which it springs. The meaning of the object, at least for us, is the meaning it possesses as a result of, and not in spite of, its particular career of translation; and the social contexts we supply to make comprehensible to ourselves the several successive episodes of that career are but an additional chapter in the history of its translation and one which is colored by our own needs and biases as translators. Thus Geertz is surely correct when he argues that "the application of critical categories to social events and sociological categories to symbolic structures is not some primitive form of philosophic mistake, nor is it another mere confusion of art with life" ("FIT," p. 803). But he can go on to argue that "it is a way into the thing itself" only if he is willing to concede that the act of social framing, of "bordering" the phases of that career "with the tenor of the life around them," constitutes another translation of our own, and that, like the others, ours, too, is conditioned by a hermeneutical setting in whose tenor one presumably finds much of its meaning.

Even more serious, perhaps, is the ambiguity latent in

Geertz's use of those slippery words "moral" and "imagination."
When Trilling challenged that axiom dearest to humanistic scholarship by raising questions about "the moral instructiveness of
past cultures," and of other cultures generally, the real issue
for him was ethical and not epistemological. He was nowhere
near as anxious about the possibility of obtaining knowledge of
other minds, of other sensibilities, as he was about the problem
of deciding what such knowledge is good for. And what simultaneously interested and worried him was not the kind of recognition such knowledge affords but the kind of changes such
knowledge does or, more alarmingly, doesn't effect. Geertz,
on the other hand, seems to have reversed the order of importance of these issues. It is not that he lacks interest in the effects
of such knowledge but only that his interest is more severely cir-
cumscribed than Trilling's. While Geertz is willing to admit that
exposure to other minds as to other cultures, can (or at least
should) considerbly expand the range of our own, and often "at
the expense of its inward ease" ("FIT," p. 799), he is less interested in the consequences of such expansion than in the mystery
on which it is based. What evokes his greatest curiosity is not the
difference other peoples' imaginations make to the moral constitution of our own, but "how it is that other people's creations
can be so utterly their own and so deeply part of us" ("FIT," p.
810).

If Geertz is here inclined to subsume moral considerations
under aesthetic ones, one could justifiably argue that this is
merely of a piece with a semiotics that conceives of "the interpretation of cultures," as Geertz suggests in his essay on
anthropological understanding, on the model of reading a poem.
But his analogy presents a problem which derives from Geertz's
rather restricted notion of poetic interpretation in the same article. As Trilling hinted in his nuanced reply, Geertz's attempt to
discount the importance of empathetic understanding in literary
and cultural interpretation alike, and therefore to dissociate
both literary and cultural interpretation from any effort to
achieve a unification of perspectives or a shared sense of identity,
is, whatever its merits on anthropological grounds, questionable
on literary grounds. If as readers we cannot put ourselves completely in the place of others, we can at least be lifted sufficiently
out of ourselves to change as a result of our exposure to the
sensibilities of others; if we cannot fully assimilate forms of humanity alien to our own, we can at least accomodate the intru-

sion into our own of forms of humanity that are not exactly identical with it. And we can do this as Trilling might have added if he were mindful of Geertz's other work, on the testimony of Geertz's own theory. For, according to Geertz's own theory, what makes communication between poem and reader possible in the first place is their mutual participation in a wider field of experience than any that either represents alone. And yet what do the variations in that wider field of experience suggest if not that the relations between poem and reader, as between the poet and the broader historical audience to which his poem is addressed, need be reconceived as reciprocal rather than merely representational, as interactive rather than simply expressive?

If cultural interpretation can be conceived in terms of the model of literary interpretation, then it would be fair to say that elsewhere and quite properly Geertz construes artistic interpretation generally in terms of the rhetorical model of responding to an argument or more specifically in terms of the dramatistic model of reacting to a situation. In either case, the interpreter is confronted with a symbolic form which purports not simply to transmit understanding but to challenge and revise it, that seeks not just to inform but also to influence. Works of art, as Kenneth Burke, Geertz's mentor, would have it, must be thought of as furnishing "equipment for living." In sizing up situations and conveying an appropriate attitude toward them, their purpose is to serve as nothing less than "strategies for selecting enemies and allies, for socializing losses, for warding off evil eye, for purification, propitiation, and desanctification. . . ."[9] These are social functions with a vengence, and Burke calls for a method of artistic interpretation which is correspondingly "sociological." Predicated on the supposition that all artistic forms represent tactics for coping with situations, Burke sponsors an interpretive theory which, in addition to breaking down such forms into their component parts, would seek to determine their typical ingredients, explore their relation to typical situations, and assess their comparative values, all with the hope ideally "of formulating a 'strategy of strategies,' the 'overall' strategy obtained by inspection of the lot" (*PLF*, p. 262).

While it is difficult to say whether Geertz's proposal for a "social history of the moral imagination" would encompass Burke's ideal formulation of "a strategy of strategies," there is little doubt that Burke's "sociological" agenda for literary interpretation, no less than Geertz's socio-moral agenda for cultural interpretation, is a far cry from the narrowly textual theory of poetic interpretation Geertz advances in the essay on anthropological understanding to which Trilling responded, where reading a poem amounts to no more than a determination of what it is about, an understanding of the relation between its generalized view of life and the specific vehicles in which that view is embodied. If Geertz is to be consistent with the larger implications of his own cultural theory, then reading a poem entails at the very least a comprehension of the sorts of claims it makes on us and an assessment of how, accordingly, we should respond. More typically, it involves a confrontation with modes of being other than our own and a requisite attempt to make the necessary adjustments.

Reading a poem, like interpreting another culture, thus depends upon a fundamental distinction between all that we are and all that we are not, between all that we could be and all that we cannot be or will not be. It is this "dialectic," to use one of Trilling's favorite words, which occasions those interpretive workings and reworkings that Geertz rightly perceives as the essence of cultural life and the central subject of cultural study. Yet the impact such interpretive reworkings have upon the moral lives of those who undertake them and those who respond to them—this remains an unresolved issue for Geertz. Not that he doubts that such interpretive reworkings have an impact or make a difference; only that he is reluctant in any given instance to say whether that impact, that difference, is for good or ill. And while Geertz's restraint at this point may well be an indication of his own moral integrity, it still remains, as I think Trilling sensed, the most troubling feature of his whole theory of culture and constitutes the chief threat to its moral basis.

NOTES

[1] "Why We Read Jane Austen," *Times Literary Supplement*, March 5, 1976, pp. 250-52.

[2] Geertz's response was initially prepared for delivery at the Lionel Trilling Memorial Seminar held at Columbia University on 17 February 1977. It was simultaneously published as "Found in Translation: On the Social History of the Moral Imagination," *The Georgia Review*, 31 (Winter, 1977), pp. 788-810; subsequently referred to as "FIT."

[3] "Why We Read Jane Austen," p. 251.

[4] Clifford Geertz, "On the Nature of Anthropological Understanding," *American Scientist*, January-February, 1975, p. 14. In the form in which Trilling encountered it, this essay appeared under the slightly more interesting title, "From the Native's Point of View: On the Nature of Anthropological Understanding," *Bulletin of the American Academy of Arts and Sciences*, Vol. 28, No. 1.

[5] Clifford Geertz, *The Interpretation of Cultures* (New York: Basic Books, 1973), p. 5; subsequently referred to as *IC*.

[6] Clifford Geertz, "Art as a Cultural System," *Modern Language Notes*, 91 (December, 1976), p. 1499; subsequently referred to as "ACS."

[7] In his brilliant essay entitled "The Symbolic Inference; or Kenneth Burke and Ideological Analysis," *Critical Inquiry*, 4 (Spring, 1978) pp. 507-23, Fredric R. Jameson points to a related but not identical phenomenon when he notes that Burke's dramatistic conception of art as a form of symbolic action helps explain the illusion that every work of art seems to be a response to a context that it has created itself. Stated differently, every text seems to be a response to a subtext of its own invention. Jameson here is doing more than pointing to the ontological priority of context over text; he is suggesting that any cultural object viewed as a text, as a symbolic mode of responding to a situation, brings into being, as

though for the first time, "that situation to which it is also, at one and the same time, a reaction. It articulates its own situation and textualizes it, encouraging the illusion that the very situation itself did not exist before it, that there is nothing but a text, that there never was an extra-or contextual reality before the text itself generated it" (p. 512). Yet against those who tend to accentuate the dominance of the text over its own subtext in order, presumably, to argue that the text's referent, the situation that provoked it, never existed in the first place, Jameson wants to argue that the situations are in fact real, no matter how much they may be "textualized" by the initial symbolic act which, as Jameson points out, can't help measuring them in terms "of its own active project" (p. 512).

[8]See Jameson, "The Symbolic Inference; or, Kenneth Burke and Ideological Analysis," pp. 507-23.

[9]Kenneth Burke, *The Philosophy of Literary Form*, rev. and abr. (New York: Vintage Books, 1957), p. 262. Subsequently referred to as *PLF*.

PARABIOGRAPHY:
THE VARIETIES OF CRITICAL EXPERIENCE*

by
Ihab Hassan

The varieties of critical experience are endless. I shall speak only of three: desiring, reading, acting (which here includes making). These are all fragments of an autobiography, itself but a sentient reed in the universe.

Autobiography has become rife, running both in high and low repute: it enjoys the sublime attention of literary theory, suffers the base association with cultural narcissism. More to the point: it has become the form that the contemporary imagination seeks to recover, as recent works of Saul Bellow, William Styron, John Barth, Bernard Malamud, Elizabeth Hardwick, and Michael Herr variously intimate. Yet autobiography remains an impossible—and deadly—form.

Impossible: how can a life come alive to itself without winding in the infinite folds of its own hermeneutic circle? How can self apprehend itself in the very act of its flight from death? But deadly too in this sense: autobiography is abject unless, in the words of Michel Leiris, it exposes itself to the "bull's horn." For writing about ourselves we risk cowardice and mendacity; and more, we risk changing ourselves by that writing into whatever an autobiographer pretends to be.

Grazing the bull's horn, we become, Leiris says, tangents to ourselves and the universe. I have no access to such grace.

*©Ihab Hassan, 1980. This essay was first presented in November 1979 at a conference on "Autobiography," sponsored by the Center for Twentieth Century Studies of the University of Wisconsin—Milwaukee, and appeared in *The Georgia Review* (Fall 1980).

My defense against the peril of autobiography consists only in naming the peril. I name it in several voices, rendering, perhaps, less a discourse than a human cacophony of the critical spheres. Attend, perpend, what voice you please.

I

> *The little boy—almond eyed, hair parted and combed smoothly to each side—stands in velvet bolero and black toreador pants. His uncle frowns down upon him from an ogre's height.*
> *"And what will you be when you grow up?"*
> *"A warrior. Greater than Hannibal or Caesar."*
> *"A general?"*
> *"And also a saint."*
> *Faint smiles. Later, something, neither shame nor pride, scalds his eyes.*

We know that Freud, a grown man, admired Hannibal inordinately, and thought himself more conqueror than man of science. In thinking so, Freud tacitly admits that thought itself, even in its most reflexive mode, is founded on power and desire. But what kind of desire, and of which desiring self? I call upon four thinkers—Hegel, Nietzsche, William James, and Freud himself—to set the question before us.

Hegel first: in *The Phenomenology of Mind,* desire radically constitutes consciousness. What we call self is but active desire for the recognition of another, which the self sublates—at once negates and maintains—and so affirms its being, *for* itself. The struggle for recognition ends when one, risking death, becomes Master, the other, preserving his life, becomes Slave. Thus history comes into dialectical existence. We need not pursue further the profound paradoxes of the Hegelian dialectic, in which the Master wins an empty victory—since he has won recognition only from a Slave; in which the labor of Slaves, not of Masters, transforms nature into history; in which, finally, freedom comes to the Slave who "overcomes" his bondage rather than the Master who perpetuates his desire. For our purpose, we need only recall that death and desire are complicit in the formation of language and mind from the start. For language not only mediates between self and other; it also becomes "the form in which spirit finds existence," as Hegel puts it, "Self-consciousness which as such is there immediately present, and which in its individuality is universal."

Nietzsche, too, perceives language as the supreme problematic of thought, making rhetoric—Paul de Man notes—"ground for the furthest-reaching dialectical speculations." Outside the "prison-house of language," we may vaguely imagine, but never speak, any "thing." No less than Hegel, Nietzsche assumes ontological desire, which he calls "will to power," and from which he derives, without benefit of Hegel's World Spirit, all things human. Virtues are but "refined passions," interpretations but affects of power; and the very "ought" at the heart of language arising from the ineluctable gap between desire and world, seeks to overcome that world. Thus desire derives from its own insufficiency more power, its aim never simply to be but always to be *more!* The Nietzschean self may be a "fiction," an empty space where various personages come to mingle, squabble, and depart; yet it remains a "fiction" more dense in its desires—including self-annihilation—than any neutron star. This is the burden of Nietzsche's great posthumous work, *The Will to Power.*

> *He asks his son: "Why do you 'sky gods' like to sky dive?" Long pause, uncertain reply: "Every time you jump, you save your life."*
> *The father thinks to himself: But what if someday the diver decides otherwise? Who knows the circumference of the self? Even Lucifer—in the unimaginable density of pride he cried: "I myself am hell"—even Lucifer evokes the rarity of light.*

Whatever the self may be, its earthly form reveals a fierce intricacy of asseveration that no human endeavor escapes. Hegel and Nietzsche define a horizon of that being; in *The Varieties of Religious Experience*, William James defines another. James knows that "civilization is founded on the shambles, and every individual existence goes out in a lonely spasm of helpless agony." The insight is as stark as any Freud gave. Yet James knows as well the need of the self to risk itself at the edge of the ineffable. What he calls "the ontological imagination" realizes "unpicturable being" with a sensuous intensity exceeding a lover's ecstasy. Such a faculty overflows the self's finitude, and touches the moral and intellectual center of mystical experience. Thus the mystic or saint accedes to a higher type than the warrior or hero precisely because the former is more adapted to "the highest society conceivable." Ethereal as James's speculations may seem to self-devoted realists, his major hypothesis stands solidly enough: mystics connect to something which, whatever it may be on its *farther* side, "is on its *hither* side the subconscious continuation of our conscious life." This is not far from Freud.

> *An adolescent still, he sought the desert, walking away from the feculent city, the river, red-brown in his native October, the soft impedients of family. He aspired to fire; his element was air; the desert offered a sterile compromise. He walked day and part of the night, past the tracks of caravans, to burn a palm leaf in the desert.*

Freud, we know, holds mysticism in suspicion; his "Nirvana principle" or "oceanic feeling" owes more to the dubious death instinct than to any numinous vision. Yet his theory, more than any other, shapes the modern languages of desire. The theory shifts, changes, as Jean Laplanche shows in his *Life and Death in Psychoanalysis*. The binary terms "ego" and "sexual instincts" become "ego" and "object instincts," become finally "life" and "death." But great Eros, the binding force of life, holds no sway over Thanatos, or death; their titanic struggles, Freud dismally concludes in *Civilization and Its Discontents*, compose the infant's cry to heaven. For instincts demand only their pleasure; Ananke, or scarcity, forbids; the harried ego in the service of reality withers. How, then, resolve this tragic conflict? Perhaps, as always, through another tragedy; that is, through life perceived under new terms of its exigencies.

Freud perceives these exigencies in an earlier work, *Beyond the Pleasure Principle*, which first posits the death wish. Since no ruse of substitution or sublimation can really appease the instincts, the self never maintains itself in balance. Yet death, terminus of the organic project, also proves to have fathered the first instinct: "the instinct to return to the inanimate state." As Laplanche concludes for Freud: "Absent from every unconscious, death is perhaps rediscovered in the unconscious as the

the most radical—but also the most sterile—principle of its logic. But it is life which crystallizes the first objects to which desire attaches itself, before even thought can cling to them."

There are, of course, many other views of the matter, notably René Girard's theory of "mimetic desire"—"the subject desires the object because the rival desires it"—advanced forcefully, even obsessively, in his *Violence and the Sacred*. Yet all views press upon us images of being in its most complex ferocity. That ferocity, from Hegel to Freud, seems instinct with varieties of death or violence; and even Girard, who dissents with both thinkers in his ontology, insists that "violence is always mingled with desire." The point is epistemological no less than metaphysical. Thus Michel Foucault remarks in his "Theatrum Philosophicum": "We should not restrict meaning to the cognitive core that lies at the heart of a knowable object; rather, we should allow it to reestablish its flux at the limit of words and things. . . . Death supplies the best example, being both the event of events and meaning in its purest state."

Death, then, is more than our ultimate reunion: it is immanent in our desires as in our knowledge or speech. But how can all this affect a critic's "job of work"? Only thus: no critical gesture—in reading or writing, in praxis or poesis—that fails to confess even as it questions the intricacies of violence and desire—desire for love or death, for being or power—can come near to wisdom, which may itself be our most "refined passion."

The principle is hardly novel; it animates the psychoanalytic movement from the old masters—Freud, Jung, Adler—to the visionary epigones—Marcuse, Brown, Laing. Yet it is in France, of course, that the discourse of desire has recently reached full philosophical loquacity—and opacity. I have in mind the utterances of Jacques Lacan, Roland Barthes, Michel Foucault, Gilles Deleuze, Jean-Francois Lyotard, of whom only the first is a professional analyst. I can do no justice here, or even injustice, to the clouded brilliance and high casuistry of that movement; nor should I dwell on strictures and tergiversations of various sophists and schoolmen on the critical scene. I hope simply to disengage from the current debate certain ideas that the critical self may find seductive.

He suffers from a certain logophobia. Once, in another

> *country, he declined to speak for two months, in spite of words. Occasionally, he still feels his brain barely bobbing on a sea of silence. He loses always at scrabble. From time to time, he thinks of Charlie Starkweather who shot some dozen people in a tavern because "there was too much talk." Unlike those far ancestors, their brains still bicameral, he hears no voices in the head; his readiest intuitions are mute. What, then did mad Hölderlin hear "wenn die Stille kehrt"?*

Like his predecessors, Lacan also locates desire in the interplay between self and other. The interplay, beginning with the infant's "mirror stage," is specular; it constitutes a reflexive alienation from which all subsequent identifications derive. For Lacan, then, desire is still *for the desire* of the other, "not so much because the other holds the key to the object desired, as because the first object of desire is to be recognized by the other." This admits Hegel's "recognition" and Freud's "primal cognition"—on the bodies of our mothers we first learn to construe—and admits as well Nietzsche's insatiable "will," perceived here as the perpetual demand of language, a language never commensurate to self and other. Lacan's genius informs his attention to the question of language, which his own paludal style both reveals and conceals. For not only is the unconscious ("the discourse of the Other") structured as a language; what we call the self is but itself an instance of the "symbolic order." Thus the philosophical status of the subject, from Descartes to the present, remains wholly contingent on the duplicities of discourse.

In his seminal essay, "The Function of Language in Psychoanalysis" (originally delivered in 1953 as the *Discours de Rome*), Lacan says: "In order to liberate the subject's Word, we introduce him into the Language of his desire, that is, into the *primary Language* in which, beyond what he tells us of himself, he is already talking to us unbeknownst to him, and in the symbols of the symptom in the first place." Yet language, we know, implies negation, the absence of the thing signified; this symbolic "murder" or death, Lacan insists, "constitutes in the subject the eternalization of his desire." What follows is Lacan at his outrageous best: "Therefore, when we wish to attain in the subject what was before the serial articulations of the Word, and what is primordial to the birth of symbols, we find it in death, from which his existence takes on all the meaning it has. It is in effect as a desire for death that he affirms himself for others; if he identifies himself with the other, it is by fixing him solidly in the metamorphosis of his essential image, and no being is ever evoked by him except among the shadows of death." Thus, again we see death (or *béance*), language, and desire coterminous in the self, a self articulated by signifiers—the most "privileged" being the phallus—that are the body's own displaced speech.

> *He has never seen anyone dead. His father and mother, long exiled, were nearly dead to him when they died very old. He was himself more than half a century old when a death finally touched him. He remembered her dying face, as she tried to speak, to recognize his presence, in words, in vain. She died—he was not there—without speaking again. Later, he dreamed of her as a little girl, dressed in white, weightless, whom he carried away from some harm no one could see or name.*

II

The human universe is made of lack: such is Lacan's gravamen, and that of his poststructuralist claques. This is because, for them, the human universe is made of language. Thus the language of desire leads to the aesthetics of absence—note the currency of such terms as *degree zero, silence, chiasmus, tear, fissure, crack, rupture, fragment,* and *lapse* in the discourse of, say, Roland Barthes. Though I believe the *human* universe to be neither Full nor Empty, neither Deed nor Word, but rather what we choose continually to make of it, I now turn to the work of Barthes, which joins for us the issues of desire and reading, the first two terms in my triad.

Barthes's later work seems as much a meditation on the reading self as an amatory ritual or verbal caress—no doubt polymorphous—of certain texts, or perhaps of textuality itself This does not inhibit the author from proposing several moot distinctions in *The Pleasure of the Text.* The arch distinction refers to the experiences of pleasure (*plaisir*) and of

bliss (*jouissance*) in reading—the first expressible, the latter un-
utterable (*in-dicible, inter-dit*). The text of pleasure fills, "grants
euphoria," even as it enters the purview of culture and history;
that of bliss, asocial, permits no "recuperation," especially
of the self in bliss. Yet even pleasure is "atopic," and so evades
ideological "prattle" and praxis. Pleasure does serve, however,
to link "the reading neurosis to the hallucinated form of the
text," thus revealing the true individuality of the subject. Based
on that conjunction between personal neurosis and imagined
text, Barthes further distinguishes four kinds of readers: "the
fetishist," haunted by parts and division of the text; "the ob-
sessive," including philologists, semioticians, metalinguists; "the
paranoiac," argumentative, ideological, egotistic; and "the hys-
teric," immersed in the text, surrendering to it in near bliss.
(Armine Kotin gives an excellent reading of these four types of
readers in the first issue of *The Journal of Practical Structuralism* [July 1979].)   Yet Barthes quickly confesses that such
distinctions waver—"I stumble, I err," he slyly cries—and so provide no solid ground for a science of reading. In any case, the
text is gossamer; the critic's business is *hyphology* (from *hyphos,*
the spider's web); and the reader, in near bliss, "unmakes himself, like a spider dissolving in the constructive secretions of
its web."   Talismanic, full of subtle subversion rather than
theory, this slim work ends by reviving, with infinite delicacy,
the Nietzschean dualism of Apollonian and Dionysian as modes
of reading.

Fragments of a Lover's Discourse affords us a more febrile
experience; for pain and solitude here attend the subject more
than pleasure, as do jealousy and spite. Simulating discretely
a lover's speech, rendering it in broken "figures," such as a
modern dancer may perform, the book also presents us with an
"encyclopedia of affective culture," ordered by no principle
other than the alphabet of desire. Yet the spirit of the Erinyes
pervades its pages; and the text to which it always returns, without ever leaving, is that incontinent book of love, death, and
madness, *The Sorrows of Young Werther*, which so many in
Europe read and, reading, learned to sigh and die. Thus both
love and suicide become textual mimesis: the question is still
one of reading. Barthes suggests that his book should be ideally
dedicated to lovers and readers united. But united in what?
In the sense of death? In the inadequacies of love? Certainly

in the immanence of a language that continually creates and betrays, speaks and silences, desire itself. Here the contradictions of readers and writers, lunatics and lovers, seem in the dis-ease of language compact.

These contradictions converge on the erotic self whose very words we read. For if Barthes writes to simulate a lover's plaintive or morbid discourse (the lover is never a *"sujet saint"*), he offers us also a counterfeit autobiography, cunning in its confessions, artful in its masks. This is not merely because Barthes is wily, or that his lovers are condemned to stealth by their love; it is also because language and desire meet at the limits of their mutual destructions in the subject of love. There is really no possibility of explication, of hermeneutics, in this forlorn confession. Indeed, for Barthes, true knowledge depends on the "unmaking of the *I*, superb organ of miscognition [*méconnaissance*]." This "unmaking of the I" is a political, a utopian, project, affecting reading and writing, self and society. In the book of Barthes, the erotic undoing of the articulate self comes finally to this: "I want to change systems: no longer to unmask, no longer to interpret, but to make of consciousness itself a drug, and thus to accede to a vision of irreducible reality, to the great dream of clarity, to prophetic love." Suddenly, Barthes calls us closer to Boehme than Quintillian.

> *Venus influenced his house in the zodiac. Yet for many years in his life, he suffered the tug of two obsessions: women and work. (He can almost recall all the "perfect legs" he has seen, climbing out of cabs, crossed in restaurants, clicking on the streets of cities; and see, in the glaucous mirror of desire, those golden-thighed women of the north, with their lupine eyes). Women and work: how can intellect choose perfection of desire or the spirit? No tantrist, he ages, locked a little in the banality of fantasy and time.*

> *Yet Venus, at last, who influenced his birth, sent an emissary to his house.*

The stance of Roland Barthes toward the text is radical, anarchic—he would prefer to say ideolectic. Yet the political terms are apposite; for a textual theory assumes a theory of society as well as of desire, and reading is an act we perform in the name of tacit cultural constraints. Such constraints do not preclude for Barthes the possibility of innovation. A political revolution and a mutation in desire share the same *telos,* which is "the absolute New." Similarly, in reading, by choosing the Lover against the Interpreter or Priest, Barthes chooses the uncodified, the enchanted, the *"intraitable,"* and so invokes the New. Yet the New, as we all sadly know, never remains novel. Thus Barthes espouses the sexual and textual politics of permanent revolution.

In George Steiner, however, we meet a critic of nearly antithetical persuasion. His censures of pornography, too famous to reiterate here, express his acute discomfort with a discourse that at once corrupts and coerces human polity. In the recent collection, *On Difficulty,* Steiner confronts the wider question of literacy. Recognizing the manifold nexus of literature and sexuality throughout history, he still deplores the devaluation of erotic as of religious language in our world. "The two devaluations . . .," Steiner argues, "are obviously related. Together they amount to an almost programmatic 'thinning out' of the interior medium." Such loss of "internality," such incursions on the privacy of love or worship, strike him as a baleful aspect of our modernity. To this process, even psychoanalysis has lent its prestige; for its voluble therapies help to erode "the autonomous energies of inward diction and plenitude." As the balance of "internal speech" shifts toward "public verbalization," toward publicity in its largest sense, the self risks its own "voidance"; "less lodged in ourselves," we become less adequate to the very stresses we generate. (Characteristically, Steiner cannot resist to add: "the American house is, or was until very recently, open to all comers.")

It is the economy of the speaking and reading and writing self, then, that vitally concerns George Steiner, and his concern puts to challenge the "empty subject" of Nietzsche, Derrida, and Barthes. Nor does Steiner favor democratic or idiosyncratic readings of texts, which help to undermine informed authority. The extroversion of the self, the prepotence of technology, the dispersal of judgment in mass society—who knows what serves as cause here and what as effect?—have instituted a new kind of illiteracy, hostile to reading as to thought. For right reading is a stringent and solitary act, requiring disciplined attention and remembrance, honed skills of language, a tensed will. It requires, too, a cultural tradition or central syllabus, assuring that density of allusion and range of reference, that interactive power of sympathies, we now call "intertextuality." "The 'text' flourishes in a context of authority," Steiner starkly asserts. The "humanities," in their classic sense, entail no "ready equivalence," no "unforced co-existence with 'humanism' in a mass-liberal or socialist scheme of values." Now that affluence seems on the wane in the West, the latent incongruence of culture and democracy may break out. Steiner stoically views the dismal prospect, and calls for "houses of reading," where a few can still be taught to read again with rigor and delight, "proudly, *con amore*," so that the text may remain for us "the vital circumstance, the informing 'context' of our being."

I may have lent the argument more austerity or asperity than Steiner intended. Certainly, he recognizes that "texts are inexhaustible to our needs," and that a degree of "disinterested irresponsibility"—one thinks of deconstruction—may enhance our quickness to literature. Moreover, in a recent essay entitled "'Critic'/'Reader'" (*New Literary History* [Spring 1979]), Steiner seeks to discriminate between literary experiences in a more optative mood. Nor is the distance between Barthes and Steiner absolute; between them, various theorists—for instance, Geoffrey Hartman, Wolfgang Iser, Norman Holland, David Bleich—mediate the reading act. Still, the issue becomes clearest when we maintain contrastive space between the two critics. For their advocacies remain antithetical; and Steiner's catholic priesthood of reading, reverting to Péguy and Benda, would find no welcome in the heteroclite culture of desire of Barthes.

Such varied dispositions toward text, self, and society lead us again to wonder: can the act of reading ever acquire consensual definition? My own contention, throughout, has been that no epistemology of literature can usefully answer the question, though an ontology of desire may help us to start. As an aspect of the primal will, reading consists of a complex *fiat* of our being in Language—which is to say, in relation to the Other, be it mother, rival, history, death, or the unconscious. Hence "reading" is always party to a continually broken, perpetually revised "social contract." Inescapably, we ask: who reads? But, imperatively, we must also know: to what end does that reader construe the text and in what historical context?

> *As if by accident, he comes upon a text, vaguely auto-biographical, published more than a quarter of a century ago. He reads from that text, written between him and birth, interposed between him and death, thinking wryly that every reading gives life to the dead, even if the latter prove to be only himself, in another country. He reads these words in a text that may be this text's context:*

. . . schoolboys of all classes jostled their prejudices and bandied their enmities with characteristic ferocity in the drab classrooms of governmental schools. At the black, iron-grilled gates, which shut at five minutes past eight with frightening finality, and opened only at five minutes to three, the parental Mercedes, Rolls, or Packard may have been waiting for the fortunate students. But once inside, these abandoned all hope, and shifted for themselves as best they could, relying on wit and fist (some fought also with their unbreakable skulls), to absolve themselves bloodily of cowardice, effeminacy, and good breeding. One played at soccer between classes, with a makeshift ball of old socks—the rest was work. . . . It was not unusual for students who failed their final examinations—the lists were there, tacked to peeling walls—to attempt suicide.

> *He thinks of another scene, decades later, a graduate student, subsisting mainly on apples and Hershey bars, earning his doctorate in a foreign tongue. The department chairman—renowned, a former president of his professional association—stares at him through fishbowl glasses and gently rasps:*

> *"We've given you scholarships and fellowships. But we can't give you a teaching assistantship now: you have elements in your speech that are not standard."*
> *Quite true, he thinks. But then, there were "nonstandard" elements even when he spoke his "mother tongue."*

III

In desiring, in reading, in making, the critic acts out his autobiography, compounded of many selves. Such enactments, though personal, refer us also to history. Thus Hans-Georg Gadamer—who clearly sees that prejudices constitute our being far more than judgments—avers in his *Philosophical Hermeneutics:* "It is not really we ourselves who understand: it is always a past that allows us to say, 'I have understood.'" This active pastness of the self, this vital historicity of understanding—so different from the *passéisme* of genteel academics—projects itself into the future and so engages the critic's praxis.

This is plain in Foucault's "archaeology of knowledge," which bares encoded patterns of power and so brings me to the last term in my triad. Of Foucault's many archaeologies—of words and madness, of penal and medical systems—that of sexuality is the most proximate to my theme. In an early work, *The Order of Things,* Foucault had noted that Death, Language (or Law), and Desire delimit the foundations of human society, the edge of the "unthought" (*l'impensé*). In his recent *History of Sexuality* (the first volume), he goes farther to assay the various languages of desire. These, he strikingly maintains, far from being repressive, richly articulate given powers. But what does Foucault mean by power? This: an immanence of effective discourse, an interplay of relations, a field of dispersed forces; in short, power "is the name one lends to a complex strategic situation in a particular society." This view, anathema to Marxists, perceives sexuality as the seam between the human body and the body politic, the suture between personal freedom and social control. By making sexuality sexy and desire desirable, by privileging eroticism as a signifier, the discourse of power further creates a manageable identity for each of us—whether homosexual or heterosexual—and so perpetuates itself. The ancient right of tyrants to kill their subjects now yields to the right of states to enforce a particular life on their citizens; the old *"symbolique du sang"* gives way to the new *"analytique de la sexualité."* Thus, for Foucault, true freedom invokes not the idea of *"le sexe-désire"* but "bodies in their pleasure."

We may challenge this peculiar concept of power, as Jean Baudrillard does in *Oublier Foucault.* (Power for Baudrillard, incidentally, is not an immanent field or grid, but a seduction, a provocation, a *leurre*.) But we cannot refuse Foucault's grand insight: that all discourse implicates itself deeply in the structures of power. For him, the very idea of epistemic continuity shields society from break, crisis, and change—hence the aversion of families, churches, states, to discontinuities of every kind. Similarly, the creed of Humanism reinforces social organization by prohibiting shifts both in the shape and intent of power. At the center of the Humanist creed lies the concept of the Western self, which Foucault wants to attack doubly: "either by a 'desubjectification' of the will to power (that is, through political struggle . . .) or by the destruction of the subject as a pseudosovereign (that is, through an attack on 'culture' . . .)," he writes in *Language, Counter-Memory, Practice*. In brief, the critic acts not only by demystifying the languages of desire but also by assaulting both the epistemic and political structures of society; or, in Foucault's words, by the "simultaneous agitation of consciousness and institutions. . . ."

Yet the critic's praxis—here Michel Foucault and Gilles Deleuze agree—cannot mesh completely with theory; for there are always *blockages,* disruptions, that neither can nor should be eliminated by "totalization." This last, of course, appears to poststructuralists as the ultimate abomination. Hence their justified equivocations about Freud or Marx. Can Freudian biological instinct desire against itself? Can Marxist class interest overrule desire? Deleuze would answer: interest gives no final answer to the riddle of power, since "there are investments of desire that function in a more profound and diffuse manner than our interests dictate"; to which Foucault would add: "the relationships between desire, power, and interest are more complex than we ordinarily think, and it is not necessarily those who exercise power who have an interest in its execution; nor is it always possible for those with vested interests to exercise power."

This politics of dispersal or displacement renders praxis ambiguous if not anarchic. Deleuze—and also Lyotard as we shall see—happily avow this tendency. Deleuze's major work, *L'Anti-Oedipe,* coauthored with Félix Guattari, carries the telling subtitle: "*Capitalisme et Schizophrénie.*" Declaring itself against both the Marxist thesis of social production and the Freudian principle of Oedipal repression, the book dazzlingly propounds the immanent "flux" of desire, which various systems, conjunctive or disjunctive, regulate. Men and women thus appear as "desiring machines," the latter being the authors' term for any system of breaks (*coupures*) which "schizo-analysis" aspires to liberate. This summary, though grossly simplified, may still educe the stubborn tendency of the book: to disrupt the structures of power and desire, and disrupt even more our understanding of these structures.

The disruptive, dispersive tendency extends to that slim anti-tract, *Rhizome.* Here Deleuze and Guattari coyly choose the figure of the rhizome—a living, amorphous plant stem—to convey their sense of emergent things: a diffuse self, fugitive forms, a culture open to syntagma and parataxis instead of hierarchic or generative models of organization. In their view, the rhizome, unlike the root, shows no direction or center, only circumference, growing by variation, a jumble of self-modifying systems. The authors end breezily by enjoining us: "Faites rhizome et pas racine, ne plantez jamais! Ne semez pas, piquez! Ne soyez pas un ni multiple, soyez des multiplicités! Faites la ligne et jamais le point!" ("Make rhizome, not root; never plant! Do not sow, puncture! Be neither one nor many, be multiplicities! Make the line, and never the period!")

Deleuze clarifies the politics of this rhizomology in another brief work, *Dialogues,* with Claire Parnet. History, he believes, consists of various lines of motion or flight, "fluxes of deterritorialization," fluid like the wandering of the Jews or Vandals or Tartars, or like the Long March of Mao. Society itself follows certain lines of flight, which direct change at the deepest level. The true revolutionary perceives these lines and poses the practical question: what covert organization of energies, refusing the State, refusing its binary models of power, can still summon a new state? Deleuze concludes with a query of his own: instead of presaging the impossibility of revolution or the advent of world totalitarianism, why not concede that a *new kind* of change may already be in progress, and that various mutant and living "machines" may now conspire to subvert the known forms of World and State? The question, Deleuze insists, is neither utopian nor improvisational: it simply assumes another perspective on desire, knowledge, and power.

Possessed by a certain idea of America, he ended

his first book with these words:

A country without prehistory, it has suddenly entered history with the intention to rape and redeem time in its heart. A country of illimitable spaces, it has confronted men with nature in the raw, inducing in them permanent and atavistic solitude, and it has been turned by them into the most profoundly denatured spectacle on record. Conceived as a dream, it has shown that dreamers may also awake in the cold sweat of a nightmare, and sleep to dream again. . . . The curse of Columbus is still with us: everyone must rediscover America—alone!

Foreign born, he still recalls that nothing terrified him more than the prospect of forced repatriation. He opened every letter from the Immigration and Naturalization Service with dry mouth, leaden hand. But now his impatience with America grows. For there is a crank in him, organ-grinding Jeremiah, ill-tempered, unreasonable, uncouth—a creature twisted of dream and hope. This is how the organ-grinder rasps:

"What's wrong with us now? A 'crisis of confidence'? You wouldn't know it, the way America rides on roller skates. But in the parks, the future walks with transistors instead of ears. The dollar's down, the dollar bills themselves torn and dirty. Everywhere, gas-guzzlers, gouged hulks, rust-cankered. The streets cracked, the lawns alitter; subways, whole cities, reeking harm in the night. We do love funk and horror; so, like Mom and Dad, Television and the Mafia give us what we need. For the rest, flabbiness like ocean to ocean carpeting, up to the knees.

"We have become a nation of first names. Oleaginous egos, spread thinly, like a smile or stain. Occlusions of desire, seeking in violence release. Perhaps this is what the poet had in mind when he wailed:
                    'For the error bred in the bone
                    Of each woman and each man
                    Craves what it cannot have,
                    Not universal love
                    But to be loved alone.'"

The crank now pauses, then turns political on his hurdy-gurdy:

"Fractious Factions everywhere, claiming Justice. But Justice— fragile, frangible, fugacious—soon yields to Vengeance, her darker sister. No hope in political Parties: the Right acts on fear, the Left on spite, except when fear and spite exchange their places. The Right, cramped in crotch, lies against time's infractions. The Left, infantile, remains fixed in futile abstractions. And the Middle, soft as always, whispers: 'death happens to other people, we're not responsible for their actions'."

The crank in him ceases cranking. Now the accuser stands accused. He thinks of his own life, full of losses and lapses. How make of personal slippage a veridical politics?

Truth, the idea of Truth itself, must be placed in doubt: so maintains Jean-Francois Lyotard, pushing the politics of desire to its limit. In *Economie Libidinale*, a work energized by a Nietzschean poetics of intransigence, Lyotard conceives human reality as *"la grande pellicule éphémère,"* a libidinal membrane on which history inscribes itself, much as it did in the work of Deleuze. Ubiquitous, Möbius-like, without "depth," this great pellicule acts, however, more as a pulse than a strip. In its "figural space," desire "connives" to "transgress" textual organization and the habitual order of signifiers. Thus poetry, ally of desire, instigates change more than the alienated discourse of politics; and Marx himself emerges as *"le désir nommé Marx,"* an author of liberating lunacies rather than stodgy theories. Zanily, wittily, Lyotard invites us to stroke Marx's beard as a "complex libidinal volume," without contempt, without devotion, simply as an affective gesture, a conflation of passions. Indeed, the "Old Man" contains an erotic and subversive creature, "little Miss Marx" (*la petite Marx*), whom Lyotard compares to Madame Edwarda, George Bataille's notorious prostitute.

Scandalous as all this may seem, Lyotard knows no cynicism in his effort to release the Human Abstract from systemic bondage. In this effort, Marxist discourse—endless chatter, perpetual revision—seems to him nugatory. The pulses of intensity, the exchanges of power, prove life to be a secret currency, running through all domains, sacred and profane, practical and theoretical. A libidinal economy *is* a political economy.

Lyotard ends with this appeal: "Nul besoin de déclarations, de manifestes, d'organisations, de provocations, nul besoin même d'*actions exemplaires.* Faites jourer la dissimilation en faveur des intensités. Complot invulnérable. . . . Nous n'inventons rien, ça y est, oui, oui, oui, oui." ("No need for declarations, manifestoes, organizations, provocations, no need even for *exemplary actions.* Put in play dissimilarities in favor of intensities. Invulnerable conspiracy. . . . We invent nothing, it is already here, yes, yes, yes, yes.")

Lyotard's politics may appear, as Matei Calinescu has noted ("Marxism as a Work of Art," *Standard French Review* [Spring 1979]), fundamentally aesthetic, their spirit tropic or figural. Yet his politics are also humorously pragmatic, enacted by a terrorist, a marginal, and a trickster all in one. Two short works, *Instructions païennes* and *Rudiments païens,* speak playfully to the point. In the first, Lyotard invokes both justice and impiety, or rather justice *in* impiety, to create a "pragmatic narrative"— made up of anecdotes, riddles, conversations, fragments—meant to undermine the Great Signifier of society. This tactic requires "riposte" rather than "reaction"—requires, that is, a constant and exultant shift of perspectives on the enemy. In the second work, Lyotard resorts to the English word "patchwork"—instead of Lévi-Strauss's *"bricolage"*—to designate the tactics of displacement. Aggravate nihilism, he cries; hasten the crisis of values; become enterprising in decadence! At the same time, permit no class to control the discourse—specifically the metalanguage—of all society. And though conflict and violence may ensue, as the American example has rabidly shown, promote the cause of minorities in a "heterogeneous space." This "new perspective," Lyotard claims, resists Unity, Finality, Truth (all in capitals), following the "logic of sophists," not of "master logicians," the "time of opportunity," not of "world history." Like the pagan gods, politic, protean, unveridical, and so often cruel, Lyotard would free praxis at the expense of all human pieties—except some vehement, some joyful idea of justice that even the gods lack.

Taut at its limits, Lyotard's thought helps us to refine, if not define, our own. In so far as it sentimentalizes terrorism, it seems blind to an arrogance which it calls justice, and so strikes us as rebarbative. Yet in its audacious vision, it confronts us with the Gorgon-stare of the age. The challenge to a critic's praxis comes finally to this: how act *in extremis,* and in whose name, without making a monster of oneself, turning self into stone:

> *He jogs, pumping blood and adrenaline, and conducts imaginary conversations.*
>
> *A Marxist colleague accuses him: "You put truth before praxis. This is bourgeois, decadent." He answers, feet pounding: "Separate truth from action, and you end with terrorism or its bigger brother, totalitarianism. I choose neither: both serve themselves while claiming to serve others."*
>
> *A friend admonishes him often: "We must make distinctions, we must make sharp distinctions." Panting, he retorts: "Indeed we must, and must distinguish between distinctions: some inert, habitual, others creative, mindbracing."*
>
> *A colleague twits him: "That's just macho." He thinks: "Machismo can be puerile and can be deadly. But its thrust got us out from the back of the cave into this dubious light. Besides, Hemingway and Mishima, Malraux and Mailer, are more emotionally literate than most men and women I meet.*
>
> *Another junior colleague boasts to him: "I am becoming more conservative every day." Sweating now, as another jogger is about to overtake him, he mutters, "So am I, if conservative means exacting. Otherwise, never! Let a thousand risks bloom."*
>
> *Laced with small aggressions, his mute conversations are less imaginary than ontological, a running critique of being in the world, as he runs to delay his dying.*

IN-CONCLUSION

Finally, no one knows of what the self is made, though luck, genes, and achievement help us to gain some working sense of it. That self is certainly a construct, an interpretation, to various degrees effective or ineffectual, yet never so capable—despite the Grandees of Neurosis—as when least anxious in its skin. The construct, however, remains unfinished, as Ortega said long ago, "a personage . . . never completely realized, a stimulating Utopia, a secret legend, which each of us guards in the bottom of his heart." It is this legend that I have tried to elicit from the critical self in three continuous movements: desiring, reading, acting. In the process, elicitation became solicitation as I called on certain authors to provide both a cultural and theoretical context for the argument. Calling on various authors, did I then betray my self?

Betrayal is always double: it discloses even as it deceives. The texts I have chosen speak a tendency in myself no less than in the culture of which we are all a part (apart). The tendency is radical in that, searching for the roots of knowledge and being, it risks itself in strenuous gestures of discontinuity, bellicose illusions of newness. Gestures and illusions rarely alter reality; yet they may vex both reality and ourselves into a larger, stronger, quicker apprehension of things. How many of us walk like somnambulists through existence, harkening to ancestral voices which are but the sound of our own fearful breath?

Half of the authors I have discussed are French. This is not adventitious. England offers nothing bracing in criticism now; Germany in reaction to its past may have locked its mind, with some rare exceptions, in academic Marxisms; and America, excepting a handful of critics, has become a virtuoso of sullen scholarship or gallic parody. Nor is French thought itself impeccable. I have elsewhere registered my impatience with its fanatic unmakings and Gongoresque styles. Yet no other thought, I think, has opened for us so many perspectives of theory as of praxis, sharpened our sense of the verbal self, and so enriched the critic's life. Moreover, no other thought, despite its cant, has moved us closer to that perception of our contemporaneity that constitutes the postmodern épistémè.

The nature of our contemporaneity merits some attention, though it defies clarity. For we live in an interstitial moment, one both of barbarism and decadence, a time both of violence and timidity in the West, which now includes the Russian Empire. What beast slouches toward Bethlehem then? I suppose it to be the dream or specter of planetization, transhumanization. For the "decline of the West" will not yield the Earth to another rising civilization, as it has so often yielded in the past; it will cede it, rather, to peaceable or savage planetization, one world yet ever so various, the North/South axis collapsing convulsively into the East/West. We may wonder: what role can the critic play when history shakes? Perhaps only a modest but dual role: one of subversion, the other of making.

We require versatile subversion to free the mind from that deadening, *and* deadly, discourse that both Right and Left impose. (An anti-ideology may constitute a kind of ideology, yet it remains one of very different kind.) For once, Lacan speaks lucidly: "It is the irony of revolutions that they engender a power all the more absolute in its actions, not because it is more anonymous, as people say, but because it is more reduced to the words which signify it." We need "subtle subversion," by which Barthes means: "what is not directly concerned with destruction, evades the paradigm, and seeks some *other* term: a third term, which is not, however, a synthesizing term but an eccentric, extraordinary term." Precisely, what I have called side-stepping, slippage, the politics of displacement, the praxis of self-surprise.

As for the critic's making—which I have expounded elsewhere—I need claim for it here only what we would claim for any act of the plenary intelligence: both imaginative freedom and moral force. I insist on the imaginative relation in the critic's life because I sense that without it, without *poesis*, the critical relation becomes a form of Nietzschean *ressentiment*, a consummation of the ironic self, a spite of mind. For beyond irony, subversion, or deconstruction—here I part decisively with Derrida —our presence and absence, like warp and woof in the loom of the universe, call us to an asseveration that few critics have been willing to make. This asseveration, perhaps fiercer than those I have earlier remarked, finds its voice not in any pale grammatology or white semiology but in the tradition of Goethe, Blake, and Emerson—a "visionary company," as Harold Bloom knows, lacking in neither dialectical awareness nor political acumen.

The strongest self is least self-absorbed; it opens and imperils itself continually. Its best achievement, both mystics and non-mystics (Nietzsche) say, may consist in self-overcoming. Yet for all that, it is neither single nor insubstantial. "What else am I who laughed or wept yesterday," Emerson asks in "History," "who slept last night like a corpse, and this morning

stood and ran?   And what see I on any side but the transmigra-
tions of Proteus?"

> *He tries to imagine precisely the unimaginable : his own*
> *death.   He succeeds only in making it literary.   Unlike*
> *Ivan Karamazov, he does not prize Justice over Reality,*
> *and so will not "return his ticket" to God.   He would*
> *rather drown in Reality :*

> "Not drowned entirely, though.   Rather carried down alive to won-
> drous depths, where strange shapes of the unwarped primal world
> glided to and fro before his passive eyes; and the miser-merman,
> Wisdom, revealed his hoarded heaps, and among the joyous, heart-
> less, ever-juvenile eternities, Pip saw the multitudinous, God-omni-
> present, coral insects, that out of the firmament of waters heaved
> the colossal orbs.   He saw God's foot upon the treadle of the loom,
> and spoke it. . . ."

> *Drown in Reality.   But then, grasping at a straw, he*
> *thinks : not yet, not yet.*

NOTES ON CONTRIBUTORS

CHARLES ALTIERI is Professor of English at the University of Washington. In addition to several essays on literary theory and Modern and Romantic poetry, he has published two books: *Enlarging the Temple: New Directions in American Poetry of the 1960's* (1979) and *Act and Quality: A Theory of Literary Understanding* (1981). He is currently working on the theory of value in relation to literary questions and the nature of abstraction in modernist poetry and painting.

DAVID BLEICH teaches in the English Department of Indiana University. He is the author of *Readings and Feelings* (1975) and *Subjective Criticism* (1978). His many essays have appeared in *American Quarterly, Psychoanalytic Review, Literature and Psychology, American Imago, College English, College Composition and Communication, English Record, Genre, New Literary History, The Sphinx* and *Style.*

MATEI CALINESCU is Professor of Comparative Literature at Indiana University. His interests include subjects from the avant-garde to wider questions of cultural criticism, the philosophy of religion, and political theory. His book *Faces of Modernity* appeared in 1977, and his numerous essays have been published in European and American journals.

GERALD GRAFF is chairman of the department of English at Northwestern University. His *Literature Against Itself* was published in 1979, and his earlier book, *Poetic Statement and Critical Dogma* has recently been republished. His essays have appeared in numerous journals including *Critical Inquiry* and *The Georgia Review.*

GILES GUNN is Professor of Religion and American Studies at

the University of North Carolina at Chapel Hill. He is author of *F. O. Matthiessen: The Critical Achievement* (1975), and editor of *Literature and Religion* (1971), *Henry James, Senior: A Selection of His Writings* (1974), and *New World Metaphysics: Readings on the Religious Meaning of the American Experience* (1981). His *The Interpretation of Otherness: Religion, Literature, and the American Imagination* was published in 1979. Professor Gunn is currently at work on a study of the moral tradition in modern American criticism and has just finished editing a book on *The Bible and American Arts and Letters.*

IHAB HASSAN is Vilas Professor of English and Comparative Literature at the University of Wisconsin in Milwaukee. He is author of *Radical Innocence* (1961), *The Literature of Silence* (1967), *The Dismemberment of Orpheus* (1971, 1982), *Paracriticisms* (1975), and *The Right Promethean Fire* (1980). Most recently, he has edited with Sally Hassan *Innovation/Renovation: Perspectives of Change in the Humanities* (1983). He is currently at work on *Imaginary Autobiography.*

NORMAN N. HOLLAND is Milbauer Professor of English at the University of Florida. He founded the Center for the Psychological Study of the Arts at the State University of New York at Buffalo. He is the author of many articles and seven books, five of which treat the psychology of literary response: *Psychoanalysis and Shakespeare* (1966), *The Dynamics of Literary Response* (1968), *Poems in Persons* (1972), *5 Readers Reading* (1975), and *Laughing* (1982).

VICTOR A. KRAMER is Professor of English at Georgia State University where he teaches American literature and literary criticism. His book *James Agee* appeared in 1975. Numerous essays of his have appeared in a score of journals. His co-edited collection *Olmsted South* was published in 1979 and his co-authored *Reference Guide for Andrew Lytle, Walker Percy, and Peter Taylor* in 1983. His book *Thomas Merton/Father Louis* will appear soon.

MURRAY KRIEGER is University Professor of English, University of California, with primary teaching duties at Irvine. His many books include, *The Apologists for Poetry* (1956), *The Tragic Vision: Variations on a Theme in Literary Interpretation* (1960), *A Window to Criticism: Shakespeare's Sonnets and Modern Poetics* (1964), *The Play and Place of Criticism* (1967), *The Classic Vision: The Retreat from Extremity in Modern Literature* (1971), and *Theory of Criticism: A Tradition and its System* (1976). His book *Poetic Presence and Illusion: Essays in Critical History and Theory* was published in 1979. *Arts on the Level: The Fall of the Elite Object* appeared in 1981.

VINCENT B. LEITCH, Associate Professor of English at Mercer University, is the author of *Deconstructive Criticism* (1982) and the editor of Robert Southwell's *Marie Magdalens Funeral Teares* (1975) and *The Poetry of Estonia: Essays in Comparative Analysis* (1982). In addition, he has published essays and reviews in his two areas of interest: critical theory and lyric poetry. Professor Leitch has received awards from The American Philosophical Society, The School of Criticism and Theory, The Mellon Foundation, The Fulbright-Hays Program and The National Endowment for the Humanities.

J. HILLIS MILLER is Frederick W. Hilles Professor of English and Comparative Literature at Yale. His books include *Charles Dickens: The World of His Novels* (1958), *The Disappearance of God* (1963), *Poets of Reality: Six Twentieth Century Writers* (1975), *The Form of Victorian Fiction* (1968), *Thomas Hardy: Distance and Desire* (1971), and *Fiction and Repetition: Seven English Novels* (1982).

STEVEN MAILLOUX is Associate Professor of English at the University of Miami. He has published on modern literary criticism in various journals including *Critical Inquiry, Genre, Centrum, Comparative Literature*, and *MLN*. He is the author of *Interpretive Conventions: The Reader in the Study of American Fiction* and the editor of a special *Bucknell Review* issue on theories of reading.

HERSHEL PARKER is H. Fletcher Brown Professor of American Romanticism at the University of Delaware. After a year as a fellow of the Center for Advanced Studies at the University of Delaware, he is completing *Literary Authority*, a study of the authority an author has over his literary works and some ways such authority can be lost.

JOSEPH N. RIDDEL teaches at UCLA, and writes on modern poetry, and on poetic and critical theory. He is the author of books on Wallace Stevens, C. Day Lewis, and William Carlos Williams and "modernism," the last of which addresses the question of the interweaving of poetry and analysis, or poetic and critical "deconstruction." He is presently at work on a book to be called *Purloined Letters*, on "American poetics" from Poe to post-modernism.

NATHAN A. SCOTT, JR. is William R. Kenan, Jr., Professor of Religious Studies and Professor of English at the University of Virginia, where he also serves as Chairman of the Department of Religious Studies. Among his numerous books are *Negative Capability: Studies in the New Literature and the Religious Situation* (1969), *The Wild Prayer of Longing: Poetry and the Sacred* (1971), *Three American Moralists—Mailer, Bellow, Trilling* (1973), *The Poetry of Civic Virtue—Eliot, Malraux, Auden* (1976), and *Mirrors of Man in Existentialism* (1978).

WILLIAM V. SPANOS teaches in the department of English at the State University of New York, Binghamton where he also edits *boundary 2*. Professor Spanos has written on a wide variety of subjects including philosophical and literary topics. His *Martin Heidegger and the Question of Literature: Toward a Postmodern Literary Hermeneutics* was published in 1979.

MICHAEL SPRINKER teaches English at Oregon State University in Corvallis. He has published essays in a wide range of periodicals including *Mosaic*, the *Journal of the History of Ideas, Diacritics*, and *boundary 2*. His book *A Counterpoint of Dissonance: The Aesthetics and Poetry of Gerard Manley Hopkins*, appeared in 1980. He is currently co-editor of *the minnesota review*.

MICHAEL STEIG is a member of the Department of English

at the Simon Fraser University in British Columbia, Canada. Professor Steig has published over thirty essays in journals such as *Victorian Studies, Nineteenth-Century Studies, Studies in the Novel,* the *Journal of Aesthetics and Art Criticism.* His book *Dickens and Phiz* appeared in 1978, and he is presently at work on a book called *Meaning, Intention, and Response in the Victorian Novel.*